AMERICAN POETRY AFTER MODERNISM

Albert Gelpi's *American Poetry after Modernism* is a study of major poets of the postwar period from Robert Lowell and Adrienne Rich through the Language poets. He argues that what distinguishes American poetry from the British tradition is, paradoxically, the lack of a tradition; as a result, each poet has to ask fundamental questions about the role of the poet and the nature of the medium, has to invent a language and form for his or her purposes. Exploring this paradox through detailed critical readings of the work of sixteen poets, Gelpi presents an original and insightful argument about late twentieth-century American poetry and about the historical development of a distinctively American poetry. *American Poetry after Modernism* offers literary history and critical argument along with readings of many of the best and most important poems written in the last sixty years.

ALBERT GELPI is Coe Professor of American Literature, emeritus, at Stanford University. His previous books include *Emily Dickinson: The Mind of the Poet*, *The Tenth Muse*, and *A Coherent Splendor*. Gelpi has also edited the work of, and written criticism on, a wide range of poets, including Wallace Stevens, Robinson Jeffers, Adrienne Rich, Denise Levertov, Robert Duncan, and William Everson. *The Letters of Robert Duncan and Denise Levertov*, coedited with Robert Bertholf, received an award from the Modern Language Association as the best scholarly edition of a literary correspondence. Gelpi continues to teach in the Stanford Continuing Studies Program.

AMERICAN POETRY AFTER MODERNISM

The Power of the Word

ALBERT GELPI

Stanford University

CAMBRIDGE
UNIVERSITY PRESS

CAMBRIDGE
UNIVERSITY PRESS

32 Avenue of the Americas, New York, NY 10013-2473, USA

Cambridge University Press is part of the University of Cambridge.

It furthers the University's mission by disseminating knowledge in the pursuit of education, learning, and research at the highest international levels of excellence.

www.cambridge.org
Information on this title: www.cambridge.org/9781107025240

First published 2015

Printed in the United States of America

A catalog record for this publication is available from the British Library.

Library of Congress Cataloging in Publication Data
Gelpi, Albert, author.
American poetry after modernism : the power of the word / Albert Gelpi.
pages   cm
Includes bibliographical references and index.
ISBN 978-1-107-02524-0 (hardback)
1. American poetry – 20th century – History and criticism.   2. Literature and society – United States – History – 20th century.   I. Title.
PS323.5.G39   2015
811'.509–dc23   2014038211

ISBN 978-1-107-02524-0 Hardback

This book is dedicated to my loved ones
BARBARA
CHRISTOPHER   JANET   MITCHELL   GRACE
ADRIENNE   PAUL   BENNET
LUCIANA   JOCELYN
and to the memory of my friend
ANDREW BROWN

Contents

Preface

This book resumes and extends an argument that runs through two previous books of mine about the American poetic tradition: *The Tenth Muse*, which focuses on American Romantic poetry, and *A Coherent Splendor*, which studies American Modernist poetry. The defining issues of a distinctive American poetics, as I see them, are introduced in Chapter 1 and summed up in the brief coda. *American Poetry after Modernism* does not presume or require a knowledge of the earlier volumes, but it does extend the lines of argument into the second half of the twentieth century, a period whose poetry and "poetry wars" were overshadowed and informed by the horrors of World War II, the threat of nuclear holocaust, the anxieties of the Cold War with the communist bloc, and the conflicts in Korea and Vietnam.

My intention, as in the earlier volumes, is not a survey of the period and its groups and movements but a more detailed examination of those poets who most effectively helped me focus and substantiate my argument. Consequently I don't discuss a number of poets whose work is less relevant to the questions of form and language that I am pursuing. In particular, I should note the emergence of African-American, Latino, and Asian-American poets in this period, but the strong focus on issues of ethnic identity in the dominant culture, important for all Americans as these issues are, mean that most of this poetry starts with and is sustained by a different set of questions. The poets examined in these chapters are all important figures in American poetry of the second half of the twentieth century, but among the poets I regret having to leave out I think particularly of Theodore Roethke, Langston Hughes, Richard Wilbur, James Merrill, J. V. Cunningham, Charles Olson, Sylvia Plath, Wendell Berry, Gary Snyder, Nathaniel Mackey, Robert Hass, and Mary Oliver.

This project encompasses the whole span of my scholarly life. It began to take direction in lectures for a two-semester course on American poets from the Puritans to the present that I taught as a beginning assistant professor at

Harvard in the mid-1960s. Reading and teaching those poets over the years that soon took me to Stanford, I kept returning to the question of whether they came to represent a poetic tradition distinct from the British tradition, and, if so, what the defining issues and differences are. A number of good and enlightening historical surveys of American poetry have been published over the last fifty years, but nothing quite like my line of inquiry. As my thinking clarified and developed, what I had presumed would be a single volume evolved into two, and now into a third segment that carries the argument up to the contemporary scene. Looking back, I see how much my reading of American literature was influenced by the great intellectual historian Perry Miller; and I feel my indebtedness to him, as I have so many times before, for the courses I took from him, especially the one on American Romanticism, and for his guidance in writing my dissertation on Emily Dickinson, which became my first book. So I feel gratified and satisfied, and also a little wistful, at completing a project conceived almost a half-century ago at the beginning of my professional life. *Mirabile dictu et deo gratias.*

As I bring this book to completion, Andrew Brown is very much in my mind and heart. Among his many achievements in his career at Cambridge University Press has been his steady advocacy of American literature. Andrew asked me more than thirty years ago to be the first academic editor of a new series we called Cambridge Studies in American Literature and Culture, which is still actively publishing. During the decade of my editorship we became good friends. The Press published my two earlier volumes about the American poetic tradition, and Andrew and I were in conversation about this third installment since its inception three summers ago. On one occasion he remarked that the book would be a fitting culmination of our long association through the Press, and, in one of my last e-mails to him before his death in January 2014, I was able to report that I had just about finished the draft of the conclusion.

In closing I also want to thank friends and colleagues who read parts of the book and generously offered incisive and helpful suggestions, especially Robert Kiely, Marjorie Perloff, Gareth Reeves, Brett Millier, and Robert Grenier, who turned his sharp proofreader's eye and pencil to my typed text. Thanks also to Ryan Haas for his sure-handed assistance in the final preparation of the book manuscript. And, as always, to Barbara Charlesworth Gelpi, whose unfailing editorial eye and deep love of poetry have seen every chapter through.

Albert Gelpi
Stanford University
August 7, 2014

CHAPTER I

Twentieth-Century American Poetics: An Overview

From Romanticism to Modernism

Terms embracing large cultural and aesthetic ideologies – Romanticism, Modernism, Postmodernism – change their protean shape and color in different hands and perspectives, but they are nevertheless useful markers in defining and comparing successive periods of cultural history. Indeed, the very imprecision of such epithets – the fact that they enfold inconsistencies and rest in contradictions and paradoxes – allows us to identify and trace the volatile play and counterplay of issues and values as a given period defines itself in relation to its antecedents and sets the terms for what will follow from it. The sections of this chapter trace three intertwined lines of descent that comprise a large historical argument about the poetics of twentieth-century American poetry.

In *A Coherent Splendor*, I argued that the Modernist period, bracketed by the two world wars, bore a complicated and ambivalent relation to Romanticism, the dominant aesthetic and cultural ideology of the nineteenth century; that Romanticism had itself evolved out of and explicitly against Enlightenment rationalism; and that the Enlightenment, in its turn, had deepened the growing skepticism since the Renaissance about theological or metaphysical absolutes capable of sustaining a reliable relation between subject and object, mind and matter, physics and metaphysics. Enlightenment rationalists might declare that they had disproved the authority of established systems of belief, but the Romantics saw the rationalist arguments as reducing metaphysics to physics, the supernatural to the natural, and thus as exposing the limits of mere human reason as a faculty for comprehending the nature of reality and the mystery of existence. In response to the epistemological and religious crisis, the Romantics sought to ground insight into reality neither in reason nor institutional systems of belief but in the felt experience of the individual. Induction and deduction yield to personal intuition of the universal in the particulars of experience, of the absolute in the passing contingencies of time and space. These moments of perception constitute acts of genuine signification that offer the deepest human understandings and proceed from the highest human faculty of cognition, which philosophers, following Kant, called transcendental Reason and artists called Imagination. And for the artist, the Imagination moves to expression in a form inspired, inspirited by the generative experience.

Thus Romantic epistemology, psychology, and aesthetics proposed an organic triad of correspondences between the perceiving subject, the perceived world, and the medium of expression in the subtending activity of Spirit. The most influential theoretician of the Romantic Imagination in England was Coleridge, and in America Emerson; its most influential exemplars were Wordsworth and Whitman. But visionary insight is difficult to attain, much less to maintain, and Romanticism put such stress on the individual's momentary experience that the Romantic synthesis of subject and object, poet and nature through the agency of the Imagination began to deconstruct almost as soon as it was ventured. The literature of the nineteenth century records the dissolution of Romantic ecstasy into Romantic irony and paradox: from Blake's visions and Wordsworth's early nature mysticism to the decadence of the Romantic ideology in fin de siècle aestheticism.

In the opening years of the new century, erupting in the war that seemed to many besides Spengler symptomatic of the "decline of the West," Modernism aggressively advanced a counter-ideology to an exhausted Romanticism, explicitly rejecting its epistemological and metaphysical idealism, its aggrandizement of the individual ego, its organic model for the instantiation of seer and seen, word and meaning. As the experience of organic continuity gave way to a deepening sense of the discontinuity between subject and object, the consequent fracture of perceiving self and perceived world required a different notion of the function of form. Where Romantic form assumed and strove for an organic wholeness, Modernist form required invention and artifice, the construction of the art object from the fragments. The Modernist artwork stood as an often desperate, even heroic insistence on coherence against the instability of nature, the unreliability of perception, and the tragedy of human history. For the Modernist, therefore, form came to mean not a discovered correspondence with nature, but almost the opposite: form organic only in the internal functioning of its parts, abstracted from nature and pieced together into an artifact that aimed to be – T. S. Eliot's adjective – "autotelic"[1]: its own end, its meaning literally manufactured (handmade) in its construction.

From this point of view, Modernism can be seen as arising from the intensification of Romantic tensions to the point of rupture. The critical discussion of Modernism has concentrated on the shattering of formal conventions as an expression of the disintegration of traditional values, and this is indeed the aspect of Modernism that anticipates Postmodernism. Marjorie Perloff has dubbed the Modernist aesthetic, in the title of her influential study, *The Poetics of Indeterminacy*, and in *The Futurist Moment* she traced how writers learned, from avant-garde artists' turn to collage, experimental techniques for verbal bricolage. The fixing of bits and pieces in an arrested arrangement compelled a dramatic shift from the temporal aesthetic of natural process to a spatial poetics of invented arrangement: in painting, three-dimensional objects flattened into a surface design; in poetry, the lyric speaker splintered into contrasting voices, sequentiality reassembled in juxtapositions; in music, chordal juxtaposition in place of melodic development. Thus Picasso's Cubism, Kandinsky's abstractions, Pound's ideogrammic method, Schönberg's jarring atonalities.

However, as I have already begun to suggest, although Modernism as an aesthetic and cultural ideology began in indeterminacy and rupture, it did not end there, because most Modernists could not accept and abide in indeterminacy and rupture. Even the patterning of bits and pieces into collage and bricolage, I would argue, is evidence not just of the disintegration of self and world but, at least as importantly, of a counter-determination to resist disintegration. Fragmentation aroused in artists an urgent need to build, to press the imagination to create form from formlessness. If order could not be found, it could be made, and that aesthetic coherence constituted the high function of art. Wallace Stevens spoke for his Modernist peers when he said that a "blessed rage for order" conferred on the driven artist a heroic nobility in an ignoble time and a vital function in society, since the work of imagination "helps us to live our lives."[2] Similarly, when Ezra Pound charged his contemporaries to make it new, the fiat of that aesthetic genesis claimed for the artist a creative and transforming power in social and cultural life.

So I read poetic Modernism differently from many distinguished commentators on the subject, Marjorie Perloff and Hugh Kenner among them, in arguing that the Modernists were aiming not at, or not finally at, a poetics of indeterminacy but rather – as suggested by the Poundian title of my study of Modernism – at achieving a coherent splendor. Despite the manifestos and axiomatic pronouncements against Romanticism, Modernism in fact represents an extension and reconstitution of the salient issues that

Romanticism set out to deal with. In the face of the intellectual, psychological, moral, and political turmoil that had propelled the last two centuries into more and more violent crises, Modernism continued to exalt the imagination as the agency of coherence. Not, the Modernists insisted, the Romantic Imagination with its capital I; but an imagination that, though shorn of mystical and idealist claims, was still the supreme human faculty of cognition, empowering the artist (echoing Stevens again) to decreate disordered experience into aesthetic creation. Even in their most experimental phases, Pound, Eliot, James Joyce, Gertrude Stein, William Carlos Williams, and Stevens all wanted the pieces in their collages to make some kind of picture, however complex and difficult. Against detractors Pound pressed forward with his life's work in the conviction that he would be able to name his cantos, when the pattern was complete, with a single ideogram that would subsume the thousands of pieces. And Stevens, acknowledging that his poems were aimed at intimating bit by bit the supreme fiction, wanted at the end of his life to call his collected poems "The Whole of Harmonium."

Nor need the coherence possible in an artwork, by being autotelic and self-completing, be merely aesthetic, art merely for art's sake, as leftist critics of the 1930s and contemporary Marxists would dismissively have it. Charles Altieri's *Painterly Abstraction in Modernist American Poetry: The Contemporaneity of Modernism* (1990) mounts a compelling argument for the moral efficacy of the Modernist aesthetic. Working from abstraction as a hermeneutic of perception in painting, Altieri reads Eliot, Williams, Pound, and Stevens to show how in poetry as well as painting the abstracting process of decreation and re-creation, hermetic though it be, requires subtle discriminations of perception, and so of consciousness. Such exacting discriminations permit, indeed compel, us to understand ourselves and our situation more precisely and thereby to define the values and commitments on which responsible choice and moral action depend. For Altieri, the Modernist aesthetic comprises not just an epistemology but an ethics: for many in the twentieth century, the only valid way of coming to discernment and commitment.

I would push Altieri's argument and claim that many of the great Modernist poets came by different paths to realize the psychological and moral limits of the poetics of indeterminacy and superseded them. The period of High Modernism – what Perloff called the Futurist Moment – was relatively brief, roughly from 1910 to 1925. The task of superseding indeterminacy served to extend these poets' active careers into mid-century and made for much of their best work. At issue are the nature and function of form: whether, on the one hand, poetic form makes an aesthetic coherence out of the fragments of experience and the incoherence of reality, or whether, on the other hand, the effort at coherence in poetic form strives to reflect or intimate or arrive at a coherence in reality outside the poem. The shift in poetic stance between High Modernism and later developments can be grasped in the contrast between *The Waste Land* and *Four Quartets*; between "Mauberley" and *A Draft of XXX Cantos* on the one hand and *The Pisan Cantos* and the final *Drafts and Fragments* on the other; between H.D.'s Imagist *Sea Garden* and her long hermetic sequences *Trilogy* and *Helen in Egypt*; between Stevens's poems in *Harmonium* and *Parts of a World* on the one hand and the poems in *Transport to Summer* and *The Rock* on the other; between the Williams of *Spring and All* and the Williams of *Paterson* and the triadic poems of his last decade.

Different understandings of Modernism make for different evaluations of the earlier and later work of these poets. For Perloff and Altieri, for example, Eliot's masterpiece is *The Waste Land*; for me it is *Four Quartets*. The prophecy of "What the Thunder Said" at the end of *The Waste Land* finds completion in the epiphany in the chapel at Little Gidding when tragic history is grasped through the mystery of the Incarnation as "a pattern / Of timeless moments." Out of the confusing polyglossia of *The Waste Land* Eliot's own voice has emerged and identified itself within a circumambient reality extrinsic to art.

Poetry need no longer be autotelic; in fact, "the poetry does not matter," "East Coker" tells us, at least not in the way that it has to matter to a High Modernist.[3] It was Eliot's particular Christian perspective – a Calvinist version of Catholicism – that impelled him to conclude that the poetry as poetry does not matter. But other Modernists came to similarly anti-Modernist positions. For all Pound's disputes with his old friend about religion, he came to a kind of Neoplatonist pantheism synthesized from the Greek mysteries and the Chinese *tao* that allowed him, in *The Pisan Cantos* and the last *Drafts and Fragments*, to repudiate Modernist aestheticism. "Le Paradis n'est pas artificiel" is a refrain in the later *Cantos*; paradise is not a narcotic fantasy, as Baudelaire had said, but "terrestre," realizable in the eternal round of nature. In Canto 81, the goddess's eyes attend Pound in his prison tent and reveal a vision in which the chastened ego consents to "[l]earn of the green world what can be thy place / In scaled invention or true artistry." By Canto 116, when Pound has to acknowledge that he will never complete and name his life's work, he is able to give his incomplete poem an unexpected affirmation by concluding: "it coheres all right / even if my notes do not cohere." "I have tried to write Paradise," but if the poem has failed in "true artistry," the failure is – only – aesthetic, not metaphysical; coherence lies in the ongoing *tao*. Meaning surpasses the "scaled invention" of Modernist means.[4]

Neither Stevens nor H.D. nor Williams would ever question the integrity of the poem in so fundamental a way as Pound or Eliot did, but the late work of all three intimated a point of reference and relevance outside their poetry. H.D.'s late autobiographical sequences intend to cast a spell as they voice prayers and invocations weaving a syncretic myth from the Christian, Greek, and Egyptian sources, which finally spells out the bare initials of her name into her "Hermetic Definition." Stevens's lengthening meditations turn and turn on archetypes – father, mother, anima, ephebe – constellated around images of the completed self as giant, hero, major man; and increasingly the language of the poems invests its fictive images with an aura of mystery, as though those images were portents of a further and numinous reality: "like rubies reddened by rubies, reddening."[5] The quasi-religious vocabulary and transcendental aura of late Stevens point away from the humanist agnosticism of an early poem like "To an Old Christian Woman" and anticipate his acceptance of Catholicism during the last weeks of his life. Even Williams found, by the time of *Paterson V* and the triadic poems in *Pictures from Brueghel*, that his resolutely anti-metaphysical humanism had deepened to the point that it had to express itself in mythic and even, occasionally, religious terms.

The longer, late poems of these poets temper their early Modernist stance by opening the visualized, spatial constellation of the poems into sequences in which time dictates both the form and the theme. Canto 30 had stipulated the Modernist dread of time: "Time is the evil. Evil."[6] Poems like *The Cantos* and *The Waste Land* fracture history into spatial juxtapositions in many voices, but in *Four Quartets* and in the later *Cantos* the poet's voice emerges from the various speakers to meditate on living in time and history. Eliot wrote the essay on "The Music of Poetry" as he was finishing the *Quartets*, and he was not alone in invoking music rather than painting or sculpture as an analogue for poetic form. Indeed, just at the point when younger, mid-century poets like George Oppen and Louis Zukofsky began adapting Williams's objectivism, Williams was himself complaining of its static constraints and turning from spatial arrangement of lines to an urgent search for a new, more flexible measure capable of extension. His discovery of what he called the variable foot,[7] based on the musical bar and stepped in tercets down the page like a score, opened the way into *Paterson* and the autobiographical voice of the late poems. Stevens smoothed out the jagged angularities of "Domination of Black" and "Thirteen Ways of Looking at a Blackbird" into the endless silken iambics of the late sequences following the year's, and life's, seasons: *Transport to Summer*, *The Auroras of Autumn*.

In my view, then, the key to Modernism resides in its attempt, in the wake of declining faith and debunked reason and decadent Romanticism, to affirm the imagination as the supreme human faculty of cognition for (and against) a secular, skeptical age. The dialectic with Romanticism that constituted and defined Modernism took place, as I have suggested, in two phases. First, the avant-garde High Modernism of the 1910s and 1920s sought to replace Romantic claims for the metaphysical and mystical insight of the imagination by redefining the function of the imagination in terms of a constructive formalism with the capacity and authority to decreate/re-create inchoate experience into a quasi-absolute, autotelic assemblage. Then, in the 1930s, the strict formalism of collage and juxtaposition came increasingly to seem not so much a solution as a static and unresolved dead end, and Modernism opened up to temporal and historical process, recovering or discovering thereby sources of cognition beyond the aesthetic: in the case of Eliot, by a renewal of faith in the Incarnation; in the case of the others – Stevens, Pound, Williams, H.D. – by an exploration of the powers of insight that had been the legacy of Romanticism latent yet active in Modernism all along.

From Modernism to Postmodernism

The epithet "Modernism" came into currency not from the artists themselves (they thought of themselves as moderns, as opposed to Romantics or Victorians, but not Modernists), but from retroactive commentary of critics and literary historians. In fact, the currency of the term marked the end of the period, and critics soon coined the term "Postmodernism" to distinguish subsequent developments. The Postmodernist break with Modernism serves to define the poetry of the Cold War decades, but just as Modernism defined itself not just against but, in many ways, in dialogue with Romanticism, so Postmodernism defined itself not just in opposition to but in dialogue with Modernism, as the transition played itself out over two generations of poets.

The poets who began to publish just after World War II found themselves awed and overshadowed by the enormous achievements of their legendary predecessors, most of them still alive and writing. Lynn Keller's

Re-making It New: Contemporary American Poetry and the Modernist Tradition (1987) focuses on the continuities and discontinuities between Modernist and Postmodernist poetics by studying four exemplary pairings: Stevens and John Ashbery, Marianne Moore and Elizabeth Bishop, Williams and Robert Creeley, and W. H. Auden and James Merrill. But other pairings across the generational divide and the years of the war also spring to mind: Allen Tate and Robert Lowell, Pound and Charles Olson or Robert Duncan, Williams and Denise Levertov, Robinson Jeffers and William Everson, W. B. Yeats and John Berryman, Frost or Stevens and Adrienne Rich. What these pairings confirm is not just the lingering presence of the long-lived and larger-than-life predecessors but also the deepening sense of a different poetic sensibility that initiates the transition from Modernism to Postmodernism in the poetry of the Cold War period.

Modernism had formulated, out of a yawning fear of impotence before the gathering forces of indeterminacy and chaos, a determined, if sometimes anxious, assertion of the authority of the imagination and the integrity of the medium. In the ashes of Berlin and Tokyo, Hiroshima and Auschwitz, that effort came to seem, to many postwar poets, an untenable and doomed retreat from history into an overreaching aestheticism. The word had to rise from those ashes: test the ground of reference, investigate the possibilities and limits of meaning, speak in the face of its own uncertainties. Postmodernism took shape as a poetics of indeterminacy without the Modernist counter-resolve to resist indeterminacy. At the same time, I would contend, Postmodernist is too categorical and simplified a label for the poetry of the Cold War period. That generation of poets was still so imbued with Modernist values and with the residual Romanticism inherent in those values that while many of them yield to a poetics of indeterminacy, others exhibit a Neoromanticism that offers an alternative pole to Postmodernism. The chapters of this book make the argument that just as the Modernism of the first half of the century maintained a dialogue with Romanticism, so the poetics of the second half of the century is most accurately seen as a dialogue between Postmodernism and Neoromanticism.

A number of postwar poets exhibit a self-questioning and a scaling back of expectations that point to what would be called Postmodernism, but the decisive and deliberate break came not with the generation of Lowell and Bishop and Rich but rather in the 1970s and 1980s when a number of critics, along with a number of younger poets, mounted a critique of Modernism. These poets looked back not to Pound and

Williams, much less to Eliot and Stevens, as forebears, but rather to the mid-century Objectivist poets George Oppen and Louis Zukofsky. Much as *Poetry (Chicago)* and *The Dial* had championed Modernism half a century before, so now the Postmodernist poets and Poststructuralist critics, based principally in New York and the San Francisco Bay Area, grouped themselves under the mastheads of *L=A=N=G=U=A=G=E*, edited by Bruce Andrews and Charles Bernstein; *Acts*, edited by David Levi Strauss; and *Poetics Journal*, edited by Barrett Watten and Lyn Hejinian. *The L=A=N=G=U=A=G=E Book* (1984) and Michael Palmer's *Code of Signals: Recent Writings on Poetics* (1983) collected manifestoes and position papers establishing the new work as Language poetry.

The postwar cultural crisis was theorized politically through a Marxist critique of late capitalism; scientifically through Einstein's relativity and Heisenberg's uncertainty principle; psychologically through Lacan's dissection of Freudian ego-psychology; linguistically, via Wittgenstein and Husserl, through a semiotics of the word as free-floating signifier with no clear signification; and literarily through Derrida's deconstruction of language. The designation "Language Poetry" was intended to declare that all we know is language. Moreover, language is not a medium of connection and communication but a code of arbitrary signals determined by extrinsic cultural patterns and political systems and psychological mechanisms, and so closed on itself, and so detached from a reliable apprehension of reality. Kathy Acker writes:

> I write with words which are given me ... I am given meaning and I give meaning back to the community ... I am always taking part in the constructing of the political, economic, and moral community in which my discourse is taking place. All aspects of language – denotation, sound, style, syntax, grammar, etc. – are politically, economically, and morally coded.[8]

Although the function of the writer is to use "given meanings and values," thereby "changing them and giving them back" to the community's discourse, the scope and efficacy of such transformation is severely restricted by the terms of the culturally enforced code.

Language poetry, then, reformulated Modernism into Poststructuralist deconstruction. In "Postmodernism: Sign for a Struggle, the Struggle for the Sign," Ron Silliman says that "Modernism ... is but the moment in which the postmodern becomes visible," but "the end of modernism was inscribed" in the spurious "yearning to recapture a lost unity in the functions of language."[9] This Modernist yearning merely put the mask of impersonality on the Romantic ego-genius; stripping off the mask reveals "an esthetics of fragmentation and discontinuity."[10] The breach between subject and object, word and world, fragments both. The word does not designate a reality but substitutes for its loss; language expresses not presence but absence. So the theory goes, and it posits a poetics that turns the poem into self-referencing semiotic code.

What, in the end, did L=A=N=G=U=A=G=E writing prove to be? If the lyric "I" is eliminated, who is speaking, and to whom? Does not a disconnection between signifier and signified disconnect poem and reader? Watten and Hejinian called issue Number 7 of *Poetics Journal* "Postmodern" but hung it with a question mark, suggesting that the term itself was so indeterminate that they were uncertain about or uneasy with it. At the end, not the beginning, of his essay on Postmodernism Silliman asks, "What is the nature and history of a writing that no longer asks for a unified sign?"[11] and leaves the question open and unanswered. The last chapter of this book undertakes a response by examining the efforts of several Language poets to find the words for an indeterminate mode of meaning.

From Modernism to Neoromanticism

As we have seen, Modernism reformulated Romanticism in the fragile conviction that through the powers of the imagination formal aesthetic coherence could, if faith and reason and mystical insight could not, perform a vital psychological, moral, even political function that could, or might, make personal and social life possible. "It is," in Stevens' words, "the imagination pressing back against the pressure of reality. It seems, in the last analysis, to have something to do with our self-preservation."[12] Postmodernism correctly sees Modernism as a reformulation of Romanticism and – wrongly in my view – takes that fact as the source of Modernist errors and self-deceptions. Bernstein sees Modernism as initiating a poetics of deconstruction but then reverting to "a poetry primarily of personal communication" that is in fact "looking for the natural in 'direct experience,' both in terms of recording the actual way objective reality is perceived (the search for the objective) & making the writing a recording instrument of consciousness."[13] Similarly, Silliman sees the contradiction of Modernism in its being at once "the announcement of the postmodern" and yet "a lingering hangover from the previous realist paradigm," and his discussion identifies realism with Romantic notions of "organic form" and an "artificial holism" that posit "a unity between signifier and signified." He cites the art critic Clement Greenberg for the aspect of Modernism that is the constellating point of Postmodernism: "[T]he work of art is a self-referential object which is in a self-critical relation to itself, particularly to its medium."[14]

In fact, the shift in the aesthetics of the two halves of the twentieth century might be telescoped into the following formula:

$$\text{Modernism} - \text{Romanticism} = \text{Postmodernism}$$

A poetics of indeterminacy is what is left when Modernism is severed from its residual Romantic inclinations. But Postmodernism, I would argue, is only half of the story, because those Romantic inclinations persist in postwar American poetry alongside, and often in active contention with, Postmodernist inclinations.

The issue can hardly be more fundamental: what we can know and how we can know it. The difference in conceptions of poetic form and structure discussed earlier in the chapter – whether form is autotelic and strives for coherence out of the incoherence of experience, or whether form strives to express a coherence in experience outside the poem – registers at the level of the word: whether language is self-referential or not, whether indeed "[a] poet's words are of things that do not exist without the words,"[15] or whether a poet's words strive, often against their own opacity, to apprehend and express an extralinguistic truth and reality.

Moreover, the power of the word – and challenges to it – were of explicit and central concern to American expression from the outset. The Puritans were a people of the word, and their conviction that the word could and would arrive at the truth about this world and the next issued not just in Scriptural commentaries, sermons, and theological tracts but also in histories, autobiographies – and the first American poems. In literary expression the Puritans distinguished between images that were "types" and "tropes." Tropes were mere metaphorical inventions of the human imagination, and so were to be used with caution and with an awareness of the danger that they could distract from or even distort truth to fit the individual fancy; types, by contrast, were true symbols that expressed the divinely ordained truth as it is embodied and revealed in the natural world and in human experience. Nature, if read right, was a second book of revelation after Scripture itself; Jonathan Edwards read nature as "Images or Shadows of Divine Things."[16] Edwards's alternative titles for his treatise included "The Book of Nature and Common Providence" and "The Language and Lessons of Nature."

The waning of Puritanism coincided, in literature, with the stirrings of Romanticism, as emblemized in Emerson's resigning his pulpit to become a poet- philosopher responsive to the new ways of thinking and writing in Germany and England. The deep-seated sense of typological language was reinscribed most powerfully in Emerson's Transcendentalism, whose assumptions are summarized in the "Language" chapter of his manifesto *Nature* (1836): "1. Words are signs of natural facts. 2. Particular natural facts are symbols of particular spiritual facts. 3. Nature is the symbol of spirit."[17] Outside of intellectual and doctrinal systems, the Imagination gave the receptive individual an inner eye that extends sight into metaphysical and transcendental insight. Emerson's calm and magisterial words quickened Thoreau's meticulous recording of his experiences at Walden, Whitman's expansive prophecies, and Dickinson's involuted exchanges with nature and God and self, different as those poets were from each other and from Emerson.

At the same time, the dissolution of the Romantic synthesis began with Emerson's contemporaries Poe and Melville. *Moby-Dick* can be read, at one level, as an epic testing of the symbolic truth of nature and of language. Melville's initial excited response to Emerson gave way to a disillusionment that turned the Transcendentalists into satiric caricatures in *Pierre* and *The Confidence Man*. Similarly, the bitterness of Poe's dismissal of the Transcendentalists is a measure of his disappointment at his own failed Transcendentalist yearnings. If, as Poe says in "Israfel," "Our flowers are merely – flowers,"[18] then they are merely tropes, not images of divine things, and nature is a charnel house. Poe's obsession with puzzles, hieroglyphs, and secret codes comes from panicked compulsion to decipher the seemingly undecipherable.

In the succession of New England nature poets after Emerson, Frost saw himself as an ironic pragmatist testing nature and language to "make something of a diminished thing"; the emphasis is on the act of making something of less than something. In "For Once, Then, Something" Frost peers down a well into the heart of nature and sees a blur. Is "that whiteness" "[a] pebble of quartz?" and is that pebble a typological "Truth"? The unanswered questions end in a repetition of the title, rounding the poem on itself: "For once, then, something." It is a rueful affirmation, but an affirmation nonetheless; for "[t]he figure a poem makes" can, if well enough made, end "in a clarification of life – not necessarily a great clarification," but at least "in a momentary stay against confusion."[19]

The deepening awareness of the subject/object split would lead through Modernism to Postmodernism and Language poetry. In *A Coherent Splendor* I read Modernist poetics, in terms reconstituting the distinction between types and tropes, as a dialogue between Imagism and Symbolism.

Imagists and Symbolists both thought of the imagination as a constructive faculty and of the poem as a made thing. But Imagist poets – Pound, Williams, H.D. – assumed an encounter between subject and object, between word and thing; the making of the poem strives to render a genuine experience of the world. In Pound's dictum, the Imagist aimed at "[d]irect treatment of the 'thing' whether subjective or objective."[20] If the poet could no longer speak of types or say with Emersonian assurance that nature is the symbol of spirit, he or she could still say that in some sense, words are signs of natural facts. *Spring and All* (1923) is Williams's declaration, "without calling upon mystic agencies," that the imagination is the "supreme" faculty "[t]o refine, to clarify, to intensify" our "consciousness of immediate contact with the world." The "actual force" of the imagination recreates that encounter into an artifact not opposed to reality but "apposed to it."[21]

The Symbolists – Eliot, Hart Crane, Stevens, with the French Symbolistes Laforgue and Valéry as forebears – tended to see poems as impressionistic figures of speech expressing internal psychic states and imaginative inventions. Form, measure, and metaphorical elaboration constitute, by suggestion and indirection, the elusive interiority of the poem. Eliot's influential early essays argued for the impersonality of the poet as maker and the "autotelic" character of the poem as "objective correlative" of its emotional affect. But for him the source of the poem and the articulation into form is a subjective process: "The poet's mind is in fact a receptacle for seizing and storing up numberless feelings, phrases, images, which remain there until all the particles which can unite to form a new compound are present together."[22] "Poetry," Stevens says, "is a revelation in words by means of the words"; "[a] poet's words are of things that do not exist without the words." "[T]he *mundo* of the imagination" presents a parallel world: the mind "constantly describing itself."[23]

Yet Stevens goes on to say that the "escapist process" of making the *mundo* works to create "an agreement with reality" that "enables us to perceive ... the opposite of chaos in chaos."[24] An escape, therefore, not just from reality but, paradoxically and thereby, into a changed and renewed reality. The paradox leads into the formal construct of the poem – and then, startlingly, through and beyond it. Maintaining his distance from what he saw as the aestheticism of both the Imagists and the Symbolists, Jeffers justified his versifying only as it pointed to, rather than away from, the vision of Nature as God. But, as Stevens's remark has indicated, many Modernists, Imagist and Symbolist alike, came to reach through the formalism of the poem to a recovered or redeemed sense of reality. We have heard Pound leave *The Cantos* unfinished in the Neoplatonist/Confucian conviction that "all things that are are lights" under the eternal radiance of the "Light tensile immaculata."[25] We have heard Eliot conclude in "East Coker" that "[t]he poetry does not matter"; that is to say, the artifact does not matter except as it apprehends the truth: "The hint half guessed, the gift half understood is Incarnation." Lines from *Ash-Wednesday* (1930) turn on the connection and disconnection between the word and the Word:[26]

> If the lost word is lost, if the spent word is spent
> If the unheard, unspoken
> Word is unspoken, unheard;
> Still is the unspoken word, the Word unheard,
> The Word without a word, the Word within:
> The world and for the world ...

Hart Crane charged his lines – in the "Voyages" sequence and in his epic *The Bridge* – with sound and rhythm and metaphorical leaps to push language toward absolute vision in the hope that "[p]oetry, in so far as the metaphysics of absolute knowledge extends, is simply the concrete evidence of the experience of a recognition (knowledge, if you like)."[27] For his part, Stevens came to invoke the "vatic stature" of the poet: "The theory of poetry, that is to say, the total of the theories of poetry, often seems to become in time a mystical theology[,]... a mystical aesthetic, a prodigious search of appearances, as if to find a way of saying and of establishing that all things, whether below or above appearance, are one."[28] The line "We say God and the imagination are one" can be read as reducing God to a projection of the imagination – or as correlating imaginative invention with "the miraculous influence," or inflowing, of the divine.[29]

  This persistent effort to confirm the word's communicable referentiality to reality and truth, even a transcendental reality and truth, extrinsic to language I am calling Neoromanticism, as it extends from the Romantic through the Modernist period into the second half of the twentieth century. In a 1973 interview, Robert Duncan admitted: "I read Modernism as Romanticism; and I finally begin to feel myself pretty much a 19th century mind ... my ties to Pound, Stein, Surrealism and so forth all seem to me entirely consequent to their unbroken continuity from the Romantic period."[30] A number of poets – Crane, H.D., Jeffers, Pound, Stevens, even Williams – were sometimes described, sometimes condemned as Romantic. And in what has sometimes too reductively been called the Postmodernist era, I find a Neoromantic sensibility – often in dialogue with a Postmodernist sensibility – in the work of a range of poets of the

Cold War period: Theodore Roethke, Lowell, Berryman, Ginsberg, Jack Kerouac, Gary Snyder, Charles Olson, Robert Duncan, Everson, Levertov, Rich, Amiri Baraka, Wendell Berry. Indeed, even in some poets usually associated with Language poetry: Ronald Johnson, Robert Grenier, Susan Howe, Fanny Howe. My contention is not that the poets I am calling Neoromantic in one way or another are imitating or even modeling themselves on nineteenth-century Romantics, but rather, that those poets are echoing, adapting, carrying forward, in one way or another, attitudes, assumptions, and aims that came into poetry with the nineteenth-century Romantics.

Neoromantic as a term of historical continuity has to be a roomy rubric to encompass the mystical Roethke, the prophetic Lowell, Rich the radical feminist, Everson the Dionysian Catholic, Duncan the occultist, Berry the agrarian, and Baraka the Black nationalist. And several of the poets would in all probability be uncomfortable with or dismissive of that designation. However, these poets, on their particular terms and in their particular ways, speak from a passionate desire to press limits and extend possibilities, insisting that language penetrate rather than maintain surfaces. They all are impelled and sustained by a sense of vocation: a calling to language as an act of signification, a vision of human life that gives direction and purpose to their words. W. H. Auden's much-quoted remark on the brink of World War II that "poetry makes nothing happen" serves as one marker for the collapse of Modernism into what was to be Postmodernism. The poets I am designating Neoromantic believe, even in the face of the violence of contemporary history, that the word can effect personal and even social change, that poetry can, sometimes almost against the odds, make things happen – psychologically, morally, politically, religiously.

The large historical argument of this chapter circles around the power of the word as the persistent and defining issue in the American poetic tradition, as the Puritan opposition of types and tropes plays out successively for the Romantic period in the dialectic between Transcendentalism and anti-Transcendentalism, for the Modernist period in the dialectic between Imagism and Symbolism, and for the postwar period in the dialectic between Neoromanticism and Postmodernism. The remaining chapters explore that argument by studying the interplay of those imaginative poles in the work of major poets of the Cold War period.

CHAPTER 2

The Language of Crisis
Robert Lowell
John Berryman

I feel I know what you have worked through, you
know what I have worked through – we are words;
John, we used the language as if we made it.

"For John Berryman I"

I

Robert Lowell is in the line of dark prophets of American letters who
have questioned the rhetoric of this country's Manifest Destiny and the
assumption of God-given exemption from the failures of history. Even the
Puritans, with their Calvinist conviction of sin, liked to pronounce their
colony a reversal of the tragedies of Europe; their history would record, as
Cotton Mather's title puts it, *Magna Christi Americana*, the great deeds of
Christ in the New World. In the increasingly secular nineteenth century,
Emerson and Whitman were the public poet-prophets of optimistic idealism. A close reading of Emerson and Whitman shows their awareness
of human fallibility and social injustice, but they both suffered through
their crises to a reaffirmation of the American spirit over American materialism. Nonetheless, in our poets and fiction writers, the Puritan sense
of sin and judgment persisted beneath the noisy bustle of progress and
expansion. Poe and Hawthorne were Emerson's contemporaries; Melville
was Whitman's, and he praised Hawthorne for recognizing "the power
of blackness."[1] Mark Twain's fame as an American humorist masked but
did not hide a deepening despair at human depravity. Jeffers so identified
the human species with original sin that at times he looked forward to
its extinction; "Shine, Perishing Republic" was his response to Whitman
and Emerson. In *The Great Gatsby* Fitzgerald composed a lament for
the degeneration of Emersonian idealism into capitalist profiteering.
Faulkner's Yoknapatawpha novels chronicle Southern history as a record
of the sins of the fathers dooming their sons and daughters.

Lowell inflected the power of blackness and the sins of the fathers for the America of World War II and the Cold War. For him, as for Hawthorne and Faulkner, the local and personal were the universal and political; autobiography became apocalypse. Being a Lowell and, on his mother's side, a Winslow and a Stark gave him a privileged perspective and responsibility. What he saw was the transformation of Puritan rigor into Yankee entrepreneurship, the hollowing out of Puritan zeal into complacent social conformity. His distant relative Jonathan Edwards haunted his imagination because Edwards's fate typified New England's, as his powerful theological vision and charismatic sermons of sin and judgment only brought rejection by his community and exile among the Indians. The decline of Lowell's own family became, for him, the immediate instance of the burden of history; his own life and heritage recapitulated the tragedy of America and of humankind.

Lowell's serious poetic vocation dates from the late 1930s. As a nineteen-year-old Harvard freshman in 1936, he wrote to Ezra Pound: "I want to come to Italy and work under you and forge my way into reality."[2] But by the next year he had begun a very differently oriented, formalist apprenticeship under Allen Tate, and left Harvard for Kenyon College to study under Tate's friend John Crowe Ransom: "no more free verse, use of rimes, rational use of material instead of impressionistic fanwork of sympathetic particles." "In the beginning," he acknowledged, "[Tate] was not only an influence but often *the* (my) style of writing." But the challenge to the young poet was not just to find a style but also to find a sustaining message: "a substance or symbolism dense enough and concentrated enough to bear and coordinate the huge energies necessary to produce poetry of vital impact."[3] And indeed Lowell not only absorbed into his writing the dense verbal and metaphorical formalism espoused by the New Criticism but also found in Tate and Ransom a kindred disgust with secular materialism as the antithesis of Christian humanism. Much as his mentors read the tragedy of American history in the victory of Yankee capitalism over Southern agrarianism, Lowell read it in the history of his own region, specifically in the godless mercantile greed that had supplanted the piety of his Winslow and Stark forebears.

How could he regain the power and authority of Edwards' vision and call for judgment? Lowell's response was to search beyond New England history for a religious conviction that would offer the possibility of salvation from the tragedy of human existence. That search led him to the Catholicism that had been anathema to the Puritans and was still socially unacceptable to the Bostonians he knew. As a graduate student

at Louisiana State University, studying with Tate and Ransom's friend
Robert Penn Warren, he began to read Church history and the writings of
neo-Thomists like Jacques Maritain and Etienne Gilson, asked for instruction in the faith, and was baptized Catholic on March 23, 1941. And in
a country waging a war on two fronts he began writing the poems that
would bring national recognition. Lowell found his poetic voice in World
War II as a Catholic firebrand and declared his conscientious objection
to the war in an open letter to President Roosevelt published on the first
page of the *New York Times*. He tried to explain the Catholic source and
intention of his poems to his bewildered parents: "All of them are cries for
us to recover our ancient freedom and dignity, to be Christians and build
a Christian society."⁴ And he continued to sound his jeremiads, even after
he had left the Church, against the self-destructive materialism and imperialism of postwar America.

Lowell's early career was remarkable not just because his poetry was
widely seen as deeply expressive and symptomatic of this uncertain and
troubled period but also because of the singular vision he brought to bear on
the period. The title of his first, small-press book, *Land of Unlikeness* (1944),
was lifted from Etienne Gilson's *The Mystical Theology of Saint Bernard*
(1940), and its epigraph comes from St. Bernard: "When the soul has lost
its likeness to God it is no longer like itself."⁵ Tate auspiciously introduced
Land of Unlikeness with a magisterial flourish: "There is no other poetry
today quite like this."⁶ Contemporaries like R. P. Blackmur and Randall
Jarrell joined in hailing it as a literary event. John Berryman saluted Lowell
as "the most powerful poet who has appeared in England or America for
some years, master of a freedom in the Catholic subject without peer since
Hopkins."⁷ When *Lord Weary's Castle* (1946) brought together ten poems
revised from the earlier book with twenty new poems, it won Lowell the
first of his three Pulitzer Prizes before the age of thirty. Two decades later
Irvin Ehrenpreis was able to speak plausibly, if hyperbolically, of "The Age
of Lowell."⁸ Lowell's years as a practicing Catholic were intensely fervent but
relatively brief; he stopped active observance in the late 1940s, just at the
time when *Lord Weary's Castle* was making his reputation as a Catholic poet.
Over the years Lowell himself tended to deprecate the early poems as overdetermined, overwrought, overwritten and so, by implication, as superseded
by his later poems. However, Lowell's Catholicism continued to be for him
a touchstone and point of reference, and his early Catholic period remains
central to any measure of his life's work.

In retrospect, *Lord Weary's Castle* can even be seen as an anticipation
of what was to come; the book's poetic modes and genres persist in the

later books through the successive shifts in perspective and technique. Thus dramatic monologues like "Between the Porch and the Altar," "Mr. Edwards and the Spider," and "After the Surprising Conversions" lead directly into the dramatic and narrative poems in the next book, *The Mills of the Kavanaughs* (1951). Autobiographical poems like "Rebellion" and "In the Cage" and family elegies like "In Memory of Arthur Winslow" and "Mary Winslow" point to *Life Studies* (1959). Verse renderings of a range of poets – Propertius, Villon, Rimbaud, Valéry, Rilke – into what the prefatory "Note" called imitations anticipate the 1961 volume of *Imitations*. The sonnets on historical subjects, both those about New England ("Salem," "Concord") and those on European themes ("Napoleon Crosses the Berezina," "Charles the Fifth and the Peasant"), look down the line to the various *Notebook* versions of the late 1960s and early 1970s.

The dramatic changes in style and form and intention in the volumes after *Lord Weary's Castle*, beginning with *Life Studies*, constitute part of what makes Lowell's career symptomatic of the period. The tension between agonized belief and agonized disbelief is reflected in his oscillation, over the years, between closed and open forms, between symbolic and direct statement. Reviewing *Lord Weary's Castle*, Jarrell, who had studied with Lowell under Ransom at Kenyon, observed that these early poems of Lowell "have two possible movements or organizations: they can move from what is closed to what is open, or from what is open to what is closed," and Jarrell associates those poles with the tension between necessity and freedom, law and grace.[9] Tate explicitly associated Lowell's formalism with his Catholicism: "T. S. Eliot's recent prediction that we should soon see a return [from avant garde experimentation with free verse] to formal and even intricate metres and stanzas was coming true, before he made it, in the verse of Robert Lowell ... Lowell is consciously a Catholic poet, and it is possible to see a close connection between his style and the formal pattern."[10] (Tate would himself become a Catholic around the time that Lowell was leaving the Church.) There is of course no inherent and necessary correlation of religious belief with closed form or of agnosticism with open form (as the poems of William Everson and Denise Levertov will demonstrate in later chapters). However, in Lowell's case Tate is correct. Lowell's desperate need to assert the salvific intervention of the divine into human history led him as poet to indicate or summon that intervention by imposing aesthetic order on the disorder of personal experience and history.

Indeed, the explicitly religious message of *Lord Weary's Castle* gives the book its distinctive voice and place in Lowell's work. In the early 1940s

Lowell was reading, along with Tate, Gerard Manley Hopkins and Eliot; in a 1943 review he called *Four Quartets* "the most remarkable and ambitious expression of Catholic mysticism in English" and made this large claim for the poetic vocation: "My own feeling is that *union with God* is somewhere in sight in all poetry, though it is usually rudimentary and misunderstood."[11] The early poems strain to break through the drive and energy of the words into a vision of the Word. To that end Lowell tightened the strong iambic rhythms with alliteration and assonance and packed densely metaphorical language into intricate rimes and stanzas. The exertion of maximum pressure against maximum constraints, enjambment overrunning the strict measures, gives the effect of language resisting, battering, and almost exceeding its constraints and limits. It is not surprising, then, that the lapsing of Lowell's prophetic vision would require a shift in the 1950s from a rigorous and elaborate formalism to more varied, flexible versification and more direct, less exclamatory statement, as Williams and Ginsberg and his friend Elizabeth Bishop displaced the example of Tate and Eliot and Hopkins.

Without question the language of *Lord Weary's Castle* is pitched at the eruptive breakpoint of form and metaphor and even meaning; the violence marks these as poems in which the poet is at war with self, family, region, country, as well as with the war the country is waging. Lowell and Flannery O'Connor were not close friends, but they had come to know each other as resident writers at Yaddo in the late 1940s, and they corresponded. Lowell made a brief, manic return to the faith after experiencing God's presence while attending Mass with her in February 1949. Their work, different as it is, links them as Catholic prophetic writers who shared an apocalyptic sense that the moment of violence could be, by divine reversal, the moment of grace.

The violent rhetoric of *Lord Weary's Castle* not only renders the condition of war but draws on the sensual, oral, nondiscursive resources of language – strong stresses, insistent rhythms, heavy sound effects, proliferating metaphors – to extend language into a dimension beyond denotation and even connotation, to push communication to its limits and (if possible) beyond, toward intimations of the incommunicable. The prophet, speaking for God (or the gods or the transpersonal force) must therefore propel language above or below – in any case, outside – the range of customary human speech. The words must break through rational proposition and demonstration, and the energy, even violence, of the language is the record of that effort. Listeners or readers are meant to be overwhelmed and carried along the rhythmic and sonar propulsion toward an area of perception otherwise beyond comprehension.

Listen to "Death from Cancer," the first section of "In Memory of Arthur Winslow," Lowell's elegy for his maternal grandfather. It is the second poem in *Land of Unlikeness* and was included in *Lord Weary's Castle* with only minor changes. The verses rumble and rattle like a roller coaster through the stanzas, driving the powerful images headlong to the glimpse of inexplicable mystery at the end-stop climaxing each stanza:

> This Easter, Arthur Winslow, less than dead,
> Your people set you up in Phillips House
> To settle off your wrestling with the crab –
> The claws drop flesh upon your yachting blouse
> Until longshoreman Charon come and stab
> Through your adjusted bed
> And crush the crab. On Boston Basin, shells
> Hit water by the Union Boat Club wharf:
> You wonder why the coxes' squeakings dwarf
> The *resurrexit dominus* of all the bells.
>
> Grandfather Winslow, look, the swanboats coast
> That island in the Public Gardens, where
> The bread-stuffed ducks are brooding, where with tub
> And strainer the mid-Sunday Irish scare
> The sun-struck shallows for the dusky chub
> This Easter, and the ghost
> Of risen Jesus walks the waves to run
> Arthur upon a trumpeting black swan
> Beyond Charles River to the Acheron
> Where the wide waters and their voyager are one.[12]

The sentences unreel in the tight stanzaic structure and rhyme scheme, but the grid cannot encompass, or can barely encompass, the verbal propulsion. The rhymes serve not to separate verses from each other but to emphasize their almost complete enjambment. Far from slowing the sentence down or dividing it into discrete units of sense, they add to the rising clamor, as the local details (Phillips House, Union Boat Club, Public Gardens) pile up, only suddenly to yawn on illimitable vistas: the Charles now the Acheron, the children's swanboat now Charon's ferry, the dying and bedridden patient now the farthest voyager. The verbal pressure against syntactic and prosodic restraints propels the sense of the scene toward awed apprehension of the absolute. Sentences stretch themselves, sometimes excruciatingly, as if the poet were trying to sweep his whole world into each statement, and the buildup stops only at the period concluding each stanza in wordless and terrified wonder. There had been no American writing of such apocalyptic and religious ferocity since the Puritans, and among them none, not even Edward Taylor, charged his religious expression with such baroque energy and Catholic sensuality.

The Christian vision centers on the mystery of the Incarnation, and the incarnational imagery in these poems focuses again and again on Christmas and Calvary, on the birth and the death and resurrection of Jesus. Here the last lines conflate the "risen Jesus" with the earlier Gospel narrative of Jesus walking on the waters of the lake toward the boat carrying the Twelve. This second image recurs in other poems; "The Drunken Fisherman" ends: "On water the Man-Fisher walks" (p. 35; henceforth page references to Lowell's *Collected Poems* will be indicated parenthetically in the text). In the account in Matthew:14, Peter jumps out of the boat at the Lord's command, walks on water toward Him, until he hesitates in self-doubt and begins to sink, only to be rescued from drowning by Jesus' saving hand with the admonition: "You have so little faith. Why did you doubt?" Lowell does not mention Peter, because here the speaker of the poem serves as the wavering witness, as he does in "The Slough of Despond": "I walk upon the flood: / My way is wayward; there is no way out: / Now how the weary waters swell, – " (p. 63).

The fullest development of the image comes as the climax of "Colloquy in Black Rock." The kinesthetic imagery, the enjambed versification, the combustive sound effects, the strongly stressed rhythms and thudding rhymes, characteristic of the early poetry, build to an apocalyptic image that renders the power – and also the limits – of Lowell's Catholic vision. At one point of its composition in 1944 the poem was called "Pentecost"[13] after the feast day celebrating the descent of the Holy Spirit on the Twelve after Jesus' ascension, but the completed poem is specifically written for Corpus Christi, the day in the liturgical calendar that commemorates the Incarnation of God as Christ's Body (p. 11):

> Here the jack-hammer jabs into the ocean;
> My heart, you race and stagger and demand
> More blood-gangs for your nigger-brass percussions,
> Till I, the stunned machine of your devotion,
> Clanging upon this cymbal of a hand,
> Am rattled screw and footloose. All discussions
>
> End in the mud-flat detritus of death.
> My heart, beat faster, faster. In Black Mud
> Hungarian workmen give their blood
> For the martyre Stephen, who was stoned to death.

Black Mud, a name to conjure with: O mud
For watermelons gutted to the crust,
Mud for the mole-tide harbor, mud for mouse,
Mud for the armored Diesel fishing tubs that thud
A year and a day to wind and tide; the dust
Is on this skipping heart that shakes my house,

House of our Savior who was hanged till death.
My heart, beat faster, faster. In Black Mud
Stephen the martyre was broken down to blood:
Our ransom is the rubble of his death.

Christ walks on the black water. In Black Mud
Darts the kingfisher. On Corpus Christi, heart,
Over the drum-beat of St. Stephen's choir
I hear him, *Stupor Mundi*, and the mud
Flies from his hunching wings and beak – my heart,
The blue kingfisher dives on you in fire.

The details of the poem specify the time and place. In September 1943, Lowell had refused to report to an induction center for military service; he based his conscientious objection on his conviction that the saturation bombing of German cities and the Allied insistence on unconditional surrender violated Catholic teaching on the conditions and circumstances that might constitute a just war. Sentenced to prison for a year and a day, he served time at a federal correction center in Danbury, Connecticut, until he was paroled in March 1944, to complete his sentence by working as janitor in a student nurses' dormitory in Bridgeport. During these last months of his sentence, Lowell lived in an apartment in the working-class neighborhood of Black Rock that overlooked an inlet from the sea. The Hungarian immigrants who were his neighbors worshipped in the local Catholic church of Saint Stephen, protector of Hungary, but worked in the local defense plant supporting the war effort.

The speaker looks out at the scene but communes with himself; his colloquy is a soliloquy addressed to his own heart. Lowell's fevered mind seizes on the violent pounding of wave on rock as symbolic of all material existence, as he feels his throbbing heart threaten to batter the machine of his body to pieces; the phrase "rattled screw and footloose" telescopes his physical and mental disintegration. Things wear each other down, wear each other out: Black Rock to Black Mud to black water. And physical processes of deterioration are hastened by human destructiveness. The fishing tubs are armored for war; the Hungarians piously contribute to the Red Cross blood drive to save those mangled by the munitions they manufacture for pay. "All discussions / / End in the mud-flat detritus of death."

Is death, then, the finality? The reversal is implied in the death of Stephen and made explicit in the apparition of Christ walking on the black water. This Stephen is not the Hungarian nationalist patron but the Christian proto-martyr, who, in being "stoned to death" and "broken down to blood" in imitation of "our Saviour who was hanged till death," typifies the Christian as redeemed victim. Death in Christ is our ransom *from* the world; redemption comes in the death of the mortal and sinful body. Incarnation means into the flesh, but Lowell's dark vision offers no salvific baptismal immersion *in* the waters of life. Here Christ walks risen and uncontaminated *on* the black water. There is a descent, but it represents not the initiation of new life but the end of the old. In a startling sequence of transformations, Christ becomes the kingfisher, and then the "blue kingfisher" becomes a divebomber, the mud of material existence shed in the hunched intensity of its descent to blast the speaker out of a world at war with itself. The descent here is not into bodily existence but into release from bodily existence. In the repeated exhortation to his thudding heart to beat faster in order to rattle the body screw and footloose, the speaker anticipates and acquiesces in his violent release from the violence of life. The present-tense verbs of the closing stanza herald the apocalypse here and now.

Lowell sought to use his Catholicism to scourge the lapsed Puritanism of his people, but, ironically, his Calvinist sense of sin made it difficult for him to accept the Incarnation as redemption *of* the human condition. The Incarnation posits the immanence of God *in* matter, personified in Jesus and sustained through history in the indwelling Spirit. But a gnostic dualism[14] that resisted the Gospel vision of Incarnation could only conceive redemption in terms of release *from* the human condition. Even a sympathetic reader like Tate sensed Lowell's anxiety about the Incarnation when he pointed to "the willed effect" of some of Lowell's symbolic language.[15] And that anxiety is precisely the issue in "The Quaker Graveyard in Nantucket," the central and most ambitious poem in *Lord Weary's Castle*. Praised by Berryman for its "drenched magnificence,"[16] it stands as one of the great elegies of the English language.

Lowell began writing the poem in the summer of 1944, after his cousin Warren Winslow, serving on the U.S. Navy destroyer *Turner*, was killed and lost at sea in an accidental explosion that sank the ship off the New York harbor. His death becomes the occasion for a sweeping view of salvation history from Genesis to Apocalypse. The epigraph from Genesis cites God's words establishing a covenant with humans under the sign of the rainbow and charging them with responsibility for the care of His whole creation, and the poem then presents the repeated and catastrophic violation of that covenant down to the present world war. Lowell was consciously working in the literary tradition of the elegy, with Milton's "Lycidas" and Hopkins's "The Wreck of the Deutschland" most prominently in mind. The poem's evolution into seven sections from two unpublished poems, "To Herman Melville:" and "Words with Ahab,"[17] points to *Moby-Dick* as the other major literary presence, and the association of the sinking of the warship with the sinking of the Quaker *Pequod* encapsulates the history of human violence against nature and our shared humanity. The poet addresses his drowned cousin as the Everyman of this drama, and he speaks from the Nantucket graveyard where the markers contain no bones for the Quakers drowned at sea, who were, for all their professed pacifism, major actors in the whaling industry and slave trade of nineteenth-century New England.

The propulsive surge and sonorous sound of the rhetoric drive through the rhymed but enjambed lines, and the sections alternate between moving out to sea and back to home port. The death drama plays out to its seeming end (the word "end" is repeated three times) in the fourth section, whose last lines pose the question of resurrection: "Who will dance / The mast-lashed master of Leviathans / Up from this field of Quakers in their unstoned graves?" The question is ironic, since divinity acts as avenging agent in the tragic action: Poseidon is the sea's "hell-bent diety," "the earth-shaker, green, unwearied, chaste"; Ahab's God is "IS the whited monster," the faceless and omnipotent "I AM" whose instrument and symbol is the white whale. The irony is clearest in the "if" of the Quakers' reiterated invocation of God's favor (from Psalm 124) as they drown "[i]n the sperm-whale's slick" (p. 16):

> "If God himself had not been on our side,
> If God himself has not been on our side,
> When the Atlantic rose against us, why,
> Then it had swallowed us up quick."

But Section V presents a different understanding of divine agency when a graphic description of the slaughter of the whale ends with an astounding revelation. The first hint comes in the phrase "the death-lance churns into the sanctuary." The whirling rhetoric and gory details suddenly contract into a terse prayer: "Hide / Our steel, Jonas Messias, in Thy side"

(p. 17). The extraordinary compression of the blunt statement identifying Jonah with the whale that swallowed him allows for different but convergent readings of the whale as IS. What if the whale is not the faceless Yahweh whose face is Moby-Dick but, almost incredibly, is Iesus Salvator, God incarnate slain by our sins for our own salvation? What if Jonah is not the whale's victim but, within the whale, the type of the crucified Jesus? If our slaying of Jesus is, paradoxically, our salvation, then the slayer's prayer has to be for Jonas Messias to take into Himself the deadly violation of our sin and thereby, mysteriously, absolve it. The double sense of "hide" as "conceal" and "shield" pivots on the turn of the line and enacts the miraculous transformation.

Then the final sections of the poem move through two further and different modulations. Section VI imagines the Sailor on pilgrimage as a penitent to the shrine of Our Lady of Walsingham, who was also revered as Our Lady of the Sea. The medieval shrine is near the sea in Norfolk, and the sanctuary was built as a replica of the room in Nazareth where the Annunciation took place and the Incarnation began. The description of the approach, paraphrased from E. I. Watkin's *Catholic Art and Culture* (1942),[18] evokes the peaceful and calm faith of the pilgrims: "Sailor, you were glad / And whistled Sion by that stream." But the description of the Virgin in the second stanza, again paraphrased from Watkin, moves out of history, as the mystery of the Incarnation recedes into the inscrutability of the transcendent Godhead: the face of the Romanesque statue of Mary, "[e]xpressionless, expresses God" (p. 17). That remote face, past all human emotion and human experience, could hardly be more different from the Mary who is addressed in the last section of "In Memory of Arthur Winslow" as the mediatrix between God and humans, the Great Mother nourishing and redeeming her wayward children (p. 25):

> O Mother, I implore
> Your scorched, blue thunderbreasts of love to pour
> Buckets of blessings on my burning head
> Until I rise like Lazarus from the dead ...

But here Our Lady of Walsingham, united not with the Incarnate Son she bore but with the transcendent Father, "knows what God knows, / Not Calvary's Cross nor crib at Bethlehem / Now, and the world shall come to Walsingham" (p. 17).

The future tense of "shall come" anticipates ultimate resolution, but not in this conflicted world, and the seventh section turns back to the violence of the sea and the fate of the drowned sailor. The sixth line says "It's well," as if looking beyond the tragic scene to a resolution, but it does not indicate how or why it's well. Instead, the concluding lines of the elegy sweep us back to Genesis and the rainbow of God's covenant (p. 18):

> When the Lord God formed man from the sea's slime
> And breathed into his face the breath of life,
> And blue-lung'd combers lumbered to the kill.
> The Lord survives the rainbow of His will.

After the pitch and roll of the enjambed lines, the final line stands as a self-enclosed and gnomic declaration: God transcends the covenant he has willed and signed with the rainbow; human violations have made that covenant seem as evanescent as the rainbow, but God is untouched by the human tragedy. The poem does not return to the redemptive imagery of Section V or even the muted assurance of "and the world shall come to Walsingham."

Lowell sought to give the volume a more positive conclusion by placing last a poem whose title makes it a kind of coda to "The Quaker Graveyard." The title of "Where the Rainbow Ends" (p. 69) again invokes Genesis, but the text invokes Revelations, the last book of the Christian Bible. The speaker adopts John's prophetic voice ("I saw," "I saw") to imagine the end of time ("the rainbow's epitaph") and the Last Judgment descending on contemporary Boston, where the metal construction of the Pepperpot Bridge spanning the Charles River makes it an "ironic rainbow" at this Apocalypse. The poem, however, does not end in irony, and the speaker's final prayer adopts the triumphal imagery of John's Revelation: "Hosannah to the lion, lamb, and beast / Who fans the furnace-face of IS with wings: / I breathe the ether of my marriage feast." Jesus here is not the suffering Jonas Messias, nor the dive-bombing kingfisher, but the dove whose appearance in Scripture signals a divine revelation: the dove who brings an olive branch to Noah at the end of the flood; the dove of the Holy Spirit who descends on Mary at the Annunciation to conceive Jesus and then descends on Jesus at his baptism as the Father proclaims his Sonship. Here the rainbow ends in a conflation of Noah's olive branch with Jesus incarnate in the life-giving Eucharist: "Stand and live, / The dove has brought an olive branch to eat." As Lowell told his friend Peter Taylor in 1946, "Belief ... is 'at bottom' belief in Christ i.e. when he said 'This is my Body' and the other passages He really meant it. Only prayer can bring this faith."[19]

But, as Lowell remarked in "Domesday Book," a poem in his last, mostly backward-looking collection *Day by Day* (1977), "The reign of the kingfisher was short" (p. 766). "Beyond the Alps," the first poem in *Life Studies*, marks the end of that reign by dramatizing Lowell's move out of the Church metaphorically as a train ride from Rome to Paris. He and his recently married second wife, Elizabeth Hardwick, were in Rome in 1950, when Pope Pius XII declared the dogma of Mary's Assumption, and Lowell's explicit connection of his departure from the Church with that declaration is deliberate and revealing. Mary had been invoked in several earlier poems in very physical and sensual imagery ("Mary, hear, / O Mary, marry earth, sea, air and fire" from "The Dead in Europe"), and the depiction of the Assumption in "Beyond the Alps" – "Mary risen – at one miraculous stroke, / angel-wing'd, gorgeous as a jungle bird!" (p. 364) – recalls the powerful Great Mother from "A Prayer for My Grandfather to Our Lady." But the deflation in the next line – "But who believed this? Who could understand?" – turns the miraculous image into a gaudy deception.

This passage is the closest that Lowell came in the poetry to accounting for his failure of belief. But why does he hang it on the matter of the Assumption? As numerous prayers and commentaries and paintings attest, the belief that Mary's body was assumed into heaven directly upon her death has a long history; the papal pronouncement was the formal doctrinal acknowledgment of that ancient Catholic tradition and devotion. But doctrinally the Assumption is significant because it carries the Incarnation to its completion in human destiny. The Incarnation means that God became flesh to redeem human beings *in* their bodily humanity, and the Assumption of Mary, as the archetypal representative and mother of all humanity, symbolizes our redemption and resurrection in the body. Lowell's gnostic inability to comprehend or accept the Assumption stands metonymically for his inability finally to accept the Incarnation, and that sad realization requires the journey from Rome: "Much against my will / I left the City of God where it belongs" (p. 364). A 1955 letter to Elizabeth Bishop says: "That God should really be Christ – that does seem strained ..."[20]

The move out of the Church had actually begun in the fall of 1946, along with (ironically) the publication and acclaim for *Lord Weary's Castle* and with the divorce from the novelist Jean Stafford. His brief resumption of Catholicism in early 1949 preceded the first of the many subsequent psychiatric hospitalizations for what would be diagnosed as a manic-depressive condition that plagued him for the rest of his life. Between two periods of hospitalization, which took up much of the year, he married the novelist and critic Elizabeth Hardwick, and upon his release they marked this new phase of his life with the extended stay in Europe that brought them to Rome for the papal declaration. That same year Lowell wrote to the philosopher George Santayana, whom he had met in Rome and who was himself a lapsed Catholic: "I too can cry out 'O Altitudo' – all Christ's violence and love" but "I am back where I was in my faith – fallen or standing in disillusion."[21] On the train ride from Rome to Paris "[t]here were no tickets for that altitude" (p.114). What he was left with was his "blear-eyed ego kicking in my berth," and the pun on berth/birth looks forward to "Life Studies."

The shock and stress of these changes were registered in a radical shift in Lowell's poetry and poetics, most notably in the autobiographical sequence "Life Studies," which provided the title for his 1959 volume. For many, it is his most significant work, and its focus on the anxieties, disturbances, and neuroses of the tormented psyche made Lowell the central figure in what was dubbed the confessional school of poets that included Berryman, Theodore Roethke, W. D. Snodgrass, Sylvia Plath, and Anne Sexton. As the title suggests, the sequence is not a sustained autobiographical narrative, but a loosely chronological series of vignettes, moving from sketches of his conflicted relations with his parents to a grim, unsparing confrontation with his vulnerable and volatile psychiatric state.

Lowell addresses these painful personal materials with a candid directness and an ironic lack of self-pity that make the poems all the more moving and persuasive. He wrote to Elizabeth Hardwick in 1953, after returning from Europe and shortly after writing "Beyond the Alps": "I've been gulping Freud and am a confused and slavish convert ... Every fault is a gold mine of discoveries – I am a walking gold mine."[22] He would later recall: "When I was in Iowa – '50 or later in '52 [–] I read 2/3 of Freud, like reading Tolstoy. In that sense ... *Life Studies* is full of him; a replacement for the Christian church, more intimate but without boundaries or credo, or philosophy."[23]

The change in content and perspective required a change in form and language. Lowell had to break open the tight formalism he had developed under Tate's influence and was looking for different models. He was reading Williams and reviewed the first two books of *Paterson*; he encountered the Whitmanian free verse of the Beats on a reading trip to the West Coast; and among his contemporaries he most keenly responded to the tone and idiom of Elizabeth Bishop. In the mid-1950s, after stalling for several years, he began writing "Life Studies" poems in a looser versification and a more conversational voice with freer rhythms and rhymes. But his sense of what he had lost can be felt in his ambivalent remark to Williams in 1957: "I feel more and more technically indebted to you" through "experimenting with mixing loose and free meters with strict in order to get the accuracy, naturalness, and multiplicity of prose," but at the same time "I also want the state and surge of the old verse, the carpentry of definite meter that tells me when to stop rambling."[24]

Nevertheless, the "state and surge," the stretch and strain, the thunder and lightning of *Lord Weary's Castle* are gone with the prophetic vision. The difference can be most tellingly felt in "Skunk Hour," written in August 1957, and dedicated to Bishop. Lowell called it "the anchor poem" of "Life Studies" because it seeks to pull the sequence together into some kind of larger statement. In Lowell's commentary on the structure of the poem, the first four stanzas present ironic, seemingly offhand glimpses of "a declining Maine sea town," strung on images of fall and autumn. But suddenly "all comes alive in stanzas V and VI" as the speaker becomes the focus and narrates his descent into the dark night of the soul. These were the first sections written, and the poem evolved backward out of them. Lowell invokes St. John of the Cross's dark night to underscore the contrast: "My night is not gracious, but secular, puritan, and agnostical. An Existentialist night." In an extended explication of the poem titled "Despondency and Madness," Berryman described its "occasion" as "the approach of a crisis of mental disorder," which breaks out in the final stanzas, and Lowell called Berryman's reading "too close for comfort."[25] Agonized in his own spiritual Golgotha ("the hill's skull"), the speaker experiences damnation, and out of his echo of Marlowe's *Faustus* and Milton's Satan emerges the vision of the "moonstruck" (lunatic) skunks (p. 192):

> I myself am hell;
> nobody's here –
>
> only skunks, that search
> in the moonlight for a bite to eat.

Mary as Mother of humankind is here grotesquely displaced by "a mother skunk with her column of kittens," and the last image is, in Berryman words, a "greedy parody of the Eucharist": "She jabs her wedge-head in a cup / of sour cream, drops her ostrich tail, / and will not scare." Lowell's response is that the skunk's tough tenacity and animal survival is as much of an "affirmation" as he can muster, albeit "an ambiguous one."[26]

On the heels of *Life Studies* and in response to a commission from the Boston Arts Festival, Lowell began to write "Colonel Shaw and the Massachusetts 54th" and read it to clamorous applause at the festival on the

Boston Common in June, 1960. The poem was tipped into the paperback edition of *Life Studies* after "Skunk Hour," and, renamed, became the concluding and title poem of *For the Union Dead* (1964). Lowell rose to the occasion with his last apocalyptic vision of Boston: a secular jeremiad voiced now not with prophetic outrage but with chillingly ironic condemnation. "For the Union Dead" evolved out of two earlier pieces, "The Old Aquarium" and "One Gallant Rush: The Death of Colonel Shaw."[27] Col. Shaw embodied the old Puritan rectitude in action as he led his black troops into slaughter in the Union assault on Confederate Fort Wagner, South Carolina, on July 18, 1863. The image of Col. Shaw is contrasted with the deracinated apathy and gross materialism of the contemporary scene. The poem moves gradually and by indirection to find Shaw as its moral center. Lowell's boyhood memories of the now ruined South Boston Aquarium lead to the contemporary excavations on the Boston Common, where the gouging of an underground parking garage by "yellow dinosaur steamshovels" so threatens Bullfinch's golden-domed Statehouse atop Beacon Hill that it has to be encased in a protective cocoon of girders. The Latin epigraph says of Col. Shaw and his men: "They gave up everything for the Republic," and the famous St. Gaudens bas-relief commemorating their courageous and resolute sacrifice has to be propped up "against the garage's earthquake." In the closing stanzas, the Republic is still torn by racial strife, and now so heedlessly engrossed in Cold War prosperity that the apocalyptic destructiveness of the atom bomb can be used as a sales pitch on a commercial billboard. The final image pulls the meandering movement of the poem into a terrifying image of universal degradation. The old aquarium is gone, but all of Boston has reverted to "the dark downward and vegetating kingdom / of the fish and reptile" (p. 378):

> Everywhere,
> giant finned cars nose forward like fish;
> a savage servility
> slides by on grease.

Lowell remarked shortly after writing this poem, "I have tried to keep religious imagery out of my poems" but "the dramatic dark of Calvinism remains."[28]

Ian Hamilton correctly claims that, although this powerful image recalls momentarily "the poet-prophet of *Lord Weary's Castle*," the poem's "manipulation of historical, personal, and political elements" in fact points "a way forward to the next phase of Lowell's work."[29] From here on what remains of the prophet with an urgent message gives way to the ironist who has no answers. Lowell's sense of human yearnings and failures – and of his own yearnings and failings – continues to be heartbreaking, and his eye and ear for words – their sounds, their rhythms, their affinities and ruptures, their capacity to focus and blur – remain; there is hardly a poem that does not have striking images, startling metaphorical leaps, haunting language. But, as William Everson observed, "When you are a Christian poet, or a communist poet, and lose your faith, the loss of commitment reduces you to a different level of activity."[30] The poem that follows "For the Union Dead" in the *Collected Poems* is the much-admired "Waking Early Sunday Morning" at the beginning of *Near the Ocean* (1967). But here the effort to rise to a judgment about the human tragedy can only express rueful desperation (p. 386):

> Pity the planet, all joy gone
> from this sweet volcanic cone;
> peace to our children when they fall
> in small war on the heels of small
> war – until the end of time
> to police the earth, a ghost
> orbiting forever lost
> in our monotonous sublime.

The questioning of the power of the word to apprehend and communicate the truth about reality inevitably left Lowell unsure of himself and of his medium, of what he could say or how he should say it. The "blear-eyed ego kicking in my berth" found itself alone in what Fredric Jameson would call "the prison-house of language,"[31] reshuffling words with only "Valéry's idea of revision as both improvement and change, many versions and possibilities, none final."[32] Because language was his only lifeline, the lack of finality, the open-ended proliferation of uncertain and momentary possibilities necessitated that he keep writing, revising, arranging, rearranging – often, by his own account, at a fevered pitch. Lowell wrote to his old friend Peter Taylor in 1970: "Doesn't writing something keep you afloat and breathing? I've been turning out poems at a great rate. They almost keep out depression [cancelled out with a line through the word] the shadows."[33]

Lowell's feverish persistence issued, in part, out of his vacillation about the appropriate and workable form to express his psychological and metaphysical uncertainty: "I clutched at different methods until they wore out."[34] In 1964 he wrote to Adrienne Rich, at a point when she was herself exploring a more open form in her own work: "[T]he keeping open, the keeping daring etc. has everything to do with having some frame or form to hold with."[35] *For the Union Dead* "tries to be an advance, whatever that means, or a sort of combination of *Life Studies* and the more metrical style of my earlier stuff."[36] Then *Near the Ocean* adopted an even tighter form in the eight-line, rhymed stanzas used by the metaphysical poet Andrew Marvell. In the late 1960s, feeling that he needed a more flexible and open space, Lowell loosened up the sonnet by eliminating the rhyme scheme and internal structure of the traditional sonnet to allow him to move with associational freedom within the fourteen lines, and he used that form through the several configurations and elaborations of the *Notebook* poems and *The Dolphin*. In a final reversal the poems written in the last year of Lowell's life and published in *Day by Day* broke into free and irregular verse reminiscent of *Life Studies*.

The continuity through the tightening and relaxing of formal modes is the effort to give effective shape to the agon of Lowell's psychological, emotional, and political life. What kept confessional poetry from being merely narcissistic and therapeutic was the assumption that personal dislocations and neuroses expressed the dislocations and violence of political life. Personal history mirrored and enacted public history; the turmoil of Lowell's emotional and domestic life, punctuated by the recurrent psychiatric breakdowns and periods of hospitalization, transpired within the national travail of the civil rights movement and the heating up of the Cold War in Vietnam. There had been a political dimension to the poetry from the beginning, but in the 1960s Lowell became a very visible public figure through his antiwar protests, his refusal of an invitation to the White House, and his association with Eugene McCarthy and Robert Kennedy in the tumultuous presidential campaign of 1968.

The intense stresses of his personal and political life made for the rapid writing and rewriting of the sonnets, which appeared first as *Notebook 1967–68* (1969) and the next year as an expanded and revised *Notebook*. The title meant to indicate the disjointed openness of daily jottings and momentary associations, but, dissatisfied with the seeming randomness of the sonnets and the baggy shapelessness of their accumulation, Lowell sorted out the personal and political, with further additions and revisions, into the companion volumes, *History* and *For Lizzie and Harriet* (1973), and published them along with "a small scale sequel"[37] in a new collection of sonnets called *The Dolphin*. The sonnets addressed to Lowell's wife and daughter, and in *The Dolphin* to Lady Caroline Blackwood, lay out in intimate detail the emotional and moral muddle of his affair with Blackwood, the separation and divorce from Hardwick, and the subsequent marriage to Blackwood and move to her country estate in England.

His paraphrasing of some of Hardwick's letters into sonnets was particularly excruciating for her, embarrassing for close friends like Bishop and Tate, outrageous to Rich.

The fact of the matter is that, for all his engagement with the political and national scene, the underlying and sustaining impetus behind all the poetry is the life-and-death need to bring the disorder of what he called "a rather grinding autobiography"[38] to some kind of coherent comprehension and expression, however tentative and unresolved. If he could not come to a final understanding, he had, then, to keep adding, revising, revisiting, reformulating. "Eye and Tooth" (from *For the Union Dead*) ends (p. 335): "I'm tired. Everyone's tired of my turmoil." However, not only did he make his exhaustion into a searing poem with a memorable last line, turning on "tired," "tired," "turmoil"; he kept on doggedly writing his turmoil into poems. Even in the volume nominally dedicated to *History*, about half of the poems are in fact autobiographical. And the valedictory poems in *Day by Day* recall, with a deepening premonition of death, old meetings, old friends as well as ongoing anxieties about love and death, transience and transcendence. "Dolphin" concludes the volume of that name with these lines (p. 708):

> I have sat and listened to too many
> words of the collaborating muse,
> and plotted perhaps too freely with my life,
> not avoiding injury to others,
> not avoiding injury to myself –
> to ask compassion … this book, half fiction,
> an eelnet made by man for the eel-fighting –
>
> my eyes have seen what my hand did.

"North Haven," Bishop's elegy for Lowell, invokes Nature's injunction to "*repeat, repeat, repeat; revise, revise, revise*" and ends:

> And now – you've left
> for good. You can't derange or re-arrange,
> your poems again. (But the Sparrows can their song.)
> The words won't change again. Sad friend, you cannot change.[39]

The Postmodernist critics and Language poets have tended to attack Lowell programmatically. He was the leading confessional poet, whose song of himself was the poetry of personality; indeed, he was the most honored and celebrated heir to all that they wanted to repudiate in the Romantic/Modernist aesthetic. In Jed Rasula's *The American Poetry Wax Museum* (1996), the title of one of the chapters repeats the title of

Ehrenpreis's 1965 essay "The Age of Lowell" and then mockingly strikes out the first three words with a canceling line. Admittedly, Lowell's poetry could hardly be more alien to theoretical notions of the death of the author, although he writes often about death and his own death: in "Reading Myself," from *History* (p. 591): "this open book ... my open coffin." Lowell would never see language as an autonomous semiotic code that determines the poem's indeterminacies. On the contrary, language was an extension and expression of his being; in the lines from the sonnet to Berryman cited as epigraph to this chapter, "we are words; / John, we used the language as if we made it" (p. 600). They were language poets but not Language poets. Nevertheless, the trajectory of Lowell's work that this chapter traces places him centrally in the postwar period precisely because it records the deconstruction of the Romantic/Modernist aesthetic from which it arose into a skeptical, fractured sense of self, a growing concern for the contingencies of language, a suspicion of final answers that anticipate and in many ways inaugurate what would coalesce under the term "Postmodernism."

Following the poet's lead in downplaying the early Catholic poems, almost all of the considerable body of Lowell criticism focuses on the poems from *Life Studies* onward, and thus offers an almost inverted perspective on Lowell's work from the one presented here. In a book chapter called "Lowell and History," Helen Vendler (whom Rasula excoriates as Lowell's principal champion) takes almost no account of the poems before *Life Studies* in parsing out the interplay of history and autobiography.[40] Vereen Bell sums up Lowell's achievement in his subtitle: *Nihilist As Hero*.[41] And indeed, "The Nihilist as Hero," from the *History* sequence, gives a good sense of late Lowell (p. 590):

> "All our French poets can turn an inspired line;
> who has written six passable in sequence?"
> said Valéry. That was a happy day for Satan ...
> I want words meat-hooked from the living steer,
> but a cold flame of tinfoil licks the metal log,
> beautiful unchanging fire of childhood
> betraying a monotony of vision ...
> Life by definition breeds on change,
> each season we scrap new cars and wars and women.
> But sometimes when I am ill or delicate,
> the pinched flame of my match turns unchanging green,
> a cornstalk in green tails and seeded tassel ...
> A nihilist wants to live in the world as is,
> And yet gaze the everlasting hills to rubble.

Lowell stripped the sonnet of set rhyme scheme and fixed structural units like the octave and sestet or three quatrains and a closing couplet so that, within the frame of fourteen, mostly iambic pentameter lines, he could have the open space to record his consciousness in "the immediate moment": "Things I felt or saw, or read were adrift in the whirlpool, the squeeze of the sonnet and the loose ravel of blank verse."[42] The generative stimulus of "The Nihilist as Hero" is the quotation from Valéry, a charge of poetic failure so devastating as to seem to Lowell satanic, and from there, as the ellipses indicate, the sonnet follows a meandering sequence of private associations. What is clear is the paralyzing sense of being stuck with a fixation on the past in a life breeding to death moment by moment, season by season: the unalterable fact in a world of change. But on occasion the "cold flame" of fixation gives way to the indelible and "unchanging" flare of insight into changeable mortality. Then "monotony of vision" quickens into a poem that allows the nihilist to live "in the world as is," despite the fact or because of the fact that his withering gaze sees in the seeming obduracy of the physical world its fundamental friability. In "Colloquy in Black Rock," "All discussions // End in the mud-flat detritus of death" but paradoxically "Our ransom is the rubble of his [the Savior's] death"; here the nihilist's discussion ends with a vision of the finality of "rubble."

William Everson made a distinction between the poet who "stands witness to a world beyond the world of his making" and the poet who "creates a world of his own making" and, accurately enough, saw Lowell as evolving from the first kind of poet to the second.[43] Everson's distinction is one way of approaching the distinction between Neoromanticism and Postmodernism that is outlined in the introductory chapter and runs through the various chapters of this book. It was the Neoromantic in Lowell that believed in the power of the word to stand witness to a truth about reality beyond the word, but Lowell was never in fact reconciled to the Postmodernist's fractured forms and indeterminate meaning. He could not finally rest in the finality of rubble and always saw the heroism of the nihilist as a lamentable diminution. To his poet-friends he would confess his regret at feeling reduced in scope and power: to Bishop, 1962: "My inspiration seems to have become minute – little lines, little subjects"; to Bishop the next year: "The best I have done seems wizened"; to Berryman, 1962: "small clear half anguished things . . . the end of one way of life, whittled down and whittled down"; to Jarrell, 1964: "a hunt for the knack and power to fly"; to Rich, 1964: "starting again, a little threadbare having junked too much in desperation"; to Bishop, 1970, about *The Dolphin*: "I am disheartened by the whole."[44] Thinking back to *Lord Weary's Castle* in

1974, Lowell sees *Notebook* as somehow "an attempt to get back its present instant, moment of struggle and occasional grand style."[45] Lowell told Ian Hamilton: "I don't read my early books with full sympathy. Those I like best are *Life Studies* and the last two" – that is to say, in 1971, *Notebook* and *The Dolphin*, still unpublished.[46] Nevertheless, near the end of *History*, "Last Night" mourns the death of friends and his own looming death, and then, with startling bravery or bravado, quotes, as a damning obituary, Donald Hall's scathing summary of his life's work (p. 601):[47]

> the deaths, suicides, madness
> of Roethke, Berryman, Jarrell and Lowell,
> "the last the most discouraging of all
> surviving to dissipate *Lord Weary's Castle*
> and nine subsequent useful poems
> in the seedy grandiloquence of *Notebook*."

Day by Day, the title of the volume published a month before Lowell's death in September 1977, suggests a continuation of the notebook format and manner, but in fact, whatever Lowell made of Hall's critique, he abandoned the sonnet form. These last poems, begun in the year after the appearance of the three sonnet volumes, were written in the open form and free verse, regulated by a roughly iambic measure, of *Life Studies*, and the poems resume the confessional mode of that book. He told Caroline Blackwood: "I have written a minor *Union Dead* fifteen years idler [sic] – fatigued, bright and elegiac."[48] Despite his concern about comparison with those earlier poems, he had in fact not written a book of such emotional immediacy and verbal energy since *Life Studies* and *For the Union Dead*. The poems probe wounds, old and recent, but with tender care. They are at once a gathering in, a rounding up, and a signing out: elegiac valedictions to and about his wives, children, parents, friends, summoned again, this time to say goodbye.

Lowell told Steven Axelrod that *Day by Day* "comes close to tragic, though that's not clear in either the book or life."[49] The language moves repeatedly into negatives: "no," "none," "nothing," and adjectives like "immeasurable," "unaccountable," "indistinguishable," "illicit," "inexcusable," "impossible," "unspeakable," "unpardonable," "insupportable," "unredeemable," "unforgivable." For example, these lines (p. 758) from "Death of a Critic":

> I ask for a natural death,
> no teeth on the ground,
> no blood about the place ...

> It's not death I fear,
> but unspecified, unlimited pain.

Or these lines (p. 797) from "Grass Fires":

> I –
> really I can do little,
> as little now as then,
> about the infernal fires –
> I cannot blow out a match.

What saves the book from unrelieved tragedy, however, are the startling moments that break suddenly into prayer at the end of the poem. "Logan Airport, Boston" moves to these lines (p. 786): "I thank God for being alive – / a way of writing I once thought heartless." "St Mark's, 1933" recalls an injury to "my closest friend" and concludes: "*Huic ergo parce, Deus* [So have mercy on him, God]" (p. 801). "Thanks-Offering for Recovery," written about a Brazilian carved votive head that Bishop gave Lowell after a psychiatric hospitalization in early 1976, expels nihilism and then addresses the votive head as his alter ego (p. 837):

> Goodbye nothing. Blockhead,
> I would take you to church,
> if any church would take you …
> This winter, I thought
> I was created to be given away.

"Epilogue," the last poem in the book, justifies his life's work with: "Yet why not say what happened? / Pray for the grace of accuracy" (p. 838). An elegy "For John Berryman" finishes (p. 738):

> To my surprise, John,
> I pray *to* not for you,
> think of you not myself,
> smile and fall asleep.

Most startlingly and powerfully, "Home," written after another hospital bout, invokes the Virgin Mary for the first time since "Beyond the Alps," and, as if in negation of that poem's negation ("But who believed this? Who could understand?"), she appears here as the "Queen of Heaven" after the Assumption, and, as in *Lord Weary's Castle,* she is the mediatrix of all graces (p. 825):

> I cannot sit or stand two minutes,
> yet walk imagining a dialogue
> between the devil and myself,

> not knowing which is which or worse,
> saying,
> as one would instinctively say Hail Mary,
> *I wish I could die.*
> Less than ever I expect to be alive
> six months from now –
> *1976,*
> a date I dare not affix to my grave.
>
> The Queen of Heaven, I miss her,
> we were divorced. She never doubted
> the divided, stricken soul
> could call her Maria,
> and rob the devil with a word.

"Beyond the Alps" decreed the divorce, "[m]uch against my will," but here the plural "we" weds the "I" and "her" of the previous line, and the passive-verb of the construction "we were divorced" elides his agency in the severance. With a word, all the poems' negatives – "unpardonable," "unforgivable," "unredeemable" – would be reversed: the devil's death wish converted into a hankering for heaven. Lowell's end would come almost as soon as he expects it here, but he comes close, in these lines, to bringing his life and his life's work full circle.

II

From their first meeting in 1944, Lowell and Berryman tracked each other through a long and competitive friendship. They wrote to and about each other in verse and prose; they regarded each other as the leading figures in the generation after the great Modernist poets. They both wrote elegically about Eliot, Pound, Frost, and Williams as towering predecessors whose influence it was necessary to acknowledge – and to question, because they felt themselves representative of a generation in intense crisis. Lowell's sonnet addressed to Berryman a couple of years before his death asserts: "I feel I know what you have worked through, you / know what I have worked through."[50] Modernism was generated out of crisis – social, political, spiritual, moral – but asserted the revitalizing and mastering of the artistic medium as the means of making out of the disorder an aesthetic order that might even, some thought, create the possibility of a renewed political, moral, and spiritual order. Pound's dictum "Make it new" put equal emphasis on "make" and "new" to proclaim the creative and recreative power of the medium.

Both Berryman and Lowell were close enough to their forebears to feel the authority and responsibility of the Modernist poet as word-maker, as maker through words; Lowell's sonnet continues with the lines quoted earlier: "we are words; / John, we used the language as if we made it." But that "as if" registers a hesitation that haunted them and foreshadowed, in the generation after Lowell and Berryman, the Postmodern deconstruction of the Modernist insistence on the art work's integrity and the power of the medium to find or make order. For if literary and artistic Modernism arose out of the crisis that culminated in World War I, it did not survive the horrors of World War II: bombardment of London and Hamburg and Berlin, the death camps of Auschwitz and Dachau, the nuclear destruction of Hiroshima and Nagasaki. Berryman and Lowell are transitional figures between Modernism and Postmodernism in their efforts, against mounting skepticism, to find ways to use the language as if they made it – and made art with it.

At the same time, the trajectories of the poetic careers of Lowell and Berryman make a striking contrast. They met in the year when Lowell was writing "Colloquy in Black Rock" and "The Quaker Graveyard in Nantucket" and other poems that would appear in *Lord Weary's Castle*, win a Pulitzer Prize, establish Lowell's prophetic voice and style, and catapult him in his early twenties to the forefront of contemporary poets. When Berryman's early poetry appeared in *The Dispossessed* in 1948, it won the Shelley Memorial Award from the Poetry Society of America but created no great stir; indeed, as Berryman himself knew, those poems showed a poet with potential but still in search of a voice and style and stance. The energy of Lowell's Catholic apocalyptic vision propelled the language and form of his early poetry, and after that vision waned, the shifting of styles and forms, the restless revising and rewriting chart his strenuous effort to sustain belief in the power of the word to transcend the flux of mortal experience. Berryman did not find his voice until the early 1950s, but then his career moved steadily through three major phases: *Homage to Mistress Bradstreet*, completed in 1953, published in *The Partisan Review* in 1953 and as a book in 1956; *The Dream Songs*, begun in the mid-1950s, published in two volumes in 1964 and 1968 and collected in 1969 (winning the Pulitzer Prize, the National Book Award, and the Bollingen Prize); and the extraordinary series of prayers that began in the last section of *Love & Fame* (1970) and ran through *Delusions, Etc.* (1972, published after his death earlier in that year) and *Henry's Fate* (1977), and that brought him back, in the last two years of his life, to the Catholicism he had practiced fervently till his teens.

In his introduction to *Henry's Fate* John Haffenden cites and agrees with Christopher Ricks's comment that Berryman's work constitutes a theodicy.[51] Leibniz coined the term "theodicy" as the title of his 1710 philosophical treatise, and the OED defines it as the "vindication of divine attributes, especially justice and holiness, in respect to the existence of evil; a writing, doctrine, or theory intended to 'justify the ways of God to men.'" Throughout his life Berryman's mind turned on questions of ultimate belief and disbelief; he avidly read – and in his classes taught – philosophy and theology, scripture and church history. He wrote, however, not as a philosopher or theologian but as a poet registering, from the quivering nerve endings of his sensibility, a daily sense of life as a prolonged dying, agonized by a conviction of sin and guilt. As a result, he admitted, "I have been interested not only in religion but in theology all my life"; "[t]he idea of a theodicy has been in my mind at least since 1938,"[52] and his work from *Homage* on does undertake a poetry of theodicy, that is to say, a poetry of dialogue with and about God concerning sin and the possibility of redemption, suffering and the possibility of rescue.

One indication of the religious inclination that energized Berryman's skepticism and agnosticism over the years is a New Year's resolution he drew up for himself for 1943: "To learn to know Christ."[53] In 1959, with *Homage* acclaimed as a masterpiece and *The Dream Songs* already begun, Berryman described the power of the word as a prayer of conversion: "Poetry is a terminal activity, taking place out near the end of things, where the poet's soul addresses one other soul only, never mind when. And it aims – never mind *either* communication or expression – at the reformation of the poet, as prayer does." Yeats and Eliot are the "grand cases" of such development in the Modernist generation, but Berryman universalizes the reforming of the poem and the poet: "something of the sort happens, on a small scale, a freeing, with the creation of every real poem."[54] This is what Berryman meant by "the freedom of the poet," the title he gave his collected prose. Berryman saw his poetry as developing, like Eliot's, through a series of "spasms,"[55] and the rest of this chapter follows Berryman's "theodicy" through the three major phases or "spasms" of his work as he finds a voice and form to articulate, out of his experience of pain and desolation, a desperate dialogue with God.

Berryman acknowledged that the shadow of literary forebears made him "very late in developing."[56] In a letter to his friend and editor Robert Giroux, he said: "Poe was our first imagination after Edwards, then Emerson, *then* Walt."[57] More immediately he saw his imitation of "middle and later Yeats" and of W. H. Auden in the poems from the late 1930s and early 1940s as at least saving him "from the then-crushing influences of Ezra Pound and T. S. Eliot," but none of them, in the end, could "teach me to sound like myself (whatever that was) or tell me what to write about."[58] Thematically at least, the early poems indicate his abiding concerns. "The Statue" depicted art, exemplified in the statue of Humboldt in a park, as elevated above the flux of mortal and temporal existence, but its very permanence and escape from the flux makes it seem "cynical" and "intolerable." "The Ball Poem" turns the chance observation of a young boy's watching his ball drift out to sea into an exemplum in which he learns "[t]he epistemology of loss." "The Disciple" is a dramatic monologue in which the elderly speaker witnesses Jesus' execution and surprising survival: "performing still what tricks he could / For men to come, rapt in compassion still." "Fare Well" is the first of many subsequent elegies for his father, whose suicide (when his son was twelve) Berryman associated with his loss of faith and his own neurotic obsession with loss and suicide: "As I sink, I weep."[59]

What held up Berryman's poetic development was finding a voice and form to "sound like myself." To his ear, "Winter Landscape" was the first intimation of his own voice, and characteristically he linked voice to formal structure: "mounted in five five-line stanzas, unrhymed, all one sentence" with a colon in the middle.[60] But it was in the writing of "The Ball Poem" that Berryman made the crucial discovery about verbalizing the speaker's identity that released him into the Bradstreet poem and *The Dream Songs:* namely, that the fluidity of personal pronouns permitted the folding and unfolding dialogue between the "I" of the poem and "you," "he," "she." "The Ball Poem" tells the narrative about the boy and his ball in the third person but then shifts in the last lines:

> I am everywhere,
> I suffer and move, my mind and my heart move
> With all that move me, under the water
> Or whistling, I am not a little boy.[61]

Berryman had listened to his mentors. These lines could come from Walt in "Song of Myself," and Berryman had heard Yeats move in and out of one persona or another, sometimes as an alter ego, sometimes as an opposite or anti-self. Berryman fully recognized the momentousness of what he had learned about the permeability of pronouns in relation to a persona:

> The discovery here was that a commitment of identity can be "reserved," so to speak, with an ambiguous pronoun. The poet himself is both let out and put in; the boy does and does not become him and we are confronted with a process which is at once a process of life and a process of art. A pronoun may seem a small matter, but she matters, he matters, it matters, they

matter. Without this invention ... I could not have written either of the two long poems that constitute the bulk of my work so far.[62]

Haffenden's assertion that Whitman is "the American poet he [Berryman] most resembles"[63] might seem at first surprising. Berryman did not subscribe to Whitman's Transcendentalist optimism and belief in cosmic and national progress. But Berryman wrote perceptively and enthusiastically about Whitman and called "Song of Myself" "the greatest poem so far written by an American." Moreover, Whitman's presentation of a fluid identity that connected poetry with lived experience helped Berryman resist the Modernist aesthetic of "the artwork made, finished, autonomous" (institutionalized by the New Criticism in "the critical quarterlies since I was an undergraduate") and instead affirm the Romantic notion of the poem as "a work of *life*" rather than merely "a literary performance." The poet as "a *voice*," "not as *maker* but as spiritual historian," means that "[t]he poet – one would say, a mere channel, but with its own ferocious difficulties – fills with experiences, a valve opens; he speaks them." Berryman stood vociferously with Whitman for poetry of personality against "Eliot's amusing theory of the impersonality of the artist."[64]

Of course, as Berryman well knew, the poem did not simply pour out in final and finished form with the opening of the valve, but took shape with the revisions, additions, and deletions of the poet as maker. In practice, Berryman revised – often, he said, "heavily," so that the initial efforts were "unrecognizable by the time I'm finished with them."[65] Nevertheless, the realization of the poet as voice and of the poem as a work of life opened the way for Berryman's first long poem, *Homage to Mistress Bradstreet*. The composition of the poem spans the years of acclaim for *Lord Weary's Castle*, and Berryman felt that he had "seized inspiration, I think, from Lowell, rather than imitated him."[66] In 1948, Berryman wrote the first eight-line stanza and the first three lines of the second stanza of *Homage*, thinking that it might run to five or six stanzas, perhaps fifty lines. There he got stuck for almost five years; as he researched Bradstreet's life and Puritan history, he realized the scope and ambition of what was gestating. Later he recalled the excitement that propelled the poem from those 11 lines to completion in 57 stanzas and 450 lines during three fevered months of sustained composition: "Narrative! let's have narrative, and at least one dominant personality, and no fragmentation! In short let us have something spectacularly NOT *The Waste Land*, the best long poem of the age."[67] Berryman's poem did avoid the structural fragmentation of *The Waste Land* and the ideogrammic method of Pound's *Cantos*, but its narrative developed not as a monologue but as a dialogue between the poet and Bradstreet. The exchange and even interchange between "I" and "you" initiated Berryman's first extended experiment with the fluidity of pronouns to dramatize the contrasting aspects of "one dominant personality." After all, for all Whitman's talk of synthesis, his "effort to put *a Person*" on record shows "what a deeply divided personality" he was.[68] For five years Anne Bradstreet held a central place in his psychological, spiritual, and moral life: "I did not choose her – somehow she chose me ..."; "I loved her – I sort of fell in love with her." One "point of connection" with "our first American poet" as "the tenth muse" was "the almost insuperable challenge" of "writing high verse" in "a land that cared and cares so little for it."[69] But Berryman was interested in her less as a practicing poet than as at once his muse and anti-self. He was drawn to her precisely because those very factors that would seem to differentiate her from him – she was a seventeenth-century woman and an avowed Puritan Christian – spoke to and for his own deep yearning for belief and forgiveness. The four stanzas at the beginning and at the end in his own voice serve as "exordium and coda" to enclose his imagining of Bradstreet's words; in the middle of the poem his voice interrupts hers and initiates a direct conversational exchange that recounts their convergence and divergence.

When Berryman wrote the opening lines in 1948, he did not foresee the direction of the poem, but he had invented a stanza with sufficient conventions to keep the language in control and focus and sufficient openness and variation to allow it scope and development. Berryman said that he had adapted the stanza from the one Yeats used in "In Memory of Major Robert Gregory."[70] In addition, in 1947, Berryman had written a sequence of sonnets about his first adulterous affair (published as *Berryman's Sonnets* in 1967), and the eight-line stanza of *Homage* can be seen as a variation on the octave of a Petrarchan sonnet (just as the six-line stanza *of The Dream Songs* can be seen to adapt the sestet of the sonnet). The meter is basically iambic, and the eight lines contract and expand the iambic pentameter: 5-5-3-4-5-5-3-6; stanzas 24 and 39, marking major transitions in the poem, have an extra hexameter in the middle of the stanza. The rhyme scheme works within and against that pattern in its own combination of recurrence and variation, with x indicating open, unrhymed lines: a-b-x-b-c-c-x-a. There are deviations from the rhyme scheme, especially in the intense complexities of the second half of the poem, but all three rhyming pairs (a-a, b-b, c-c) occur in thirty-six of the fifty-seven stanzas, and two pairs, (a-a, c-c) appear in fifty-four stanzas.

The voice that Berryman devised for his engagement with Bradstreet strikes the ear as oddly formal yet fractured, at once decorous yet colloquial. The often idiosyncratic diction, the compressed phrasing, the eccentric word order create a verbal space that sounds both familiar and unfamiliar, both contemporary and historically removed, where the poet and his seventeenth-century muse can converse and understand each other. For example, the poet displaces Anne's husband Simon in the twists and turns of these lines from the second stanza:

> I doubt if Simon than this blast, that sea,
> spares from his rigour for your poetry
> more. We are on each other's hands
> who care. Both of our worlds unhanded us.

Anne's words can be no less contorted:

> Chapped souls ours, by the day Spring's strong winds
> swelled,
> Jack's pulpits arched, more glad. The shawl I pinned
> flaps like a shooting soul
> might in such weather Heaven send.[71]

A less scrambled and compressed wording might be: "Our souls were chapped, but had become more glad by the day when Spring's strong winds swelled and Jack's pulpits arched." But what makes the poem so powerfully successful is that Berryman's strange, contrived, private language works to accommodate and modulate both speakers in a range of tones from the violence and exaltation of childbirth in stanzas 19 though 21, to an intense and rapid-fire exchange of conversation in stanza 25, to a lyric description of the gentle awakenings of spring after a hard New England winter in stanza 31.

The drama of the poem turns on the mutual recognition – and self-recognition – between seeming opposites: the Puritan wife and mother, accepting the hardships of her life in loving submission to God, and the twentieth-century agnostic man, driven by lust, tormented by guilt, and fearful of death. The poem has rightly been hailed as an extraordinary feat of historical imagination, and it does follow Anne through the years of her life in the New World to her death; but she speaks as Berryman's Mistress Bradstreet. By the end of the exordium, as the poet summons Anne from the grave of the past, his voice dissolves into hers. His assumption of her voice allows him to use a moment of distress recorded in her diary on her first sight of the unpeopled wilderness ("at which my heart rose") before submitting to God's will[72] and expand on it to give his Bradstreet a more independently "modern" spirit. She confesses to her interlocuter her grumblings about the domestic routine and theocratic patriarchy and even her sympathy for Anne Hutchinson, the excommunicated and expelled heretic, as her "[b]itter sister" and fellow "victim": "Still-all a Christian daughter grinds her teeth / a little." In turn, he sees their outcast state as their special bond: because "[b]oth our worlds unhanded us," "[w]e are on each other's hands / who care"; we "care" for each other in loving concern and mutual responsibility. Moreover, Berryman attributes to his Bradstreet a worldly vanity about her youthful beauty (providentially blighted by smallpox) and an erotic carnality suppressed by Puritan suspicion of the body: "Brood I do on myself naked." Berryman's projections onto his Bradstreet leave her vulnerable to the sexual advances of the poet: "You must not love me, but I do not bid you cease."[73]

The heart of the poem (25–39) initiates an intense and passionate conversation that becomes a verbal seduction whose consummation would "[s]ing a concord of our thought." In Berryman's extraordinary fantasy ("I decided to tempt her") she is drawn to him as "demon lover,"[74] wavers, almost succumbs to the pressure of his words – before rejecting the Devil ("Father of lies, / a male great pestle smashes / small women"), seeking divine protection ("my God, / mercy for him and me"), and resuming her life as a Christian daughter, wife, and mother (stanzas 39 to the coda in the poet's voice).[75] Of course, convincing as the poem makes the temptation seem, it can only be a verbal seduction, and by writing the poem Berryman has come to possess her imaginatively.

What's more, the psychological and religious point of the poem requires that she refuse his sexual advances, because as anima and muse, his Bradstreet represents the longing in the guilt-ridden and agnostic poet to believe in God and in divine mercy for sins of lust. When he confesses to her his violent fantasies of lust and murder, she dismisses them: " – Dreams! You are good ... In green space we are safe. / God awaits us ..." Her faith is the counter-temptation for the poet, but his response expresses the depths of his agnostic doubts: " – I cannot feel myself God waits. He flies / nearer a kindly world; or he is flown"; "Man is entirely alone / may be. I am a man of griefs and fits / trying to be my friend."[76] The coda confirms his loneliness in a violent world: "I am a closet of secrets dying, / races murder, foxholes hold men ..." Nevertheless, the poet, chastened and comforted, gathers her "benevolent phantom" to himself in the concluding stanza:

> O all your ages at the mercy of my loves
> together lie at once, forever or
> so long as I happen.

In the rain of pain and departure, still
Love has no body and presides the sun,
and elfs from silence melody. I run.
Hover, utter, still,
a sourcing   whom my lost candle like the firefly loves.[77]

It took Berryman two years to recover from the manic intensity and subsequent exhaustion of writing *Homage to Mistress Bradstreet* ("I was on fire every second"[78]), but in 1955 he wrote the first of the poems that he was soon calling *The Dream Songs*. He would continue to write them, even after their supposed completion and publication in 385 songs, until his death. It is an indication of the different trajectories of Berryman's and Lowell's careers that where Berryman had had *Lord Weary's Castle* in mind when he undertook *Homage*, Lowell had Berryman's poem-in-parts very much in mind when he set out in the late 1960s on the sequences of *Notebook* sonnets. But in fact, Berryman's intention was very different from Lowell's. Whereas Lowell's forewords to the various editions of reshuffled and revised sonnets indicate his anxiety about coherent form and meaning, Berryman made large claims for *The Dream Songs*. For him the songs comprised not a sequence but a single poem grounded in the personality of a persona, "a character named Henry, who also has a friend who calls him 'Mr. Bones.'" In a 1970 interview he declared "I saw myself only as an epic poet," and where *Homage* was written against the example of *The Waste Land*, "the model in *The Dream Songs* was the other great American poem – I am very ambitious – 'Song of Myself' ..."[79]

The Romantics turned the epic narrative of the mythic hero into a journey into the psyche of the protagonist. Berryman's ambitions link *The Dream Songs* to Romantic epics like "Song of Myself" and Wordsworth's "The Prelude" and Thoreau's *Walden* – but also to Modernist epics like *The Cantos* and *The Waste Land* which displace the poet/protagonist into personae: Pound into Ulysses and Confucius, Eliot into many voices, Berryman into Henry and his "Friend." But those analogies with Romantic and Modernist inflections of epic also indicate the relative limits of Berryman's ambition, the more restricted world of his poem. *The Dream Songs* lacks Wordsworth's sublime Nature, Whitman's vision of America, Pound's historical and mythic scope; it records the implosion of the epic impulse into the introverted dreamworld of Henry's lacerated psyche.

A number of the songs do in fact engage postwar America, often trenchantly: racism and the civil rights struggle; the consumerism and hucksterism of the Eisenhower years; American expansion and Cold War conflicts and the Vietnam War. But Berryman suggests the hermeticism of his project when he claims that a long poem with a "hero" requires "the construction of a world rather than the reliance upon one already existent which is available to a small poem." Whitman asserted that *Leaves of Grass* should not be judged merely as a literary performance; Berryman cites that remark in his essay on "Song of Myself" but insists that Henry's world is literary performance, fictive constructions: "Henry both is and is not me, obviously ... But I am an actual human being; he is nothing but a series of conceptions – my conceptions." Whitman boasts, "I sing myself and celebrate myself"; Berryman can sing himself most openly as Henry. The poem's "I" is more "myself" as Henry, but Henry is "nothing but" a world of dream and images so hermetic that "observation of nature" can offer no objective term of reference or solace, reflection or transcendence, as it does to Wordsworth and Whitman, Pound and Hopkins and Jeffers. Song 265 says: "next time it will be nature & Thoreau / this time is Baudelaire."[80] Berryman might have cited Whitman instead of Thoreau in juxtaposition to Baudelaire; *Leaves of Grass* and *Fleurs du Mal*, published in 1857, just two years after Whitman's first edition, have often been juxtaposed as the janus-face, radiant and outgoing vs. dark and inward-looking, of Romantic poetry as it turned into modern poetry.

In constructing Henry's world Berryman undertakes a complicated experiment in the fluidity of pronouns: "the 'I,' perhaps of the poet, disappears into Henry's first and third persons (he talks to himself in the second person, too, about himself)."[81] "I," "you," and "he" intersect and interchange as the poet recounts Henry's encounter with self and world on the cusp between dream and reality. To construct Henry's verbal world, Berryman invented a "metrical plan – which is original, as in *Homage*": "eighteen-line sections, three six-line stanzas, each normally (for feet) 5-5-3-5-5-3, variously rhymed and not but mostly rhymed with great strictness."[82] As with *Homage*, the discipline of stresses and lineation and rhyme provided the needed focus and shape, while the lengthening and tightening of line length and the variations in meter and rhyme provided sufficient openness to allow free movement from image to image, emotion to emotion, and also to sustain the succession of poems over the years.

The style that Berryman devised for Henry is also idiosyncratic: a rapidly shifting mix of intimate conversation, slang, minstrel blackface, blues, jazz, fluid pronouns, broad humor, outrageous puns, sly irony, and soaring rhetoric. This "polyglot" speech, Adrienne Rich said, was a "new language" for contemporary American angst.[83] Henry speaks always in extremis, and his speech is a quirky but effective vehicle for negotiating the wild twists and turns of Henry's dream world. Song 13 is a good introduction to Henry and the polyglot speech of *The Dream Songs*:[84]

> God bless Henry. He lived like a rat,
> with a thatch of hair on his head
> in the beginning.
> Henry was not a coward. Much.
> He never deserted anything; instead,
> he stuck, when things like pity were thinning.
>
> So may be Henry was a human being.
> Let's investigate that.
> ... We did; okay.
> He is a human American man.
> That's true. My lass is braking.
> My brass is aching. Come & diminish me, & map my way.
>
> God's Henry's enemy. We're in business ... Why,
> what business must be clear.
> A cornering.
> I couldn't feel more like it. –Mr. Bones,
> as I look on the saffron sky,
> you strikes me as ornery.

Song 13 presents Henry, early in his "epic," as a kind of American antihero everyman whose fantasies of lust and nightmares of violence are somehow a consequence of or compensation for a lifelong sense of dying, of suffering and loss in a fallen and guilty world, of being trapped in diminishing life with God as either redeemer or enemy. Henry speaks to and about many people, but the songs are all elegies, for his friends (especially poet friends: Theodore Roethke, Delmore Schwartz, Randall Jarrell, Dylan Thomas) and, through it all, for himself. Song 21 sums up Henry's obsession with death "Appalled: by all the dead: Henry brooded. / Without exception! All. / ALL." Henry is appalled (the word contains "pall" and anticipates the reiterated "all") yet mesmerized by the seductive refrain from "underground": " 'O Come on down. O come on down.' "[85]

In Song 76, near the end of Book III, Henry laments " – *If* life is a handkerchief sandwich, // in a modesty of death I join my father," but his minstrel friend hands him a handkerchief to dry his tears and teaches him the steps needed to keep going and resume his song:

– You is from hunger, Mr. Bones,

I offers you this handkerchief, now set
your left foot by my right foot,
shoulder to shoulder, all that jazz,
arm in arm, by the beautiful sea,
hum a little, Mr. Bones.
– I saw nobody coming, so I went instead.

The next poem ends the first published volume of songs with Henry, like
a madly inspired prophet, preparing to "move on" with *Homage* and *The
Dream Songs* brandished as talismans:

it is a wonder that, with in each hand
one of his mad books and all,
ancient fires for eyes, his head full
& his heart full, he's making ready to move on.[86]

Thus Book III concludes with Henry resolved to live; but Book
IV, the middle of the seven books, is the only one with a title, "Opus
Posthumous," in the course of which Henry dies, comes back to life,
and moves on again through the three remaining books. So the poem
advances through a series of reversals and counterreversals with death.
Moreover, as Berryman's alcoholism deepened and his mental and physical condition deteriorated in the 1960s, the songs focus more insistently
on a choice between survival and suicide. The more strongly Henry feels
drawn to "come on down," the more insistently he pulls himself up short.
He mourns Sylvia Plath but finds her "exit" "a poor exemplum, one more
suicide / to stack upon the others" (Song 172); "relevant experts / say the
wounds to the survivors is // the worst of the Act, the worst of the Act!"
(Song 345). Consequently, Henry counsels himself against suicide: "My
desire for death was strong / but never strong enough. I thought: this is
my chance, / I can bear it" (Song 259); "Now at last the effort to make
him kill himself / has failed" (Song 359). After all, "Henry has much to
do" (Song 175); "there are secrets, secrets, I may yet – / hidden in history
& theology, hidden in rhyme – / come on to understand" (Song 159).[87]

All along, the rhyming of the songs has been Berryman's lifeline. Song
75 follows the exfoliation of the book as tree from the initial indifference
of the universe through the comic indignity of dogs' "friendly operations"
and punning wisecracks (dog bark / tree bark, tree leaves / book leaves) to
glorious rhetorical heights hymning the heroic, life-sustaining power of
language:

Turning it over, considering, like a madman,
Henry put forth a book.
No harm resulted from this.
Neither the menstruating stars   (nor man) was moved
at once.
Bare dogs drew closer for a second look

and performed their friendly operations there.
Refreshed, the bark rejoiced.
Seasons went and came.
Leaves fell, but only a few.
Something remarkable about this
unshedding bulky bole-proud blue-green moist

thing made by savage & thoughtful
surviving Henry
began to strike the passers from despair
so that sore on their shoulders old men hoisted
six-foot sons and polished women called
small girls to dream awhile toward the flashing & bursting
      tree![88]

What sustains Henry is what Berryman called his "theodicy": his need to unriddle the "secrets" of his relation to God and God's relation to him. As with the Bradstreet poem, Berryman asserted, "there is a lot of theology in *The Dream Songs*."[89] Henry "would be prepared to live in a world of Fáll / for ever, penitent Henry," but a postlapsarian world has no "for ever." In Song 64 his anonymous minstrel friend tries to resign the desolate Henry to the existential dualism that keeps our broken world from insight into a transcendent order of Being: "Here matters hard to manage at de best, / Mr. Bones. Tween what we see, what be, / is blinds. Them blinds' on fire." A song, written in 1968 after the published poem, recalls the innocence and happiness of "the altar boy … on freezing twilit mornings, after good dreams. / Since when my dreams have changed." Henry has a dim sense that "once" he knew an edenic wholeness and happiness (see Songs 1 and 26), but "[t]hen came a departure." When his friend asks, "What happen then, Mr Bones?," Henry's answer sees the "fall" into poetry as a compensation for the original fall: "Fell Henry back into the original crime: art, rime …" In Song 201, "Henry in twilight is on his own: … pondering, making" because "[o]n the philosophical side // plus religious, he lay at a loss."[90]

But in all his pondering and making Henry, never an atheist, is focused on God as the heart of the mystery. The question that he ponders has troubled many hearts and minds: how to reconcile a God of love and

blessing with a world of suffering and sin. "[P]erishing Henry" at times
blames and holds God responsible for his desperate situation: "long experience of His works / has not taught me his love." Henry "can advance
no claim" to answer the question "God loves his creatures when he treats
them so?"; but this negation moves characteristically to a plea for inclusion in the divine remembrance: "he studied thy Word & grew afraid, /
work & fear be the basis for his terrible cry / not to forget his name." In
Song 194, in addition to the physicians and psychiatrists helping him to
survive, Henry calls on "Dr God" for spiritual aid; "Púsh on me. / Give it
to Henry harder."⁹¹

A number of songs reiterate Henry's struggle to accept Jesus as God's
"Word" of love to sinful humans. In Song 29 the eyes of Jesus gaze "blind"
from "a grave Sienese face" in "still profiled reproach." But Song 47 takes
Mary of Egypt as his patron saint and tells her legend: visiting the Church
of the Holy Sepulcher in Jerusalem, Mary was overcome with remorse for
a life of prostitution and "rushed from The Crucified" in shame to live
out her penitence as an ascetic in the desert. For agnostic Henry, however,
her feast day coincides, ironically but appropriately enough, with "April
Fool's Day": "We celebrate her feast with our caps on, / whom God has
not visited."⁹²

Nevertheless, the combination of compressed language and wild metaphorical leaps in the next song works its way torturously to the redemptive promise of Jesus' death and resurrection renewed through all time in
the sacramental "bread" of communion. The poem plays out the death
and resurrection through the Gospel image of the wheat that must die
into earth to rise again and make the bread of life: "the seed goes down,
god dies, / a rising happens, / some crust, and then occurs an eating."
To the question "[W]here's the bread?," the "implausible" but "necessary"
answer is: "the rising in the Second Gospel, pal." The last stanza enacts the
inversion or conversion: Henry, "[B]itter" and "full of the death of love"
comes to "sybil" of that rising as "the death of the death of love."⁹³

"The Carpenter's Son" (Song 234) is another communion song, celebrating Jesus' message – "Repent, & love" – with a eucharistic Christmas
"cookie": "Pass me a cookie O one absolutely did / lest we not know
him. Fasten to your fire / the blessing of the living God." For what if,
Henry wonders, "the final wound of the Cross" is in fact "the terrible
tree / whereon he really hung, for you and me"? In "The Secret of the
Wisdom" (Song 20) when we ask God to "[h]url" some intimation of
the secret, what "we hear" echoes the felix culpa, the fortunate fall at the
heart of Augustinian theology ("St. Augustine ... is a particular interest

of mine"): "the more sin has increast, the more / grace has been caused to abound." In Song 58 "the mystery is full": Henry is "shaky" in his "shame," but is nonetheless emboldened to address God or Jesus as "Sire" and proclaims himself, in a mad jumble of faux-medieval and faux-blackface, Sire's "serf" and "male Muse": "Sire, damp me down. Me feudal O, me yore / (male Muse) serf, if anyfing; / which rank I pull."[94]

The theodicy pieced together here from texts scattered throughout *The Dream Songs*, is never summed up with finality. It remains "shaky" and can only break through in fragments and bits because the tension between the desire to believe and the pain of experience is never resolved in the poem. Nevertheless, what the last several paragraphs draw out and draw together is the underlying narrative of Berryman's song of Henry: the psychological and spiritual impulse from which his songs emerge, the ground in which they cohere as a poem. It is Henry's shaky theodicy that makes *The Dream Songs* an "epic" of consciousness comparable to "The Prelude" and "Song of Myself" and *The Cantos*.

As after the Bradstreet poem, the completion of *The Dream Songs* left Berryman wiped out physically and emotionally – and unsure about the next project, especially about another long poem. The publication of the sequence of love sonnets, written in 1947 but only published in 1969, temporarily filled the gap and opened the way to Berryman's return to a more nakedly confessional mode. In early February 1970, he began to write poems about his undergraduate years at Columbia College in New York, written in unrhymed four-line stanzas that he associated with Emily Dickinson's quatrains. The poems continued to pour out in a second group about his years as a fellow at Clare College, Cambridge, and then in a third group about himself in the present, many about interactions with fellow patients in alcoholic treatment. These poems did not involve the mask of a persona or the dialogue with an interlocuter – distancing strategies that had sustained his poetry for more than fifteen years. "I wiped out all the disguises and went to work"; "it didn't resemble anything I had ever written in my entire life, and the subject was entirely new, solely and simply myself."[95]

From St. Mary's Hospital in Minneapolis Berryman sent the typescript of these three clusters of poems under the title *Love & Fame* to a dozen people, mostly poet friends, but including (to my surprise) me. I had met Berryman only on the occasion of his 1966 reading at Harvard, but he liked my recently published study of Dickinson. His cover letter asked for criticism but clearly hoped for reassurance about the new direction in his poetry. I found many of the new poems disappointingly diffuse, gossipy, even adolescent in their fixation on sexual conquest and poetic celebrity, but I held off responding because I was painfully aware of his fragile mental and physical condition. However, when *Love & Fame* appeared as a book later in 1970, I was able to respond because the poems I had read now led up to a new fourth section, "Eleven Addresses to the Lord," which moved the sequence into a new, explicitly religious dimension and cast the carnality and worldliness of the first three sections into ironic perspective. In the "Afterword" to the English edition and the second American edition of *Love & Fame*, Berryman generously credited me, in contrast to what he felt was the mostly "uncomprehending" reception of the book, with seeing that "it is – however uneven – a whole, each of the four movements criticizing backward the preceding, until Part IV wipes out altogether all earlier presentations of the 'love' and 'fame' of the ironic title."[96]

In his next book Berryman voiced his anxiety about the critical response to his new work in "Defensio in Extremis," a wacky appeal to his divine "Father" against those commentators who "splinter at my immusical procedures & crude loves": "Tell them to leave me damned well alone with my misunderstood orders."[97] But the tenth "Address" had already cited his final and authoritative defense: "Father Hopkins said the only true literary critic is Christ." In an interview Berryman cites the source of Hopkins's remark as a letter to his friend Robert Bridges and glosses it: "Fame is in itself nothing. The only thing that matters is virtue. Jesus Christ is the only true literary critic." Berryman is mistaken in his attribution; Hopkins's remark occurs in a letter to another friend, Rev. Henry Watson Dixon. Hopkins is consoling Dixon for the dejection he feels at the lack of recognition and acclaim Dixon's poems have received:[98]

> The only just judge, the only just literary critic, is Christ, who prizes, is proud of, and admires, more than anyone, more even than the receiver himself can, the gifts of his own making. And the only real good which fame and another's praise does is to convey to us ... some token of the judgment which a perfectly just, heedful, and wise mind, namely Christ's, passes upon our doings.

Berryman obviously took Hopkins' words to heart.

He need not, however, have been as anxious as he was about the new work. William Heyen, for example, goes so far as to claim that Berryman came to fully "inspired form" only "at the end of his life in *Love & Fame* (1970) and *Delusions, Etc.* (1972)."[99] The longest and culminating chapter of Tom Rogers's recent study of Berryman's work is devoted to the late poems.[100] Even at the time, Lowell told Elizabeth Bishop: "his heroism was in leaping into himself in the last years, bravely." (The word "amazingly" is crossed out before "bravely.") And in what is probably his last letter to Berryman, dated December 27, 1970, Lowell wrote:[101]

> I've read your marvelous prayer at the end of your book, and can hardly find words to praise it. Though cunning in its scepticism, it feels like a Catholic prayer to a personal God ... Anyway, it is one of the great poems of the age, a puzzle and triumph to anyone who wants to write a personal devotional poem. Along with your posthumous poems [Book III, "Opus Posthumous" of *The Dream Songs*], to my mind, the crown of your work.

The "Eleven Addresses" inaugurated the third and final outburst or "spasm" of Berryman's career: a series of prayers that runs through *Delusion, Etc.* and the posthumous *Henry's Fate & Other Poems*. Berryman left no doubt about the source of the prayer-poems of his last two years, as he struggled, with some success, to stop drinking and control his alcoholism:[102]

> They are the result of a religious conversion which took place on my second Tuesday [May 12, 1970] in treatment here [the Intensive Alcohol Treatment Center in St. Mary's Hospital] last spring. I lost my faith several years ago [as a teenager after his father's suicide], but it came back – by force, by necessity, because of a rescue action – into the notion of a God who, at certain moments, definitely and personally intervenes in individual lives, one of which is mine.
>
> . . . .
>
> I never lost the sense of God in the two roles of creator and sustainer – of the mind of man and all its operations ... But my experience last spring gave me a third sense, the sense of a God of rescue, and I've been operating with that since.[103]

"Eleven Addresses to the Lord" and "Opus Dei," the sequence that opens *Delusions, Etc.* and is based on the hours of the Divine Office, along with the other prayers scattered through that collection, are psalms of a twentieth-century Christian, tormented by doubts and a profound sense of sinfulness but rapt at times by an equally profound sense of blessing and hope. "A Prayer for the Self" ends: "Lift up / sober toward truth a scared self-estimate," and the word "sober" here takes on painful urgency. Where Lowell's Catholicism had foundered early on his inability to believe in the Incarnation, Berryman's late encounter with the benevolent Father unlocked the block that his father's suicide had created (see "Lauds" and "Overseas Prayer") and led to an acceptance of Jesus as the incarnate Son (see "Ecce Homo") and of Mary as Queen of Heaven (see "A Prayer After All.")[104]

As Lowell noted, there is nothing like these late Berryman poems in all modern poetry, except perhaps Hopkins's "terrible sonnets," but without the percussions and contortions of Hopkins's diction and syntax. After the verbal hijinks of the exchange between the poet, Henry, and his minstrel friend in *The Dream Songs*, Berryman's psalms speak, with fierce clarity and unmasked honesty, in words directed in extremis to the wordless Word. There is no fluidity of pronouns here, no slippage or confusion about who the "I" and "You" are; the sentences move with declarative directness and undisguised imperative need. The poetry lies precisely in the chastened, almost Lear-like bareness, the inability any longer to hide in being poetic:[105]

> Sole watchman of the flying stars, guard me
> against my flicker of impulse lust: teach me
> to see them as sisters and daughters. Sustain
> my grand endeavours: husbandship and crafting.
>
> . . . .
>
> Make me from time to time the gift of the shoulder.
> When all hurt nerves whine shut away the whiskey.
> Empty my heart toward Thee.
> Let me pace without fear the common path of death.

These poems do not require a literary critic, only a receptive reader. The question "How Do You Do, Dr Berryman, Sir?" elicits this candid answer, gasped out with dashes and an open parenthesis:

> and as for Henry Pussycat   he'd just as soon be dead
>
> (on the Promise of – I know it sounds incredible –
> if he can muster penitence enough –
> he can't though –
> glory

But "if He loves me He must love everybody / and Origen was right & Hell is empty / or will be at apocatastasis."[106]

Why, then, the suicide at this point in Berryman's life? Did the depression he had contended with till his late fifties win out at last? Berryman underlined in his copy of the 1967 *Catholic Catechism* the passage on suicide which said that sometimes "hypertension or depression," "grave psychological disturbances or anguish or grave fear" – all of which Berryman suffered throughout his adult life – could affect the judgment of the suicide and diminish responsibility, so that final judgment should be left to a merciful God.[107] Berryman blamed his father's choice of death for damaging him for life, and the years of psychological stress and alcoholism, of obsessions and insomnia had left him shaken and frail, consumed by anxiety and difficult to live with. But the poems say that the God of rescue had found him, sustained him in Alcoholics Anonymous, blessed his marriage to Kate with young daughters. We can never know conclusively what led to the suicide. But the final lines of a poem, flatly but tellingly called "The Facts & Issues," may offer a glimpse into Berryman's state of mind.

The poem was written on May 20, 1971, a little more than seven months before his death, on a sleepless night when he was staying in Hartford, Connecticut, on his way to a reading at Goddard College in Vermont. He had been reading Graham Greene's novel *The Power and the Glory.* Like Berryman, Greene was a Catholic, tormented by a Jansenist sense of sin and guilt. Scobie, the adulterous protagonist of *The Heart of the Matter,* was a suicide. In *The Power and the Glory,* the Mexican whiskey priest dies before the firing squad of the anti-Catholic revolutionaries, burdened by his own failings, particularly the adultery that violated his vow of chastity and fathered a child, but Greene's narrative makes the reader see him as a heroic martyr unfailing in the faith that transcends his sins. In the early hours of the morning, unexpectedly and incongruously, "in a motor hotel in Wallace Stevens' town" Berryman was sublimely lifted up by a sense of the divine presence "all over this room." In the closing lines the language explodes in exclamation points and commas, capitals and italics to render his ecstatic elation as human perception and articulation and endurance reach their limits:[108]

> It is plain to me
> *Christ* underwent man & treachery & socks
> & lashes, thirst, exhaustion, the bit, for *my* pathetic &
>   disgusting vices,
> to make this filthy fact of particular, long-after,
> far-away, five-foot-ten & moribund
> human being happy. Well, he has!
> I am so happy I could scream!
> It's *enough!*   I can't BEAR ANY MORE.
> *Let this be it.*   I've *had* it.   I can't wait.

The poem Berryman placed after "The Facts & Issues" to close what would be the last book he put together for publication is "King David Dances." The old King, painfully mindful of the adultery and vanity and violence that marred his life as God's chosen, nonetheless ends wildly on his feet: "yea, / all the black same I dance my blue head off!"[109]

III

In a time of crisis and in lives filled with crises, Lowell and Berryman saw each other as bonded in the heroic determination to test and demonstrate the adequacy of the medium and the authority of the word. The next generation took an increasingly dim view of that effort, and the reputation and standing of Lowell and Berryman have declined among poets and critics since the 1970s. For feminist poets and ethnically identified poets, they were representatives of privileged white patriarchy. For deconstructive Postmodernists they represented the disastrously erroneous notions that blighted Romanticism and Modernism: the self-regarding hubris of the artist as personality and subject; the naiveté of the artist as master craftsman, trusting the power of language and the integrity of texts to make meaning.

Whatever one makes of these revisionist second thoughts, the achievement of Lowell and Berryman and their importance in the American poetic tradition stand secure. In terms of this book's argument about the dialectic between Modernism and Romanticism, Postmodernism and Neoromanticism, the trajectories of their careers cross, and it was their Catholicism that impelled and followed their different trajectories. When Lowell lost a sense of the vital connection between his words and the incarnate Word, he moved from the rhetorical sublimity of the early prophetic poems in the direction of Postmodernist slippage and indeterminacy. By contrast, Berryman moved in the direction of what I am calling Neoromanticism. The refractions and dislocations of the long poems give way to plain statement as his slippery human speech seeks center in the significance of the Word. In the tenth "Address to the Lord" Berryman joins Father Hopkins's effort to take Jesus as his literary critic and to make his "wayward" words at least a rusty recording of the "dictation" of the divine Word: "Oil all my turbulence as at Thy dictation / I sweat out my wayward works"; "Let me lie down exhausted, content with that."[110]

CHAPTER 3

The Language of Flux
Elizabeth Bishop
John Ashbery

I

In the years before the Second World War, Elizabeth Bishop made her initial appearance on the literary scene as a protégée of Marianne Moore, and Moore remained an important presence even after Bishop's life and poetry took its own direction. After Bishop and Lowell met in January 1947, they became close and trusted friends whose correspondence documents the crucial role each played in the other's life and work. At the same time, David Kalstone's *Becoming a Poet* (1989) traces the ways in which Bishop, while admiring her mentors' poetry and relying on their friendship and support, quietly and consistently maintained her independence from Moore and then from Lowell in establishing her own poetic voice.

In 1962, Lowell would write to Bishop: "I don't see any reason to compare you with Marianne: you so beautifully exist together equally good, alike and opposites."[1] In a review of Bishop's first book, *North and South* (1946), before Lowell had met her, he had described his sense of "the differences in method and personality" between Bishop and Moore:[2]

> Bishop is usually present in her poems; they happen to her, she speaks, and often centers them on herself. Others are dramatic and have human actors. She uses dreams and allegories. (Like Kafka's, her treatment of the absurd is humorous, matter-of-fact, and logical.) She hardly ever quotes from other writers. Most of her meters are accentual-syllabic. Compared with Moore, she is softer, dreamier, more human, and more personal; she is less idiosyncratic, and less magnificent.

The next year Lowell met Bishop at a major turning point in his life: the publication of *Lord Weary's Castle*, the breakup of his marriage to Jean Stafford, and his drift out of the Church. They both immediately recognized how "indispensable" (Lowell's word[3]) as friends and poets they were to each other, both in what they shared and in what their differences could teach the other.

Though Bishop greatly admired Lowell's new poems, which became *Life Studies*, the inclination that linked Bishop to Moore made her uncomfortable with the self-exposure and self-dramatization in Lowell's (and Berryman's) work. She would never herself be a confessional poet. Her physical and psychological problems, her lesbian relationships, and her struggles with depression and alcoholism informed the sensibility that shaped the poems, but they never became the immediate and explicit subject matter of the poems. Bishop's poems record a life in crisis as acute in its way as Lowell's, but she resisted the autobiographical bent and rhetorical tone of Lowell's response to crisis. And it is precisely the qualities of her work closest to Moore's that distinguish hers from Lowell's: a modest and steady tone of voice, keen and exact observation, carefully controlled understatement, prosy rhythms, quiet wit, and self-protective irony. In a letter to literary critic Joseph Summers in 1967, Bishop admitted that what he called her "meticulous attention" is "a method of escaping from intolerable pain" – a strategy that she had observed in "Marianne Moore long ago" but "had just begun to realize myself."[4] Yet it was those same Moore-like qualities in Bishop's poems that Lowell learned from to modulate his voice and rhetorical tone in the transition from *Lord Weary's Castle* to *Life Studies*: an indebtedness acknowledged in dedicating "Skunk Hour," the concluding poem of the "Life Studies" sequence, to Bishop.

The most personal poem Lowell wrote for and about Bishop is "Water." They had spent some time with friends on the Maine coast in Stonington during the summer of 1948. In a 1957 letter Lowell confessed to Bishop that at the time he assumed that it "would be just a matter of time before I proposed, and I half believed you would accept." Whatever Lowell's and Bishop's intentions and assumptions might actually have been at the time, their lives and loves were on different courses and would soon take them in different directions: him to a marriage with Elizabeth Hardwick, her to a long relationship with Lota de Macedo Soares in Brazil. But the poem commemorates that summer and particularly "that long sunning and swimming Stonington day"[5] when the two of them "sat on a slab of rock" and faced the blank infinity and obliterating anonymity of the sea that "kept tearing away" at the rock "flake after flake":[6]

> We wished our two souls
> might return like gulls to
> the rock. In the end,
> the water was too cold for us.

The imagery in the lines preceding this concluding stanza is drawn from a fantasy that Bishop had described (in a September 1948 letter to Lowell) in which she was "a gasping mermaid" under a dock "trying to tear the mussels off the piles for something to eat." Lowell began the poem soon after Bishop's departure at summer's end but finished it only in 1962, when it became the lead poem in *For the Union Dead*. " 'Water' I like very much," Bishop told him, and in 1968 she sent him a Winslow Homer postcard, "for obvious reasons," recalling the summer and the poem.[7] As for Lowell, "Water" persisted in his imagination as well; he revised it into the present tense and re-lineated its quatrains into an unrhymed sonnet, the first of four sonnets for Bishop in the 1973 *History*.

Lowell had good reason, besides the Stonington summer, to associate Bishop with water, more precisely with the meeting of land and sea. With Bishop's father's death the year of her birth and with her mother's commitment to a mental institution when she was five, she lived those early years in Nova Scotia with grandparents, and returned there periodically for the rest of her life. In 1938 she bought a house in Key West and spent much of the next decade there. Her years in Brazil, almost two decades starting in 1951, centered on Lota Soares's apartment in Rio fronting the beach and the Atlantic. Her last residences, after her return to teach at Harvard, were on Lewis Wharf, looking out on the Boston harbor and the Mystic River, and, in summers, Sabine Farm on North Haven Island, Maine (the site of her elegy for Lowell).

Bishop once told Lowell ("rather humorously yet it was truly meant") that her epitaph should say that she was "the loneliest person who ever lived."[8] Her books map her lonely peregrinations: *North & South*, *Questions of Travel*, *Geography III*; the poems often place her on her travels at the liminality of land's edge. "The Map," the first poem in *North & South*, begins, "Land lies in water"; "Arrival in Santos," the first poem in *Questions of Travel*, begins: "Here is a coast; here is a harbor"; the epigraph to *Geography III* offers a school-book lesson: "*What is Geography? A description of the earth's surface ... Of what is the Earth's surface composed? Land and water.*" Her rueful image of the poet is the sandpiper, running the misty beach "in a state of controlled panic": "Poor bird, he is obsessed!" "[P]reoccupied" but "focused" the sandpiper stares at "the dragging grains" of sand – "black, white, tan, and gray": "(no detail too small)," because, like a baffled "student of Blake," who had said that he saw the whole world in a grain of sand, the sandpiper is "looking for something, something, something" in the multicolored sands.[9]

"Land lies in water": an image of the beached and marginal human situation between foreign land and unknown sea. "The Map" goes on to ask which shapes which, which is formed by which. The question is left open, but the final line – "More delicate than the historians' are the map-makers' colors" (p. 3; page references to the *Collected Poems* will henceforth be indicated in the text) – identifies the poet's aim less with the historian's immersion in temporal flux than with the mapmaker's attempt to fix boundaries in a visual image. The sandpiper-poet wants to map the shifting boundary of sand and wave that she runs. Reviewing *North & South*, Lowell saw Bishop's early poems as seeking to negotiate the "two opposing factors" of flux and form: "The first is something in motion, weary but persisting, almost always failing and on the point of disintegrating, and yet, for the most part stoically maintained ... The second factor is terminus: rest, sleep, fulfillment, death."[10] In its artifice and formality the poem is a map that pictures yet contains the fluctuations of time and history, the fact of failure and disintegration; it is the rock flaked by the sea it fronts.

Or "The Imaginary Iceberg." That poem – the title sounds like a Marianne Moore poem – follows "The Map" in *North & South* (p. 4). It begins with an unsettling statement: "We'd rather have the iceberg than the ship," even if that meant shipwreck and "the end of travel." Why? Because, unlike the ship running the waves under running clouds, the iceberg "takes repose" by standing "stock-still" on the "shifting stage" of the sea's "moving marble." "Icebergs behoove the soul" precisely because the iceberg is self-sustaining ("it saves itself perpetually and adorns / only itself") and self-contained (it "cuts its facets from within"). The solid stanzas of the poem, each finely faceted into eleven smoothly enjambed lines, become the iceberg, the steadying apprehension of which can behoove the cruising, wave-tossed soul.

The structure and language of Bishop's poems are calculated to seem casual, but she often took years to craft that effect. Lowell thought her "command of shifting speech tones" comparable to Frost's. The typical Bishop poem begins with a keenly observed "description or descriptive narrative," and its course (again, like some of Frost's poems) seems to meander, taking time for pauses and diversions, noting each thing closely. Along the way it may be difficult to know where the poem is going and what its conclusion will be, because the poet, like the sandpiper, is looking for "something, something, something" significant and meaningful in the details of the description or narration. The poem finds its way in looking, and the conclusion in an arresting image or phrase reveals what is found and not found. "On the surface," Lowell says, "her poems are observations" – the title of Moore's 1924 book of poems – but then "the poet or one of her characters ... reflects" on what has been seen and lived through to arrive at what Frost called "a clarification of life – not necessarily a great clarification, such as sects and cults are founded on, but in a

momentary stay against confusion."[11] Bishop's expert craftsmanship guides
the meandering search through a range of meters, rhyme schemes, and
stanza patterns so that each poem seems to fit snugly into and fulfill its
chosen form. As a result, she sounds no more like Frost than Moore or
Lowell; she inhabits her poetic world herself, and almost alone.

Images of seashore, fragile ship, and threatening sea persist into the
later poems of *Geography III*. "Crusoe in England" is a monologue voiced
by the most famous shipwreck victim, reminiscing about the strategies
for survival on his volcanic island surrounded by the blank expanse of the
Pacific. His investigations make him sound like that other beachcombing
surrogate of Bishop's, the sandpiper (p. 163):

> The beaches were all lava, variegated,
> black, red, and white, and gray;
> the marbled colors made a fine display.
> And I had waterspouts.

"In the Waiting Room" recalls a turning point in the young Elizabeth's
unexpected awakening, all at once, to identity and sexuality, to suffering
and mortality as she reads a *National Geographic* article while waiting for
an aunt in her dentist's office. The epiphany has no logical connection
with the sea, but Bishop's imagination veers to the sea for the climactic and dramatic image that pulls the poem together. Elizabeth's sudden
awareness of alienation from the world around her makes her see the
microcosm of the waiting room "sliding / beneath a big black wave, /
another, and another" (p. 161). In the narrative of "The End of March" the
poet is walking the beach in Duxbury, Massachusetts, with two friends on
a "cold and windy" day beside water "the color of mutton-fat jade," when
she sees a tangle of kite string in the water as a drowned man (p. 179):

> a thick white snarl, man-size, awash,
> rising on every wave, a sodden ghost,
> falling back, sodden, giving up the ghost ...

This beach-march, like others in Bishop's poems, projects a fateful "end."

Bishop's fondness for and indebtedness to Moore is acknowledged in
her many letters to Moore and, more extensively, in "Efforts of Affection,"
the memoir she wrote after Moore's death.[12] But Lynn Keller made the
astute observation that "[i]n regarding herself adrift in an unpredictable
and unknowable universe Bishop seems closer to Stevens (and to Ashbery)
than to Moore,"[13] whose rock-ribbed Presbyterian conviction sinewed her
observations and her poems. Bishop started reading Stevens in the 1930s,
and though she was wary of writing essays about other poets, her letters to

Moore report her enthusiasm for Moore's friend Stevens: "I am so pleased to have" *Ideas of Order* (1936); "I like *The Man with the Blue Guitar* [1937] more and more …"; "what strikes me as so wonderful about the whole book [*Owl's Clover*] … is that it is such a display of ideas at work – making poetry, the poetry making them, etc. That, it seems to me, is the way a poet should think …" Twice she named Stevens in a triumvirate of the great modern poets, once along with Moore and Lowell and once with Moore and Auden. In a letter of 1940 Bishop reported the flurry of excitement in Key West at one of Stevens's sojourns there away from the New England winter: "Wallace Stevens was here too at the 'fancy' hotel, and Robert Frost. I went to lunch there with Louise's aunt, almost provided with opera glasses, but the only person I saw of any importance was [labor leader] John L. Lewis chewing a cigar."[14]

At the same time, as with Moore and Lowell, Bishop distanced her own poetic practice from Stevens's, criticizing particularly his indulgence in what she saw as soaring and sonorous rhetoric: "the way he occasionally makes blank verse *moo*."[15] As for the much older Stevens, he was aware of Bishop's poems but in a 1946 letter offers no further comment in an uncharacteristically monosyllabic remark: "I know Miss Bishop's work. She lives in Key West."[16] Indeed, reading Stevens's and Bishop's versions of Key West against each other reveals their tellingly different sense of how a poet thinks in poetry and thereby illustrates the shift in poetics that began about mid-century with the Second World War.

"The Idea of Order at Key West," which provided the title for Stevens's second collection of poems, is a major statement of his poetics and of the Modernist contention that the imagination as a human faculty can assuage our "[b]lessed rage for order" by decreating a world in flux and recreating elements of that world into aesthetic order. Stevens called that alternate aesthetic world the *mundo* of the imagination and saw it as an escape from reality – but as a creative escape that adumbrated an idea of order that could actually affect one's sense of reality and thereby perhaps even eventually affect that reality itself. The elaborate machinery of Stevens's poem presents itself as a dramatic monologue, addressed to an interlocutor, about his seeing a woman on the beach in Key West. She walks beside the "meaningless plungings of water and the wind," but as she walks she sings a song so transfixing and transforming in its power that it becomes the poet's song and, in the poet's ears and in the poet's own words, it

> Mastered the night and portioned out the sea,
> Fixing emblazoned zones and fiery poles,
> Arranging, deepening, enchanting night.[17]

"The Bight," Bishop told Lowell, is "a long and complicated [poem] about Key West,"[18] and it leaves no doubt that, despite her admiration for Stevens, she was not the singer whose song could enchant the night. Written in 1948, the poem's unrhymed lines, more irregular and conversational than Stevens's stately blank verse, give a flat, low-keyed description of the Garrison Bight (p. 60):

> At low tide like this how sheer the water is.
> White, crumbling ribs of marl protrude and glare
> and the boats are dry, the pilings dry as matches.
> Absorbing, rather than being absorbed,
> the water in the bight doesn't wet anything,
> the color of the gas flame turned as low as possible.
> One can smell it turning to gas ...

The poem's leisurely progress, noting the dreary details of the scene, depicts a place disfigured by the ugly clutter and delapidated machinery of human activity. It is a scene of detritus comparable to Lowell's Black Rock at low tide, but no Christ walks on these waters. When the rage for order is confounded by the insistent fact of disorder, the rhetorical heroics of Stevens's *mundo* can sound to ears like Bishop's a bit absurd and perverse, making the blank verse moo. Bishop's poem admits – and discards – Stevens's imaginative strategy when, immediately after the lines above, comes this sly aside: "if one were Baudelaire / one could probably hear it turning to marimba music." Stevens's indebtedness to the French Symboliste poets is well established, and "Esthétique du Mal" proclaims his affinity specifically for Baudelaire in its echo of *Fleurs du Mal*. The "marimba music" is the giveaway; the alliterated, syncopated phrase sounds like Stevens, not Baudelaire, and of course Baudelaire would never have heard marimba music. Baudelaire here stands for Stevens and, more broadly, for the Symboliste imagination's effort to make a disillusioning reality into an exotic artifact. And Bishop's hypothetical, subjunctive "if one were Baudelaire" dismisses that strategy even as it poses it.

From start to finish, "The Bight" accepts the world as is, without marimba music: water that doesn't wet, that turns to gas; the crumbling of the beach's marl foundation; the boats and pilings abandoned to dry rot; the dredge clanking away. At the same time, the poem's personal self-dedication, tucked in parenthetically but prominently under the title – "[On my birthday]" – turns the bight into a metaphor for the observer's psychological landscape. Bishop remarked to Lowell that the "mess" of Garrison Bight "reminds me a little of my desk."[19] Indeed, the poem is not all factual description; what makes it a poem are the

unobtrusive metaphors and similes with which Bishop defamiliarizes
the all-too-familiar and transforms the prosy description into an understated but ominous image of the human situation. The protruding shelves
of marl are the "ribs" of earth's crumbling skeleton. The pilings "dry as
matches" sunk in water with the color and smell of gas are a combustion
and conflagration waiting to happen. The pelicans hit the water "like pick-
axes"; the man-of-war birds open their tails "like scissors" or tense them
"like wishbones, till they tremble"; the sponge boats bristle with "gaffs and
hooks"; the shark tails hang on the chicken wire fence "like little plow-
shares": workaday blades and points that can turn into weapons and cut
to the bone. Except for the speaker on her birthday, there are no people,
only autonomous machines without occupants or operators: sponge boats
approach the beach like retrievers after a hunt; the dredge rips up "a drip-
ping jawful of marl" from the seabed like a hungry dinosaur; the boats lie
"piled up":

> stove in,
> and not yet salvaged, if they ever will be, from the last
>   bad storm,
> like torn-open, unanswered letters.
> The bight is littered with old correspondences.

In these seemingly casual lines near the end of the poem the broken boats scattered on the beach become "letters," and in the next line
"letters" become "correspondences," with further wordplay on the
near-correspondence in "letters" and "littered." It is the most extended
and developed metaphor in the poem, and the nimble wordplay raises, by
implication and indirection, the metaphysical questions underlying the
poem. Beyond the immediate epistolary metaphor of the boats as unanswered letters, the word "correspondences" introduces an issue crucial to
Romantic and post-Romantic literature, so that the letters in question
become, literally, the words of the poem itself. "Correspondences" picks
up on and elaborates the earlier reference to Baudelaire and extends it specifically to his sonnet "Correspondances," from *Fleurs du Mal* (1857). Its
octave reads in a quite literal translation:[20]

> Nature is a temple in which living pillars
> Sometimes give voice to confused words;
> Man passes there through forests of symbols
> Which look at him with understanding eyes.
>
> Like prolonged echoes mingling in the distance
> In a deep and tenebrous unity,

> Vast as the dark of night and the light of day,
> Perfumes, sounds, and colors correspond.

The reference to the bight littered/lettered with old correspondence, then, unobtrusively brings to bear on the scene at Garrison Bight the Romantic theory of the material world as symbolic of spiritual truth. In post-Enlightenment Western culture, as credence in philosophical and theological systems was increasingly questioned, the Romantics had sought, outside creeds and institutions, to affirm the world of experience as revelation of transcendental truth. The belief in correspondences is the basis for Wordsworth's poetry and for Coleridge's exposition of the Romantic imagination. Emerson gave the most influential American articulation to the notion when he pronounced that every physical fact is a symbol of spiritual fact because Nature is symbol of Spirit.

In "The Idea of Order at Key West" Stevens voices his yearning for Romantic correspondence but, concluding sadly that "the sea is not a mask" revealing, or even concealing, Spirit, proposes the Modernist notion of the *mundo* as a compensation: no correspondence but an alternate world of aesthetic artifice. But for Bishop, as her earlier dismissal of Baudelaire/Stevens suggests, the marimba music of the mundo no longer offers compensation or consolation; even the desire for correspondence, however poignant, is "like torn-open, unanswered letters," discarded and outworn literary and metaphysical notions. The broken boats spell no meaning, nor do the words of the poem; they are not so much letters as litter. The phrase "the last bad storm" anticipates another storm, perhaps igniting at last the potential for conflagration in the scene, but the poem ends before the catastrophe with the poet's unblinking, clear-eyed bemusement at the blind, unthinking persistence of life at Garrison Bight (pp. 60–61):

> Click. Click. Goes the dredge,
> and brings up a dripping jawful of marl.
> All the untidy activity continues,
> awful but cheerful.

The only correspondence that the poem admits is the correspondence between the disordered world of experience and the disordered world of the psyche. Sight yields no insight; having the wit to see things as they bleakly are and say so is the only strategy for sanity and endurance in a world of flux: the wit to say "jawful," "awful," "cheerful." Bishop sent a copy of "The Bight" to her psychiatrist with the remark: "I still think if I can just keep the last line in mind, everything may still turn out all right."[21]

The untidy activity at the Bight is more cheerful than the poem. Bishop seldom lost her wit in writing disaster, but sometimes she could not manage even a semblance of cheer. Emily Dickinson began a poem with the cheerless line: "The loss of something ever felt I." "One Art," Bishop's "one & only villanelle," written early in 1976,[22] plays, through the repetitions of the form, with the line "The art of losing isn't hard to master" (p. 178), and each insistent repetition makes it clearer how much control, metrical and emotional, it takes to master, or at least compensate for, losing by turning it to art. The other repetition, programmed into the villanelle, insists, against the mounting evidence in the poem itself, that a life of losing things "is no disaster." What makes it bearable – or more bearable – is the art and wit of turning it to form. The rhymed words come together in the last lines to fulfill the form of the villanelle in an act of verbal mastery: "the art of losing's not too hard to master / though it may look like (*Write* it!) like disaster."

Among her life's major losses "One Art" mentions "three loved houses." After her place in Key West in the late 1930s and 1940s, there were two cherished Brazilian residences. Samambaia is the modernist house that Lota Soares designed and built on a hillside in Petropolis outside Rio, with an adjacent study for Bishop besides a cascading waterfall. And in 1965 Bishop bought for herself an old colonial house in remote Ouro Prêto and named it Casa Mariana, in part after Marianne Moore, but she lived in it only briefly after Soares's death in 1967 and her move to Harvard in 1970 (to replace Lowell in the Boylston Chair, after he moved to England). "The End of March" (pp. 179–80) was written in 1974, two years before "One Art," but Bishop placed it after the villanelle because it resumes the theme of homelessness in an alien world.

"The End of March" is dedicated to John Malcolm Brinnin and Bill Read because they often lent Bishop their house in Duxbury, a suburb of Boston, as a welcome retreat from Harvard. In the poem she is taking her Duxbury friends on a walk to show them a house down the beach that, though she described it in a letter to Lowell as only an "ugly little green shack,"[23] she here idealizes as "my proto-dream-house, / my crypto-dream-house." The middle section of the poem imagines how "perfect" living there would be: as it turns out, "perfect! But – impossible"; perhaps impossible because perfect. The way there, described in the first section of the poem, is forbidding on the cold, wet, windy day. The footprint of a dog looks large enough to be that of a lion (March weather proverbially comes in like a lion); the water is "mutton-fat jade," which, as Brett Millier points out,[24] is the color of a corpse; a snarl of kite string in the waves looks like a drowned person. So menacing, in fact, are the weather and the beach scene that they turn back before they reach their destination, and in any case, the poem observes wryly, "the house was boarded up." (The next year Bishop reported to Brinnin: "My House is GONE! ... a flimsy, gray but 'moderne' affair is rising on the site ..."[25]) In the briefer section of the poem recounting their return walk, the day breaks briefly into sunshine that transforms the "drab, damp" stones into "multi-colored" beauty (like the beach stones in "The Sandpiper" and "Crusoe in England"). But the repeated phrase "for just a minute" measures the unpredictable ephemerality of the moment of illumination. What they found on their walk are nature's indifference to life and death; the "lion sun" had left its "big majestic paw-prints" at "the last low tide" when it "batted a kite out of the sky to play with" and discarded its corpse in the sea-wash. Faced with the overwhelming force of nature and the inhuman power of the lion sun, Bishop prudently retreated in self-preservation.

Most of the time Bishop chose, like the pragmatist Frost but unlike contemporaries like Berryman and Sylvia Plath and Anne Sexton, not to push the tragedy of life to its conclusion in oblivion and silence, but instead to employ wit as a verbal defense against the menace of time and nature. But occasionally, like Frost in the sonnet "Design," she allowed wit to approach and test the abyss. Bishop's metaphysically darkest poem is "At the Fishhouses," written in Key West in 1947, the year before "The Bight," from notes taken from the previous summer at Lockeport Beach in Nova Scotia. When Bishop sent it to Lowell early in their friendship, he thought it probably "your best" yet, and, thinking of "The Drunken Fisherman" and other poems in *Lord Weary's Castle*, Lowell lamented: "all my fish become symbols, alas!"[26]

"Geographical Mirror," the heading that Bishop gave the descriptive notes from which "At the Fishhouses" would evolve, acknowledges again (like the dedication of "The Bight") her correlation between geography and psychology, the correspondence between outer and inner landscapes. The return to the scene of her Nova Scotia childhood brings Bishop's sense of her life full circle. The poem breaks almost exactly into two parts. The first half meanders down to the sea, describing the five fishhouses and the fishing paraphernalia at land's end, all silvered and sequined with fish scales. She has the beach again to herself, except for an old fisherman ("a friend of my grandfather") with whom she exchanges words briefly about codfish and herring and "the decline in the population." In retrospect, the first half reads as though she is postponing the confrontation with the sea as long as possible. That confrontation comes in the second half in a carefully and skillfully paced passage that needs to be cited in full. Under the gathering pressure of a gradually quickening succession of repeated words and internal rhymes and a quickening succession of "then"s, the poem finds its direction and moves to its conclusion, the rush of adjectives and participles pushing into deeper and darker perceptions (pp. 65–66):

> Cold dark deep and absolutely clear,
> element bearable to no mortal,
> to fish and to seals ... One seal particularly
> I have seen here evening after evening.
> He was curious about me. He was interested in music;
> like me a believer in total immersion,
> so I used to sing him Baptist hymns.
> I also sang "A Mighty Fortress Is Our God."
> He stood up in the water and regarded me
> steadily, moving his head a little.
> Then he would disappear, then suddenly emerge
> almost in the same spot, with a sort of shrug
> as if it were against his better judgment.
> Cold dark deep and absolutely clear,
> the clear gray icy water ... Back, behind us,
> the dignified tall firs begin.
> Bluish, associating with their shadows,
> a million Christmas trees stand
> waiting for Christmas. The water seems suspended
> above the rounded gray and blue-gray stones.
> I have seen it over and over, the same sea, the same,
> slightly, indifferently swinging above the stones,
> icily free above the stones,
> above the stones and then the world.
> If you should dip your hand in,
> your wrist would ache immediately,
> your bones would begin to ache and your hand would burn
> as if the water were a transmutation of fire
> that feeds on stones and burns with a dark gray flame.
> If you tasted it, it would first taste bitter,
> then briny, then surely burn your tongue.
> It is like what we imagine knowledge to be:
> dark, salt, clear, moving, utterly free,
> drawn from the cold hard mouth
> of the world, derived from the rocky breasts

forever, flowing and drawn, and since
our knowledge is historical, flowing, and flown.

The passage begins whimsically enough, postulating a correspondence between the speaker and a particular seal in the harbor. Both, she claims drolly, are believers in "total immersion," hence both Baptists, hence both solaced by the providential security promised in old hymns like "A Mighty Fortress Is Our God." Our God: But do they really share a God, a sense of salvation by baptism? The speaker knows that the correspondence is fanciful whimsy, and the seal calls her bluff when it does immerse totally in the watery element, and she shrewdly does not, because she has known all along that the sea is an "element bearable to no mortal," only "to fish and to seals."

After that false start the passage has to begin again, repeating, more grimly this time, the litany of adjectives – "Cold dark deep and absolutely clear" – that sets the sea against land life. And in the remaining lines the disastrous and paradoxical conflagration of water, deferred in "The Bight," seems to have ignited to consume the world: "as if the water were a trans-mutation of fire / that feeds on stones and burns with a dark gray flame." Onshore stand the shadowed trees (punning on a "stand of trees") like anxious and helpless watchers, hoping for the advent of Christmas rather than the advance of the fiery ice of the sea. But in this poem Christmas will not arrive, and everything on land is doomed to an annihilating baptism by "total immersion." The only reference to the sea in the first half of the poem depicts it as "swelling slowly as if considering spilling over." Now the spilling comes in the rocking rhythms of these lines:

> I have seen it over and over, the same sea, the same,
> slightly, indifferently swinging above the stones,
> icily free above the stones,
> above the stones and then the world.

At the imagined moment of total immersion and wipeout, the earth's drowned "stones," repeated five times, become the "bones" of the human skeleton. The poem abruptly shifts pronouns from the first-person "I" to "you," strategically deflecting the focus of the action away from the speaker but also involving the reader in the immersion. "If you should dip your hand in," "[i]f you tasted it," you would begin to know something of the fiery ice of the absolute wherein utter freedom and utter necessity lock together to annihilate human contingencies. The sea is twice described as "absolutely clear"; its touch and bitter, briny taste are of the absolute, "like what we imagine knowledge to be." In the closing sentence "I" and "you" become "we" in the common and shared fate of that absolute clarity.

Thus the last lines mythologize the absolute not as the Christmas Christ-child, born to bring resurrection out of death, but instead as the Terrible Earth Mother whose "rocky breasts" feed but also "feed on" her offspring, whose "cold hard mouth" engorges what it births. The concluding image here is not "awful but cheerful" but awesome and terrifying. The repetitions and internal rhymes continue to point the way: "stones," "bones," "drawn," "flown." And the present participles are, in the very moment of articulation, becoming past participles: "moving" but "drawn," "flowing and drawn," "flowing, and flown." For us, then, "since / all our knowledge is historical" and transpires in time and of time, "knowing" becomes instantaneously "known," but sometimes, with luck and skill, caught and known in the form of the poem. "The Map," the first poem in Bishop's first book, preferred the geographer's art to the historian's temporal fact, but here the geographer-artist acknowledges that the historian's swelling and obliterating truth is precisely the basis for her preference for the geographer's art.

"At the Fishhouses" draws out the unexamined but dark implications of "The Bight." The long poem "The Moose" had its genesis at the same time as "At the Fishhouses," but was only completed in 1972. The poem narrates the long bus ride Bishop took back from Nova Scotia in the summer of 1946. In the course of the first four pages of the poem, which seem just a chatty account of the people on board and the snatches of conversation overheard, the bus becomes a microcosm and the ride recapitulates the vagaries of human life. Then, suddenly and startlingly, the slow progress of the bus is stopped by the intrusion of another female manifestation of nature's inhuman otherness. A cow moose, "grand, otherworldly," "looms" out of "the impenetrable wood," "looks the bus over," and after inspection allows it to proceed (pp. 172–73):

> Towering, antlerless,
> high as a church,
> homely as a house
> (or, safe as houses).
> A man's voice assures us
> "Perfectly harmless . . ."

This once, unlike the lion sun in "The Bight" and the mother-sea in "At the Fishhouses," nature shows no menace or malice, only curious indifference to the human plight, and the riders' alarm gives way to a "sweet sensation of joy" at the moose's clumsy size and "otherworldly" imperturbability.

That experience of wonder is unusual in Bishop; her early poem "The Fish" catches another such moment, the monosyllabic last line grounding the expanding arc of the preceding line: "everything / was rainbow, rainbow, rainbow! / And I let the fish go" (p. 44). For the most part, however, like her sandpiper-poet, Bishop, while keeping an alert but wary eye out for some intrusion of the absolute, maintains her momentum by staying focused on sensing and making an accurate account of the world at hand: the natural world in the precise discriminations of its subtly shifting ephemerality, the human world in the complex mesh of its feelings and responses, desires and losses. Language, for all its slipperiness, and form, for all its limitations, is what we humans have to locate ourselves stoically and without illusions, even if only for a moment, in a world of flux: knowing but also known, even as it is "flowing, and flown."

In terms of the larger argument of this book, reading Bishop against predecessors like Moore, Stevens, and Frost helps to define the shift from the prevailing Modernism of the poetry of the first half of the twentieth century to what came to be called, by the 1970s, the Postmodernism of the second half of the century. There is no sharp break but a wavering line of continuity and discontinuity. But that line traces a declension in the function of the imagination and of language so that, for a poet of the generation after Lowell and Bishop, such as Ashbery, the imagination brings to a world in flux only the freedom to play with words in their indeterminate signification and ambiguous reference. Coleridge and Emerson would have said that such a view reduces the metaphysics of the imagination to the artifice of fancy; Pound and Williams, Stevens, and even Frost would have said that it undermines the essential constructive work of the imagination in (Pound's dictum) making it new and thus (Stevens's phrase) helping "us to live our lives."[27] But Postmodernists like Ashbery saw themselves as stripping away the false and ego-inflated notions of the power of words that Modernists had adapted from their Romantic forebears, and thus freeing words from culturally determined denotations and connotations into the free play of semiotic self-determination: words piecing out, through their interaction, their own frame of reference and reality.

II

John Ashbery won the triple crown – the Pulitzer Prize, the National Book Award, and the National Book Critics Circle Award – for *Self-Portrait in a*

Convex Mirror, published in 1975, two years before Lowell's death and four years before Bishop's. Earlier in this chapter we heard Lynn Keller suggest a continuity back from Bishop to Stevens and forward from Bishop to Ashbery. In fact, there are only a few passing references to Ashbery in Bishop's letters and no comment on his poetry. But the lack of connection is not surprising; they were not personal friends and were on opposite sides of the poetry wars of the 1950s and 1960s, whose frictions divided self-consciously avant-garde poets, experimenting in open form, from more traditional poets. What is more surprising, given Ashbery's place in the New York avant-garde, is his stated enthusiasm for Bishop's work.

Reviewing her 1969 *Complete Poems*, he declared himself "an addict of her work" who had "read, reread, studied and absorbed Miss Bishop's first book and waited impatiently for her second one." Ashbery could not resist a bit of a Postmodernist sniff: "Establishment poet" though Bishop was, "the establishment ought to give thanks" for her presence, because "she is proof that it can't be all bad." And when Bishop was awarded the 1976 Neustadt Prize Laureateship, Ashbery took the occasion to review her career at some length and commend her poetry for "the looking so intense that it becomes something like death or ecstasy, both at once perhaps."[28]

Beyond the poetry wars, however, the configuration of Stevens, Bishop, and Ashbery yields a telling insight into the development of American poetry in the twentieth century. "Self-Portrait in a Convex Mirror," like "The Idea of Order at Key West" and "The Bight" and "One Art," is an important statement of the poet's poetics – that is to say, of the relationship of language and form to meaning – so that reading those poems in succession traces one wavering line from Modernism to Postmodernism. Faced with flux, Bishop and Ashbery felt Stevens's longing for a "permanent realization" that never came as "the flecked river ... kept flowing and never the same way twice,"[29] but where that realization aroused in Stevens a "rage for order" and a call for the imagination to slake that rage in creating its own *mundo*, Bishop tempered her language with measured understatement and stoic resignation, and Ashbery accepted and assumed flux as the state and condition of language.

The different ways in which Bishop and Ashbery deal with flux have defined their engagement with poetry. Bishop published only four quite slim volumes over the forty years of her career; Ashbery has published some two dozen volumes of poems since 1953, not counting translations. Bishop labored over poems, sometimes for many years, so that the form might bring the flux to apperception. Ashbery, on the other hand, tends to yield his poems to flux; their diffuse prolixity and lack of focus and direction, their hesitations and reversals and divigations articulate the flux not just in the subject matter but in the form, or formlessness, of the poems. Therefore, although a number of individual poems display a formal virtuosity and variety comparable to Bishop's, his most persistent and characteristic inclination runs to long, discursive, lightly stressed lines stretching out into long, low-pressured, prosy poems that meander their course not to a conclusion but to a pause in the flow.

Ashbery belongs to the group of poets who became dubbed the New York School because they were centered in that city during the creative ferment that included the emergence of Abstract Expressionism with painters like Jackson Pollock and Willem de Kooning and the musical experimentation, including chance operations, of musicians like John Cage and David Tudor. The group included Kenneth Koch and Frank O'Hara, both of whom Ashbery had met at Harvard, and they were joined in New York by James Schyler and Barbara Guest. The New York poets were closely involved in the art and museum world, and, as with other confederations of experimental poets, the exploration of open form freed them to develop their particular stances and voices. O'Hara's chatty, jazzy poems sound as though they were spoken on the run in the loud rush of metropolitan streets and subways, reporting rat-a-tat-tat: "I saw this, I saw that; I did this, I did that." In contrast, Ashbery's cool, seemingly offhand poems, never too dejected or too elated, seldom raising or lowering the voice, characteristically concoct surreal, sometimes wacky fantasies that keep up a steady murmur in the shadow-box of consciousness ("the room of our forethought," as he put it in "A Wave," "the amazingly quiet room in which all my life has been spent"[30]). In that shuttered space the flat, uninflected voice muses with disarming diffidence: "Right at the moment this occurs to me, or that, or the other; let's suppose this, or, maybe, let's suppose the opposite."

It was *Self-Portrait in a Convex Mirror* (1975), with its triple prizes, that propelled Ashbery from the obscurity of his earliest published poems into the glare of the changing poetry scene and established him as an avant-garde experimentalist who needed to be reckoned with. The long title poem has been called his masterpiece, and is still probably the Ashbery poem most widely read and discussed, in large part because it is the least characteristic and most accessible of the major poems. The poem's very accessibility has led some Ashbery aficionados to complain about the disproportionate attention it has received, and the poet seems to agree: "I've never really cared for 'Self-Portrait' very much"; "[i]t seems to have given people the idea that I was actually dealing with a subject matter in some recognizable way, and this was a great relief; but I think really it's just as random and unorganized as my other poetry is."[31] Asked in this 1985 interview for his favorite poems, Ashbery mentioned immediately "The System" from *Three Poems* (1973) and the recently published "A Wave."

Despite these protestations, "Self-Portrait" is a key poem because it does deal with subject matter in a more recognizable way than do earlier and subsequent poems. Moreover, it is a landmark in American poetry because it articulates a major shift in postwar poetics from a waning Modernism toward what critics were beginning to call Postmodernism, for lack of a more substantive term. One aspect of "Self-Portrait" that signals this transition is the fact that it is the most Stevensian of Ashbery's poems not only in its aestheticism but in its diction. Here, for example, are the closing lines:

> One feels too confined,
> Sifting the April sunlight for clues,
> In the mere stillness of the ease of its
> Parameter. The hand holds no chalk
> And each part of the whole falls off
> And cannot know it knew, except
> Here and there, in cold pockets
> Of remembrance, whispers out of time.[32]

On many occasions Ashbery acknowledged Stevens as a strong early influence, and reading "Self-Portrait" against "The Idea of Order at Key West" clarifies Ashbery's thinking in moving from a Modernist poetics to a Postmodernist poetics.

The "recognizable" focus that gives Ashbery's ruminations their loosely organizing point of reference is a sixteen-century self-portrait by Francesco Mazzola, called Parmigianino because he hailed from Parma, painted on a curved ball of wood the exact size of the convex mirror in whose circle the artist viewed himself. The poem reminds the reader that the self-portrait's innovation lies in its being the first mirror painting and marks a significant moment in the practice of art as self-reflection. Parmigianino became one of the leading Mannerist painters after the Italian Renaissance, and the association of Mannerism with Postmodernism runs through the poem. Moreover, the direct address of the poem's speaker to Francesco ("The Idea of Order" is Stevens's address to the aesthetician Ramon Fernandez) makes explicit Ashbery's identification with Parmigianino and makes the poem into a dramatic monologue that constitutes, at a further remove, Ashbery's own self-portrait. Ashbery has said that he started from a Romantic outlook but that "the modernist tradition that I grew up with" provided the "foundation for further experimentation," which led in turn to the Postmodernist stance that he is working out in "Self- Portrait."[33]

What requires the fifteen pages of the poem is Ashbery's convoluted reflection on the issue of whether, and how, the artist can plausibly present his inner self or "soul" in a portrait of face and physiognomy. The first pages of the poem reiterate again and again the paradox of how the soul is presumed to present itself in the face and especially the eyes of the portrait. What does the artist see with and in his eyes? Is the soul thus seen "lively" or "embalmed," hidden or visible and expressive, open or secret and "captive," "in repose" or "restless," "englobed" or reaching a hand "[o]ut of the globe"? The enigmatic paradoxes soon knot themselves into contradictions and negations: "the soul is not a soul"; the "plain" secret is that there is "no secret"; there is "no way" out of the self-circling. The uncertainties and shifting perspectives call into question the power of the medium to convey reality. "[N]o words" can "find the meaning"; the convexity of language makes words "only speculation / (From the Latin *speculum*, mirror)" (pp. 68, 69).

Modernists were painfully aware, as Eliot also put it in *Four Quartets*, of "the intolerable wrestle / With words and meanings"; "[w]ords strain, / Crack and sometimes break ... / Decay with imprecision, will not stay in place ..." But Modernism rests on the conviction that wrestling words into "pattern" and "form" can make meaning by creating an artifact with the integrity and endurance of Keats's Grecian urn or Eliot's "Chinese jar" or Stevens's jar, placed in the Tennessee wilderness that takes "dominion everywhere" in a world "no longer wild." In those Romantic and Modernist works that Ashbery grew up with he can feel the "rage for order" but only nostalgically; he can no longer summon and channel its energy because for him the fissures and slippages of language make order, even aesthetic order, unattainable in the old way.[34] Ashbery's unshakable sense of flux, here and in poem after poem, issues in Heraclitean tropes of flowing water. Gazing into the convex mirror of Francesco's painting and his poem, he sees the image "swim"; the verb recurs twice on the first page. The painted face and its verbal analogue manifest themselves "in a recurring wave / Of arrival." But the moment of arrival is itself the moment of disintegration, "[l]ike a wave breaking on a rock, giving up / Its shape in a gesture which expresses that shape": the momentary shape of flux and fragmentation (pp. 68, 73).

Historically, Ashbery sees Parmigianino's position on the cusp of Mannerism as parallel to his position on the cusp of Postmodernism. Parmigianino's early self-portrait antedates his Mannerist works and still retains much of "the consonance of the High Renaissance," but already "distorted by the mirror" and anticipating his later Mannerist style. Echoing Stevens's *The Necessary Angel* as the title for his books of essays outlining his poetics, Ashbery sees Francesco's face as "an angel" that "looks like everything / We have forgotten, I mean forgotten things … lost beyond telling, / Which were ours once." Yet in the poem "I go on consulting / This mirror that is no longer mine" because what remains of its consonance seems like "a vase" that "is always full" and "accommodates everything" – "everything," that is, "as it / May be imagined outside time." Such a vase, like Stevens's jar, is what he called, in *The Necessary Angel*, the *mundo* of the imagination: an alternative aesthetic world that none-theless has the power to initiate an agreement with reality. In Ashbery's words, "it is a metaphor / Made to include us, we are a part of it and / Can live in it as in fact we have done …" "Once," indeed, "it seemed so perfect" that "[t]his could have been our paradise: exotic / Refuge within an exhausted world, but that wasn't / In the cards." Making exotic and artificial paradises, as Stevens did, seems to Ashbery, despite nostalgia for their "investing aura," uncomfortably "out of style," like "the games of an old man": "You can't live there" (pp. 74, 77, 76, 79, 82).

The turning point comes mid-poem with the suggestion of "something new … on the way," a new "wave / Of arrival," "a new preciosity / In the wind." "Can you stand it, / Francesco?" the poet asks the painter and him-self, "Are you strong enough for it?" He cannot yet name it Postmodernism or describe it in detail, because the deflation of Modernism has left a sense of impotence or "inertia" that "saps all activity." But this, he says, is only the "negative side" of the "change," the residual "whispers of the word" that has now spent itself in "the bathed, aired secrecy of the open sea." Its "positive side" is harder to discern, but the effort may make "you notice life," indeed may make one live more self-consciously each day, "crest-ing into one's present" as "the waterwheel of days / Pursues its unevent-ful, even serene course." Merely living self-consciously in the flow of "[t]odayness" – without illusions or preconceptions, without any "big the-ory to explain the universe," but with an acceptance of the multitudinous "otherness" each day presents – may be the new Postmodernist "game," the "metaphor / Made to include us" so that we "[c]an live in it" (pp. 68, 75, 76, 78–79, 81).

This commentary assembles a more linear argument than the wave-like movements of the poem trace with their overlapping advances and retrac-tions and returns. But it makes clear how "Self-Portrait" is a pivotal poem not just in Ashbery's work but in the history of American poetry. By the end of the poem's fifteen pages Ashbery, buoyed by the possibilities of change, consigns Parmiginiano's painting to the past and turns back to the challenge of exploring the possibilities of the new poetry and inventing the language to verbalize the self-reflexive ebb and flow of his sense of todayness – what Stevens (in "The Man Whose Pharynx Was Bad") had lamented as "the malady of the quotidian." The flat clumsiness of the word "todayness" accepts and even embraces what Stevens had deplored in fastidious Latinate mellifluousness.

What might a Postmodern poetry be? A central tenet of Modernism affirmed the craftsman's mastery of the medium in deconstructing reality and reconstructing it into an artifact. Even Stevens the aesthete saw the trap of aestheticism and argued that the *mundo* was intended to create an agreement with reality, although he never spelled out the terms of that agreement. For Williams, less the aesthete than Stevens, the verbal construct stood in vital apposition to the world of experience and entered it as a new thing. It was Gertrude Stein's radical experiments with language that most pointedly anticipated deconstructive Postmodernism more than anything in Stevens or Williams. Ashbery called Stein's long "Stanzas in Meditation" "the most successful of her attempts to do what can't be done, to create a counterfeit of reality more real than reality." Indeed, he saw "Stanzas" as "a hymn to possibility; a celebration of the fact that the world exists, that things can happen," but the possibility it explores is the deconstruction of the world into words, so that the things that happen are first and foremost linguistic and semiotic. Yet in sensibility and language Ashbery was from the outset closer to Stevens than to Stein. Her minimalist means of deconstructing reality through simplification of syntax and flat repetition of words and images were antithetical to what Ashbery saw as his "so European and maximalist" means, which were closer to Stevens's.[35] Indeed, Ashbery mediated the transition from Modernism to Postmodernism principally through Stevens, and "Self-Portrait" marks that mediation most explicitly.

The most formative influences on Ashbery, after Stevens, were the French Symbolistes whom Stevens revered. Ashbery absorbed their attempts to write a *poésie pur* during the decade he spent in Paris in the late 1950s and early 1960s. But where Stevens felt particular affinity with Paul Valéry, Ashbery inclined more to Arthur Rimbaud and Stéphane Mallarmé and to their more contemporary descendants coming out of French Surrealism. Ashbery has translated a number of these poets, including a Baudelaire poem in rhymed couplets in *A Wave* (1984), poems from Mallarmé's *Nursery Rhymes* (in the Fall 2005 issue of the journal *Conjunctions*), and, more recently, a highly acclaimed translation of Rimbaud's *Illuminations* (2011).

Ashbery's comments on his favorite French poets highlight what have come to be recognized as defining features of his own poetry. Pierre Reverdy's experiments "with language and syntax," Ashbery noted, make it "often difficult to determine whether a particular line belongs with the preceding sentence or the one following it. The lines drift across the page as overheard speech drifts across our hearing ..." Thus with Reverdy "one can have the impression one moment of contemplating a drop of water on a blade of grass; the next moment one is swimming for one's life." Ashbery particularly singled out Raymond Roussel, whose work he helped to introduce to the American public, as the poet "whose experiments with language can be likened to those of Mallarmé." His fractured, heavily parenthetical sentences seem calculated "to speed the disintegration of language," or perhaps to invent "a language that seems always on the point of revealing its secret, of pointing the way back to the 'republic of dreams' whose insignia blazed on his forehead." Ashbery cites the observation by Pierre Janet, Roussel's psychiatrist, that for Roussel "the work of art must contain nothing real, no observation of the real or spiritual world, only totally imaginary arrangements."[36]

Marjorie Perloff's suggestion that we consider Ashbery's poems dream songs summons up Berryman's dream songs for comparison. If Berryman's dream songs read like wide-eyed nightmares, Ashbery's read like shadowy daydreams. But the point for the argument of this book is that the juxtaposition illustrates the declension of a residual Modernism into a Postmodernist poetics.[37] Ashbery has always been candid about the challenging complexity and obliqueness of his poems: "There are no themes or subjects in the usual sense, except the very broad one of an individual consciousness confronting or confronted by a world of external phenomena"; "I write with experiences in mind, but I don't write about them, I write out of them." As a result, "there is no message, nothing I want to tell the world particularly except what I am thinking when I am writing"; "[c]haracteristic devices are ellipses, frequent changes of tone, voice (that is, the narrator's voice), point of view, to give an impression of flux." To that end, "I write rapidly usually ... [W]hen I've finished writing I go over and make a few changes, but usually not very extensive" – usually excisions and rearrangements rather than alterations in the words of the text – because "I am more interested in the movement among ideas than in the ideas themselves, the way one goes from one point to another rather than the destination or origin."[38]

Ashbery's poetry of todayness, then, records not descriptions of the "world of external phenomena" but the drift of consciousness. The appropriate vehicle for tracing the free association of images and ideas is not the verse line, with its history of artifice, but the sentence, often a long, loose sentence stretching syntactical connection and grammatical structure in modifying phrases and qualifying clauses that open out into other phrases and clauses. Ashbery has written hundreds of short or shortish poems, and some use meter and rhyme and traditional forms like the sestina or the sonnet. But the conventions and structures of form serve as a witty and pointed dissonance from the material and shape of the sentences so enclosed. Ashbery's expressed aversion to iambic pentameter indicates his attitude to all structural forms, even those he uses in ironic play: "It has an order of its own that is foreign to nature." And for him nature signifies not the organic form of the Romantics but Heraclitean flux. Consequently, language tracing the self-consciousness of a day or a series of days naturally seeks the open, flat, unmapped space of long poems: sentences loose enough to accommodate modifying phrases and qualifying clauses, running on through long and prosy lines or block paragraphs of prose. At the end of the process, Ashbery insists, "[f]or me, my poems have their own form, which is the one I want, even though other people might not agree that it is there."[39] For the "form," like the "form" of a wave, is merely whatever shape and length the movement of the poem itself takes.

Reading and talking about an Ashbery poem is, therefore, significantly different from unraveling the tight-wound jeremiads of Lowell, or from following Bishop's narratives to their appointed conclusions, or even from analyzing Berryman's dream songs in which, in contrast to the blur of Ashbery's diaphanous pronouns, the play of Berryman's pronouns enacts the drama of a fractured self. The usual strategies and devices for a critical reading of thematic, prosodic, and formal development get little traction in poems like "The System" or "A Wave," to cite two of Ashbery's most admired poems, which are also among his own acknowledged favorites. The reader and critic can only enter the flow of language to seek and then swim with the elusive, submarine current carrying the wash of pronouns, images, dangling modifiers in successive waves of arrival and subsidence. The usual strategies of critical analysis and commentary run counter to the intended drift of the poem.

"The System" antedates "Self-Portrait in a Convex Mirror." It is the central and by far the longest of the prose poems collected under the title *Three Poems* (1972). "The System" has been called Ashbery's most philosophical, even metaphysical poem, and perhaps for that reason Ashbery chose it, despite its length, for inclusion in his 1985 *Selected Poems*. The first sentence, uncharacteristically short and declarative, opens the flood-gates of discursive speculation: "The system was breaking down"; and the ensuing paragraphs of speculation spill over forty pages from left margin to right. The current carrying this poem follows the commitment to live in "[t]odayness" – that is to say, the psychological need to account for "the size of today" in "life's rolling river," and to do so without the inherited certitudes and assurances of the religious and philosophical tradition.[40] The impersonal "one" of the first paragraph soon morphs into "we," elid-ing the reader into the speculation, and then contrasts "we" with those third-person "others" of the old traditional "system" (pp. 53–54). "They" accepted a central "truth," which vouchsafed that "the life uncurled around it in calm waves" and that "[t]he words formed from it and the sentences formed from them were dry and clear, as though made of wood" (pp. 54, 55). But, on the contrary, precisely because life's "flood" is no longer a mir-ror in which one sees "the comforting reflection of one's own face," in this poem "we propose to explore," with "the enthusiasm not of the religious fanatic but of the average, open-minded, intelligent person," what "other tradition" might be in "a kind of fiction" or "a kind of sequence of fantas-tic reflections" (pp. 57, 55, 56).

From the perspective of the other tradition, the assumption of cos-mic "love" on which the old system was founded roiled "the clear waters of the reflective intellect." The "*hubris*" of the old system was "bent on self-discovery in the guise of an attractive partner who is *the* heaven-sent one," and offered the assurance that life's "river journey" could be sus-tained, through the "eddies and shallows" and "rapids," because of a "celestial promise of delights to come in another world and still lovely to look at in this one" (pp. 57, 59, 57–58). This sense of "upward path" gave flux the seeming "stability" of "steady advancement" and served "to stifle any burgeoning notions of the formlessness of the whole, the mud-dle really as ugly as sin." The emergent new and "other" system arises, on the other hand, from the assumption that "the real thing … has to be colorless and featureless if it is to be the true reflection of the primeval energy from which it issued forth." But this negation of certitude par-adoxically opens unexplored "possibilities" that provide "a mirror reflect-ing the innermost depths of the soul" (pp. 59, 60, 58, 61). Throughout the poem (and elsewhere in his work) Ashbery uses available religious and implicitly Christian language – here "sin" and "soul," and elsewhere in the poem "the way," "redemption," "damnation," "grace," "heaven," "angel," "a god come down to instruct us," the Good Samaritan, the resurrection of Lazarus, and so on (pp. 69, 64, 72, 77, 81, 96) – to evoke both a nostalgia for the lost faith and the quasi-religious impulse behind his own secular and skeptical speculations.

The two systems are epitomized by "two kinds of happiness." The old system rests on an epiphanal moment adumbrating "an ideal toward which the whole universe tends and which therefore confers a shape on the random movements outside us." Such an epiphany comes only "through the obscure workings of grace as chance" but is taken to reveal something of what "the souls 'in glory'" must feel as "a state of permanent grace." Nevertheless, though we may feel that "this is truly what we were brought into creation for," "we" of the other tradition "do not bother our heads too much about it" because "we know that very few among us will ever achieve it." For those convinced of flux ending in "inundation," the idealizing "castaways of the eternal voyage" seem "spiritual bigots" who only imagine that they are headed "for the promised land when in reality the ship is sinking under them" (pp. 71, 72, 73–74, 75). On the other hand, speculation about what a moment of happiness might signify for those seeking a possible postmodern system in the "colorless and featureless" flux triggers a remarkable fourteen-page paragraph that is the crux of the poem. For unless the isolated moments of consciousness can be intelligibly reconciled with the flux, no system is conceivable.

In the preface to his 1853 *Poems*, Matthew Arnold defined the pain and anxiety of the modern condition as the consequence of a radical fall into self- consciousness: "The dialogue of the mind with itself has commenced; modern problems have presented themselves; we hear already the doubts, we witness the discouragement, of Hamlet and of Faust." The mind's turning in on itself denoted a tragic disconnection from the world outside the mind that split organic nature into the diverse particularity of individual phenomena and fractured the coherence of time into a succession of separate moments. Walter Pater's "Conclusion" to *The Renaissance* (1873) is a more extended reflection on "the race of the midstream, the drift of momentary acts of sight and passion and thought," with the deracinated mind "keeping as a solitary prisoner its own dream of a world." That same dilemma is what transfixes Ashbery a hundred years further along in the devolution of modernity into alienation.

How, then, can "we" negotiate todayness, "the business of day-to-day living" (87) from moment to moment? The language of that long, central paragraph of "The System" spins that epistemological dilemma into a blur of criss-crossing paradoxes: particularizing senses / abstracting reason; moments / eternity; flux / fixity; doubt / knowledge; instant / pattern;

part / whole; open / closed; indeterminacy / teleology. Charles Altieri sees an underlying epistemological motive and purpose in Ashbery's slippery language:

> Ashbery's purpose is probably not simply to present indeterminate discourse or even to show the inherent duplicities of language. What matters is how forms of indeterminacy intensify our engagement in complex reflections on precise relations among loss, belatedness, the desire to know, and the play of transition and transference.[41]

For Ashbery, as the future rushes through the present into the past, as potentiality dies into the muddle of memory, our ability to live "a preordained succession of moments" (p. 76) pivots perilously on the moment of happiness that can come unexpectedly from time to time. The senses seize it not as a transcendence of time, which Ashbery would suspect as an illusion, but merely as

> almost a moment of peace, of purity in which what we are meant to perceive could almost take shape in the empty air, if only there were time enough, and yet in the time it takes to perceive the dimness of its outline we can if we are quick enough seize the meaning of that assurance, before returning to the business at hand ...   (p. 79)

The qualifiers testify to the elusiveness of the momentary peace and purity: "almost ... almost ... if only ... dimness of its outline." Nevertheless, those "fragments" of "revelation" and their "traces in the memory" persist as a "divine enigma," "as a god come down to earth to instruct us in the ways of the other kingdom." In sacramental language of Eucharist and Spirit, the moment "may be eaten, and breathed"; it is "bread and meat left by the wayside ... by an anonymous Good Samaritan." Those remembered traces "come to you like fragments of a buried language you once knew" (pp. 79, 80, 81, 77, 86).

Ashbery comes to realize that "this second kind of happiness" turns out to be, for him and maybe for "us," "merely a fleshed-out, realized version of that ideal first kind, ... the faithful reflection of the idealist concept." Even if in the rush of time its potential "cannot be realized," it is "more to be prized" as a "singular isolated moment that has now already slipped so far into the past that it seems a mere spark." The paradox is that "[y]ou cannot do without it and you cannot have it" (pp. 81, 84, 85). Even if that incarnate moment were to turn out to be unique and unrepeated in the "preordained succession of moments," it was, nonetheless, "a *new arrangement* that existed and was on the point of working." Indeed, "it mattered precisely because it was a paradox and about to be realized here on earth, in human terms"; "it *was* real, and therefore it *is* real" – at least within the individual consciousness, taken "inside us to be the interior walls of our chamber, the place where we live" (pp. 85, 82). In the most assertive and expansive speculation of the poem, this rearrangement of consciousness is seen to have the potential "to change us on every level" of our engagement with the teeming world outside of us (p. 82). For Ashbery, this postulation is the closest intimation of a possible alternate system that the "other tradition" can at this point manage. Consequently, the long paragraph ends with the assurance that because of "the speed with which you advance," this inflection of consciousness "has become the element in which you live and which is you. Nothing else matters" (p. 86).

Once again, it is important to note that this extrapolation, though composed from the language of the poem, does not render the many diversions and doublings back in the erratic course of the paragraph. Ashbery could rightly object that such a summary does not give the effect of the poem, but it does follow the ongoing current underlying the surface eddying. Where Bishop used the form of the line and the stanza to control and measure the flux that is the matter of the poem, Ashbery's fluid sentences and paragraphs of such sentences are the very vehicle and form, for want of a better word, of the flux it mimics and conveys.

However, the climactic declaration "Nothing else matters" does not conclude the poem. After rejecting, earlier in the poem, the idea or ideal of cosmic or "universal love" on which the old system was based, the last third of the poem circles back and begins to test whether "my solipsistic approach" can allow, hesitantly and tentatively, the contingencies of human love, "the only human ground that can nurture your hopes and fears into the tree of life that is as big as the universe" (pp. 58, 94, 98). Human love, in all its chanciness and uncertainty, is a shadow theme throughout Ashbery's work. The possibility that "self could merge with selflessness, in a true appreciation of the tremendous volumes of eternity" (p. 71) offers a counter to and rescue from alienated self-consciousness, but here, as in other poems, the speculation about the possibility of such love circles back to solipsism.

The speaker of the poem turns to "the eyes of the beloved," of "the person sitting opposite you who asked you a question" (pp. 94, 95, 97). Who is the beloved? Does the person opposite have a name and reality? In life David Kermani was Ashbery's longtime partner and his bibliographer, and both *Self-Portrait* and *Flow Chart* are dedicated to him. But in the tentative exchange between speaker and beloved in "The System," the pronouns "I" and "you" become so slippery and interchangeable that the beloved fades into a shadowy figure in the speaker's imagination. In the first person, for example, "I'm just a mute observer," wondering "What am I going to say?" to the beloved's question; but the speaker elides into the second person "you," as he faces "[t]he person sitting opposite you" who is "waiting for this word that must come from you and that you have not in you." The "new voice" needed for a response should be "turning you both in on yourself and outward to that crystalline gaze" of the beloved. But, as the pronouns turn into each other, is the responder "I" or "you"? While I await "your inevitable reply," "I am listening. From now on the invisible bounty of my concern will be there to keep you company ..." By now "I" and "you" have blurred into mirror images of each other: "You have been talking a long time without listening to yourself" (pp. 94, 95, 97, 98, 99). Altieri remarked that because in Ashbery "the self is imaginary, or comprises itself in positions ... he can play all the functional roles in dialogue."[42] So the brief exchange or interchange between lovers comes "full circle." The speaker rejects "the idea of oneness in favor of a plurality of experiences, earthly and spiritual, in fact a plurality of different lives that you lived out to your liking"; "in order to avoid extinction," one must gather this plurality in a semblance of "yourself," but self "under the aegis of singleness" and "separateness" (p. 101).

The personal pronouns keep disappearing into and reappearing out of one another, as the conclusion turns on the trope of the poem as "a movie of yourself." This movie/poem would "show us" how – through "these ample digressions of yours," through "the meandering stream of our narration" – "we" have made the "shapeless blur" of all those past moments into the "shape of the plot of a novel." But then, when "the allegory is ended," there inescapably comes the realist's recognition that "the plurality of experiences" implodes into the solipsistic first person: "I am quite ready to admit that I am alone, that the film I have been watching all this time may be only a mirror, with all the characters ... played by me in different disguises." In the final image, "we" – the janus-face of "I" and "you" – return "together" from the theater to the todayness of an afternoon "as wide as an ocean. It is the time we have now, and all our wasted time sinks into the sea and is swallowed up without a trace" (pp. 102, 103, 104, 105, 106).

Perhaps Ashbery favored "The System" over the other two of the *Three Poems* not just because it was the most fully developed but also because, at least in those central paragraphs, it reached, ever so tentatively, a kind of life-affirming possibility. However, the poem as a whole and the other two prose poems that frame that possibility acknowledge its fragility and vulnerability. In "The New Spirit," the "continual pilgrimage" down life's temporal course "carries you beyond, alarmingly fast out into the confusion where the river pours into the sea. That place that seems even farther from shore ..."[43] And the last page of "The Recital," and thus of the *Three Poems* volume, takes a grim retrospective look at the speculation about renewal and resolution:

> But already it was hard to distinguish the new elements from the old, so calculated and easygoing was the fusion, the partnership that was the only element now, and which was even now fading rapidly from memory ... A vast wetness as of sea and air combined, a single, smooth, anonymous matrix without surface or depth was the product of these new changes.[44]

Tropes of water recur in Ashbery's work because they are metaphors both for what the poems say and for how they say it. Life's river pours its current, poems pump their words into the sea's "single, smooth, anonymous matrix without surface or depth." Reading "A Wave" and *Flow Chart* after "Self-Portrait" and "The System" confirms that both formally and thematically Ashbery's long poems have become increasingly watery, flowing steadily through the reader's mind and leaving increasingly faint, deliquescent tracings of their passage. We have heard Ashbery say that to his mind the poems have the appropriate form; if form as flux is not a paradox or even a contradiction, it certainly proposes a notion of artistic form contradictory to Keats' Grecian urn or Eliot's Chinese jar or Stevens' jar in Tennessee.

For that very reason, perhaps, Ashbery's long poems have been hailed as landmarks in Postmodernist poetry: Dennis Brown calls "A Wave" "the 'Tintern Abbey' of poetic postmodernism"; John Shoptaw cites *The Prelude* as the "most prominent book-length forerunner" of *Flow Chart*.[45] Whitman is also sometimes cited for comparison, but it is noteworthy that Modernist landmarks are seldom invoked as forerunners of or analogues for Ashbery's long poems. In fact, searching for historical links and precedents reveals discontinuity more than continuity. Even in long open-form poems such as "Song of Myself," *The Cantos*, *The Bridge*, and *Paterson* the seemingly disparate parts are meant to reveal their connectedness, are meant to unfold as a process of – or at least toward – discovery and realization. Unlike flux, process assumes and seeks to articulate its underlying and evolving form: a subtending direction and an end-point that will integrate the parts into a coherent whole. The historical importance of the long poems of Ashbery is that they constitute a radical rupture of form unlike anything in Romantic and Modernist experimentation.

"A Wave," the title poem of Ashbery's 1984 volume and the final poem in his 1985 *Selected Poems*, is twenty-two pages of loose and predominantly long lines broken into verse paragraphs. Ashbery has said that he wrote not about experiences but out of experiences, and "A Wave" begins by saying that it emerges from an experience of pain: "To pass through pain and not know it, / A car door slamming in the night. / To emerge on an invisible terrain."[46] Shoptaw guesses that the pain was "brought on by a romantic break-up (or parental flare-up),"[47] but in the text the occasion is unspecified: "By so many systems / As we are involved in, by just so many / Are we set free on an ocean of language that comes to be part of us" (p. 71). The vague course of the first half of the poem offers various images of polarity: landscape with a river or road / house; journey / stasis; ageing / childhood; flux / permanence; moment / memory; play / systems. The wave crests into something more like a discernible tension and movement roughly in the middle of the poem. As in "The System," this passage does seem to correlate the emergence of the poem with the possibility of experiencing love. The poem comes "questioning the old modes / And the new wondering" and is "[t]he empty space in the endless continuum" that "can be filled only by you." Again, as in "The System," the question immediately arises: Is the "you" who fills the temporal space a beloved, or the poet/speaker himself? The pronouns switch from "you" to "I," "choosing / Myself now," as "the place I have to get to / Before nightfall" (p. 79).

But what about the possibility of "our love"? The anxiety of finding "something to say" on that subject – especially after the generations of poets and poetic styles on the subject of love – releases this cascading passage that twists and turns down the page to its repeatedly deferred destination (pp. 80–81):

> Even just one word with a slightly different intonation
> To cause it to stand out from the backing of neatly invented
> Chronicles of things men have said and done, like an
> 　　　English horn,
> And then to sigh, to faint back
> Into all our imaginings, dark
> And viewless as they are,
> Windows painted over with black paint but
> We can sufficiently imagine, so much is admitted, what
> Might be going on out there and even play some part
> In the ordering of it all into lengths of final night,
> Of dim play, of love that at last oozes through the seams

In the cement, suppurates, subsumes
All the other business of living and dying, the orderly
Ceremonials and handling of estates,
Checking what does not appear normal and drawing
                together
All the rest into the report that will finally be made
On a day when it does not appear that there is anything
                to receive it
Properly and we wonder whether we too are gone,
Buried in our love,
The love that defined us only for a little while ...

Here – as in Ashbery's most memorable passages – the prosy, discursive language finds an image, moves into a phrasing and cadence that lift the passage into a poignant eloquence and haunting beauty. The clear note of the English horn sustains these twenty lines with a dying fall. But the sentence keeps deferring naming its urgent concern, and even then the word "love" does not appear till mid-sentence, buried mid-line in a cluster of prepositional phrases. Love is invoked as a response to, even a resolution of death's "final night" and life's "dim play," subsuming the "business of living and dying." It is "our love," then, that defines "us," yet "we" cannot but "wonder whether" we are "[b]uried in our love," since love defines us only for the passing moment – and dies. The verb "subsumes" follows and alliterates with "suppurates." If love be the "one word" that can finally sound out with the clarity of an English horn, it is sadly destined to "faint back / Into all our imaginings, dark and viewless as they are, / Windows painted over with black paint." Since love does not open these blinded windows, we can only imagine "what / Might be going on out there."

The myth of Psyche and Cupid cautions us that "love in the dark" is "the only way / That love determines us." In a rare instance of sustained rhetoric in the poem, our very "singleness, separateness" makes us see love retrospectively as one of those "infrequent pellucid moments" (p. 81):

                in which all lives, all destinies
And incompleted destinies were swamped
As though by a giant wave that picks itself up
Out of a calm sea and retreats again into nowhere
Once its damage is done.

The image for love turns out to be the wave's passage. Buried in the giant wave, the drowned "émigrés" can only tell "how love came and went, /

And how it keeps coming and going, ever disconcerting ..." (p. 82). From
this point the poem wanders uncertainly to a low-keyed effort at resignation; here are the final words (p. 89):

> And so each of us has to remain alone, conscious of
>   each other
> Until the day when war absolves us of our differences. We'll
> Stay in touch. So they have it, all the time. But all was
>   strange.

For "each of us," consciousness of the other confirms mutual isolation.
What kind of conflict or altercation will finally bridge the breach? Will
that "until" ever come to be? The deadly violence of "war" jars with the
sacramental efficacy of its verb "absolves." How can war end our differences except through annihilation? Three abrupt sentences break up the
last line. The line break in "We'll / stay in touch" keeps us from touching. In fact, the breezily chummy conversational cliché may even maintain disconnection under the pretense of wanting contact. What do "they"
have that we do not? Are they in touch while we remain at odds? "But" –
the conjunction begs and concedes the question – "all was strange" and
estranged. After the dying clarion note of love on the English horn, the
terse staccato of the last line, with its repetition of "all," sounds the bumpy
dissonance of universal alienation.

The 213 wide pages of the book-length *Flow Chart* (1991) represent
the most extreme development of Ashbery's poetics, perhaps its *reduc-
tio ad absurdum*. Its genesis was the suggestion from the artist Trevor
Winkfield, who would paint the design of the dust jacket, that Ashbery
write a hundred-page poem about his recently dead mother. Ashbery
avoided any such direct autobiography and began the hundred-page
poem on December 8, 1987, deciding ahead of time to complete it on
his sixty-first birthday, July 28, 1988. The governing convention was
both arbitrary and predetermined. Shoptaw has examined the typescript
and reports that the single-spaced sheets have no breaks or interruptions
other than stanza breaks, the division into six sections or books coming later to serve as rest stops on the reader's way through. The other
arbitrary but fixed convention was the one-hundred-character limit to
the line on the typewriter, and Ashbery's long lines, uncapped here for
the first time to move closer to prose, do not exceed that limit by more
than one word. Yet so loose and chancy was the movement from line to
line and page to page that the omission of a page of typescript from the
printed text was not noticed by either the author or the publisher, and

when Shoptaw pointed out the omission to Ashbery, he merely said that it must have accidentally occurred when the typescript was transferred to the computer.[48]

Shoptaw claims that the genre of *Flow* Chart is autobiography: nothing so predictable, needless to say, as a "chronological, personal story, buttressed by specifics of time, place, and event" but purportedly, in its diary of more than six months of more or less daily speculation, "anybody's autobiography" and so "nobody's in particular." Shoptaw cites Ashbery's slyly hyperbolic remark: "My own autobiography has never interested me very much. Whenever I try to think about it, I seem to draw a complete blank."[49] Of course anybody's autobiography is not everybody's autobiography but, as Shoptaw admits, nobody's. The lack of identifiable focus and reference points frees the accumulating particulars from assuming sequentiality, much less consequentiality. Marjorie Perloff describes Ashbery's poems as consisting of "parts that belong to no whole – an absent totality."[50] *Flow Chart* can perhaps best be understood as the realization of the poststructuralist theorists' postulation of the death of the author in a semiotic sea of indeterminate words.

Ashbery tries to resolve, or disguise, the tension between the two words of the title in the blurb he drafted for the dust jacket:[51] "he charts the internal ebb and flow of a life perceived – perhaps even lived – through the somehow sacred act of self-reflection." More than one reader has complained of finding the uninterrupted interior dialogue more flow than chart: "chart" claims an evolving structure that the poem's associative mode, especially at novel-length, undermines. The last words in the poem sum up the dilemma in an image: "By evening the traffic has begun / again in earnest, color-coded. It's open: the bridge, that way."[52] The colon implies some kind of correlation across the punctuation between open flow of traffic and overarching, underlying bridge, but the last words instead suggest disjunction. Any bridge-like structure will be found not here but "that way" – outside the poem, off the "chart."

In an enthusiastic review of *Flow Chart*, Fred Muratori gathers the opacities and disconnections of the poem into the huge claim that it "comes as close to an epic poem as our postmodern, nonlinear, deconstructed sensibilities will allow."[53] Is the relevant genre, then, not autobiography but epic? But the contrast between *Flow Chart* and Romantic and Modernist experiments in the epic form are very revealing. Whitman kept revising and reordering *Leaves of Grass* in an effort to arrive at an organization he found adequate to the ambition of his project. Joyce's *Ulysses* and Eliot's *The Waste Land* constellate their parts and fragments into structures so complex that the poems have generated library shelves of commentary and exposition. When Pound was unable to complete the periplum of *The Cantos* to his satisfaction, he considered his life's work a failure. For all its gaps, the sections of Hart Crane's *The Bridge* hang, in rough historical sequence, suspended between the pylon supports of the Proem and the climactic section, evoking the architectural strength and soaring sublimity of the Brooklyn Bridge. In *Flow Chart*, however, Romantic and Modernist energies as formal agents yield to Postmodernist passivity and play. Nevertheless, Muratori may, after all, be correct in the sense that *Flow Chart* approaches something like the furthest stretch of the Postmodernist sensibility, after Poststructuralist literary theorists have declared the death of the author and the decentralization of the poem, after post-Freudian psychiatrists have analyzed consciousness into a narcissistic labyrinth of smoky mirrors, after deconstructive linguists have reduced language to a semiotic code at once radically closed and radically open, at once overdetermined and indeterminate.

At the beginning of section III, near the middle of *Flow Chart*, Ashbery projects – with uncharacteristic rhetorical flourish, almost inescapably with Whitman's Bridge and Crane's Bridge in mind – the construction of a heroic, almost god-like bridge, in order immediately to demolish it (pp. 84–85):

> A bridge erects itself into the sky, all trumpets
>   and twisted steel,
>   but like the torso of a god, too proud to see itself, or
>   lap up
> the saving grace of small talk. And when these immense
>   structures go down, no one hears:
>   a puff of smoke is emitted, a flash, and then it's gone,
>   leaving behind a feeling that something happened there
>   once,
>   like wind tearing at the current, but no memory or crying
>   either; it's just
> another unit of space reduced to its components. An
>   empty salute.

The poem as bridge is too vauntingly self-important in its claims of quasi-divinity to sustain itself, and its collapse leaves neither recollection nor regret: only a vacancy to be filled with small talk. Its ruins present at best "[a]n empty salute" to its preposterously "proud" claims. Earlier the poem had said (p. 25):

now the bridge will never be built,
if that is all time had in the wallet at his back. Scaled-down
        surprises
here and there, a puttering about in dust, and once again
        it seems as though it
were all up to us. Well, why not?

Flow Chart professes no vain aspirations to be a bridge, only the river that burbles and chatters along with the day's self-reflections till it debouches into the unlettered ocean of language, returning to the "matrix without surface or depth" from which it had flowed: "[t]he words have, as they / always do, come full circle, dragging the meaning that was on the reverse side / all along and one even / expects this . . ." (pp. 25–26).

Burbles and chatters along, as in this characteristic passage, chosen utterly at random by flipping the book open and seeing what the page presented (p. 111):

Since the last heist I sense a quintessential weariness;
        I can
neither lay my barrel down nor look directly into it. I think
        I'll have a go at the food –
h'mm, squirrel ragout again. No, I'll opt, I'll ope my
        eyelids for this next one
coming, without food. It was the cutest darned haunted
        house you ever saw. It had blue
shutters with squirrel cutouts in them. Inside everything
        was clean and neat.
But haunted houses are like whores – there's no such thing
        as a nice one, no matter
how prim they act, or how the spotted sun greets them as
        the warm morning is painted.
And then such a one, some other one, would want to know
        why in the name of thunder
these repairs were necessary. After all, the place looked
        all right. Even the bailiff
who lived next door said so. In the event of a storm or
        flood, the door
could be shut, and there was an end to it. But it never
        occurs to anyone that when the
light of the sun does reach the deep pools which are
        almost always bathed in shadow,
why then a short plop is heard and two people are unable
        to occupy the same space.
It sounds simple enough in my book.

Simple enough? Hardly, as Ashbery well knows. For some readers the openness and disconnection of his language and imagery make for a playful, campy form of *poésie pur*, but for many that kind of game constitutes a dangerous abrogation of the power and agency of the word to find or make coherent meaning. Early in *Flow Chart*, however, Ashbery, ever candid about his assumptions and practices, forewarns readers that he had waived a certain kind of linguistic responsibility: "Words, however, are not the culprit. They are at worst a placebo, / leading nowhere (though nowhere, it must be added, can sometimes be a cozy / place, preferable in many cases to somewhere), to banal if agreeable note-spinning" (p. 24).

Flow Chart makes no pretense of having much to offer those who seek a "subject" in the subjective, a "Logos" in language (pp. 33–34):

> Without further ado bring on the subject of these
> negotiations. They all would like to collect it always, but since
> that's impossible, the Logos alone will have to suffice.
> A pity, since no one has seen it recently.

Characteristic offhand dismissal of finality, with a nudge in the ribs for the sophisticates. At the same time, here as elsewhere in Ashbery's poetry, especially in the longer poems, the pity of what will "have to suffice" is anything but "simple enough"; the image in the self-reflecting mirror looks ironically but wistfully both ways. The seemingly casual skepticism that seeks to shrug off the satisfactions of signification does not quite mask the lingering disquiet that dogs Ashbery's life in language: the hankering actually to name and identify the subject of all these verbal negotiations, even to catch momentarily the Logos in the wave of words flowing to the anonymous sea. In "Self- Portrait" he gave this haunted longing Stevensian diction and cadences:

> Whispers of the word that can't be understood
> But can be felt, a chill, a blight
> Moving outward along the capes and peninsulas
> Of your nervures and so to the archipelagoes
> And to the bathed, aired secrecy of the open sea.[54]

CHAPTER 4

The Language of Incarnation
Allen Ginsberg
Jack Kerouac
William Everson

I

The New York School arose out of the meeting of Ashbery, O'Hara, and Koch at Harvard in the late 1940s. The Beat Movement arose in New York out of the 1944 meeting of Jack Kerouac, a Columbia dropout, with Allen Ginsberg, a Columbia undergraduate, William Burroughs, Lucien Carr, and later Gregory Corso. In the mid- to late 1950s, while Ashbery and O'Hara were beginning to work out a Postmodernist poetics, Kerouac and Ginsberg were voicing a counter-poetics that was unapologetically and unabashedly Neoromantic. The two groups first coalesced in New York, but they occupy and speak from utterly different poetic and metaphysical worlds.

Beat beat beat beat-up beat-down beat downbeat beat heartbeat upbeat beat beat beatific: the word has many and contrary inflections and connotations. Beat poetics invokes the rhythms of contemporary speech – quick and syncopated, brassy and spontaneous as jazz and blues – to move the speaker and hearer, body and soul, to wail the woes and sound the highs of human existence. In rejection not just of the formalist poetic norms established in the academy as the New Criticism but also of the cool sophistication of the New York School, Beat poetry was oral, performative, deliberately confrontational; it flaunted its outrageousness and took many risks – emotional nakedness, incoherence, banality, sentimentality, madness – to voice the extremes of despair and ecstasy muted and repressed in the consumer capitalism and Cold War politics of postwar America. Kerouac picked up the word "beat" from Herbert Huncke, a Times Square junkie and drug trafficker ("Man, I'm beat"), and in 1948 grandly proclaimed of his band of friends: "this is really a beat generation."[1]

In the late 1940s Ginsberg and Kerouac's friendship with Neal Cassady, who came from Denver and worked the railroads from his home base near San Jose, brought them west, and San Francisco and the Bay Area became a center of countercultural activity when Ginsberg and Kerouac's frequent and extended visits coincided with the arrival there of Lawrence Ferlinghetti, Michael McClure, Gary Snyder, and Philip Whalen and when these newcomers connected with the poets of the already flourishing San Francisco Renaissance: Kenneth Rexroth, William Everson, Robert Duncan, and Jack Spicer. Together they formed a fluid but close-knit little community of literary and social dissent and affirmation, whose survivors and remnants are still active and vocal more than half a century later.

Volumes have been written, pro and con, about the Beat counterculture as an alternative to the dominant postwar culture. But it is important to note that both the culture and the counterculture were riven by deep-rooted and volatile contradictions that bound the two in symbiotic opposition. On the one hand, American culture was characterized by nationalistic pride in becoming a victorious superpower; after the stresses and shortages of the war years, an unprecedented economic prosperity and industrial boom drove capitalist competition masked by a complacent conformity to bourgeois values. At the same time, postwar culture was haunted by the apocalyptic possibilities of the newly unleashed atomic power, and gripped by a Cold War with global Communism that ratcheted up an arms race to meet the Red advances in Korea and Vietnam. To the nascent counterculture, however, the American Century proclaimed triumphantly by Henry Luce made for moneyed materialism at home and reckless brinksmanship and imperialism abroad. The dissenting response was itself conflicted by contradictions that veered between mania and depression, despair and ecstasy.

Socially, psychologically, and morally, the Beats lived on the edge and sometimes over the edge. In terms of social class, with the exception of Burroughs, the central figures came from immigrant stock (Ginsberg, Jewish; Kerouac, French-Canadian; Gregory Corso, Italian), and their working-class background sought identification with the downtrodden and rejected (what Kerouac called "the fellaheen"). They dropped out, refusing to compete in the capitalist marketplace. They sought to prove liberation from bourgeois morality with narcotics, drink, and sex, and even naively ventured into the criminal underworld of drug dealing, theft, and murder.[2] The psychological stresses of their deracinated lives and disorderly relationships ended frequently in despondency and crack-up; Ginsberg and Kerouac both spent time in psychiatric hospitals. The overwrought avowals of love and friendship in the tight, closed band of sworn male comrades were periodically rent by anger, jealousy, and resentment.

In the opening lines of *Howl* Ginsberg saw "my generation" as "angel-headed hipsters," but William Carlos Williams concluded his introduction of the *Howl* poems: "we are going through hell." Kerouac's characterization of their generation as "desolation angels" catches the tension between the demonic and angelic in the Beat psyche.[3]

For both Ginsberg and Kerouac Rimbaud was the archetypal *poète maudit* who sought transcendence in transgression and disorientation. Yet, amidst the messiness of their lives and the often hostile furor in the press after the publication of *Howl (1956)* and *On the Road* (1957), Kerouac wrote: "I don't think the Beat Generation is going to be a moronic band of dope addicts and hoodlums. My favorite beat buddies were all *kind*, eager, good kids, sincere ... such tender concern."[4] And, indeed, the flip side of what seemed to many commentators the riotous self-indulgence of emotionally retarded adolescents was, in fact, an intense idealism, a vehement seeking after transcendence and vision that also seemed to those same commentators naïve and self-deluded. In the sudden glare of publicity Kerouac tried repeatedly to insist to his dubious interlocutors that this mystical inclination is the affirmation emerging from the negative protest: "The word 'beat' originally meant poor, down and out, deadbeat, on the bum, sad, sleeping in subways," but now does not mean that "so much as it means *beato*, the Italian for beatific: to be in a state of beatitude, like St. Francis, trying to love all life ..." In fact, he said, "it was as a Catholic" in his parish church in Lowell, Massachusetts, that on November 21, 1954, "I heard the holy silence in the church ... the vision of the word Beat as being to mean beatific ..."[5] Ginsberg also insisted on the "religious" inflection of beat in a long response to the Eastern establishment poet Richard Eberhart, who had written about the Beats in "West Coast Rhythms" for *The New York Times Book Review*. What Eberhart had taken "as a negative howl of protest" was, on the contrary, "an act of self-realization, self acceptance" and the "*realization of love*. LOVE"; "I am saying that what seems 'mad' in America is our expression of natural ecstasy (as in Crane, Whitman) ..."[6]

The radical contradictions in the Beats' attitudes and responses made their effort to revolutionize America fizzle out as a movement by the time of Kerouac's early death in 1969. Ginsberg and Snyder were pursuing peace and harmony in their different strains of Buddhist thought, and Kerouac, increasingly alarmed by the hippies of the 1950s and the revolutionary anarchists of the 1960s, retreated to his version of Catholic mysticism. Nevertheless, the Beat phenomenon is historically important, for all the noisy excesses and highjinks of its manifestation, because it opposed the self-satisfied complacency of postwar society with a populism as deep-rooted in the American psyche as capitalist individualism and an idealism as fundamental as American materialism. The political, ethical, and spiritual contradictions, the aspirations and failures of this seemingly fringe movement are woven into the troubled history of the nation.

However, what principally concerns the argument of this book is the Beat poetics that Kerouac and Ginsberg worked out between them in the 1950s, as they worked through versions of *On the Road* and *Howl*. Beat poetry first burst on the startled literary scene with the famous/infamous reading at the Six Gallery in San Francisco on October 7, 1955. McClure, Snyder, Whalen, and Philip Lamantia read poems, with Kenneth Rexroth presiding as impresario, but what made the evening a landmark event was Ginsberg's reading of the just-written first part of *Howl*, with Kerouac a loudly cheering member of the audience. And what made *Howl* possible was the conception of literary expression – its genesis and end – that Kerouac had worked out in writing his fiction.

The Town and the City (1950), Kerouac's first novel about his early life in Lowell and his transition to New York as a Columbia undergraduate, was written under the inspiration of Thomas Wolfe's fiction; it was respectable but quite conventional autobiographical fiction. However, in struggling to render truthfully his meeting with Cassady and their cross-country car trips, he discovered a narrative technique that he called "sketching" and a style that he called "spontaneous prose." The result was the version of *On the Road* that Kerouac typed out, high on drugs, as a continuous unparagraphed narrative on a single scroll of paper in three weeks in April 1951.[7] Almost immediately he began an even more experimental version, published only posthumously as *Visions of Cody* (1973). After reading the typescript of *The Subterraneans*, written, again on drugs, in three nights in 1953, Ginsberg and Burroughs asked Kerouac in amazement to explain his method of composition. His response was "Essentials of Spontaneous Prose" (published in Robert Creeley's *The Black Mountain Review* in 1957) and "Belief & Technique for Modern Prose" (published in *The Evergreen Review* in 1959), and those manifestos defined Beat poetics in much the same way that Charles Olson's "Projective Verse" catalyzed Black Mountain poetics during these same years. From the West Coast Ginsberg told his former Columbia professor Lionel Trilling that, with the Beats centered in San Francisco, Black Mountain was now the "only Eastern center of real poetic discipline, i.e. freedom."[8]

Kerouac had completed six novels (*The Town and the City, On the Road, Visions of Cody, Doctor Sax, Maggie Cassidy*, and *The Subterraneans*) as well as a book of poems, *San Francisco Blues*, and had begun *Mexico City Blues* and his book on Buddhism, *Some of the Dharma* – all before Ginsberg came to write *Howl* in 1955. In fact, when Kerouac first wrote to Ginsberg about "sketching" ("It's the *only way to write*") in 1952, Ginsberg was at first dubious about *On the Road* and its method: "I think book is great but crazy in a bad way, and *got*, aesthetically and publishing-wise, to be pulled back together, re constructed." Up to that point Ginsberg had been writing "fixed iambic rhyme, and 4 yrs. work with Williams' short line free form." However, by August 1955, Ginsberg was pouring out his uncensored feeling of desolation in long lines that would become Part I of *Howl*, and he immediately sent the typescript to Kerouac with this acknowledgment: "I realize how right you are, that was the first time I sat down to blow, it came out in your method, sounding like you. An imitation practically. How advanced you are on this." For his part, Kerouac would tell Ginsberg that "it was not only from Neal's letters but from your wild racing crazy jumping dontcare letters that all that sketching came out, it broke me off from American formalism à la Wolfe …"[9]

Behind the principles and techniques for "a new literature," summarized in Kerouac's two manifestos, is the conviction that "[t]he requirements for prose & verse are the same, i.e., *blow* –"[10] "[S]ketching language is undisturbed flow from the mind of personal secret idea-words, *blowing* (as per jazz musician) …" The central injunction is to focus "the eye within the eye" on the "image at *moment* of writing, and write outwards swimming in the sea of language to peripheral release and exhaustion …" Consequently there should be no "preconceived idea," "[n]o pause to think of proper word," "*no revisions* (except obvious rational mistakes, such as names or *calculated* insertions …)," "[n]ever afterthink to 'improve' or defray impressions." Facilitating the flow of words and images as they follow the "laws of Deep Form" requires the elimination of periods, "false colons and timid usually unnecessary commas" in favor of "the vigorous space dash" to mark "rhetorical breathing (as jazz musician drawing breath between outblown phrases)." Taking Whitman as precedent, Kerouac's imperatives and italics and dashes urge the writer to "tap from yourself the song of yourself, *blow! – now! – your* way is your only way – 'good' – or 'bad' – always honest, ('ludicrous'), spontaneous, 'confessional' interesting, because not 'crafted.' Craft *is* craft." The pun on "craft" turns technical sophistication into a thwarting of the power of the word that imposes artificial form on natural flow. At the pitch of intensity that Kerouac is attempting to reach, language can exceed its limits and break through, to "[t]he unspeakable visions of the individual." At this pitch language is not merely private and individual but public and performative, in the sense that it seeks to enact what it proclaims, so that the hearer or "reader cannot fail to receive telepathic shock and meaning-excitement by same laws operating in his own human mind."[11]

Ginsberg echoed Kerouac in using the image of flow for poetic composition: "mental flow," "the natural flow of the mind," "the unspoken visual-verbal flow inside the mind." Not mind as rational ego-consciousness, but mind as locus and conduit of the flow from below and above consciousness. Moreover, where for Ashbery mental flow meant drift without direction or end except final dissipation, for Ginsberg and Kerouac flow had an anticipated teleological climax: "exciting or mystical moments or near mystical moments"; "[t]he unspeakable visions of the individual."[12] In "Essentials of Spontaneous Prose" Kerouac mentions Yeats's "trance writing," but he came to claim for the writer a more explicitly religious function as prophet in the root sense of that word: the writer channels the energy of God or whatever one calls the transcendent power and speaks for and with that authority. The Beats were sometimes discussed, and sometimes saw themselves, as descendants of the nineteenth-century Transcendentalists with a very different ethos and lifestyle. And indeed they were tapping into a prophetic strain in American letters that extends from Emerson and Thoreau through Whitman to Pound and Jeffers and Crane – and, among their contemporaries, to Everson and Duncan.

Looking back in a 1967 essay titled "The First Word," Kerouac cites Buddhist and Christian scripture as the justification for pursuing that prophetic mission. In the *Surangama Sutra*, the Buddha teaches: "If you are now desirous of more perfectly understanding Supreme Enlightenment, you must learn to answer questions spontaneously with no recourse to discriminative thinking." And in Mark 13:11, Jesus sends the disciples out to preach to a hostile world with this injunction: "Take no thought beforehand what ye shall speak, neither do ye premeditate: but whatever shall be given you in that hour, that speak ye: for it is not ye that speak, but the Holy Ghost." When Kerouac reiterated Mark's imperative to me in conversation, he added with emphasis: "That's what it's all about." In order to "break through the barrier of language through WORDS," the writer must push "to the edges of language where the babble of the subconscious begins, because words 'come from the Holy Ghost' first in the form of babble [glossolalia] which suddenly by its sound indicates the word truly intended ..." Hence Kerouac's injunction to "stick to what you first thought, and to the words the thought brought," and Ginsberg's mantra "first thought, best thought."[13]

Beat language aims at transcendence not to escape the materiality of words but, on the contrary, to incarnate the transcendent in the materiality of words. Ginsberg says that poetry then becomes "a physiological thing," an "expression of the whole body": "*use* your body, use your breath, use your full breath." Beat poetics is professedly incarnational, and, as we shall see, Buddhist and Christian conceptions of incarnation inform the poems themselves, give the poems at once their form and meaning. This is what Kerouac meant by "following laws of Deep Form, to conclusion" and what Ginsberg meant by taking "mental flow" as "the model for Form as Cézanne took nature."[14] Spirit-breath into body-words: the Latin "spiritus" as both "spirit" and "breath" makes the link; inspiration is, then, breathing in the inspirited body of the world, and poetic expression the inspired body's breathing out into words. Ginsberg's poems and Kerouac's prose and poems present a carnival of not just carnal but incarnational language.

The paradox at the heart of a poetics of incarnation – indeed, of the mystery of incarnation in any religious tradition – lies in the body as the locus at once of mortality and immortality, of death and transcendence, of sexuality and spirit. The paradox is in the very nature of carnival. In the liturgical calendar "carnival," which means literally "farewell to the flesh," is followed by the penitential season of Lent leading to Easter; it celebrates the flesh, paradoxically, as mortal and sinful and thus in need of inspiriting incarnation: what Buddhists call the enlightened body, what Christians call the graced body incorporated into the Mystical Body of Christ; what Blake saw as "the human form divine"; what Whitman saw as "yourself spiritual bodily," "the body lurking within thy body, / The only purport of the form thou art, the real I myself."[15]

The paradox plays out both ways in images of incorporation and sublimation: spirit descending to flesh, flesh ascending to spirit. For Buddhists, the body is the corporal site of Enlightenment revealing the reality of Mind. For Christians, the person of Jesus, God-man, subsumes and resolves the paradox. Not surprisingly, then, the language and imagery that the great celibate and ascetic mystics like John of the Cross and Theresa of Avila found to express their exalting experience of God are physical and erotic. Inversely, the un-ascetic and "liberated" Beats seek the revelation of spirit in the body, often in and through sexual experience. In a course on "Spiritual Poetics" taught in the 1970s at the Naropa Institute in Colorado (founded by Ginsberg's Buddhist mentor Chögyam Trungpa), Ginsberg claimed that poetry at the highest spiritual register "became an expression of the whole body."[16] Kerouac, asked about sex by one interviewer looking for a juicy response, said instead that sexual passion was "the gateway to paradise." For an incarnationalist, inspiration cannot be divorced from sexuality, and vice versa. Kerouac points out that the word "genius" is "derived from the Latin word *gignere* (to beget)." The genius who receives a vision and gives it "Deep Form" becomes thereby a procreative begetter: "the originating force," the "person who *originates* something never known before." Whitman had boasted that sex was the generative force behind *Leaves of Grass*, speaking of words as seminal and of poems as bodily organs. In the same spirit, for Kerouac the spontaneous method of blowing and sketching operates by the "laws of orgasm" – that is to say, "from within, out" into words and images, from the body into the body of the poem.[17]

To the literary and cultural establishment, all this Beat talk about inspiration and spontaneous form was dubious blather at best, and at worst crass self-promotion. When I, as a new assistant professor at Harvard, introduced Kerouac at a reading in Lowell House in 1964, I received only head-shaking condolences from senior colleagues. Antipathy to the Beats as self-proclaimed holy barbarians led to solemn denunciations and derisive quips like Truman Capote's wisecrack that what Kerouac did was typing, not writing. To an increasingly Postmodernist culture in postwar America, the Beats were touting the Romantic notion of organic form: as Kerouac put it, "Something that you feel will find its own form."[18] In 1956, when Ginsberg sent a typescript of *Howl* to Trilling, Ginsberg correctly anticipated Trilling's disapproval by predicting in anxious self-defense: "I think what is coming is a romantic period ... Eliot and Pound are like Dryden and Pope."[19] There was good reason for the anxiety and defensiveness. In their intense exchanges and in their public pronouncements in the mid-1950s, Ginsberg and Kerouac were challenging a waning Modernism and its academic offshoot, the New Criticism, with a Neoromantic poetics that claimed spontaneous inspiration as the genesis of the creative process and visionary ecstasy as the end of that process. Like it or not, outside the academic establishment and the literary periodicals, Ginsberg and Kerouac were voicing, however outlandishly, something vital to an American psyche afflicted, beneath complacent conformity, by fearful anxiety and spiritual longing. And, as it turned out, many did indeed like it. *Howl* (1956) is probably the most widely read poem of the second half of the twentieth century, and *On the Road* (1957) the most widely read novel; both now have secure places in the literary canon.

Nevertheless, why did the Beats see themselves as "desolation angels," as *poètes maudits*? When Ginsberg let Williams read *Howl*, he saw it as a vision of hell as well as a vision from hell. "Beat" was not always "beatific." Inspiration and spontaneous form are difficult to achieve, much less sustain, especially in lives as disordered and uprooted as theirs. The body was carnal before incarnational. Consequently, despite the commitment to "first word, best word," the best form was not necessarily the first form. Both *On the Road* and *Howl* underwent several stages of revision in variant versions, available now in Barry Miles's variorum edition of *Howl* and in the initial scroll version of *On the Road*. But the poetics of spontaneous form as the way to vision underlay and motivated every stage of the process.

Ginsberg described the evolution of *Howl* toward final form in some detail. When, lonely and miserable in San Francisco in August 1955, he sat down at the typewriter, his intention, he later said, was not to "write a *poem*, but just write what I wanted to without fear, let my imagination go, open secrecy, and scribble magic lines from my real mind – sum up my life …" What emerged was a draft of Part I of *Howl*, "typed out madly in one afternoon."[20] Kerouac responded right off that "[y]our HOWL FOR CARL SOLOMON is very powerful, but I don't want it arbitrarily negated by secondary emendations made in time's reconsidering backstep."[21] As the subsequent sections of *Howl* took shape over the following months, Ginsberg came to see the emerging poem as "a series of experiments with the formal organization of the long line." In exploring the possibilities of the long line as the structural unit, Ginsberg recognized precedents among the prophets: Isaiah and Jeremiah; William Blake, whom he had heard ("like God had a human voice") in a vision in 1945, reciting "Ah, Sunflower" and other poems until "my body suddenly felt *light*" with "cosmic consciousness, vibrations, understanding, awe, and wonder and surprise"; and, in the American Romantic tradition, Whitman, followed to some extent by Pound and Jeffers, helped him develop a "new speech-rhythm prosody to *build up* large organic structures."[22]

In *Howl*, therefore, each line functions as a kind of stanza or strophe that, though variable in length, "constitutes *one speech-breath-thought*" in the thematic development of the poem as a whole. Each section, then, anchors the swell of long lines in a refrain or "fixed base" of repeated words and phrases. Anticipating complaints of the poem's formlessness, Ginsberg sought to demonstrate at some length, in his letter to Eberhart, that though "[t]he general ground plan" evolved as "an accident," it arrived at a form that was "organic" and "quite symmetrical, surprisingly." Indeed, he insisted twice, "[t]he poem is really built like a brick shithouse."[23]

Thus Part I of *Howl* is a five-page catalog of the miseries and hysteria of his generation of "angelheaded hipsters," with the fevered clauses of each long line beginning "who" as the fixed base. Part II is, then, an exorcizing invocation of Moloch as the satanic embodiment of capitalist America spreading death and oppression and imaged in the "skullface" that Ginsberg saw from his apartment on Nob Hill in the lights of the Sir Francis Drake Hotel, and the exclamatory repetition of "Moloch" at the beginning of each line serves as the fixed base for the variations. Part III singles out Carl Solomon, whom Ginsberg had met as a fellow patient in a New York psychiatric hospital in the late 1940s and who had recently had to return there for treatment, and addresses him in a litany with the fixed base of "I'm with you in Rockland / where ..." And, out of this vision of hell, the concluding "Footnote" is a chant celebrating the sacredness of life and the holiness of the body, with the "Holy!" displacing "Moloch!" as the exclamation, reiterated fifteen times in the first line and then repeated at the beginning of the subsequent lines. In "Notes Written on Finally Recording 'Howl,'" Ginsberg overlays Blake's image of the lamb with the Lamb of Revelations and glosses the thematic structure of the sequence through that unifying image: "Part I, a lament for the Lamb in America with instances of remarkable lamblike youths; Part II names the monster of mental consciousness that preys on the Lamb; Part III a litany of affirmation of the Lamb in its glory: 'O star-spangled shock of Mercy'" in the very place of madness and incarceration; and the culminating "Footnote" whose incantation is a "variation of the form of Part II" that lifts the poem into vision.[24]

The fourth part of the poem, therefore, far from being a "Footnote," is the emotional and thematic climax, and its word "Holy!" celebrates incarnation, the integration of suffering body and soul: "beat down" and "beat up" become "beatitude." Let's examine more closely how the poem seeks to effect that metamorphosis. The "angelheaded hipsters" of Part I present a kaleidoscope of bodies battered and degraded and souls hysterical and suicidal, blindly seeking escape in a narcotic or sexual fix; the fatal opposition of body and soul is summed up near the end of Part I in the juxtaposition of "the madman bum and angel" who has had "the poem of life butchered out of their own bodies." Part II names the butcher Moloch, whose money, machinery, and munitions alienate the soul and kill the body: "Moloch who entered my soul early! Moloch in whom I am a consciousness without a body! Moloch who frightened me out of my natural ecstasy!" Moloch's dehumanization becomes individualized and personalized in Ginsberg's madhouse companion and alter ego, Carl Solomon, locked in the Rockland psychiatric ward, "where fifty more shocks will never return your soul to its body again." But Part III is the turning point of *Howl* as by the end Ginsberg imagines Solomon's suffering body and soul moving toward liberation: "imaginary walls collapse O skinny legions run outside O starry-spangled shock of mercy the eternal war is here O victory forget your underwear we're free." There had been a momentary glimpse of resurrection in Part I as "the madman bum and angel ... rose reincarnate in the ghostly clothes of jazz ..."[25] But the realization more fully intimated at the end of Part III opens, in the concluding section, into a full-throated ecstatic chant proclaiming the reincarnation of soul and body:[26]

> Holy! Holy! Holy! Holy! Holy! Holy! Holy! Holy! Holy! Holy!
>   Holy! Holy! Holy! Holy! Holy!
> The world is holy! The soul is holy! The skin is holy! The nose is holy!
>   The tongue and cock and hand and asshole holy!
> Everything is holy! everybody's holy! everywhere is holy!
>   everyday is in eternity! Everyman's an angel!

The section sustains the rapture through fifteen lines, till the staccato rhythms of the penultimate line are gathered into the single sustained closure of the final clause:

> Holy forgiveness! mercy! charity! faith! Holy! Ours! bodies!
>   suffering! magnanimity!
> Holy the supernatural extra brilliant intelligent kindness of the soul!

Perhaps Ginsberg thought of this chant as a "Footnote" because it is less a conclusion and fulfillment than a prospective invocation. The intense orality of *Howl*'s language, most emphatically in this final section, is kinetic and performative with the intention of bringing into being and realization the state that it is invoking. In the letter to Eberhart Ginsberg countered the charge of the poem's immorality and lack of social value by insisting on its performative efficacy: "I have told you how to live if I have wakened any emotion of compassion and realization of the beauty of souls in America, thru the poem."[27] The moral transformation is here couched in a conditional clause, but the response of the audience at the Six Gallery and at subsequent public readings, which became a featured platform for Beat poetry, served to confirm, for Ginsberg and his friends, the poem's potential to transform people and society. The speech act itself is the agency bringing the prophetic word to realization.

But, as Ginsberg anticipated, what many people, inside and outside the academy, heard in the Beat message was not a new morality but,

on the contrary, a shedding of moral codes as puritanical and bourgeois inhibitions, liberating the body into adolescent narcissism, narcotic highs, and sexual indulgence. For them, Ken Kesey and his Merry
Pranksters summed up the carnival riot of the Beat message. The under-
graduates who invited Kerouac to Lowell House in 1964 expected "the
King of the Beats" to perform as a clown whose antics would outrage
Harvard propriety. By that time the glare of publicity after *On the Road*,
ending in the crackup recounted in *Big Sur* (1960), had made Kerouac
paranoid about public appearances. But the immigrant son from Lowell
made an exception for the Harvard invitation from Lowell House, and
then, vulnerable and insecure, got drunk and fulfilled the students'
expectations by acting the clown, as he sadly recognized the next day
from the write-up in the Harvard *Crimson*.[28] Some of the provocative
and outrageous things the Beats did and said made it easy to dismiss
them as irresponsible adolescents, but dismissal, whether amused or
unamused, overlooked or misread the essentially religious drive behind
much of the Beat dissent from the entrenched materialism of the culture. What Ginsberg and Kerouac were desperately seeking, in breaking
free from the constraints of expected social roles, was the opening to the
path to salvation.

However, as *Howl* and *On the Road*, as well as later writings, make
painfully clear, that path led through hell, or, more accurately, through
purgatory. Early in their friendship Kerouac acknowledged the desperation they shared: "Your little letter moved me, I must say ... particularly
the line, 'I was so sick that I found myself worrying about the future of
man's soul, my own in particular.' There you elicited the true picture of
things terrestrial ... namely, disease and loss and death."[29] Loud opposition to the materialist culture at once mirrored and masked the internal
struggle to liberate the sick body from the shame and guilt of its mortality. For both Kerouac and Ginsberg redemption of the body lay in
realizing the body as incarnation; the human form divine resolves eros
and thanatos, assuages shame and absolves guilt, especially sexual guilt.

"Kaddish" (1959), Ginsberg's lament for his mother Naomi, who died
lobotomized in a mental hospital shortly after *Howl* was published, pours
out, in the narrative of his mother's life, the horror and degradation of
things terrestrial. The conflicted entanglements of their relationship are
summed up in her final words to him from the letter that she had written
him after reading *Howl* the day before her death: "Get married Allen don't
take drugs." His fevered response to his mother's dying plea for sexual and
social conformity comes immediately in a section called "Hymmnn," that

echoes the "Holy!" litany of *Howl* with a chant that envelops mother and son in divine blessings:[30]

> In the world which He has created according to his will Blessed Praised Magnified Lauded Exalted the Name of the Holy One Blessed is He!
>
> . . . .
>
> Blessed be He in homosexuality! Blessed be He in paranoia! Blessed be He in the city! Blessed be He in the Book!
>
> . . . .
>
> Blessed be you Naomi in tears! Blessed be you Naomi in fears! Blessed Blessed Blessed in sickness!

We learn how to live, Ginsberg told Eberhart, "thru the poem," and the preposition "thru" indicates the transformative and performative process of the poem. That movement is performed succinctly in "Sunflower Sutra," written shortly after *Howl* when Ginsberg was living in Berkeley. It is one of his most widely anthologized poems and, arguably, his best short poem. Ginsberg noted that the poem ("composition time 20 minutes") achieves a "rhythmic buildup power equal to 'Howl' without use of repeated base to sustain it."[31] In Buddhism "sutra," from the Sanskrit for "thread, string," designates a scriptural narrative, in this case, an incarnational revelation that comes to him and his buddy Kerouac, just back from his sojourn in Mexico. Ginsberg had become interested in Buddhism through Kerouac, who began studying Buddhist texts in 1954 and wrote excitedly to Ginsberg in May: "I typed up a 100-page account of Buddhism for you, gleaned from my notes ... 'Some of the Dharma' I called it."[32]

The sutra begins with the two old friends, "hung-over like old bums," sitting "bleak and blue and sad-eyed" on the riverbank in the Southern Pacific railroad yard, "surrounded by the gnarled steel roots of trees of machinery." The graphic imagery depicts, detail by detail, a landscape defiled by human filth and bodily excrement and further defiled by industrial waste and grime. In this landscape of death the dead sunflower ("big as a man, sitting dry on top of a pile of ancient sawdust") seems a human corpse degraded by railroad grit and grime: "that smog of cheek, that eyelid of black mis'ry, that sooty hand or phallus or protuberance of artificial worse-than-dirt – industrial ..."[33]

Identification with the sunflower ("my sunflower O my soul") awakens memories of Blake's sunflower poem. (Ginsberg often wrote and spoke of the voice and vision of Blake that had come to him in 1945 in his Harlem

apartment and had given him his first sense of "the human form divine."[34])
The language acknowledges the comic absurdity[35] of the sunflower even as
it sets the sunflower in mock-epic opposition to the locomotive through a
mounting roll of o-sounds:

> Poor dead flower? when did you forget you were a flower? when did you
> look at your skin and decide you were an impotent dirty old locomotive?
> the ghost of a locomotive? the specter and shade of a once powerful mad
> American locomotive?
> You were never no locomotive, Sunflower, you were a sunflower!
> And you Locomotive, you are a locomotive, forget me not!

The revisioned sunflower then becomes a symbol of the poet's newfound
power, at once heroic and prophetic, as he sticks it "at my side like a scep-
ter" and delivers "my sermon to my soul, and Jack's, and anyone who'll
listen." The sermon ends the sutra in an extreme instance of the long line,
gathering up the swarming details of the narrative in the apocalyptic last
word, "vision":[36]

> –We're not our skin of grime, we're not our dread bleak dusty imageless
> locomotive, we're all beautiful golden sunflowers inside, blessed by our
> own seed & golden hairy naked accomplishment-bodies growing into
> mad black formal sunflowers in the sunset, spied on by our eyes under
> the shadow of the mad locomotive riverbank sunset Frisco hilly tincan
> evening sitdown vision.

For Ginsberg, as for Blake and the Hebrew prophets, vision is not just
personal but necessarily political; for Ginsberg, as for Whitman, the poem
of the body becomes the poem of the body politic; for Ginsberg, as for
Shelley, the poet can aspire to rise to the role of legislator for mankind.
Ginsberg's early poem "America," for example, launched a Whitmanian
catalog denouncing national conservatism, materialism, militarism, and
homophobia. In the 1960s, opposition to the Vietnam War intensified
the political rhetoric of Ginsberg's poems, as it did that of a number of
his contemporaries. "Wichita Vortex Sutra" (1966) represents an extraordinary moment in American poetry because of its bold assertion of the
power of the word and the strength of the prophet's voice to overcome
entrenched cynicism and complacency and convert a nation from war to
peace, from destruction to renewal.

The narrative in this sutra, which was the centerpiece of the collection *The Fall of America*, traces a long, slow bus ride that carries the
poet through the towns and plains of Nebraska and Kansas to Wichita.
The long lines, moving raggedly down the page without fixed margins,

have lost much of the raw edge and frantic energy of the poems of the 1950s, but their wandering mimics Ginsberg's journey to the heart of the American heartland. Pound had used the word "vortex" to describe cities, like London and Paris before and after the Great War, that were creative centers emanating cultural and artistic energy, but here Ginsberg sees Wichita as the vortex of Cold War America. Glimpses of landscape alternate in the poet's consciousness with road signs, advertising slogans, newspaper headlines, radio talk from politicians like Johnson and McNamara touting the success of American aggression. The fixed base punctuating the poet's progress toward Wichita is the refrain "language, language." As the poet hears the war- talk ("language abused / for Advertisement / language used / like magic for power on the planet"), he recalls the witness of his prophetic forebears – Whitman excoriating Gilded Age corruption in "Democratic Vistas," Pound inscribing the Chinese character for "man standing by his word" – as he sets himself to the task of reclaiming the language and thereby the nation. Against all that "Black Magic language" he will assert the authority of the prophet's word.[37]

That assertion is in the end strengthened rather than undercut by the poem's ironic recognition of the disparity between the poet's marginalization in American culture and the authority he is claiming. Emerson's notion of the poet as representative man had been tested with increasing bitterness by Whitman and Pound. Early in the poem/journey Ginsberg claims "I am the Universe tonite / riding in all my Power," grandly dispensing absolution ("Thy sins are forgiven, Wichita!") and inviting the lovers of Nebraska and Kansas to hear and heed him ("[c]ome, ... sing and dance with me"). But the singer's ironic unease is there in the parodic, almost comic phrasing, especially since the "national" poem is curiously unpeopled; besides the politicians' recorded cant, the only voice on this bus ride (unlike Bishop's bus ride in "The Moose") is this latterday Whitman's voice: "the lone One singing to myself / God come true"; "a lone man talking to myself, ... imagining the throng of Selves / that make this nation one body of Prophecy"; "my lone presence into this Vortex named Kansas." Nevertheless, like Jonah headed to Nineveh, the poet heads "into the heart of the Vortex," "[o]n to Wichita to prophesy!" Summoning to his purpose all the Buddhist holy men, he adds the "Sacred Heart, my Christ acceptable / Allah the Compassionate One / Jaweh Righteous One" to the litany, and sets about making his imagination come true in and through his words. At the crucial moment the ironic hedging falls away and yields to full-throated prophecy:

> I call all Powers of imagination
> to my side in this auto to make Prophecy,
>
> . . . .
>
> I lift my voice aloud,
> make Mantra of American language now,
> I here declare the end of the War!
> Ancient days' Illusion! –
> and pronounce words beginning my own millennium.

Let the Congress and the president react as they will, "this Act [was] done by my own voice, nameless Mystery ... accomplished in my own imagination."[38]

The poet knows that the war goes on ("the suffering not yet ended"), but his poem projects the war's end because "in my own imagination" prophecy has initiated the language of national renewal ("all realms within my consciousness fulfilled"):

> The War is gone,
> Language emerging on the motel news stand,
> the right magic
> Formula, the language known
> in the back of the mind before, now in black print
> daily consciousness

Are these words only an empty hope, or even a phony bluff? The conclusion of the poem has had its doubting critics, who have found it a bathetic demonstration of the failure of the prophet's voice. Others, however, have read it more sympathetically as a brave assertion of the poet's passionate intent to change America. Ginsberg, in the magnificent moment of the mantra, had the Whitmanian resilience to rise to the gravity of the historical situation and imagine a rebirth of the body politic ("waiting for Man to be born / O man in America!"). Moreover, the power of that moment ("The war is over now – ") sinews him to turn, in the last lines, from aggression abroad to address the nation's most pressing domestic problem: racial prejudice and segregation.[39]

Ginsberg remained a prolific poet, but most of his best work was done by the time of Kerouac's death in 1969. Political and visionary to the end, he became, like Whitman, a revered public figure by the time of his own death in 1997. These years of cultural assimilation coincided with a change in the poetry through his deepening commitment to Buddhism. The poems became less conflicted, less incarnational, more transcendental, more placid and serene, looser and more notational in style, as the tension between body and spirit, material existence and selfhood dissolved in the awakening of Mind: "all realms within my consciousness fulfilled." By 1976 he could attribute the transition in his poetry to the development in his understanding of Buddhist enlightenment:[40]

> At the time [of *Howl*] I believed in some sort of God and thus Angels, and religiousness – at present as Buddhist I see an awakening emptiness (*Sunyata*) as the crucial term. No God, no self, not even great Whitman's universal Self, it's still Self, as God would be. The defect in these [early] poems … is the insistence on a divine self rather than a relatively heavenly emptiness. But it was implicit that mindfulness insight and perfection of Self would lead to no-Self …

In the 1950s, Kerouac had introduced Ginsberg to Buddhist spirituality, and in Kerouac's memory Ginsberg and Anne Waldman founded the Jack Kerouac School of Disembodied Poetics at the Buddhist Naropa Institute in Colorado. But Kerouac never could move with Ginsberg to a disembodied poetics; his remained a painfully embodied poetics. Kerouac's compilation of notes and meditations on Buddhism, *Some of the Dharma*, which he had first mentioned to Ginsberg in 1955, was finally published in the year of Ginsberg's death. As early as the 1960s, however, Kerouac was already retreating from Buddhism to the French-Canadian Catholicism of his boyhood; in 1964, Kerouac told me that *Some of the Dharma* was written to reconcile Buddhism with Catholicism. His reversion to Catholicism indicated, among other things, that the issue of the body and incarnation was for him unresolved and inescapable, and that issue remained the underlying concern of his fiction and poetry.

Kerouac is, of course, better known for his fiction than for his poetry, and much of his best poetry occurs in the lyrical and meditative sketching that is a distinctive aspect of the novels. *Mexico City Blues* (1959) is the only volume of poems that appeared in his lifetime, but he wrote poems all through his literary life, many published posthumously and now brought together in a Library of America *Collected Poems*. In *Scratching the Beat Surface* Michael McClure calls *Mexico City Blues* Kerouac's "masterpiece,"[41] and James T. Jones' *A Map of Mexico City Blues: Jack Kerouac as Poet* (1992) ranks it above *On the Road* and demonstrates its centrality to all of Kerouac's work. Kerouac was working on *Mexico City Blues* when Ginsberg sent him the first part of *Howl* in August, 1955: "Myself I have knocked off 150 bloody poetic masterpieces [of an eventual 242 choruses] in MEXICO CITY BLUES, each one of uniform length and wailing."[42] The length of each blues poem was not to exceed a page in one of the notebooks that Kerouac always carried in a pocket, but each poem found its improvised shape and form. Jones claims that *"Mexico City Blues* provides a subtext for 'Howl,' and vice versa," and without question the two books together, in their affinities and differences, invented Beat poetry. Acknowledging his inspiration in jazz, blues, and bebop, Kerouac said in the opening Note to *Mexico City Blues*: "I want to be considered a jazz poet blowing a long blues in an afternoon jam session on Sunday ... my ideas vary and sometimes roll from chorus to chorus or from halfway through a chorus to halfway into the next."[43]

McClure described Kerouac's experiments in verbal jazz, often written when he was high on narcotics, as "a religious poem startling in its majesty and comedy and gentleness and vision," and Jones said that the improvisations allowed Kerouac to explore "personal conflicts" with "acute introspection" and "serious theological speculation."[44] The central conflict is rooted in his haunted conviction that the body, especially the sexual body, desperately needs to be saved from its carnality. Eros is the sign and seal of thanatos. Would-be beatniks who want to take Kerouac as simply celebrating sexual expression and dionysian liberation blind themselves to what his words actually say. Every brief moment of dionysian liberation – sex, drink, drugs, the comradeship of soulmates – ends in disappointment, remorse, isolation, depression. The tragic sense of loss and abandonment is summed up in the famous prose poem of the last paragraph-long sentence of *On the Road*. After all the boyish romps and adventures, the frantic action stops; the road reaches dead end. Kerouac's alter ego stands sad at the roadside, deserted by Dean Moriarty, the Neal Cassady alter ego, alone in America with sunset receding into night's blackout. Looking back down the road and across the broad land, he sings the blues for all things terrestrial:[45]

> So in America when the sun goes down and I sit on the old broken-down river pier watching the long, long skies over New Jersey and sense all that raw land that rolls in one unbelievable huge bulge over to the West Coast, and all that road going, all the people dreaming in the immensity of it, and in Iowa I know by now the children must be crying in the land where they let children cry, and tonight the stars'll be out, and don't you know that God is Pooh Bear? the evening star must be drooping and shedding her sparkler dims on the prairie, which is just before the coming of complete night that blesses the earth, darkens all rivers, cups the peaks and folds the final shore in, and nobody, nobody knows what's going to happen to anybody besides the forlorn rags of growing old, I think of Dean Moriarty, I even think of Old Dean Moriarty the father we never found, I think of Dean Moriarty.

In all its ups and downs, *On the Road* is, at its deepest level, a Whitmanian elegy. Even if Ginsberg did not have this paragraph in mind when he wrote "Sunflower Sutra," that poem presents a very different story from Ginsberg's two companions on the riverbank sharing a glorious revelation of their "golden hairy naked accomplishment-bodies growing into mad black formal sunflowers in the sunset." Kerouac described his blues-poems as "wailing," and it is no exaggeration to say that all he wrote is a long lament for living. I knew Kerouac a little in his later years, and he seemed to me someone almost skinless and without defenses, eager for yet suffering from ordinary human contact: as he put it in the 88th Chorus of *Mexico City Blues,* "afraid of myself simply, / And afraid a everyone else." In a letter dated October 26, 1954, to the poet and journalist Robert Lax, a fellow Catholic and a friend of the Trappist poet Thomas Merton, Kerouac made this naked confession: "I'm no saint, I'm sensual, I can't resist wine," and, like "all sentient beings," need to "find enlightenment and holy escape from the sin and stain of life-body itself" in order to attain "purity of solitude, quiescence & concentration of mind in prayer & compassion – THE WHOLE WORLD A MONASTERY, ASCETICISM, CHASTITY." In a footnote to this letter Ann Charters records an entry from a 1954 notebook in which Kerouac lays out a "Modified Ascetic Life" in "stages by which he hoped to reach Nirvana by the year 2000."[46] Kerouac declined Lax's offer to arrange a residence for him in a Trappist monastery as a guest, but in his mind and soul the monkish ideal stood in judgment of the sensual man. The lapses into drunkenness and sensuality, which he would describe in his novels, sometimes with rapturous lyricism, only served in the end to deepen his sense of "the sin and stain of life-body itself."

So let's listen to his *Mexico City Blues.* As in jazz, there is a lot of improvisational playfulness – puns and allusions and the nonsense sounds of scatting. The 213th Chorus begins:[47]

> Poem dedicated to Allen Ginsberg
> – prap – rot – rort –
> mort – port – lort – snort
> – pell mell – rhine wine –
> roll royce – ring ming –
> mock my lot – roll my doll –
> pull my hairline – smell my kell –
> wail my siren – pile my ane –
> loose my shoetongue – sing my aim –
> loll my wildmoll – roll my
>   luck –

Scatting is not nonsense; Kerouac said that inspiration sometimes begins in the "babble" of glossolalia that first emerges from the unconscious and leads to "the word truly intended."[48] They are "words to make flit / in the fun-of make-it" (227th Chorus, p. 161). So, through the wild and deceptively childish word play, the blues choruses sing pain and suffering – sexual, psychological, spiritual – in search of release, even transcendence (114th Chorus, p. 84 and Chorus 195, p. 137):

> Wailing sweet bop ...
> And every note plaintive,
> Every note Call for Loss
>   of our Love and Mastery –
>   just so, eternalized –
>
> ....
>
> And rip me a blues,
> Son, blow me a bop,
> Let me hear 'bout heaven
> In Brass Flugelmop

Many of the choruses redact Buddhist teaching on suffering and transcendence.[49] The 227th Chorus begins flatly and bluntly (p. 161):

> Merde and misery.
> I'm completely in pain
> Waiting without mercy
> For the worst to happen.
> I'm completely at a loss.
>   There is no hope ...

And hopelessness leads to the negation of material human existence:

> no shoes no eyes
> no shoetongues, lungs,
> no happiness, no art,
> nothing to do, nothin to part,
> no hairs to split,
> sidewalks to spit ...

Suffering mortality seeks resolution in the Buddhist precept that the material world is an illusion of the analyzing human intellect. The world of experience is "the verdant / Fantasm of conception," mental and sexual conception (216th Chorus, p. 152), "the movie in your mind" (67th Chorus, p. 52).

Enlightenment is the awakening to the essential emptiness of all things ("Essence is like absence of reality," 105th Chorus, p. 76), so that "Nothing-ness" is the real "SUCH-NESS" (66th Chorus, p. 51); "Eternity

/ Is the other side / Of the other part / Of your mind" (156th Chorus, p. 111). Suffering elicits compassion, but Buddhist compassion is "Love not of Loved Object / Cause no object exists," but "Love of Objectlessness, / When nothing exists / Save yourself and your not-self..." (157th Chorus, p. 122). In the pun on "Save," salvation lies in realizing that nothing exists except yourself, and that the self is a not-self.

This is the point that we heard Ginsberg say that he had reached in Buddhist enlightenment. For Kerouac too, in chorus after chorus Buddhism offers escape from the suffering of the sexual body. The 212th Chorus begins, "All of this meat is in dreadful pain /... And pricking goads invest the flesh," and poses the question "Why was I born with a body, / ... as if, to wish / For flesh was sin alone itself – ?" (p. 148). Kerouac invoked Buddhist nothingness in an ongoing argument with Cassady and his wife Carolyn about their belief in reincarnation. The 113th Chorus sums up the course of mortal life:

> Got up and dressed up
> and went out & got laid
> Then died and got buried
> in a coffin in the grave,

and then redeems it: "Man – / Yet everything is perfect, / Because it is empty / ... Because it's not even happening" (p. 83). Kerouac inscribed on the flyleaf of my copy of *The Scripture of the Golden Eternity* (1960) "Nothing Ever Happened."

At the same time, both as a poet and as a Catholic, Kerouac could never find in Buddhism the resolution that it brought to Ginsberg and Snyder. The very materiality of language seemed to challenge and contradict the nothingness of things (206th Chorus, p. 144):

> Because you cant sing
> open yr mouth with poems
> without you make sound
> and sound is wrong
> sound is noise

Since we have "only human speech," we have to presume that "[t]he essence is realizable in words." However, if those words "fade as they approach" into the essential "emptiness and silence," then the truly Buddhist poem, "white pure / spotless," would have to be a "no-poem nonpoem" (206th Chorus, p. 144; 123rd Chorus, p. 90; 202nd Chorus, p. 141). But the white and pure nonpoem can only express itself in a series of images of a sensory and material world (pp. 141–42):

                silverdawn clear
                silent of birds
                pool-burble-bark
                        clear
                    the lark of trees
                    the needle pines
                        the rock the pool
                        the sandy shore

   As a poet, then, Kerouac felt caught in the contradiction of needing
sound and metaphor to talk about the perfection of emptiness. The most
satisfying metaphor for that paradox in *Mexico City Blues* is milk: "empty
milk / Of God-Kindness" (209th Chorus, pp. 146–47); "Pleased Milk / of
Humankindness" (193rd Chorus, p. 136). Life's restless quest is to find the
spiritual mother's milk within one's self (225th Chorus, p. 159):

                I keep restless mental searching
                And geographical meandering
                To find the Holy Inside Milk
                Damena gave to all.

                Damena, Mother of Buddhas,
                Mother of Milk

A poem that Kerouac recited again and again at public readings begins:

                Praised be man, he is existing in milk
                    and living in lillies –
                And his violin music takes place in milk
                    and creamy emptiness –

and concludes: "Praised be my fellow man / For dwelling in milk" (228th
Chorus, p. 162). But the praise expresses itself not in emptiness and silence
but in the serene, sustained music of its litany of images.
   However fervently Kerouac tried to be a Buddhist, he could never, even
in *Mexico City Blues*, leave behind the incarnational character of language
and of the Catholicism of his childhood and boyhood. The spiritual milk
he most longed for was not Damena's but his French-Canadian mother's. In 1956, at the height of his Buddhist engagement, he wrote his most
Catholic novel, *Visions of Gerard*, an exquisitely touching fictional account
of the early death of his ailing older brother Gerard, whose short life was
held in sacred memory by the family and the young 'Ti jean. In the tradition of saint's lives, Gerard is presented as a child saint, the idealization of
the innocence that 'Ti jean long lost, and Gerard's funeral Mass ends the

book with a spiraling and soaring alternation of the prayers of the Latin liturgy with Buddhist meditations. A group of choruses at the heart of *Mexico City Blues* recalls his Lowell childhood with Gerard and his parents ("My father loves me, / my mother too, / I am all safe," 98th Chorus, p. 71), and the 187th Chorus extends "the milky fliss" to cover "Gerard, Pa, ... Heaven, you, me" (p. 132).

As Jones observes, Kerouac's "Buddhism seemed always to have a theistic undertone."[50] A number of choruses acknowledge his unease with Buddhist dismissal of the reality of material existence: "Heaven's inside you, but there's no you" (203rd Chorus, p. 142); "Nirvana aint inside me / cause there aint no me" (198th Chorus, p. 139). The 190th Chorus sums up the problem for him; it begins "[w]hat I have attained in Buddhism / is nothing," and ends "[n]o matter how you cut it / it's empty delightful baloney" (pp. 133–4). Increasingly in the 1960s, after *Mexico City Blues* and *The Dharma Bums* and *Scripture of the Golden Eternity*, Kerouac resisted identification as a Buddhist and insisted in interviews and essays on his abiding Catholicism.

Kerouac could never escape the body as the matrix and crux of his anxiety and vision. For a Catholic the agon of sin and redemption transpires in the body and turns on the Incarnation: God embodied to suffer human sinfulness to his death but to rise again as enduring proof of human salvation not out of the body, as in Buddhism, but, on the contrary, in the redeemed and glorified body. At the heart of Catholicism is the mystery of the Cross hung with the suffering body of the Redeemer, and his fictionalized account of his Lowell boyhood in *Doctor Sax* (1959) is overshadowed by the recollection of the gigantic crucifix atop a local shrine. But, from his mother and from the nuns who taught him, Kerouac also learned the Catholic devotion to the Sacred Heart of Jesus as solace and healing for suffering. Ed Adler's book on Kerouac as a visual artist[51] reproduces not just paintings but the sketches and drawings with which he filled notebooks and letters: most of them religious, often of crucifixions and pietás, sometimes with a bleeding heart but also with an Easter sun rising in the background.

Big Sur (1962) is a terrifying account of the low point in Kerouac's life. In 1960, he retreated to Lawrence Ferlinghetti's cabin in Bixby's Canyon on the Big Sur coast, seeking a solitary retreat to recover, physically and spiritually, from the ordeal of publicity and mayhem that followed the spectacular success of *On the Road*. Soon, however, Kerouac brings down from San Francisco a group of partying friends, and the sordid binge of sex, alcohol, and dope that ensues ends in a breakdown that threatens to engulf him, dissolute body and guilt-wracked soul, in a final madness. The climax comes in a vision of an apocalyptic battle between Satan and Jesus. The rush of the prose is strung out on series of images (I see ... I see ... I see) breathlessly punctuated by dashes and commas and exclamation points:[52]

> An argot of sudden screamed reports rattles through my head in a language I never heard but understand immediately – For a moment I see blue Heaven and the Virgin's white veil but suddenly a great evil blur like an ink spot spreads over it, "The devil! – the devil's come after me tonight! tonight is the night! that's what!" ... Suddenly as clear as anything I ever saw in my life, I see the Cross.
>
> ....
>
> I see the Cross, it's silent, it stays a long time, my heart goes out to it, my whole body fades away to it, I hold out my arms to be taken away to it, by God I am being taken away my body starts dying and swooning out to the Cross standing in a luminous area of the darkness ... "I'm with you, Jesus, for always, thank you" –

The morning after the vision of the Cross he pulls himself together sufficiently to "go back home across autumn America," where "[m]y mother'll be waiting for me glad." The last words are: "Something good will come out of all things yet – And it will be golden and eternal just like that – There's no need to say another word."[53] The road trips that had begun more than twenty years ago with Cassady had come to an end.

The extreme dualism of Kerouac's religious sensibility stems from the Jansenist reading of nature and grace that informed French-Canadian Catholic culture. Jansenism, based on the theological writings of Cornelius Jansen, was a seventeenth-century reform movement within the Church. Like Calvinism, it emphasized the utter depravity of fallen human beings, strict moral regulation and ascetic detachment from a sinful world, and salvation not by human merit but by God's election. From the early days of Christianity on, various gnostic dualisms postulated a seemingly unbridgeable dichotomy between spirit and matter, good and evil, and the influence of such dualisms on Christian thinking has worked against the full realization of the Incarnation. Although Jansenism was quickly condemned as heretical and Calvinist, it remained and remains an influence – particularly in France, Holland, and Ireland, and in their subcultures in the New World – not at the theological level but at the psychological and affective level of religious temperaments and popular devotions.

For that reason Kerouac's aspirations toward Nirvana, heaven, the golden eternity arose from a manichean and Jansenist distrust of, even disgust with the body as sexual and so sinful and so suffering. He wanted to call his collected poems *The Book of Blues*, and bodily existence itself is the lament of Kerouac's blues: "All of this meat is in dreadful pain": "Why was I born with a body … as if to wish, / For flesh was sin alone itself" (212th Chorus, p. 148). The very conception of life is the human tragedy and the original and self-perpetuating sin: "A Baby in Pain: / tell the proud seminal mother / how many more of that she wants / to satisfy her fertile ego" (216-B Chorus, p. 152); "Flap the wack I smack the hydrant / of desire, sip sop the twill – " (218th Chorus, p. 154). The 211th Chorus sums up Kerouac's Jansenism. The jazzy syncopation of the language only intensifies the horror of the vision (p. 148):

> The wheel of the quivering meat conception
> Turns in the void expelling human beings,
> Pigs, turtles, frogs, insects, nits,
> Mice, lice, lizards, rats, roan
> Racinghorses, poxy bucolic pigtics,
> Horrible unnameable lice of vultures …
>
> . . . .
>
> All the endless conception of living
> > beings
> Gnashing everywhere in Consciousness
> Throughout the ten directions of space

The lines of the Chorus shrink to a desperate longing for release and transcendence:

> *Poor!* I wish I was free
> of that slaving meat wheel
> and safe in heaven dead.

"Safe in heaven dead": for a Jansenist like Kerouac, heaven means not salvation in the redeemed body but liberation from the living death of the body.

Kerouac's vocation came early: "Always considered writing my duty on earth." And it was explicitly prophetic: to make himself the genius who might find the words and images for "the unspeakable visions of the individual." His writings do record moments of exaltation and transcendence, often but not always with the aid of drink or drugs, and often while making music or language. But those visionary moments came to him, with piercing but passing clarity, while singing the life-long blues. In the "Author's Introduction" to *Lonesome Traveler* (1960) Kerouac goes on to review his family background, his boyhood in Lowell, his young manhood on the road, his writings up to that point, and sums himself up as a "strong solitary crazy Catholic mystic." His projected hopes for a peaceful conclusion ("hermitage in the woods, quiet writing of old age, mellow hopes of Paradise ..."[54]) were sadly cut off by his early death from the effects of alcoholism.

II

Two widely noted journal articles brought William Everson to national attention as Brother Antoninus, his monastic name during the almost twenty years he spent as a Dominican lay brother. In 1957, Kenneth Rexroth had contributed a "San Francisco Letter" to the second issue of *The Evergreen Review*, discussing Antoninus first before going on to Philip Lamantia, Robert Duncan, Allen Ginsberg, and Lawrence Ferlinghetti. And the May 25, 1959 issue of *Time* reached a much wider audience with a piece on the "Beat Friar," linking Antoninus with the current excitement about the Beats. Everson/Antoninus welcomed the Beat connection because it placed his poetry in what he called the American dionysian tradition that he traced back from Jeffers through Whitman to Emerson.[55] But in fact he did not know Ginsberg and Kerouac, and his closer, more immediate ties were to the poets of the San Francisco Renaissance, particularly to Rexroth and Duncan. In *The Evergreen Review* Rexroth said that he was "probably the most profoundly moving and durable of the poets of the San Francisco Renaissance."[56] In the gallery of photographs that accompanied Rexroth's article, Antoninus wears his Dominican habit and stands beside the Washington handpress that would establish him as a distinguished designer and printer of books and broadsides.

By midlife Everson had come to think of the corpus of his poems as constituting, like Whitman's *Leaves of Grass*, a single, organic, cumulative poem-in-process coextensive with his life. He envisioned a three-volume collected poems under the title *The Crooked Lines of God*, which Black Sparrow realized posthumously in an edition edited by Allan Campo, David Carpenter, Judith Shears, and Bill Hotchkiss.[57] He intended the triadic design to reflect the classic movement from thesis through antithesis to synthesis, with the phases of his life and work hinged on three major, even convulsive turning points or conversions: in 1934 his commitment, through reading Robinson Jeffers, to pantheism and poetry; in 1949 his conversion to Roman Catholicism, followed in 1951 by his entry into the Dominican order as a lay brother; in 1969 his leaving the order to spend his last two decades in a coastal canyon north of Santa Cruz.

From childhood on, Everson was a quiet, introverted person, a man of few words and none of them idle, as he sought words and rhythms and images for the intensities and convulsions of his inner life. In the 1930s Everson grounded his Jeffersian confirmation as a pantheist poet in the cultivation of a vineyard in the San Joaquin Valley and in marriage to his high school sweetheart, Edwa Poulson. Their separation during the years of World War II, while he did alternate service in Oregon as a conscientious objector, undermined the marriage and brought that period of his life to a sad and indeterminate close. Drawn to the San Francisco area by his correspondence with Rexroth and Duncan, he joined the group that convened regular at Rexroth's apartment. There he met and in 1948 married the artist-poet Mary Fabilli. Mary, a lapsed and previously married Catholic, was in the process of returning to the Church, and she became, in Everson's account, spiritual guide and mediatrix of grace in the process of his own conversion. Out of love for her, Everson began attending Mass with her and reading theology, church history, and the lives of the saints, and he was particularly moved by Augustine's *Confessions*. After an overwhelming and ecstatic experience at midnight Mass, Christmas 1948, recounted in his spiritual autobiography, *Prodigious Thrust*, he undertook instruction for baptism. Both he and Mary were agonized by the knowledge that because her previous sacramental marriage in the Church invalidated their civil marriage, they would have to part. He was baptized in July 1949 (taking Augustine as his baptismal name), and, after spending some months living and working in the Catholic Worker house in Oakland, he entered the Dominicans at St. Albert's Priory in Oakland in the spring of 1951 as Brother Antoninus. The poems tracking this second conversion were published in *The Crooked Lines of God* (1959) and *The Hazards of Holiness* (1962).

In 1959, Antoninus met Rose Tannlund, and their relationship, while not sexual, quickly became both deeply erotic and intensely spiritual. In the book-length sequence *The Rose of Solitude* (1967), Rose is for Antoninus, as Mary had been for Everson, the apotheosis of the feminine and the agent of God's grace. With Rose's blessing and encouragement, Antoninus took his monastic vows in 1964. Not long after that, however, he met Susanna Rickson, thirty-five years his junior, when she came to him for counseling, and in December 1969 he left the order to marry her and take up life with her and her son, Jude, first at Stinson

Beach and then in a small cabin located in the canyon he called Kingfisher Flat. As *Man-Fate* (1974) and *The Masks of Drought* (1980) demonstrate, Antoninus had left the monastery, but Everson had not left his Catholic faith. His return to nature constituted, in his mind, an extension of his effort to integrate body and spirit, self and nature. Lee Bartlett caught the symbiosis between Everson and Antoninus in the title of his biography, *William Everson: The Life of Brother Antoninus.*[58]

This summary accelerates the drama of a life lived, through all these transformations, under the sign of woman. In the mid-1950s, through the Jungian Dominican Victor White, author of *God and the Unconscious,*[59] Antoninus found in Jung's archetypal psychology the schema for comprehending and articulating what he knew instinctually and emotionally: that his masculine drive and need sought resolution and transcendence through the mediation of what Jung called the anima. The anima, imaged in dreams and the imagination as a woman, represents to a man the feminine aspect of himself, the latent capacities within himself, waiting to be engaged, that the culture has figured as feminine. In the Jungian schema, therefore, the anima is for the man the source and agent of both eros and agape, physical and spiritual love. Thus "marriage" with the anima is the goal and fulfillment of the process of individuation; Jung called it the *hieros gamos*, the sacred or mystical marriage that completes the individuated man's self.

Everson/Antoninus found Jung at a crucial and clarifying point, as he was assimilating the early dionysian influence of Jeffers and D. H. Lawrence into the theological and spiritual tradition that informed his new life as a Christian and now as a monk. The result was a distinctive and powerful poetics worked out roughly in the same years in which Ginsberg and Kerouac were working out theirs. If theirs was a poetics of incarnation, his became a poetics of Incarnation, and the central concern of his life and work is what he came to call erotic mysticism. In 1960, William Lynch published a study of the Christian imagination called *Christ and Apollo*, but Antoninus had already entered unexplored territory by articulating and putting to the test of practice a theory of imagination that might be captioned Christ and Dionysus.

What sustained that Christian/dionysian poetics was a sense of the capacity of language to transcend and reach beyond itself. In Everson's formulation there are two kinds of poet: "Basically, one kind of poet or artist creates a world of his own making, while another stands witness to a world beyond the world of his making." In the first instance language made meaning through the craft of the artist in the construction of the artwork, a meaning that did not otherwise or previously exist in that form; in the second instance the making of the poem was necessary for language to express a meaning extrinsic to the poem. In the first instance meaning is centripetal, inherent in and coexistent with the patterning of words; in the second it is centrifugal, with words pointing out to the pattern of external reality. The apollonian formalist stance Everson associated with Modernists and with the academic New Critics, and would have associated it with the Postmodernists who emerged toward the end of his career. He saw himself as the other kind of poet, whom he called "the vatic or prophetic poet," and he associated vatic poetry with the American Romantic tradition from Emerson and Whitman through Crane and Jeffers (and, by adoption, Lawrence) to the Beats. It was the impulse to stand "witness to a world beyond the world of his making" that unites the Dionysian and the Christian.[60]

Chancing upon Jeffers's poems in the library of Fresno State College (now University) in 1934 was the *coup de foudre* that set the course of Everson's life as a prophetic poet and as a pantheist. His first thin pamphlet of poems, *These Are the Ravens* (1935), identifies Jeffers as his source. In "Tor House," dated July 31, 1935, Everson turns from the stone house that Jeffers built in Carmel and commits himself, in Jeffersian rhythms and imagery, to a pantheist poetry rooted in his own landscape in the San Joaquin Valley:[61]

> Now that I have seen Tor House
> And crouched among the sea-gnawed granite under the wind's throat,
> Gazing against the roll of the western rim,
> I know that I can turn back to my inland town
> And find the flame of this blunt headland
> Burning beneath the dark beat of my blood.

Jeffers was not a Transcendentalist like Emerson, for whom "Nature is symbol of Spirit," but a true pantheist for whom the material universe is "God," and the life of God was the procreative energies that sustained the "eternity" of biological and chemical processes in nature's ongoing round. Jeffers's pantheism led him to feel that the human connection with the divinity of natural process was established not in abstracting mind but in body, not through intellect but through eros. The development of human consciousness, he said again and again, is an evolutionary aberration that pits self-involved, alienated humans against nature and one another in the violent record that is human history. Jeffers's strong Calvinist bent led him to see ego-consciousness as the original sin, the violation of and fall from nature, and in his darkest moments he looked forward to the extinction of humanity in order to leave the divinity of natural processes whole again. Jeffers's double vision played out in the contrast between the meditative lyrics that evoke the brute, pantheist life-force of his California coastland and the narratives and plays that dramatize the tragic lives of the coastal people, whose self-centered will and ego-consciousness desecrate nature and destroy one another in murderous sexual violence.

The San Joaquin landscapes of Everson's early poems throb with the pantheist life-force.[62] But from the outset Everson was uneasy with Jeffers's Inhumanism (as Jeffers came to call his philosophy), and his discovery of D. H. Lawrence soon after finding Jeffers allowed him to circumvent Jeffers's Inhumanism by humanizing and personalizing pantheism. For Everson, as for Lawrence, participation in natural process through the intuitive affinities of eros was the crux of the drama of individual consciousness and identity. In Everson's words, "I became a Dionysian through Jeffers, but it was Lawrence who enabled me to make it whole within myself – subjectivize the Jeffersian cosmos as the pattern of my soul."[63] By the time of Everson's second collection, *San Joaquin* (1939), he was adapting Jeffers's pantheism and Lawrence's sexual mysticism into long Whitmanian free-verse lines whose diction and rhythms are Everson's own.

In "August," for example, nature's divine energy is symbolized in the sun that radiates the landscape and ravishes the body and consciousness of the speaker:[64]

> Smoke-color; haze thinly over the hills, low hanging;
> But the sky steel, the sky shiny as steel, and the sun shouting.
> The vineyard: in August the green-deep and heat-loving vines
> Without motion grow heavy with grapes.
> And he in the shining, on the turned earth, loose-lying,
> The muscles clean and the limbs golden, turns to the sun the lips
>   and the eyes;
> As the virgin yields, impersonally passionate,
> From the bone core and the aching flesh, the offering.
>
> He has found the power and come to the glory.
> He has turned clean-hearted to the last God, the symbolic sun.
> With earth on his hands, bearing shoulder and arm the light's touch,
>   he has come.
> And having seen, the mind loosens, the nerve lengthens,
> All the haunting abstractions slip free and are gone;
> And the peace is enormous.

The climax comes at the end of the octave of this unrhymed sonnet, as the man, recumbent on the open earth, yields to the power of the pantheistic sun. The man-virgin "comes" in the insemination of sunlight, and the elision at the turn of the line from "has come" to "having seen" converts orgasm into visionary transcendence.

Everson's lines are more carefully worked than Whitman's or Jeffers' or, among his contemporaries, Ginsberg's: more heavily stressed, more percussively rhythmic, more loaded with sound effects. In the first lines, for example, the chords of double stresses ("smóke cólor"; "háze thínly"; "lów hánging"; "sky" "steel"; "sky shíning"; "sún shoúting," "greén deép") are propelled forward by the tripping of unstressed syllables, many in anapests and dactyls. At the same time, the movement of the lines is thickened and measured by the play and counterplay of consonants and vowels. The strong alliteration is reminiscent of Anglo-Saxon verse and, closer still, of the verse of Everson's Scandinavian and Germanic forebears: "haze," "hills," "hanging," "heat," "heavy"; "smoke," "sky steel," "sky shiny," "sun shouting"; "green," "grow," "grapes"; "vineyard," "loving," "vines," "heavy." Simultaneously assonance creates a continuo beneath and through the marching consonants: "smoke," "over," "low," "motion," "grow"; "thinly," "hills"; "steel" (twice), "green-deep," "heat"; "shouting," "without." Words are repeated, sometimes with variations: "heat," "heart"; "loose," "loosens." The same vowel alternates long and short: "shiny," "vineyard," "in," "vines." The early lines are verbless images suspended on present participles until the decisive verbs: "turns," "yields." In the sestet of the sonnet, the revelation of "the power" and "the glory" is accomplished in the elision of present perfect verbs to the present tense, sealed by the sibilants of the short, declarative line: "And the peace is enormous." Ginsberg advocated "First thought, best thought," but Everson characteristically achieved the complex texture of his heavily textured rhetoric by refining draft after draft. (He attributed his perfectionism and craftsmanship to his astrological sign, Virgo.) "August," though unmetered and unrhymed, has the fourteen lines of a sonnet and the structure of a Petrarchan sonnet with a volta or turn from octave to sestet. In the genesis of his poems, Everson rightly called himself a dionysian; but in the slow gestation and making of his poems, his work habits were painstakingly apollonian, just as they were in designing and printing books and broadsheets on his handpress.

The San Francisco poets he was closest to were Rexroth and Duncan. They had initiated correspondence with him in the C. O. camp, and those ties drew him to San Francisco after the war. Like Jeffers and Lawrence, however, Everson followed his own path. Although Rexroth secured the publication of his commercially produced book, *The Residual Years* (1948), he had no significant effect on Everson's poetic focus or style. Everson often attended the literary and political sessions in Rexroth's apartment but observed from the periphery. What drew Everson to Duncan was what he felt was the dionysian impulse in Duncan's poetry of the 1940s, but when Duncan urged him to read Pound to counter the influence of Jeffers, Everson resisted Duncan's Modernist adhesions and his close association with the Black Mountain poets Charles Olson, Denise Levertov, and Robert Creeley. Indeed, by the time the Beats and the Black Mountain poets emerged in the 1950s as parallel and rival movements in opposition to the academic formalism of the New Criticism, Everson had become Antoninus and was isolated from the literary scene in the monastic life of St. Albert's.

Jeffers and Lawrence were not theists, and the turmoil in Everson's psyche and personality that sought a personal God ended in his conversion. As a Christian poet he was drawn to Gerard Manley Hopkins's powerful imagery and language and his experiments in sprung rhythm, but Hopkins's sensibility, education, and life experience were distinctly British. However, the American religious imagination was Protestant, and even Eliot acknowledged that his sensibility remained New England and Puritan. In fact, from the outset Eliot was the Christian poet against whom Everson defined himself, and their inflections of the Christian imagination could hardly be more markedly different. Eliot is the conservative classicist submitting fallen human nature to the reasonable authority of historical tradition and institutional structures in order to absolve it from the weaknesses and vulnerabilities of personality. Everson is the romantic individualist, trusting reason less than the undertow of instinct and intuition to transcend human limitations and realize self in the mystery of nature and nature's God. For what linked Everson with Whitman, Jeffers, and Lawrence is what Eliot shrank from as from the devil: a sourcing of self in the unconscious, a faith in the energies – prerational, postrational, suprarational – operative in nature and emergent in the human psyche. Consequently, where Eliot's Christianity is ascetic and apollonian, Everson's is incarnational and dionysian.

When Everson set out to rewrite Eliot's "Journey of the Magi" into "The Wise" – the third of the *Triptych for the Living* and one of his first poems as a Catholic – he was acknowledging Eliot as his opposite pole. In Eliot's version the Magi's uncertain quest is tested as they meander through the desert (through a series of clauses strung loosely by the conjunction "and") only to end with an equally uncertain epiphany. Eliot's wise man renders the finding of the Christ child with almost weary and puzzled understatement:

But there was no information, and so we continued
And arrived at evening, not a moment too soon
Finding the place; it was (you may say) satisfactory.[65]

With Eliot in mind, Everson instead renders the journey as a tumultuous gallop to an ecstatic revelation:

And they brought their camels
Breakneck into that village,
And flung themselves down in the dung and dirt of that place,
And kissed that ground, and the tears
Ran on the face where the rain had.[66]

Four Quartets are Eliot's meditations on the fleeting moments both in and out of time in which intimations of the Incarnation break into a broken, sinful, war-torn world. But what if the Incarnation were not just a single event in the historical person of Jesus, not even just a mystery to be glimpsed in what Eliot called "hints and guesses,"[67] but the ever-active indwelling of Spirit in material and corporal life? Everson's poetry explores the awesome implications and inexhaustible consequences of the Incarnation in human experience. The double helix of Incarnation: Spirit into matter, matter into Spirit; God into human, human into God. The ascetic strain in Christianity, as evidenced in the lives of the great saints and the writings of the great mystics, tended to emphasize the ascent of the human to the Godhead, the sublimation of flesh into Spirit. But Everson's dionysian temperament drew him to pursue the paradox from the opposite perspective: God's assuming a mortal, sexual body signifies, in every mortal, the inspiriting of the sexual body. The end of human striving, then, is not to free spirit from corrupt body, as ascetics and Jansenists and gnostics tend to think, but to realize the incarnation of spirit in body. Eros and agape are not antagonists but a janus-face. Even the ascetic mystics had to express their experience of God's love and love of God – agape, in theological terms – in physical and erotic imagery. If agape manifested itself erotically, then does not eros reveal itself as agape? And might not the pursuit of agape and the pursuit of eros prove to be not opposite pursuits but one and the same? For Everson, then, Jeffers's pantheism gave way to Christian Incarnation, and Lawrence's sexual mysticism gave way to Christian erotic mysticism. Everson's vocation was to pursue the convergence of eros and agape, and his years in monastic life, he felt, only served to intensify the terms of that pursuit.

River-Root is a watershed poem in Antoninus's development because it is his most extended and extreme poetic exploration of erotic mysticism and because it broke through an arid period, spiritually, emotionally, and poetically, after the intensity of his conversion and his entry into the Dominicans. The release began in 1956 with a series of dreams that he described in his journal and interpreted at length through his newfound Jungian hermeneutic. Then in 1957 *River-Root* came in a rush, although he continued to tinker with it over the years, even after its eventual publication in 1976. The poem displaces the account of erotic mysticism from the monk's personal experience to a fictional narrative located not in California but in the American heartland on the banks of the Mississippi. The narrative action describes a night's lovemaking by a married Catholic couple that resolves the disruption of an earlier quarrel. The situation could hardly be simpler, but the point is not plot or even characterization but, through the relentless drive of the rhetoric, the evocation of agape from eros, the revelation of eros as agape.

Whatever one makes of it as a poem, *River-Root* undertakes the most sustained orgasmic celebration in English, perhaps in all literature. The bluntly detailed sexuality of the language is meant to be shocking, but also shockingly innocent in its directness, and its insistent physicality is intended and necessary to embody the unexpected revelation that overwhelms the astounded couple as sexual climax yields the Beatific Vision and the procession of the Trinity becomes the kinetic drive in the sexual act. This long passage at the poem's climax is an explicit statement of the theology of erotic mysticism:[68]

> For God grows in them. In the sacramental oneness
> Presence flows and possesses; in the unsearchable
> Deeps of that contemplation
> Spirit abides; they know the wholeness of spirit.
> Its mystical knowledge moves into union,
> Makes a rapture within, and they worship.
> They gaze in worship on the deep God-presence
>   each wakes in the other,
> And night contains them.
>   For over the bed
> Spirit hovers, and in their flesh
> Spirit exults, and at the tips of their fingers
> An angelic rejoicing, and where the phallos
> Dips in the woman, in the flow of the woman on the phallos-shaft,
> The dark God listens.
>   For the phallos is holy
> And holy is the womb: the holy phallos
> In the sacred womb. And they melt.

> And flowing they merge, the incarnational join
> Oned with the Christ. The oneness of each
> Ones them with God.
>
>   For this is the prototypal
> Act of creation. Where the phallos
> Kisses the womb-nerve listening
> The Father is. And as the phallos flows
> So is uttered the Son. And as Father and Son
> Meld together, merging in love,
> So here Spirit flows. Between taut phallos and tremulous womb,
> The male nerve and the female,
> Spirit moves and is one.

The short clauses and sentences spin through the short lines, strung together by enjambment and conjunctions ("for," "and," "so"), as the words seek to render the activity of Spirit moving and melding, flowing and folding back, circling around a mystery that precludes exposition or conjecture. If the phrasing seems to echo the "Holy!" litany in *Howl*, Antoninus acknowledged that one motive behind *River-Root* was to sacralize what he felt was the prevailingly negative and violational sexuality of Ginsberg's recently published poem.

Antoninus knew full well that *River-Root* was a risky poem, that many believers would think it blasphemous and many nonbelievers would dismiss it as a willful exercise in inflated, empty rhetoric, and he left it unpublished until 1976. But it is a pivotal poem, and from his point of view the charge of rhetorical excess misses the point. The poem has to risk and even seek excess in the effort to render in the materiality of words the activity of Spirit in body. If the reader does not move with the words, the rhetoric sounds like bombast. But for Everson, the function of rhetoric is to use all the evocative resources of language – stress, rhythm, sound effects, powerful imagery – to intimate what cannot be presented. At this level the relative failure of language is, paradoxically, the demonstration of its extraordinary power. Antoninus labored over draft after draft to make the rhetoric its own performative substantiation.

Whatever the risks, whatever the responses, *River-Root* was a necessary and liberating clarification for Antoninus, and his poems constellate around it to articulate a Christ-centered erotic mysticism. His conception of incarnational language looks back in American experience to Emerson's Romantic procession from word to thing to Spirit and to the Puritan typology that reads material existence as divine revelation. But Antoninus extends Puritan types and Emersonian symbols into Catholic sacrament.

In a late interview Everson reiterated the orthodox definition of sacrament "as the concrete or physical sign signifying a mystery" and went on to say that through the Incarnation "Nature becomes sacramental" and thereby language becomes "sacramental": "language is a sacrament that I've always held to ... I can see that a good deal of the power of my poetry has been that I would relate to language as sacrament."[69]

The three-part structure of "In All These Acts," written shortly after *River-Root,* rehearses Everson's evolution into Antoninus. The first free-verse paragraph recounts in brutal and grisly detail the death and disembowelment of a buck elk in an avalanche; the second paragraph assimilates the mutilated carcass into the undisturbed cycles of life and death indifferent to the individual drama. In an inhuman world violence is the harmony of renewal; the erotics of death germinate the maternal round of nature. If the poem had ended here, it might have been written by Jeffers. But the third paragraph re-envisions the whole action:[70]

> In all these acts
> Christ crouches and seethes, pitched forward
> On the crucifying stroke, juvescent, that will spring Him
> Out of the germ, out of the belly of the dying buck,
> Out of the father-phallos and the torn-up root.
> These are the modes of His forth-showing,
> His serene agonization. In the clicking teeth of otters
> Over and over He dies and is born,
> Shaping the weasel's jaw in His leap
> And the staggering rush of the bass.

The energy driving this harrowing event is no longer the indifferent physical and biological laws of natural process but Christ as God immanent in nature's round. The phrasing in these lines deliberately echoes Eliot's monologue "Gerontion" ("In the juvescence of the year / Came Christ the tiger"; "The tiger springs in the new year"[71]) in order to convert impotence into potency. Gerontion shrinks from the advent of Christ as a terrifying and devouring force bringing death to him and his world, and chooses death over new life. In Antoninus's poem Christ's "forth- showing" is both castrated victim and inseminating agent in the "serene agonization" of death and renewal.

However, the principal challenge for Antoninus – the high-pitched psychological and moral drama of his Catholic poems – came not in imagining Christ as the life force in inhuman nature but in realizing Christ as the subsumption of the mind/body split in the human person. He almost always opened his platform readings with "A Canticle for the Waterbirds," because it invokes the round of natural creation to broach

the daunting question of how the Incarnation plays out in human consciousness. The poem is Antoninus's re-envisioning of the dilemma of
consciousness central to Jeffers's poetry. Written soon after his conversion when he was living and working in the Catholic Worker House in
Oakland, the "Canticle" addresses the waterbirds of the Pacific coast and
gathers their particularity and variety into an expansive swirl and stretch
of language:[72]

> And you freshwater egrets east in the flooded marshlands skirting
>   the sea-level rivers, white one-legged watchers of shallows;
> Broad-headed kingfishers minnow-hunting from willow stems on
>   meandering valley sloughs;
> You too, you herons, blue and supple-throated, stately, taking
>   the air majestical in the sunflooded San Joaquin,
> Grading down on your belted wings from the upper lights of
>   sunset ...

The birds all share the common glory of fulfilling their function totally as
God's creatures within the natural round, unconflicted by the bewilder-
ingly contradictory impulses of human awareness and will. Because the
birds "bear existence wholly within the context of His utter will," they
have "the imponderable grace to *be* His verification, / Outside the mulled
incertitude of our forensic choices." The irony is that they, "our lessers
in the rich hegemony of Being, / May serve as testament to what a creature is, / And what creation owes"; their cries "say His name" with an
immediate and unreflective spontaneity denied to the human creature,
fallen from nature into language. The doubling of the irony is, of course,
that the poet's words say His name with a conscious awareness beyond
the birds' thoughtless instinct. The poem's rhetoric is the poet's effort to
move human consciousness into something like the birds' spontaneous
response.

   The challenge to the conscious Christian lies in comprehending
the self not just in relation to the God of natural processes but also to
God incarnate in himself or herself. For Jung, Christ is the most potent
image in Western culture for the individuated self. For Antoninus, Jesus
as God-man is the reality through whom the self is individuated in the
Godhead. The human contradiction – body and soul, masculine and feminine – met, once and for all time and all generations, at the cross-point
on Calvary in sublime transfiguration. In a 1986 interview, long after
Antoninus was again Everson, he commented: "The reason I remain a
Christian is the drama of the Cross. For me that's the point of ultimate
reality, ultimate truth."[73]

"The Cross Tore a Hole," subtitled "A Canticle for the Feast of the Most Precious Blood, 1954," meditates on the sublime contradiction and resolution of the Cross. The violence of death becomes the conception of life; the precious blood becomes the precious semen, as "the seed sack of Christ's body" on the phallic Tree erupts at death in an orgiastic drench of engendering love into the earth's womb:[74]

> And the fierce Christ,
> Split, shaken free,
> Flings up, rejoicing,
> Upswung, outflung,
>
> . . . .
>
> For the great side splits.
> The packed incarnate Blood
> Pours to the world's black womb
> The funneling Seed.

And also pours, the poem goes on to say, into "my womb":

> My soul,
> God's womb, is seeded
> Of God's own.
>   My womb,
> God's own, is sown
> Of God's seed.
>   My soul,
> Wombed of God's wonder,
> Is seeded, sown.

My soul is womb for God's seed, and so my womb-body is seeded and souled by God: the seeded soul enwombed and the seeded womb ensouled. The runic sentences use passive verbs in short, enjambed lines to spin the alternation of "I" and "God" on the prepositional phrases and the reiterated, alliterated words to the climactic point of identification: "In Thee, God, / I am Thou." The last lines of the poem are: "Christ-crossed I bleed. // I am One."

Since a man characteristically brings to the encounter an assertive masculine ego and will to control and dominate, he has to curb those inclinations – "crack the ego," is Antoninus's phrase[75] – to release and realize his "feminine" capacity for receptivity and response. At Mass in 1950, before he had joined the Dominicans, he had experienced a dark ray emanating from the tabernacle on the altar that possessed him body and soul, and "The Encounter" presents that experience in gendered terms: "I was as woman made before His eyes."[76] A number of Antoninus's poem pursue the gendered psychology of the divine encounter. "Annul in Me My Manhood" cites St. Teresa of Avila's conviction that " 'The soul is feminine to God' / And hangs on impregnation" and asks to be made "Girl-hearted, virgin-souled, woman docile, maiden-meek":[77]

> If by that total transformation
> I might know Thee more.
> What is the worth of my own sex
> That the bold possessive instinct
> Should but shoulder Thee aside?

To the objection that such gendered language and imagery, essentializing the distinction between masculine and feminine traits, has worked historically as an effective strategy to maintain male hegemony, Antoninus did not deny the point of the argument but responded that he could only speak from his own psychological and imaginative experience.

With an epigraph from "Song of Songs," "The Song the Body Dreamed in the Spirit's Mad Behest" begins "Call Him the Lover and call me the Bride," and pursues the conjunction of eros and agape further in gendered language that describes the union with God in bluntly sexual and animal imagery. Antoninus said that in this poem he eschewed free verse and adapted the rhymed stanza that Hart Crane had employed in "The River" section of *The Bridge* because the extremity of the metaphorical language required the decorum of the stricter form as a chastening restraint, with the final line of the quatrain, shorter and rhymed, reining in the violence of the heavily monosyllabic and consonantal language into an end-stopped stanza:[78]

> The Seal is broken and the Blood is gushed.
> He does not check but boldens in His pace.
> The fierce mouth has beaked out both my eyes,
> And signed my face.
>
> His tidal strength within me shores and brunts
> The ooze of oil, the slaver of the bitch,
> The bull's gore, the stallion's famished gnash,
> And the snake's itch.
>
> . . . .
>
> Born and reborn we will be groped, be clenched
> On ecstasies that shudder toward crude birth,
> When His great Godhead peels its stripping strength
> In my red earth.

There are scriptural precedents for such erotic language. In the second chapter of the book of the Prophet Hosea, for example, God says of Israel: "I will lead her into the desert and speak to her heart," and, eliding into the second person: "I will espouse you to me forever." But it is generalized language addressed to the entire chosen people. The language in Antoninus's poem speaks of a personal encounter, like that of the great mystics, but the graphic elaboration is intentionally shocking in the effort to resist gnostic asceticism and explore the erotic dimension of Incarnation. Antoninus's gloss on this "Song" can stand as a explanatory gloss on all his poems of erotic mysticism:[79]

> The Imagination, unable to grasp the reality of pure Spirit, conceives of their union under the modality of her own nature. Longing to respond totally to the divine summons, and convinced in faith that the Redemption has rendered this possible, she struggles to cast off all the inhibitions of original sin, and evokes the deepest resources of her sensuality, in order to achieve in shamelessness the wholeness of being an age of shame has rendered incomplete.

"A Canticle to the Christ in the Holy Eucharist," which the subtitle tells us was "Written on the Feast of St. Therese of the Child Jesus, Virgin and Contemplative, 1953," is perhaps Antoninus's richest and most serene meditation on the Incarnation. Following the epigraph from Psalm 33, "Taste and see the Lord is sweet," the poem reflects on the sweet taste of the Lord and transforms the communicant's receiving the Eucharist into an allegory of a doe's impregnation by a stag on Tamalpais, the mountain that bulks above the Bay Area like a supine woman. The similes in the opening lines establish the allegorical terms: "I lay as one barren, / As the doe lies on in the laurel under the slope of Mt Tamalpais," until "you" came "like the buck that stamps in the thicket."[80]

The metaphorical linkage of communicant with doe and of Jesus with buck may seem strained and improbable at first, but the slow and cumulative turning of the metaphor again and again makes it convincing and moving. Periodic references to food and eating keep the reader reminded of the Eucharistic "communion," and the voice of the allegorical narrative, unlike that in "The Song the Body Dreamed," remains quietly attentive and contemplative. The rhythms, anapests lightening the iambs, sift and shift the repeated words and images through prepositional phrases and modifying clauses to ponder, this way and that, the mysterious conjunction:[81]

> There is nothing known like this wound, this knowledge of love.
> In what love? In which wounds, such words? In what touch?
>   In whose coming?
> You gazed. Like the voice of the quail. Like the buck
>   that stamps in the thicket.

You gave. You found the gulf, the goal. On my tongue you
    were meek.

In my heart you were might. And thy word was the running
    of rain
That rinses October. And the sweetwater spring in the rock.
    And the brook in the crevice.
Thy word in my heart was the start of the buck that is sourced
    in the doe.
Thy word was the milk that will be in her dugs, the stir of new
    life in them.
You gazed. I stood barren for days, lay fallow for nights.
Thy look was the movement of life, the milk in the young
    breasts of mothers.

My mouth was the babe's. You had stamped like the buck
    in the manzanita.
My heart was dry as the dugs of the doe in the fall of the year
    on Tamalpais.
I sucked thy wound as the fawn sucks milk from the crowning
    breast of its mother.
The flow of thy voice in my shrunken heart was the cling of
    wild honey,
The honey that bled from the broken comb in the cleft of Tamalpais.

The wound of impregnation by the Christ-buck quickens the doe-communicant to new life; semen becomes mother's milk. And through the gentle modulations of the long lines the roles are startlingly transformed; the Christ-buck becomes the wounded but suckling mother, and the doe-communicant becomes the nursing fawn-child: "For each in that wound is each, and quick is quick, and we gaze ... The double gaze and the double name in the sign of the quenchless wound, / The wound that throbs like wakening milk in the winter-dugs of the doe." As Christ becomes, doubly, father and mother, the communicant becomes, doubly and correspondingly, pregnant mother and offspring.

"A Frost Lay White on California" inverts the encounter, this time with God as the seducer of the alienated and resistant male ego. The poem narrates a frost-bitten night as a monk prowls in the chapel at St. Albert's: "My heart fisted on stubborn revolt, / My two arms crossed on my chest." The cross here is a sign of the monk's clenched repudiation, a fist to any intruder, when God's voice breaks the silence in the wooing voice of a woman. The epigraph from Deuteronomy expresses the patriarchal and gnostic association of the woman with sexual sin and animal instincts: "Thou shalt not offer the hire of a strumpet, nor the price of a dog, in the house of God . . . because both these are an abomination to the Lord thy God."

But in a reversal of that ascetic proscription, God here enters his own house at St Albert's precisely as a spurned strumpet and dog (God backward in lower case) to stalk and win the monk's clenched heart:[82]

> "*Do you know what I am?*
> *I am your woman.*
> *That is my mouth you feel on your heart.*
> *Breathing there, warming it.*
> *I am more, I am your dog.*
> *That is my moan you hear in your blood,*
> *The ache of the dog for the master.*
> *I am your dog-woman.*
> *I grieve a man down,*
> *Moan till he melts.*"

God as the rejected woman, the neglected house pet: the urgency of the short, end-stopped lines dramatizes "the terrifying helplessness of God": omnipotence powerless before the will of stubborn creatures closed to the surrender of love. Through the long night's moaning the monk refuses to answer, till at break of dawn the long-pent rains, falling out of that terrifying helplessness, melt at last the grip of the frost, quicken the spring seeds in the earth's body, and loosen the monk's tongue in sobbing capitulation.

In December 1969, Antoninus left the monastery to marry Susanna Rickson, and they settled with her son Jude into a cabin in a canyon off the coastal highway, while he taught at Kresge College in the University of California, Santa Cruz. The cabin, heated only by a Franklin stove, stood beside a creek with a waterfall half a mile upstream, and beside the cabin was an A-frame housing his books and his handpress. He marked the change from Antoninus back to Everson by trading the Dominican habit for the leather jacket and bear-claw necklace of the mountain man. In the triadic organization of his collected poems, he grouped the poems from this third phase of his life under the rubric "The Integral Years," to suggest continuity and synthesis in his return to nature, now with a Christian perspective. He saw these later poems as a search for the animistic Christ in the wild landscape of his coast: the Christ of "In All These Acts." The poems infuse the landscape round his cabin in Kingfisher Flat with a sacramental sense of the often violent power of natural processes, with "Christ / The principle in the purpose." He remained the "God-stoned monk" of Kingfisher Flat,[83] and, after his death in June 1994, his funeral mass was in St. Albert's chapel, and he was buried, with his bear claws and his Dominican rosary, in the Dominican cemetery in Benicia, California.

"The South Coast," written earlier in the 1950s, describes that stretch of sea and mountain and shore, and sums up Everson/Antoninus' sacramental vision:[84]

> God *makes*. On earth, in us, most instantly,
> On the very now,
> His own means conceives.
> How many strengths break out unchoked
> Where He, Whom all declares,
> Delights to make be.

The Spirit's delight in conception, the flesh's declaration of Spirit: the double helix of erotic mysticism. The delicate pun on clarus / light in the turn of the line at "declares, / Delights" translates word into light, light into word: the double helix of Everson/Antoninus' poetics of Incarnation.

CHAPTER 5

The Language of Witness
Adrienne Rich

I

More than is true for most poets, the word "change" stitches Adrienne Rich's poetry into a continuity. A number of critics have taken change as the key to Rich's message, but their focus for the most part has been her emergence as the poetic voice of American feminism and lesbian feminism in the 1970s. That focus is true as far as it goes, but it largely ignores what preceded and followed the 1970s in the full sweep and scope of Rich's enormous achievement. It is a poetry of transformation and conversion. For more than half a century the prospect of change – personal and historical, psychological and social, moral and political – impels the poems through their own changes in perspective and shape and technique. The titles of the volumes keep signaling the pressing urgency and ongoing challenge of change: *A Change of World, Necessities of Life, The Will to Change, A Wild Patience Has Taken Me This Far, Your Native Land, Your Life, Time's Power, An Atlas of the Difficult World, Telephone Ringing in the Labyrinth, Tonight No Poetry Will Serve.* In fact, the continuity of Rich's work consists in the changes in the character of change and her responses to those shifts; for her, "the will to change" is the key to "time's power" to mend and amend itself.

From the publication of *Snapshots of a Daughter-in-Law* in which she first established her distinctive poetic voice, Rich began dating individual poems and, on the title pages of successive collections, stated the time frame for those poems. The sections of this chapter indicate the major transitions in tracking the ongoing process of change (Rich would write a sequence called "Tracking Poems"). This first section covers the period of 1951–1963 (from *A Change of World* through *Snapshots*); the second covers 1963–1981 (from *Necessities of Life* through *A Wild Patience has Taken Me This Far*); the third section, 1981–1998 (from *Your Native Land, Your Life* through *Midnight Salvage*); the concluding section, 1998–2012 (from

Fox through *Later Poems*). Obviously the chronological subdivisions are to some extent arbitrary; the poems speak to one another within and across those demarcations. Consequently, as the commentary in this chapter proceeds through this rough chronology, it will sometimes move among poems through and across the chronology to stitch in the connections and continuities that give this record of change its sustained and powerful coherence.

A Change of World was chosen for the Yale Younger Poets series by W. H. Auden in 1951, the year Rich graduated from Radcliffe College, and the poems consistently express a sensibility afflicted by mortality and confronting a world alarmingly and violently in flux. As a precocious child, who had a three-act play called *Ariadne* published privately at the age of ten, Rich had read the Romantic and Victorian poets in her father's library in Baltimore, and at Radcliffe she read Yeats, Eliot, Frost, Stevens, and Auden. Her first published poems followed the Modernist strategy against psychological fragmentation and social upheaval: change the disintegrating world into art, into what Stevens called "the *mundo* of the imagination"; arrest impermanence in artifice to secure, in Frost's words, "a momentary stay against confusion."[1]

The title poem tries to mitigate the threat of "A Change of World" with irony, trivializing it into the feminine trope of a change in fashion; the metered, rhymed lines elaborate this initial metaphor – "Fashions are changing in the sphere" – through two neatly turned stanzas. But "Storm Warnings," placed first in the volume, anticipates devastation right from the start. The poem echoes Frost's ruminations in "Tree at My Window" on the correspondence of inner and outer weather ("Weather abroad / And weather in the heart come on / Regardless of prediction"), and Rich's blank verse, Frostian in maintaining a smooth conversational tone through enjambed iambic lines, proposes the only defense against the coming storm: stay inside, close the shutters, beware the keyhole, protect the light from the blast:

> Between foreseeing and averting change
> Lies all the mastery of elements
> Which clocks and weatherglasses cannot alter.
> Time in the hand is not control of time,
> Nor shattered fragments of an instrument
> A proof against the wind; the wind will
> rise, We can only close the shutters.
>
> I draw the curtains as the sky goes black
> And set a match to candles sheathed in glass

> Against the keyhole draught, the insistent whine
> Of weather through the unsealed aperture.
> This is our sole defense against the season;
> These are the things that we have learned to do
> Who live in troubled regions.

Master the hostile elements in the sealed and shuttered poem. And master "the weather in the heart" in the "form" of the artwork – for example, in the intricacies of a Bach fugue. "At a Bach Concert" ends in this concluding triplet: "A too-compassionate art is half an art. / Only such proud restraining purity / Restores the else-betrayed, too-human heart."[2]

In "Storm Warnings" "mastery" has no sinister implications of masculine oppression or suppression. But what would later be recognized as a nascent feminism in Rich makes for the ironic undercurrent in "An Unsaid Word" and in "Aunt Jennifer's Tigers":

> The massive weight of Uncle's wedding band
> Sits heavily upon Aunt Jennifer's hand.
>
> When Aunt is dead, her terrified hands will lie
> Still ringed with ordeals she was mastered by.

But it is more difficult to detect irony in "The Uncle Speaks in the Drawing Room"; the poem seems to speak with the alarm of the patriarch in the ancestral house as he contemplates loss of mastery and the threat of rising social violence to the family's "crystal vase and chandelier." Here is the final tight, rhymed stanza:

> Let us only bear in mind
> How these treasures handed down
> From a calmer age passed on
> Are in the keeping of our kind.
> We stand between the dead glass-blowers
> And murmurings of missile-throwers.[3]

"The centuries have a way of being male," Stevens declared without a tinge of irony.[4] The poetic culture in which Rich was trained and into which she entered earlier than most young poets was, of course, predominantly, almost exclusively, male: her doctor father's careful tutelage of his talented daughter; the nineteenth-century poets in his library and the Modernists she absorbed at Radcliffe; her favorite Harvard professors, notably Theodore Morrison (to whom she dedicated *A Change of World*), and F. O. Matthiessen (to whose memory she would dedicate *Telephone Ringing in the Labyrinth*)[5]; the centrality of Robert Lowell in the poetic world of Cambridge and Boston in which she found herself after she married economist Alfred Conrad in 1953. She would later remark: "I have had to reckon in and out of gender to do my work."[6] Neither Marianne Moore nor H.D. nor Edna St. Vincent Millay were forebears for her, and she did not discover Emily Dickinson until after the Johnson edition of the poems was published in 1955. Lowell was the catalytic figure among the Boston-area poets in the 1950s and early 1960s at roughly the same time that the Beats were constellating around Ginsberg and Kerouac, the New York poets around Ashbery, and the San Francisco poets around Rexroth. Lowell's recognition and friendship were therefore important to Rich in these early years; though Sylvia Plath and Anne Sexton joined the Lowell circle, Rich was never close to them or to their poetry. In the early 1960s Denise Levertov would offer the example of a (slightly older) woman poet who wrote with independence and integrity from her experience as a woman, and Rich dedicated "The Roofwalker" to Levertov. But before that it was the men who recognized her talent and praised her good ear and her "mastery" of the elements of craft.

At the same time, as she could not but have noticed, the praise often came laced with male condescension. In the Foreword to *A Change of World*, Auden summed up his assessment of "Miss Rich": "the poems a reader will encounter in this book are neatly and modestly dressed, speak quietly but do not mumble, respect their elders but are not cowed by them, and do not tell fibs ..." Lowell's friend Randall Jarrell called her "a sort of princess in a fairy tale" who "lives nearer to perfection (an all-too easy perfection sometimes ...) than ordinary poets do," then went on presciently, but still condescendingly, to say: "The reader feels that she has only begun to change; thinks, 'This young thing, who knows what it may be, old?'" In a review of *Necessities of Life*, titled (after Eliot's essay) "Tradition and Talent," Ashbery archly called Rich "a sort of Emily Dickinson of the suburbs" (Rich's poem about Dickinson, "I am in Danger – Sir –," appeared in that collection) but somewhat grudgingly goes on to commend some of her "new and sinewy poetry."[7]

She was indeed changing, and the new poetry was more sinewy, more tense and intense than the poems in *A Change of World*. By *Snapshots of a Daughter-in-Law* (1963), her third book in a little more than ten years, she acknowledged the change by renaming herself, dropping the middle name from the more old-fashioned and girlish Adrienne Cecile Rich; and she started to track the change by dating the poems by year. But men still opened the way. Decisive, she would recall, was a line from Rilke's poem about the marble bust of Apollo – "Du musst dein Leben ändern": "[n]o poem ever said it quite so directly. At twenty-two it called me out of a kind of sleepwalking. I knew, even then, that for me poetry wasn't enough as something to be appreciated, finely fingered: it could be a fierce, destabilizing force, a wave pulling you further out than you thought you wanted to be. *You have to change your life.*" And it was Stevens, the Modernist who meant most to her, who, despite his "'high' tone," in "The Idea of Order at Key West" "offered me something absolutely new: a conception of the woman maker, singing and striding beside the ocean, creating her own music, separate from yet bestowing its order upon *the meaningless plungings of water and the wind.*"[8]

Not surprisingly, therefore, she often imagined change in herself in terms of her ambivalent relation to a male figure. In "The Knight," for example, that heroic figure of song and story, whose helmet "points to the sun" as he "rides like a ship in sail" under "his crackling banner," conceals, beneath his glittering armor, the wounded flesh and tattered nerves of a mortal man imprisoned in and needing liberation from "the gaiety of his mail":[9]

> Who will unhorse this rider
> and free him from between
> the walls of iron, the emblems
> crushing his chest with their weight?
> Will they defeat him gently,
> or leave him hurled on the green,
> his rags and wounds still hidden
> under the great breastplate?

The pun on "mail" underscores the issue of gender, and the poem can be read as a crypto-feminist poem: "Who will unhorse this rider …?" But the knight is also a refracted image of the young poet, secure but repressed within the assurances of the male tradition and the protective formalism of her early verse, who needs to be freed from the armor she has assumed.

On the other hand, in "The Roofwalker," the closing poem in the volume, the speaker sees herself now entrapped in the structures of feminine domesticity (Rich was by then the mother of three sons) and sees the repairmen on the roof as the image of a heroic freedom she now craves:[10]

> Was it worth while to lay –
> with infinite exertion –
> a roof I can't live under?
>
> . . . .
>
> A life I didn't choose
> chose me; even

> my tools are the wrong
> ones for what I have to do.

Enclosed in the walls of the house, "I feel like them up there: / exposed, larger than life, / and due to break my neck"; "I'm naked, ignorant, / a naked man fleeing / Across the roofs ..."

The male figure as liberator, the male figure as antagonist: the paradox for the woman changing to a roofwalker. The title and central poem of *Snapshots of a Daughter-in-Law*, a sequence written between 1958 and 1960 and so between "The Knight" (1957) and "The Roofwalker" (1961), marks the psychological and poetic breakthrough. The title specifies the speaker's role under patriarchal law, and the poems in the sequence satirize with cool, keen-edged irony both the male perpetrators, historical and literary, of that system and the demeaning maneuvers and strategies of women living within it. The penultimate section satirizes Stevens's remark about the male centuries: "Sigh no more, ladies. // Time is male / and in his cups drinks to the fair." But along the way the poem also cites and allies itself with women (not "ladies") who, sometimes covertly, sometimes overtly, challenged the system: Emily Dickinson, Mary Wollstonecraft, Simone de Beauvoir. In the final section the poem suddenly leaps from the irony of the scattered snapshots and vignettes into another imaginative dimension with an image of the liberated woman as a diver/swimmer just as heroic as the roofwalker, just as exposed and larger than life.

The contrast between this diver and the wavering, almost passive diver in "The Springboard" from *A Change of World* marks the change in Rich during the decade of the 1950s. For the earlier diver, the jump will come, if it is to come at all, from a "force" beyond "any will of ours." The poem is two tightly rhymed quatrains:[11]

> Like divers, we ourselves must make the jump
> That sets the taut boarding bounding underfoot
> Clean as an axe blade driven on a stump;
> But afterwards what makes the body shoot
> Into its pure and irresistible curve
> Is of a force beyond all bodily powers.
> So action takes velocity with a verve
> Swifter, more sure than any will of ours.

The closing section of *Snapshots* also ends in "ours," as if to call attention to the contrast, but this diver makes a self-willed and self-directed leap into the open space of free verse:[12]

> Well,
> she's long about her coming, who must be
> more merciless to herself than history.
> Her mind full to the wind, I see her plunge
> breasted and glancing through the currents,
> taking the light upon her
> at least as beautiful as any boy
> or helicopter,
>   poised, still coming,
> her fine blades making the air wince
> but her cargo
> no promise then:
> delivered
> palpable
> ours.

The longer lines of the preceding sections of the sequence concentrate as they leap into the page's open space and spiral down into that final word: "ours," not just the diver's but "ours."

"Snapshots" is not overtly political, but Rich's accelerating commitment to political and soon feminist activism is implicit in that work. The dramatic change in thinking and acting requires not just a change of tone but a change in poetics: a breaking open of known forms to find the rhythms and images for the new way of seeing and being. Capitals no longer begin the verses to indicate distinct and completed structural units; lines find their own length and movement; enjambment keeps the lines moving to the climactic emphasis on three adjectives rising to closure with "ours." It is a visionary moment ("I see," "taking the light"), sustained and completed by the present participles ("taking," "still coming," "making"); and the vision seems no mere promise then but its own realization. The present participle "still coming" gives way to the past participle "delivered," as the "cargo" delivered is "ours."

II

In the early poems, a change of world – inner world and outer world – was cause for alarm and guarded defense, but through the social and cultural upheavals of the 1960s Rich came to a life-defining clarification about herself and the world. In 1966 she moved from Cambridge and Harvard to the different political and poetic world of New York when Conrad took a faculty position at City College, but she had already undertaken the mission of remaking herself as a poet. At a poetry reading in Cambridge in

1964 she was clear about the consequent shift in poetics that would open the way to still undefined purposes and discoveries:[13]

> Today, I have to say that what I know I know through making poems ... I find that I can no longer go to write a poem with a neat handful of materials and express those materials according to a prior plan: the poem itself engenders new sensations, new awareness in me as it progresses. Without for one moment turning my back on conscious choice and selection, I have been increasingly willing to let the unconscious offer its materials, to listen to more than the one voice of a single idea. Perhaps a simple way of putting it would be to say that instead of poems *about* experiences I am getting poems that *are* experiences, that contribute to my knowledge and my emotional life even while they reflect and assimilate it. In my earlier poems I told you, as precisely and as eloquently as I knew how, about something; in the more recent poems something is happening, something has happened to me and, if I have been a good parent to the poem, something will happen to you who read it.

In poems like "A Marriage in the Sixties" and "Like This Together," Rich sees her husband as companion and "twin" in facing a chancy and violent world. But for the most part *Snapshots* and the ensuing volumes portray the responsibility for change first and foremost as an individual choice and commitment. In "The Roofwalker" she saw the possibility of remaining in the enclosure of the house and only "reading – not with indifference – / about a naked man / fleeing across the roofs." "Prospective Immigrant Please Note" proposes the existential choice: "Either you will / go through this door / or you will not go through." In the dream imagery of "The Trees" she sees herself inside a house strangely filled with trees that are uprooting themselves from the cracks in the floor and pressing to smash the glass doors and re-enter the forest outside:

> Listen. The glass is breaking.
> The trees are stumbling forward
> into the night. Winds rush to meet them.
> The moon is broken like a mirror,
> its pieces flash now in the crown
> of the tallest oak.

The process of transformation is shattering and risky, but the title poem of *Necessities of Life* begins: "Piece by piece I seem / to re-enter the world ..."[14]

Re-entry is a life-or-death risk. "Like This Together," dedicated to Conrad, spurns indifference once and for all and embraces the ferocity of desire and attention required to inaugurate, piece by piece, the regenerative re-entry into self and world:[15]

> Our desiring does this,
> make no mistake, I'm speaking
> of fact: through mere indifference
> we could prevent it.
> Only our fierce attention
> gets hyacinths out of these
> hard cerebral lumps,
> unwraps the wet buds down
> the whole length of the stem.

An additional stanza that appeared in the poem's initial publication in *Poetry* again invokes the tree as the image of metamorphosis:

> But new
> life? How do we bear it
> (or you, huge tree)
> when fresh flames start spurting
> out through the old sealed skins,
> nerve-endings ours and not yet ours?
> Susceptibilities we still
> can't use, sucking
> blind power from our roots –
> what else to do but
> hold fast to the
> one thing we know,
> grip earth and let burn.

Attention focuses desire: "The mind's passion is all for singling out." And focus inaugurates response: "What we see, we see / and seeing is changing." The words "clarity" and "lucidity" recur frequently in Rich's poetry and prose, and their etymological roots mean light. The poems are filled with images of light – from the "sacramental clarity" of the "[v]eridical light" of "Focus" (1965) to "the miraculous migration / of sunshafts through the redwoods" in "Waiting for You at the Mystery Spot" (2000). The diver in "Snapshots" is seen as "taking the light upon her," and light suggest the aura of sacrament and miracle precisely because it is veridical; it tells the truth to mind and heart and spirit.[16]

During the 1960s Rich's mythology of metamorphosis would shift the source of her creative power from a masculine alter ego to a feminine one. In "Orion," she still identifies herself with the constellation dominating the night sky: the now liberated knight lighting the high heavens. He is "my genius," "my fierce half-brother," associated archetypally in the poem not only with the Greek hunter but also with the "cast-iron" Viking and the "helmed" Richard the Lion-Heart. Like Frost, Rich often turns to the stars for an elevated perspective that seems transcendent and "larger than life." Up there against the sky, Orion holds his ground. Even "with your back to the wall," "you burn, and I know it" with "a starlike eye / shooting its cold and egotistical spear." "Indoors I bruise and blunder," but out in the open "I throw back my head to take you in" as a vital "transfusion" of light. With him as "speechless" but energizing male muse, she finds the words for them both in the poem.[17]

Dickinson is the woman poet to whom Rich turned as example and against whom she measured herself. "I Am in Danger – Sir – " is the poem that occasioned Ashbery's quip about Rich as an "Emily Dickinson of the suburbs." But in that poem Rich saw Dickinson instead as a "woman, masculine / in single-mindedness" who "chose to have it out at last / on your own premises." At the same time, the pun on "premises" indicates why Dickinson could not serve as Rich's female muse in every respect. Dickinson lived and wrote on her own terms, but she did so in privacy and retirement under the shelter of her father's roof with the handwritten poems left unpublished at her death. In "Planetarium," however, Rich finds an empowering muse not in a masculine constellation but in a star-woman who "in her 98 years" ventured out among the constellations to "discover 8 comets": the astronomer Caroline Herschel, the "virile" "sister of William." Identifying with Caroline "levitating into the night sky / riding the polished lenses" among the "[g]alaxies of women," Rich is herself, by the end of the poem, a star-woman among those galaxies: a source and medium of power, the planetary light pulsing through her into words:[18]

> I am bombarded yet   I stand
>
> I have been standing all my life in the
> direct path of a battery of signals
> the most accurately transmitted most
> untranslateable language in the universe
> I am a galactic cloud so deep   so invo-
> luted that a light wave could take 15
> years to travel through me   And has
> taken   I am an instrument in the shape
> of a woman trying to translate pulsations
> into images   for the relief of the body
> and the reconstruction of the mind.

"[W]e see / and seeing is changing," and we "record / in order to see."
Clarity and lucidity are a function of language, and vice versa: "the mind
of the poet is changing // the moment of change is the only poem."[19]
Language would no longer seal the world off, as in "Storm Warnings."
Yet as Rich sought a language for the poetry of change, the most inspiring
figure among her contemporaries was not a woman, not even Levertov,
but John Berryman. She turned to him not for specific strategies and
techniques but for his determination to make a "new language" out of
the volatilities of his experience. This effort made him, in her mind,
"*the* master poet of this half-century." In a 1969 essay, written the year
after "Planetarium" and after the publication of the second collection of
Berryman's *Dream Songs*, several of which were dedicated to Rich, she
honored the heroic chanciness of that effort: "our ability to read [*The
Dream Songs*] has some relation to our own willingness to risk body and
mind in the real world. Terrible risks have gone into making this poetry."[20]

Rich's poems of the sixties acknowledge the risks and dangers to self
and others. "Face to Face" alludes to Dickinson's poem "My Life had
stood a Loaded Gun – "; and in poem after poem the taut lines, clenched
on enjambment, twist and turn on images of bombs and explosions,
flames and burning, fractures and breaks, wounds and bleeding, the cutting edges of knife, scissors, spear. "On Edges" ends:[21]

> I'd rather
> taste blood, yours or mine, flowing
> from a sudden slash, than cut all day
> with blunt scissors on dotted lines
> like the teacher told.

In a few years "Diving into the Wreck" would be able to say: "The
words are purposes. / The words are maps," and "Waking in the Dark"
would associate another of Rich's female divers – "the water opening /
like air / like realization" – with "Clarity." But in the early 1960s what the
poems express is pain, paralysis, impotence. This "woman sworn to lucidity" would not reach the clarity of purpose expressed in "Diving into the
Wreck" and "Planetarium"[22] until she found the connection between (in
Stevens's phrase) the violence within and the violence without, between
her personal dilemma and the public tragedy, between her psychological and emotional impasse and the broken social and economic systems
that convulsed the shared and communal world. Stevens's instinct was to
withdraw from the violence without into the healing harmonies of words;
Rich's commitment came to see that words had to be made to engage and

thereby change the violence without. The poet's regenerative responsibility is in exploring and moving to realization a life that is not just hers but, as she had intuited at the end of "Snapshots," "Ours." The word had to be personal and political.

With the move from Cambridge to New York in 1966 she and Conrad became increasingly active in the protest movement opposing the Vietnam War and pressing the struggle for civil rights. Rich's essays from the late 1960s and early 1970s reflect her deepening conviction that the root of inequality and oppression at home and imperialist aggression abroad was the capitalist system and its individualist ethos. The lucidity of that radical insight amounted to nothing less than a conversion – a secular conversion, but a conversion nonetheless – that would make her a poet of witness committed, as she never could have imagined in 1951, to a change of world. This "woman sworn to lucidity," "[a] woman with a certain mission ... feeling the fullness of her powers,"[23] would carry her mission through to the end. The poems begin to assume this clearer perspective and direction in the second half of *Leaflets* (1969) and in *The Will to Change* (1971). (The urgency of the political activism of those years is registered in the fact that Rich was writing *Leaflets* as the same time as Lowell's *Notebook* poems and Levertov's notebook poem "Staying Alive" and Ginsberg's journal poem "Wichita Vortex Sutra.")

But how to pursue her mission in a language corrupted by the cultural attitudes and structures she was seeking to change? "Our Whole Life" poses the challenge:[24]

> Our whole life a translation
> the permissible fibs
>
> and now a knot of lies
> eating at itself to get undone
>
> Words bitten thru words
> meanings burnt-off like paint
>
> under the blowtorch
> All those dead letters
>
> rendered into the oppressor's language

"The Burning of Paper Instead of Children" takes as its epigraph a statement by Fr. Daniel Berrigan, on trial in a much-publicized case for non-violent resistance to the Vietnam War: "I was in danger of verbalizing my moral impulses out of existence." Early in "The Burning of Paper" Rich states her risky resolve across the turn of the lines: "this is the oppressor's language // yet I need it to talk to you." The poems in *Leaflets* and *The Will to Change* proceed on the premise that continuing to talk can decreate and recreate language, that "[t]he meaning that searches for its word" can gradually and painfully begin to bring about "the fracture of order / the repair of speech / to overcome this suffering."[25]

The repair of speech would work toward a "common language," the shared speech of a people no longer riven by economic, racial, and gender inequities. Auden, disheartened that the leftist politics of the 1930s had not reformed British society or averted World War II, declared magisterially in his Yeats elegy: "poetry makes nothing happen: it survives in the valley of its making …" Rich might have agreed when she wrote *A Change of World* and received the prize from Auden, but now she was committed to an opposite poetics in which language can recover its inherent power to make things happen. And it is Rich's love of language, attention to language – the resonance of words, the power of images, the sound of syllables, the rhythms of sentences – that makes her witness into enduring poems.

As Rich would say, "poetry / isn't revolution but a way of knowing / why it must come."[26] *The Will to Change* initiates *The Dream of a Common Language.* Such a language might be for the moment only a dream; for that very reason, Rich's need to witness compelled her to accept and work with what Lynda Bundtzen has called "a partly common language," not as an admission of defeat but, on the contrary, as a strategy for liberating language from the oppressors' structures of meaning by reconstituting words, relations, significations subversively from within: "the language is a dialect called metaphor," often disjunct images spare and severe, spaced out in short lines largely stripped of punctuation.[27]

As we have seen, gender had been an issue in Rich's poetry from the beginning, but in the first two books she treated it with understated irony because she saw no way past the impasse. By the 1970s, she saw gender as the issue underlying the political and economic system: male dominance required and enforced discriminatory structures based on ethnicity, class, and wealth. The politicization of gender turned irony to what she called "my visionary anger."[28] The three collections from these years – *Diving into the Wreck* (1973), *The Dream of a Common Language* (1978), and *A Wild Patience Has Taken Me This Far* (1981) – established Rich, both nationally and internationally, as the leading poetic voice in feminism and in the lesbian feminism that emerged within the movement. Poems like "Trying to Talk with a Man," "Diving into the Wreck," "The Phenomenology of

Anger," "Power," "Twenty-One Love Poems," and "Transcendental Etude"
became catalytic texts in feminist consciousness-raising and in patriarchal culture itself. The great outburst of poems in the 1970s is marked
by important transitions in Rich's own life: the death of Alfred Conrad
in 1970; the growing up of her sons; the beginning a new life in 1976
with the fiction writer Michelle Cliff, a partnership that lasted until Rich's
death in 2012.

In "Diving into the Wreck," patriarchal history is a "book of myths /
in which / our names do not appear," and the myths disguise and perpetu-
ate a tragic history of domination and wreckage. The poem imagines the
inevitable shipwreck of patriarchy as the prelude to a new history and a
new myth. The speaker in the poem undertakes the heroic task of excavat-
ing the sunken wreck; the steady pace of the lines traces, step by perilous
step, her imaginative submersion into the "deep element" where gender
distinctions become fluid and flow into a new identity:[29]

> This is the place.
> And I am here, the mermaid whose dark hair
> streams black, the merman in his armored body
> We circle silently
> about the wreck
> we dive into the hold.
> I am she: I am he
>
> . . . .
>
> We are, I am, you are
> by cowardice or courage
> the one who find our way

Rich and her "fierce half-brother" (as she called her "genius" in "Orion")
fuse into the hero/heroine of the excavation and the elision from "We" to
"I" and "you" and from the singular "one" to the plural "our" extends the
metamorphosis performatively to the reader. The way is "Ours"; her/our
words are now "purposes" and "maps" to write the new book of myths in a
"common language" as a cartography of the changed world.

In 1970s feminism the new identity was often imagined in the Jungian
model of the androgyne: the "masculine" force of mind and will that Jung
called the woman's animus integrated into her identity as woman. Thus in
"The Stranger,"[30]

> if they ask me my identity
> what can I say but
> I am the androgyne

> I am the living mind you fail to describe
> in your dead language
> the lost noun, the verb surviving

However, as feminists, especially lesbian feminists, realized that the ideal of the androgyne accepted and reified the very gender categories that sustained patriarchy, they moved to a concept of a woman-centered identity, as Rich did in such influential essays as "When We Dead Awaken: Writing as Re-vision," "'It Is the Lesbian in Us ...,'" and "Compulsory Heterosexuality and Lesbian Existence."[31] Rich's poems begin not just to speak for all women but to incorporate other women's voices, sometimes to speak in another woman's voice. A common language required "a theater of voices rather than the restricted *I*."[32]

At the same time, many readers, including sympathetic readers, male and female, were disturbed by poems like "Trying to Talk with a Man" and "The Phenomenology of Anger" and by the polemical essays from the 1970s for what sounded like an anti-male and separatist exclusion of, even hostility to, men. In "The Phenomenology of Anger" she does say: "I hate you. / I hate the mask you wear," and these lines from the same sequence were cited as evidence of Rich's misandry:[33]

> When I dream of meeting
> the enemy, this is my dream:
> white acetylene
> ripples from my body
> effortlessly released
> perfectly trained
> on the true enemy
>
> raking his body down to the thread
> of existence
> burning away his lie
> leaving him in a new
> world; a changed
> man

The "true enemy" in these lines is directed at the false and destructive mask of patriarchy, and the "visionary anger" seeks not annihilation but conversion to "a new / world" in which men and women would be changed in themselves and in their relations. The "dream of a common language," she would insist, arose from "[t]he drive / to connect"; it was not "a call ... for a 'women's language,' or something like what French feminist theorists called 'écriture feminine,'" but, on the contrary, "poetry itself as connective urge and power."[34] Rich repeatedly denied the charge of separatism, and in the 1974 poem "From an Old House in America" she calls her dead husband to refute the charge: "If they call me man-hater, you / would have known it for a lie."[35]

III

Charles Altieri's study of postwar American poetry presents John Ashbery and Adrienne Rich as dialectical opposites, and in the argument of this book they do represent the difference between a Postmodernist sensibility and a Neoromantic sensibility.[36] Without adopting that descriptive term, Rich herself has said: "I have been a poet of oppositional imagination, meaning that I don't think my only argument is with myself" but also "for people who want to imagine and claim wider horizons."[37] Rich's poetry of the late 1960s and 1970s registered her sense of crisis and her refusal to submit to a doomed acceptance of impotence. The imagery of the poems meets the psychological and social violence of contemporary existence with vehement, even violent resistance as she sought a new grammar of personal and political connection, a new prosody of exploration and relationship, largely in the bonding between women.

In the 1980s, however, Rich's reading of the historical and cultural problem shifted in ways that changed her feminist perspective. In poems like "Sources," "Yom Kippur 1984," and "Eastern War Time" and in the essay "Split at the Root: An Essay on Jewish identity," Rich was acknowledging the Jewish experience as a defining, often denied factor in our history and in her identity. Almost from the beginning of the movement Black and Hispanic feminists were attacking its white, middle-class bias, and through Rich's association with Michelle Cliff and with the poets Audre Lord and June Jordan she was recognizing how deeply racial and ethnic discrimination was intertwined with gender discrimination. She also began reading Marx seriously and was struck by his delineation of the economic basis of the structures of oppression. The poems and prose of the 1980s begin to show a feminism no less resolute but now more conscious of the complex ways in which gender is inseparable from matters of class and ethnicity. Muriel Rukeyser became important for Rich as the poet of the previous generation who made these connections and spoke for poetry as "*an exchange of energy*, which, in changing consciousness, can effect *change in existing conditions.*"[38]

Rich's first mention of Marx in "Women and Honor" (1979) was to warn feminists of Marxism out of "the fear that class would erase gender once again, when gender was just beginning to be understood as a political category." However, her uneasiness with the bourgeois individualism of much feminist testimony, grounded in "a United States model of female – or feminine – self-involvement and self-improvement, devoid of political context or content," led her to reread Marx, beginning "around 1980." There she found "no blueprint for a future utopia, but a skilled diagnosis of skewed and disfigured human relationships" through an analysis of "capitalism and its dehumanizing effect on the social landscape." As a result, although Rich continued to believe that "a change in the concept of sexual identity" is "essential" to any change in the social order, she also came to see that the "fusion of Marx's humanism with contemporary feminisms expanded my sense of the possibilities of both." In 2004 she wrote the preface to *Three Classics for New Readers: Karl Marx, Rosa Luxemborg, Che Guevara*.[39] To the persistent question of whether poetry could or should be political, she asked back: how could it not be, if it is woven from and into the thick, rough warp and woof of living in the world.

Consequently, from the 1980s on Rich began to speak with greater inclusiveness. The titles of the volumes – *Your Native Land, Your Life*; *Dark Fields of the Republic*; *An Atlas of the Difficult World* – proclaim a national witness to a national audience. And the widening perspective changed the form and technique of the poetry. The shorter, jaggedly enjambed lines of much of the poetry of the 1960s and 1970s give way to more expansive lines that enfold more and different voices, more and different inflections and kinds of diction. Pronouns become more gender-inclusive; punctuation falls away as divisive and hindering the forward propulsion of the language. Often, too, the longer lines gather into longer poems and longer sequences, accommodating a range of modes – landscape, narration, meditation, social commentary – into great chordal modulations of rhythm and speech: "An Atlas of the Difficult World," "Calle Visión," "A Long Conversation," "The School among the Ruins." Moreover, that extension of diction, prosody, and tonal register strengthens the capacity of the language to call meaning and action into being. "Dreams Before Waking" asks: "what would it feel like to know / your country was changing? – / You yourself must change it. – "[40]; the "you" here enfolds the poet and the reader.

"Yom Kippur 1984," written in the year in which Rich and Cliff moved from the East coast to Santa Cruz, summons Walt Whitman and Robinson Jeffers, as forebears in her prophetic witness to the nation. Whitman and Jeffers spanned the country's boundaries geographically, metropolitan

New York and California coast, as well as philosophically, optimistic humanist and pantheistic inhumanist. From opposing perspectives they had both assumed a prophetic role in exhorting and decrying the America of their time. Indeed, Rich is the first woman in the American poetic tradition to assume that large collective role. What impelled their witness was the awareness, which Rich shared, of the interdependence of personal and national destiny: "your [our] life" in "your [our] native land." Jeffers's inhumanism made him withdraw from what he saw as the "perishing republic" into pantheistic detachment. Rich, newly settled in Jeffers's landscape and admiring his poetry, contemplates the example of his isolation, and, on the Jewish day of atonement, counters Jeffers with a verse from Leviticus and with her Marxist and feminist concerns: "what is a Jew in solitude? / What is a woman in solitude, a queer man or woman?" Rich's politics demanded a Whitmanian solidarity: "I am the man [woman]; I suffer'd; I was there" ("Song of Myself, #33"). "Find someone like yourself," she urges Jeffers; "[fi]nd others. / Agree you will never desert each other."[41]

In the free-verse expanses of "An Atlas of the Difficult World" Rich makes Jeffers's native land her own "on her own premises" in a long Whitmanian sequence. The concluding section of that poem, titled ("Dedications"), like the catalogues in "Song of Myself," summons the readers of the poem, one by one, scattered and alienated as we are, into an association with the poet and one another. Here are some lines from that section, as the poet calls her people and draws them together through the reiteration of her prophetic recognition of them:

> I know you are reading this poem by the light
> of the television screen where soundless images jerk and slide
> while you wait for the newscast from the *intifada*.
> I know you are reading this poem in a waiting-room
> of eyes met and unmeeting, of identity with strangers.
> I know you are reading this poem by fluorescent light
> in the boredom and fatigue of the young who are counted out,
> count themselves out, at too early an age. I know
> you are reading this poem through your failing sight, the thick
> lens enlarging these letters beyond all meaning yet you read on
> because even the alphabet is precious.

"In the last section of 'Atlas,'" she said, "I was trying to imagine an invisible collectivity."[42]

Rich became interested in the linguistic experiments of what came in the 1970s to be called Language poetry. She shared with the more politically oriented of the Language poets a concern about the corrosive effects of consumer capitalism on American society and so on American language. In their strategizing the Language poets often took the extreme position, bolstered by the neomarxist and poststructuralist theory of the 1970s, that the oppressors' language cannot be used except on the oppressors' terms and thus must be dismantled before communication can be reconstructed in new verbal and grammatical structures. Rich felt the force of that argument, but at the same time she was concerned that their deconstruction of a language already "worn thin by usage and debased by marketing" worked against the burden and responsibility of communication. Must "a radical social imagination" express itself in "a language so deracinated that it is privy in its rebellions only to a few"? "[M]ust we choose between the nonreferential and the paraphraseable?" Or "can poetry persist as a ligatory art rather than as an echo chamber of fragmentation and alienation?"[43] These are, of course, questions Rich had already answered for herself. From her perspective, the theoretically absolute position of the Language poets can be self-defeating ("pure exploration of language, a kind of 'research' into language"), and she had already set herself instead to making an admittedly impaired language "as complex as necessary, as communicative as possible."[44] And, in fact, where the Language poets have marginalized themselves into an avant-garde elite with a small academic audience, Rich has written herself from the margins to the center, where she can speak to and for all the people of her time and place – women and men, dark-skinned and white, gay and straight.

Earlier in the chapter I spoke about Rich's sense of witness as a kind of secular conversion. Commitment to the power of the word proceeds from some kind of faith, from an instinctual ground of conviction that impels speech to call that conviction into being in the reader or hearer. Prophecy as performance: the word "prophecy" means etymologically "speak for." But on whose authority was Rich speaking? She had read the Hebrew prophets and the Romantic visionaries, but she made no claim to religious inspiration or special insight and for that reason was uncomfortable with designations like prophetic and Neoromantic. She had rejected the social Episcopalianism of her early training, as the poem "Air Without Incense" in her first collection indicates: "We eat this body and remain ourselves. / We drink this liquor, tasting wine, not blood."[45] Although "in my college years T. S. Eliot was the most talked about poet," he was never an influence in her development because "as a young person" she had become "utterly disaffected with Christianity and with organized religion in general": "My experience of the suburban Protestant church was that it had nothing whatsoever to do with changing one's life."[46] She reclaimed her Jewish heritage but remained a cultural, nonobserving Jew.

Yet in "Yom Kippur 1984" she spoke about "my want or anyone's want to search for her spirit-vision," and in "1941" she asked herself: *"are you poetry's inadmissible untimely messenger? By what right? / In whose name?"* "Transcendental Etude," which concludes *The Dream of a Common Language* and is dedicated to Cliff, is a key poem in Rich's work because its long meditation answers those questions. The "etude" of the title reflects the love of music that Rich traced back to her pianist mother (see the poem "Solfeggietto"); the word suggests the Romantic piano etudes of Chopin and establishes the musical analogy that runs through the poem. The "transcendental" of the title suggests the quasi-philosophical tenor of this etude and specifically evokes the Romantic Transcendentalism that Emerson and Whitman had written into American philosophy and poetry. But Rich shied away from Romantic idealism and would have endorsed Frost's warning (about Emerson) against "getting too transcended," and her etude evokes the Transcendental impulse only to subvert, or invert, it. That impulse would make us feel "as if / our true home were the undimensional / solitudes, the rift / in the Great Nebula," but, on the contrary, "[v]ision begins to happen" in the clarifying commitment to earth, to the life of the mind in the body that links self to the natural world, to the beloved, to the human community.[47]

Rich would ground her vision in poems like "An Atlas of the Difficult World"; her atlas begins "with the geography closest in – the body" and maps the material world "against lofty and privileged abstraction." Philosophically Rich was, like Jeffers, a materialist, but Jeffers was a pantheist and she was a socialist. Her secular materialism did not speak of the divinity of Nature but of the "composition" (literally, the putting together) of "the daily conditions of our material existence": "Such a composition has nothing to do with eternity." "Time's / power" – mortal humans' ability to create their own destiny – is "the only just power," and tapping into and channeling that power would compose her etude in a "new Language," "a whole new poetry beginning here."[48] Such poems are prophetic because they call us to each other in the name of our debased yet resilient humanity. And they are performative poems because they engage language in the work of transfiguring suffering into love and community.

Rich's poems resist Transcendental moments but rise to earthly moments of elevated, sky-high transcendence. The descent into the bodily and material existence awakens a complementary response, often imaged, as also in Frost's poems, as the need to look up, grounded and embodied, into the seemingly boundless infinity of the stars in order to gauge and extend the range of the human. As we know from "Orion" and "Planetarium," Rich was a star-gazer, and the constellations were not divine but human inscriptions mapping the mind's farthest reaches. In "North American Time" the momentary feeling, "born of flying," that she has a prophetic calling and angelic powers ("angelos" means "messenger") seems dismissed as a "grandiose idea," deflated by a return to a world tragic enough to break the heart and stifle speech:

> Sometimes, gliding at night
> in a plane over New York City
> I have felt like some messenger
> called to enter, called to engage
> this field of light and darkness.
> A grandiose idea, born of flying.
> But underneath the grandiose idea
> is the thought that what I must engage
> after the plane has raged onto the tarmac
> after climbing my old stairs, sitting down
> at my old window
> is meant to break my heart and reduce me to silence.

But the poem does not end here, and in the last line the messenger refuses silence and resumes her high calling: "and I start to speak again."[49]

In a 1987 poem simply dated "6/21" the star-gazer translates starlight into enlightened human speech:[50]

> It's June and summer's height
> the longest bridge of light
> leaps from all the rivets
> of the sky
> Yet it's of earth
> and nowhere else I have to speak
> Only on earth has this light taken on
> these swivelled meanings, only on this earth
> where we are dying befouled, gritting our teeth
> losing our guiding stars
>   has this light
> found an alphabet   a mouth

Though the stars have no supernatural power, they illumine our tragic and mortal existence. Under those pulsations the human imagination finds the power to light and enlighten that world by spelling out ("an alphabet") and communicating ("a mouth") what it sees. The adjective "swivelled" catches both our capacity to warp or skew meanings and our capacity to make or remake meanings that can turn the course of things. "Dreamwood" ends: "the material and the dream can join / and that is the poem."[51]

A statement written for the jacket of *Your Native Land, Your Life* grounds Rich's poetics in what she called her "marxist humanism": "I believe more than ever that the search for justice and compassion is the great wellspring for poetry in our time, throughout the world ... I draw strength from the traditions of those who, with every reason to despair, have refused to do so." Robert Creeley – no Romantic visionary, a Postmodernist forebear of the Language poets – felt the power of Rich's vision for their generation, even linking it with Martin Luther King's:[52]

> The dream of a common language, therefore, in Adrienne Rich's proposal, becomes the hope for, the wish for, the desire for, the working toward, literally – *I have a dream*, I'm sure it echoes that – the place where the company of that dilemma will find a bonding and a way of having a life in common, a common life. It's to get to, in not too simple a manner, the imagination of a common need, a common place, a common person – a *common* ...

IV

A number of Rich's sequences from the 1980s and after – "Contradictions: Tracking Poems," "An Atlas of the Difficult World," "Calle Visión," "Midnight Salvage," "Terza Rima" – begin with the body in pain in a world of psychological and physical violence and institutionalized injustice and oppression. If the common language begins as a language of pain, can it realize its dream? Shortly after her graduation from Radcliffe and the publication of *A Change of World*, Rich was diagnosed with rheumatoid arthritis, and over the years the effects of the arthritis steadily intensified and required a harrowing series of surgeries and medical treatments. In "Transit," dated 1979, Rich sees herself as a "cripple" facing the "sister" she will never be in the athletic skier riding the mountain slopes. In one of the "Tracking Poems," she says: "I feel signified by pain"; "I'm already living the rest of my life / not under conditions of my choosing / wired   into pain." Another of the "Tracking Poems" recognizes the vulnerable body as the inescapable and common ground that all mortals share:

> The problem, unstated till now, is how
> to live in a damaged body
> in a world where pain is meant to be gagged
> uncured   un-grieved over   The problem is

> to connect, without hysteria, the pain
> of any one's body with the pain of the body's world

In "Calle Visión" the street of our lives leads not up to a transfiguring "visión" but down to the stark fact of the suffering body – the individual body within the social body: "never forget / the body's pain // never divide it" because "this is your revelation this the source."[53]

The words "patient" and "patience" suggest both suffering and endurance, endurance through suffering, and the "wild patience" that sustained her in the 1970s gave way, by the 1996 sequence "Midnight Salvage," to a different inflection of "patience":

> This horrible patience which is part of the work
> This patience which waits for language for meaning for
>   the least sign
> This encumbered plodding state doggedly dragging
> the IV up and down the corridor
> with the plastic sack of bloodstained urine

No stargazer here, the patient plods the hospital corridor, but the passage moves not to the death it seems to portend but to a stubborn commitment to life:

> Only so can you start living again
> waking to take the temperature of the soul
> when the black irises lean at dawn
> from the mouth of the bedside pitcher
> This condition in which you swear *I will*
> *submit to whatever poetry is*
> *I accept no limits*   Horrible patience

"Only so can you start living again": through the transforming power of language. The poet's italicized vow – "*I accept no limits*" – restores the stargazer; the reiterated "Horrible patience" opens the phrase to awesome, untold potentialities, but it is the stargazer who speaks the final lines of the sequence: "and when the fog's irregular documents break open / scan its fissures for young stars / in the belt of Orion." For, as Rich says in "Poetry III," "the thing comes as it does come / clarifying grammar / and the fixed and mutable stars."

Still, as she was increasingly disabled with pain year by year, the realist in Rich faced the inevitable: time's power was running down; the telephone was ringing in the labyrinth; fog threatened the starlike clarity. One of the "Tracking Poems" from the mid-1980s addressed Elizabeth Bishop's

"One Art," in which Bishop says that what life teaches is the art of losing. Rich admired Bishop's poems, but she rejects Bishop's stoic resignation to loss: although "these last few years I've lived / watching myself in the act of loss," Rich's effort has been "trying to let go without giving up."[54]

"Terza Rima," a sequence written in the centennial year, is a major poem of Rich's later years, and it is a poem of deep crisis. What is at risk is nothing less than her mission of witness to a world desperately needing change. The unmetered, unrhymed triplets do not follow Dante's verse form strictly but allude to it, and the references to *"the underworld"* and the "Ninth Circle" make it clear we are in Rich's version of the Inferno. But because, unlike Dante, the speaker has no Virgil, no "great teacher" to lead her and us through and out, she has had to "become the default derailed memory-raided / limping / teacher I never had   I lead and I follow." Now, however, deep in the circles of hell, she doubts her capacity to show the way:[55]

> I have lost our way   the fault is mine
> ours   the fault belongs
> to us   I become   the guide
>
> who should have defaulted
> who should have remained the novice
> I   as guide   failed
>
> I as novice   trembled
> I should have been stronger   held us
> together
>
> . . . .
>
> I thought I was
> stronger   my will the ice-sail
> speeding my runners

If the will to change proves a "failed will," then she suddenly feels "[s]ick of my old poems": "How I hate it when you ascribe to me / a 'woman's vision'"; "how I've hated speaking 'as a woman.'" In the final section of "Terza Rima" she tries to rally herself and us by the reiterated assurance, "I lead / and I follow," but the poem leaves us still in hell.[56] Strong poems did follow, but the titles of the collections – *The School Among the Ruins*, *Telephone Ringing in the Labyrinth* – catch their deepening darkness.

A number of Rich's poems acknowledged that her private life with Michelle Cliff was a sustaining and centering source of loving comradeship and peace, a safe haven all the more cherished in these difficult years. "Tonight No Poetry Will Serve," the title poem of the collection published the year before her death, weighs private happiness against the daily word of death and torture in the terrorist wars in Iraq and Afghanistan. Here is the whole poem:[57]

> Saw you walking barefoot
> taking a long look
> at the new moon's eyelid
>
> later spread
> sleep-fallen, naked in your dark hair
> asleep but not oblivious
> of the unslept unsleeping
> elsewhere
>
> Tonight I think
> no poetry
> will serve
>
> Syntax of rendition:
> verb pilots the plane
> adverb modifies action
>
> verb force-feeds noun
> submerges the subject
> noun is choking
> verb   disgraced   goes on doing
>
> now diagram the sentence

In "Poetry III" language comes "clarifying grammar," but can language address and redress the "[s]yntax of rendition"? Is the power of words only a Neoromantic illusion, the common language only a dream? Was she right after all, in *A Change of World,* that storm warnings leave us nothing to do but seek shelter and secure the blinds? The poem turns on the various meanings of "serve." The spacing out of the lines – "Tonight I think / no poetry / will serve" – raises haltingly the judgment she most dreads: poetry is inadequate to confronting and changing the systemic structures of violence and torture. But this hesitation occurs in the middle of a poem that nonetheless continues and in continuing refuses to serve and be used by those structures. Those lines are clumsy, but they fumblingly begin to piece out, piece together the "[s]yntax of rendition." Not serving moves from a confession of impotence to a recovery of power: "now diagram the sentence." Tonight, in the end, poetry does serve not the system but its own witness.

"From Sickbed Shores," "Emergency Clinic," and "Don't Flinch" – the poems that follow "Tonight No Poetry Will Serve" – are filled with images of sickness unto death: *"sick body in a sick country: can it get well?"* But Jeffersian retreat into isolation – that "un-belonging, being-for-itself-alone, runged / behind white curtains in an emergency cubicle, taking care of its own / condition" – remains an unacceptable option for Rich, even though "I write this / with a clawed hand," crippled by arthritis. The volume moves toward the final poem, "Powers of Recuperation," and pivots on "Axel Avákar," the extraordinary sequence in the middle of the volume.[58]

In this crisis Rich's imagination circled back to the late 1960s to seek again the clarity that she had found then and that had taken her this far. The exotic name Axel Avákar recalls the Urdu poet Mirza Ghalib, whose ghazals inspired Rich's experiment in that form in the late 1960s, and Aijiz Ahmad, whose literal English transcriptions of Ghalib's ghazals Rich read. "Ghazals (Homage to Ghalib)" were original poems, not translations, that appeared in *Leaflets*, followed by "The Blue Ghazals" in *The Will to Change*. The fourth poem of "Axel Avákar" alludes to and works off of one of "The Blue Ghazals." Rich's Axel with his strange, dreamlike name was a reimagining of a familiar figure. So "[b]ack to you Axel through the crack-ling heavy / salvaged telephone"; and the references to recent poems in the words "salvaged" and "telephone" bring Axel to bear on the present crisis. *"[F]ictive poet, counter-muse, brother,"* he is another version of her "mascu-line" animus like her "fierce half-brother" Orion in the 1965 poem.[59]

Axel is starry Orion come to earth, "boy- / comrade" from girlhood at the very beginning of her imaginative life, as if "elbow to elbow reading / in Baltimorean August- / blotted air"; and even now he remains the heroic figure leading the way:

> in all weathers you're
> crawling exposed   not by choice   extremist
> hell-bent searching your soul
>
> – O my terrified   my obdurate
> my wanderer   keep the trail

In the years since "Orion" the feminist movement had changed conscious-ness: "when we parted // I left no part behind I knew / how to make poetry happen." Yet her indelible connection with the animus ("Back to back our shadows / stalk each other Axel") is precisely what enabled and continues to enable "my decision ... to be in no other way // a woman."

So the last two sections of the sequence make no direct mention of Axel as she resumes her lifelong commitment to questioning "the Book of Questions" in search of "the true / unlocking code."[60]

Rich wrote "Powers of Recuperation" the year before "Axel Avákar," but placed the poem last in the volume to complete the thematic trajectory from sickness to recovery. The speaker is "[a] woman of the citizen's party," "the incendiary woman," and, though "old, old," she feels herself an "endless beginner." The sequence imagines a narrative of the old woman setting out yet again through the ruined city, where, at a bridge across the river, she encounters a child already planning, as "civil / engineer," to rebuild the city. The prospect of ongoing witness and mission leaves "the massive figure" of the old woman, like one of Michelangelo's sibyls, resting

> on unrest's verge
> pondering the unbuilt city
>
> cheek on hand and glowing eyes and
> skirted knees apart

The sibyl, as Rich's note on these lines indicates, is one she had cherished since childhood: the brooding image of Melancholy in the Dürer engraving that she had first seen in her father's library as a child and had evoked in the 1968 poem, "The Burning of Paper Instead of Children." However, where Melancholy in the earlier poem was "the baffled woman," here she is specifically "Melencholia Imaginativa," the kind of melancholy that fires the imagination. So "the incendiary woman" in "Powers of Recuperation" continues "to scribble testimony by fingernail and echo / her documentary alphabet still evolving."[61] Rich inscribed these two lines in a shaky hand on the title page of my copy of *No Poetry Will Serve*.

Adrienne Rich's last year, burdened with worsening pain and failing eyesight, was spent in the company of her loved ones: Michelle, her sons, and their families. Near the end she wrote to me: "So there is pain but also clarity."[62] The posthumously published volume of later poems that she labored to assemble during those final months concludes with a section of ten poems written in the last year. One of the new poems anticipates the future: "For the Young Anarchists." But the very last poem, "Endpapers," faces the fact of terminus, and its last lines stand as an epigraph and epitaph for her life's work:[63]

> The signature to a life requires
> the search for a method

rejection of posturing
trust in the witnesses
a vial of invisible ink
a sheet of paper held steady
after the end-stroke
above a deciphering flame

In the flame and flare of our reading, "after the end-stroke," the words of Rich's long witness to a change of world come indelibly present and insistently clear.

CHAPTER 6

The Language of Vision
Denise Levertov
Robert Duncan

I

For almost twenty years Denise Levertov and Robert Duncan shared poems with each other and wrote poems to and for each other. Poems flow into and out of the letters; letters occasionally are themselves poems or turn into poems. Their correspondence constitutes the most remarkable exchange between two major poets in American literary history. What sustained the correspondence was a dialogue about the function of the imagination and about the function of language in the imaginative act. Moreover, the issues that sustained the dialogue dramatize and clarify the interplay between Neoromanticism and Postmodernism that defined postwar American poetics. The back-and-forth of letters, so intense and regular that it reads like an epistolary novel, carried Duncan and Levertov through a friendship so close in the 1950s and 1960s that they called each other brother and sister, animus and anima; yet it ended in a painful breakup in the early 1970s over the very "aesthetic ethics" they had thought they shared. The phrase is Levertov's; she used it to describe what she had learned from Rilke, her first mentor, and to designate the underlying issue of her exchange with Duncan.[1]

In literary accounts of the postwar period Duncan and Levertov are linked, along with Charles Olson and Robert Creeley, as the major poets of the Black Mountain school, named after the experimental Black Mountain College, tucked away in the hills of North Carolina, where Olson was rector in the 1950s. The four of them were scattered across the map – Olson in Gloucester as well as Black Mountain, Creeley in Mallorca and New Mexico, Duncan in San Francisco, Levertov in New York – but they were connected by a crisscrossing web of friendships and correspondences. Through Olson, Duncan and Creeley had residences at Black Mountain; Levertov never went to the college and met Olson only later at a conference, but Creeley and Duncan are her link to Black Mountain poetics. In the poetry wars of the postwar decades the Beats and the Black Mountain poets represented experimental open form against the closed forms of Richard Wilbur, James Merrill, and J. V. Cunningham. But where the Beats drew their inspiration from Whitman's free verse and from jazz and blues, the Black Mountain poets coalesced around Olson's 1950 essay "Projective Verse," which in turn took as its point of departure not the Romantic Whitman but the Modernist experimentation of Pound and Williams in the first half of the century and of their Objectivist successors Louis Zukofsky and George Oppen.

"Projective Verse" headlined its theory of open form, in Olson's emphatic caps, as "COMPOSITION BY FIELD." The linguistic field of the poem followed and enacted the poet's engagement with the multidimensional field of experience. The lines of the poem were shorn of the initial caps that set them off as scanable metrical units and orchestrated themselves across the space of the page through linebreaks and indented left-hand margins, so that the spatial arrangement, like a musical score, registered the temporal measure of the lines through the field of the poem. The defining axiom of Black Mountain poetics is Creeley's formulation, again posted in Olson's caps, that "FORM IS NEVER MORE THAN AN EXTENSION OF CONTENT."[2] In other words, form is not precedent to or extraneous to content and meaning but, on the contrary, the evolving dynamics of form constitutes the poem's emergent content and meaning.

The Black Mountain poets gave their individual inflections to form as extension of content and content as realization of form. In broad terms, Olson and Duncan were closer to the Pound's epic intentions, with its investigation of history and myth and philosophy, whereas Creeley and Levertov were closer to Williams's attention to the particulars of immediate experience in finely calibrated lyrics. And, perhaps because of the attraction between their different sensibilities, Olson and Creeley were drawn into extended and voluminous correspondence, as were Duncan and Levertov.

Before Black Mountain poets were identified as a school, however, Levertov and Duncan found each other on their own, and, as the letters make clear, what drew them together at the outset was not "Projective Verse" but the Romantic conception of the imagination as a faculty of vision and inspiration. Before Levertov came to New York as the wife of American writer Mitchell Goodman, she had been publishing poems as one of the New Romantic poets in England. In an early notebook Duncan declared that he was seeking "a style and temperament in which the

Romantic spirit is revived" and that "there is a route back to the Romantic in Stevens."[3] "How many correspondences there are," Duncan exclaimed to Levertov, "between your *Double Image* (1946) [her collection of New Romantic poems] and my *Medieval Scenes*, written in 1947."[4] Levertov first encountered Duncan's "rich romanticism" in Muriel Rukeyser's review of his *Heavenly City, Earthly City* (1947) in *Poetry* magazine, and she liked the excerpts quoted in the review so much that she bought the book soon after arriving in New York.[5]

Duncan said that when he wrote the title poem of that collection, poetry was for him "a magic of excited, exalted or witch-like (exciting) speech, in which the poet had access to a world of sight and feeling, a reality, deeper, stranger, and larger than the world of man's conventional concerns."[6] The dichotomy in the title catches the essential Romantic dilemma: the tension between the aspiration to transcend human limits and the human limits that constrain and perhaps doom that aspiration, between the spirit's effort to inspirit matter and matter's failure to incarnate spirit. Duncan's opulent diction and imagery, before he encountered Olson and "Projective Verse," acknowledge Stevens, and the meditation in the third and concluding section of the poem, as the poet ponders that dilemma beside the "[t]urbulent Pacific," is Duncan's response to Stevens's "The Idea of Order at Key West." As with Stevens, the dualism is not resolved in Duncan's poem: "in the avenues of his earthly city / unearthly presences wink, / unfathomable eyes of an inward vision."[7] And that unresolved dualism is, as we shall see, the source and expression of a persistent gnosticism that over the ensuing years will more and more sharply set Duncan's "inward vision" against Levertov's increasingly incarnational vision. At this first encounter, however, what Levertov responded to in *Heavenly City, Earthly City* was a connection with "the tradition of magic and prophecy and song."[8]

By the time Duncan discovered Levertov's poems in the pages of Cid Corman's magazine *Origin* in the spring of 1953, the "Romantic spirit" of both poets had accommodated itself to and assimilated late Modernist notions of form and technique. Through Olson, Duncan had been exposed to Black Mountain poetics as extensions of the formal experiments of Pound and Williams, Gertrude Stein and Zukofsky. Upon coming to New York, Levertov had been swept up by the rhythms and diction of American speech and by a poetic culture radically different from the British, and the traditional formalism of the New Romantics rapidly gave way to American experimentalism. In particular, Levertov had become friends with Creeley, her husband's Harvard classmate, and through

Creeley had met Williams, who became the most important influence in her transformation into an American poet. For his part, Williams came to think of Creeley and Levertov as the poets of the younger generation who most creatively carried forward his sense of poetic line and structure. The Levertov poems that Duncan found in *Origin* clearly showed Williams's influence, and the poem he was most struck by was "The Shifting" – so struck, in fact, that he was impelled to address to her the poem-letter that initiated their voluminous correspondence.

When Levertov's poem appeared in *Overland to the Islands* (1958), published by Jonathan Williams, who had studied at Black Mountain, it was called "Turning":[9]

> The shifting, the shaded
>   change of pleasure
> Soft warm ashes in place of fire
>   out, irremediably
>
> and a door blown open:
>
> planes tilt, interact, objects
>   fuse, disperse,
>   this chair further from that table ... hold it!
> Focus on that: this table
>   closer to that shadow. It's what appalls the
> heart's red rust. Turn, turn!
>   Loyalty betrays.
>
>   It's the fall of it, the drift,
>   pleasure
>   source and sequence
>   lift
>   of golden cold sea.

Composition by field: the poem as process and the poem as graph; the poem following the temporal realization of experience in the spatial arrangement of words and lines on the page. "Turning" is sustained by the tension and correlation between the two exclamatory commands: "Turn, turn!" but "hold it!" followed by "Focus." It is pleasure in the shift/drift/lift that keeps the heart from rusting in place, and the strong verbs suggest a Cubist painting: "planes tilt, interact, objects / fuse, disperse." However, lest the shifting blur into indistinction, lest the particulars get lost in the "golden cold sea," the admonitions at the heart of the poem insist, moment by moment, on clarity of focus, on the distinct particularity of "this" and "that": "this chair further from that table," "this table / closer to that shadow."

Over the years it is precisely Levertov's focus on the particularity of the
moment, her sensuous and tactile experience of the physical world that
attracted Duncan as a counter to his tendency to intellectual abstraction
and his delight in shifting perspectives and configurations. "The Rights,"
the poem she wrote for him after their first exchange, begins:[10]

> I want to give you
> something I've made
>
> some words on a page – as if
> to say 'Here are some blue beads'
>
> or 'Here's a bright red leaf I found on
> the sidewalk'

In a 1965 letter Duncan tells Levertov that where she sees experience as "a
constellation raying out from and into a central focus," as in "a mandala
or wheel," he sees experience as the spinning equilibrations of "a mobile."[11]
And indeed Duncan's poems do characteristically spin out an open-ended
and ongoing process of circulation, and Levertov's characteristically draw
in the dynamic convergences of an immediate moment.

The letter from June 1953, in which Duncan meant to express his "more
than admiration" for "The Shifting," took the form of a poem – but a
poem so perplexingly different from the poems of his that Levertov had
read that she wrote back to ask if the "R.D." of the signature could pos-
sibly be the Robert Duncan of *Heavenly City, Earthly City.* The "puns,
lists, juxtapositions" of "Letters for Denise Levertov: An A Muse Meant"
seemed to her to be mocking rather than praising her poem.[12] What had
intervened were Duncan's immersion in the writings of Gertrude Stein in
the early 1950s and his composition of several sequences imitating Stein's
verbal and syntactical experiments.[13] Stein's anti-Romantic foregrounding
of the materiality of language and the mechanics of signification made her
a precursor of Postmodernism and a formative influence on later poets,
from Zukofsky and Oppen through Ashbery and Creeley to the Language
poets of the 1970s.

So Duncan's "Letters for Denise Levertov" was written in his Steinian
mode. Levertov, however, had no interest in or sympathy for Stein's strain
of Modernism. Not surprisingly, then, she felt only baffled consternation
when she read the opening lines from R. D.:[14]

> in
>
>   spired / the aspirate
>   the aspirant almost

> without breath
> it is a breath out
>> breathed spiraling – An aspiration
> pictured as the familiar spirit
>> hoverer
>> above
>> each loved each
> a word giving up its ghost
> memorized as the flavor
>> from the vowels/the bowels/
>> of meaning

Or these lines later in the letter:

> Why knot ab stract
> a tract of mere sound
> is more a round
> of dis ab con
>> traction
> a deconstruction
> for the reading of words.

Levertov's perplexed response to R. D. precipitated a back-and-forth exchange through the month of June in which Duncan, appalled that "[m]y praise is your abuse," explained his intentions, and she apologized for her "stupidity."[15]

So quickly was everything patched up in great embarrassment on both sides that by the time they met for the first time in New York in 1955, she was able to tell him in a follow-up letter that "the effect on me of your visit" made her want to write back "a real crazy letter – something like a loveletter, tho' not that." The circumstances of their lives on opposite coasts – Duncan with his life's partner, the painter Jess Collins; she with her husband and their son Nikolai – kept them apart except for occasional and brief visits. But their correspondence over the next two decades and more were in fact love letters of a special and rare kind, based, in Duncan's words, on "the special view we have ... of why and what the poem is."[16]

Nevertheless, they sensed from the start real differences. She described their initial exchange as "such a spectacle of cross-purposes," and he saw right off that "my own aesthetic is I see *not yours*." Yet they willfully passed over the underlying cross-purposes to celebrate "the happy conjunction of the two of us," wherein the symbiotic interplay of "sympathies and differences shld [sic] give rise to a dialectic."[17] Their symbiotic relationship represented, they said, the play between animus and anima, distinct but interdependent aspects of the imagination. Levertov ascribed the "big difference," the "thread of another texture among those that we held in common," to Duncan's daunting intellectual "sophistication," his "almost encyclopedic range of knowledge," including history, philosophy, and mythology. He agreed that he was "drawn by the conceptual imagination rather than the perceptual imagination," but, paradoxically, for that very reason, he was drawn to the immediacies of the perceptual imagination in her poems. She called her first American collection *Here and Now* and told Duncan that "when this *kind* of imagination – the presence of felt-through absolutely convincing details – is manifested it excites and delights me – shakes and moves me to tears," so that "even thinking of it ... is almost a sensuous, no, sensual experience, sharp and exquisite."[18]

Consequently, in the encounter between mind and world from which the poem arises, Duncan's imagination tended to turn in, to draw sensual experience into the play of consciousness, whereas Levertov's imagination tended to turn outward and seek realization in the particulars of experience. In a notebook entry Duncan attributed "the radical disagreement that Olson has with me" to the fact that Olson is "so keen upon the *virtu* of reality that he rejects my 'wisdom' ... because my wisdom is not true wisdom. He suspects, and rightly, that I indulge myself in pretentious fictions ... It is the intensity of the conception that moves me." Levertov's own dialogue with Duncan convinced her that the challenge to her was "to develop a greater degree of conscious intelligence to balance my instincts and intuitions" and the challenge to Duncan was "to keep his consciousness, his diamond needle intellect, from becoming overweening, violating the delicate feelings-out of the Imagination."[19]

Yet through the poems and essays and letters of the 1950s and 1960s, their profound trust in and empathy for each other sustained their shared commitment to the mystique and metaphysics of the imagination, to the visionary nature of the creative process. Their Neoromanticism adapted the Romantic imagination to Modernist practice; they assimilated their reading of Wordsworth and Coleridge, Emerson and Whitman with their reading of Pound and Williams and Stevens. In Duncan's words, "I read Modernism as Romanticism, and I finally begin to feel myself pretty much a 19th century mind ... [M]y ties to Pound, Stein, Surrealism and so forth all seem to me entirely consequent to their unbroken continuity from the Romantic period."[20] What transfixed them both was the ineluctable mystery shadowed yet somehow manifest in lived experience. The notion of the creative process they shared was essentially (but, as we shall see, differently) religious, as they sought to invest the formal experimentation they learned from the Modernists with the metaphysical aura and mystique of the Romantic imagination.

The juxtaposition of Duncan's *The Opening of the Field* (1960) and *Roots and Branches* (1964) with Levertov's *The Jacob's Ladder* (1961) and *O Taste and See* (1964) illustrates the dialectic, within their Neoromanticism, between the conceptual imagination and the perceptual imagination. Here, for example, is the text of the first poem of *The Opening of the Field,* with the title serving as the first line:[21]

OFTEN I AM PERMITTED TO RETURN TO A MEADOW

as if it were a scene made-up by the mind,
that is not mine, but is a made place,

that is mine, it is so near to the heart,
an eternal pasture folded in all thought
so that there is a hall therein

that is a made place, created by light
wherefrom the shadows that are forms fall.

Wherefrom fall all architectures I am
I say are likenesses of the First Beloved
whose flowers are flames lit to the Lady.

She it is Queen Under The Hill
whose hosts are a disturbance of words within words
that is a field folded.

It is only a dream of the grass blowing
east against the source of the sun
in an hour before the sun's going down

whose secret we see in a children's game
of ring a round of roses told.

Often I am permitted to return to a meadow
as if it were a given property of the mind
that certain bounds hold against chaos,

that is a place of first permission,
everlasting omen of what is.

The language shows none of the verbal quirks and ruptures of Duncan's Stein imitations of the early 1950s. Instead, its smoothly seductive rhythms and hypnotic revolving of the words and images on their vowels and consonants work their magic, cast a spell of "words within words," so that what is concealed is revealed and what is revealed is concealed: the scene seen and unseen. And the scene is a composite or composed imagined landscape.

In August 1958, Duncan sent Levertov a version of the poem, begun in 1956 and revised through many previous drafts. In the same letter his gloss on the sources of the poem indicate the whirl of associations in the imagery:[22]

> In *The Opening of the Field* there was, and I've stuck to it, a basic fiction: the field that is: The poem as composed by field. (Feel?) See Olson's "Projective Verse"; the Field that Abraham bought for the cave of Machpelah "That I may bury my dead out of sight." It's third, a field in the earliest dream I remember, a hilltop meadow with the grass in no wind bowing towards the east, and a circle of children dancing a ring around me as It, to be crowned initiating the fullness of fear and the destruction of the world by flood.
>
> Now what do I *know* here? It's the pulse I go by –

Duncan points to the poem as an instance of composition by field, and his imagery is a characteristic fusion of literary, historical/religious/mythological, and personal sources. In Genesis Abraham purchased the field and cave of Machpelah, known as the Cave of the Patriarchs, as a burial place for himself, Isaac, Jacob and their wives, and in Judaism Machpelah became hallowed ground. The "destruction of the world by flood" alludes not only to the Genesis account of Noah but also to the legend of the sinking of the island of Atlantis. Duncan's adopted parents, ardent theosophists, had convinced him as a child that he had been reborn from a previous incarnation on Atlantis. The nursery rhyme of "ring a round of roses" derives from the medieval plague ("all fall down"), and Duncan's recurrent dream fuses childhood and death with him as "It" at the center of the ritualized game. The image recurs in a number of his poems as well as in Jess's apocalyptic painting "If All the World Were Paper And All the Water Sink" (1962) (with a silhouette of Duncan watching the game) as well as in Jess's illustration for the title page of *The Opening of the Field*.

The field evoked in the poem is, then, an imagined or "dream" site, "folded in all thought," enclosing the whole lifespan from childhood to death. It is at once "mine," "so near to the heart," yet it is also "not mine" but "eternal" and archetypal: the "everlasting omen of what is." Thus it is the "place of first permission": the platonic light source that projects all the shadowy forms of life and of all that "I am" in particular; yet the field is also the burial ground or "hall" of Machpelah into which all living forms fall. The children's game is a dance of death; sunrise and sunset coexist; the Queen Under The Hill is at once the Great Mother and Proserpina of the underworld "hall." The insistent rhyming of all/hall/fall sounds the existential round, and all the circlings of images and intimations are gathered and contained in a "made place": the "property" of the central "mind" of the speaker who is both subject and object ("me as It") of the game. The poem itself – the reverberant field of "words within words" – is the conscious mind's defensive "hold against" life's death dance. The repetition of the title line at the end folds the poem hermetically on its repeated "as if" and closes the circle.

Where Duncan's "Meadow" is a work of the conceptual imagination, "The Ripple" is an instance of Levertov's perceptual imagination.[23]

> On white linen the silk
> of gray shadows
> threefold, over-
> lapping, a
> tau cross.
> Glass jug and
> tumblers rise from
> that which they
> cast.
>
> And luminous
> in each
> overcast of
> cylindrical shade,
> image
> of water, a brightness
> not gold, not silver,
> rippling
> as if with laughter.

The perceptual imagination made for Levertov's "passion … for the vertebrate and cohesive in all art." From Williams she had learned the strategic use of line breaks to measure the process of perception, focus on individual details, and highlight the syntactical play of elements within a simple declarative sentence. Line breaks, she said, provide "a form of punctuation *additional* to the punctuation that forms part of the logic of completed thoughts. Linebreaks – together with the intelligent use of indentation and other devices of scoring – represent a peculiarly *poetic*, alogical, parallel (not competitive) punctuation."[24] The delicate lineation in "The Ripple" prompts the reader to see what might go unnoticed: the silken gray shadows on the white linen; the solid jug and glasses rising from their cast shadows; the luminous shimmering of jug-water in the shadows; the configuration of the shadows into a triform cross. The careful line breaks mark the mind's active participation in and response to the objects of the moment's perception: "rippling / as if with laughter." The tau cross is a sacred symbol in Egyptian mysteries as well as in the Judeo-Christian tradition, and as the only metaphor in the visual description it renders the mind's perception of the sacramental aura investing this simplest of everyday perceptions.

Years later Levertov would remark: "This acknowledgement, and celebration, of mystery probably constitutes the most consistent theme of my poetry from its very beginnings."[25] Again and again her poems of the 1950s and 1960s are epiphanies of wonder at the *Here and Now*, the title she gave her first American collection. In "The Depths," the word "sacred" expresses no easy sentimentality but a revelation of essence:[26]

> When the white fog burns off,
> the abyss of everlasting light
> is revealed. The last cobwebs
> of fog in the
> black firtrees are flakes
> of white ash in the world's hearth.
>
> Cold of the sea is counterpart
> to this great fire. Plunging
> out of the burning cold of ocean
> we enter an ocean of intense
> noon. Sacred salt
> sparkles on our bodies.
>
> After mist has wrapped us again
> in fine wool, may the taste of salt
> recall to us the great depths about us.

As in "The Ripple," light is the agent of sight and insight, as the meeting of land and sea reconciles the opposition between fire and water.

The last lines of "Claritas" (Latin *clarus* means "light") enact the declension from the supersensory to the sensory:[27]

> Sun
> light.
> 　　　Light
> light light light.

Capital S "Sun" becomes "light"; capital L "Light" proliferates into the multitudinous world of "light light light." The thrush in the poem, known in New England as "the All-Day Bird" because of its daylong singing, becomes a type of the artist, and the speaker "prays" to make her poem of praise as precise as the bird's song in the exact rendering of its subtly nuanced modulations. When Levertov sent "Claritas" to Duncan, his reply expressing admiration for the poem breaks, in mid-letter, into his own poem, published with slight revisions as "Answering" in *Roots and Branches*. While writing the letter, he heard a bird chirruping outside his window, unperturbed by the pneumatic drill from workmen repairing the street. Joining its song and hers, he "sings out" his response, italicized in the insistence of the concluding lines: *"The song's a work of the natural will. / The song's a work of the natural will."*[28]

Nevertheless, a comparison of the title poems of *Roots and Branches* and *O Taste and See*, both published in 1964, confirms, within their sense of shared enterprise, their different inflections of seeing into song. The opening lines of "Roots and Branches" transform the swarms of orange monarch butterflies that migrate each winter to the California coast into a profusion of metaphors, "tracing out of air unseen roots and branches of sense I share in thought." In the rest of the poem the butterflies become almost completely subsumed into figments of his imagination, stimuli in his consciousness that function to perfect his "inner view of things":[29]

> There are
>
> echoes of what I am in what you perform
> this morning, How you perfect my spirit!
> almost restore
> an imaginary tree of living in all its doctrines
> by fluttering about,
> intent and easy as you are, the profusion of you!
> awakening transports of an inner view of things.

Duncan's instinctive turn to inner vision had a physiological basis; his eyesight was impaired in a childhood accident, which left him cross-eyed and seeing a double image, one slightly higher and to the left of the other. This literal blurring of the physical world made Duncan all the more responsive to Levertov's acute sensory observation, but these Stevensian lines do indeed suggest Stevens's notion of the imaginative *mundo* as an alternate world. "Roots and Branches" moves quickly from the sight of the butterflies to the branching of his "inner view" into the words of the poem.

In contrast, for Levertov insight must be grounded in the perceived world. The opening lines of "O Taste and See" invert Wordsworth's famous declaration (in the sonnet "On Westminster Bridge") to insist instead: "The world is / not with us enough," with the hang at the line break emphasizing the inversion. The poem then glosses a subway poster with the famous verse from Psalm 34, "O taste and see the Lord is sweet," to mean "if anything all that lives / to the imagination's tongue." The Lord will be tasted only in all that nourishes body and spirit:[30]

> grief, mercy, language,
> tangerine, weather, to
> breathe them, bite,
> savor, chew, swallow, transform
>
> into our flesh our
> deaths, crossing the street, plum, quince,
> living in the orchard and being
>
> hungry, and plucking
> the fruit.

In a mortal Eden the fruit is to be eaten. Even abstractions like grief and mercy, life and death are not disembodied concepts but lived experiences as palpable to the imagination's tongue as plum and quince.

As Levertov and Duncan were swapping poems and commenting on each other's poems, they were clarifying their poetics, piecemeal in the letters and more systematically in essays. She reported to him in August 1962 that she had begun putting together her thoughts on organic form for a lecture. Before she completed the long gestation of that essay and sent it to him in October 1965, he wrote her in January 1964 that he was himself at work on a lecture, commissioned by the Voice of America, about his "concept of the poem." The results were Levertov's "Some Notes on Organic Form," first published in *Poetry* magazine for September 1965, and Duncan's "Towards an Open Universe," first published by Voice of America in *Contemporary American Poetry* in 1964. The two essays present succinct statements of the conceptual and perceptual strains of the Neoromantic imagination.

Levertov's essay posits a correspondence between the "organic form" of the poem and the forms of things in the world outside the observer's mind and extrinsic to language. The "conception of 'content' or 'reality' is functionally more important" than, and prior to, the poem because "first there must be an experience, a sequence or constellation of perceptions of sufficient interest, felt by the poet intensely enough to demand of him their equivalence in words: he is *brought to speech*." Levertov is clear about the metaphysical assumptions of her position: "For me, back of the idea of organic form is the concept that there is a form in all things (and in our experience) which the poet can discover and reveal." The shaping work of the imagination commences when it is "*brought to speech*" and activated to find the most precise and resonant "equivalence in words." The organic poet is therefore not inclined to fall back on established and "prescribed forms," which often imply that "content, reality, experience, is essentially fluid and must be given form"; instead, the organic poet seeks out the "inherent, though not immediately apparent, form" of the experience.[31]

Levertov cites the Romantic antecedents to her conception of composition by field: Coleridge, Emerson ("Ask the fact for the form"), and, most importantly, Hopkins: "Gerard Manley Hopkins invented the word 'inscape' to denote intrinsic form, the pattern of essential characteristics both in single objects and (what is more interesting) in objects in a state of relation to each other, and the word 'instress' to denote the experiencing of the perception of inscape, the apperception of inscape." She finds her "religious devotion to the truth, to the splendor of the authentic" in the etymological roots of words:[32]

> To contemplate comes from "*templum*, temple, a place, a space for observation, marked out by the augur." It means, not simply to observe, to regard, but to do these things in the presence of a god. And to meditate is "to keep the mind in a state of contemplation"; its synonym is "to muse," and to muse comes from a word meaning "to stand with open mouth" – not so comical if we think of "inspiration" – to breathe in.
>
> So – as the poet stands open-mouthed in the temple of life, contemplating his experience, there come to him the first words of the poem: the words which are to be his way in to the poem, if there is to be a poem.

Since the culminating "moment of vision, of crystallization ... occurs as words," "the metric movement, the measure, is the direct expression of the movement of perception," and the rest of the essay proceeds with a nuts-and-bolts discussion of how the elements of composition – rhythm, rhyme, repetitions and variations, harmonies and dissonances, line breaks, spaces and indentations – realize the poetic organism. The essay "Line breaks, Stanza-Spaces, and the Inner Voice" is an illustrative exercise in explicating the evolution of her poem "The Tulips."[33]

When Levertov sent "Some Notes on Organic Form" to Duncan, his initial response was to note that his experience of form was more fluid and multiphasic than hers: "not a mandala or wheel but a mobile." Twice he extracts with approval her phrase "a method of recognizing what we perceive" but detaches it from the large metaphysical claim behind the phrase as it appears in the essay. She wrote: "A partial definition ... of organic poetry might be that it is a method of apperception, i.e., of recognizing what we perceive, and is based on an intuition of an order, a form beyond forms, in which forms partake, and of which man's creative works are analogies, resemblances, natural allegories. Such poetry is exploratory." Duncan responds by redefining organic form not as natural allegory but as aesthetic self-determination: organic form should not be construed to mean that it "seeks to imitate the growth forms of shell, tree, or human body," but rather must mean that "the poem itself is an organism grow-ing (living) into its own life as a form."[34] Levertov did not at the time take note of Duncan's elision from language as referential to language as self-referential: a crucial shift that would lead the Language poets of the 1970s to regard Duncan as a forebear.

The Romantic in Duncan, however, could see the danger of entrap-ment in such self-referentiality, and in "Towards an Open Universe" he described the poem of "inward vision" as "a happening in language, that leads back into or on towards the beauty of the universe itself." The con-figuration of "our own personal consciousness" in words adumbrates "also the inner structure of the universe," so that the immanence of the poet in the poem is analogous to "the immanence of the Creator in Creation." However, the differences with Levertov are significant. Where she con-centers the forms of reality and reality of forms in an apperception of the "form beyond forms," Duncan sees a radically open universe with the shifting circulations of "self-consciousness" tracing "the transcendent con-sciousness of the dance." Because of the fluidity of reality, "the poet and the poem are one in a moving process"; poems are "part of the evolving and continuing work of a poetry I could never complete."[35]

By 1968, when the crisis of the Vietnam War was making clearer the differences between him and Levertov, Duncan cites Heraclitus at the beginning of the essay "Man's Fulfillment in Order and Strife," and goes on to argue that order is indistinguishable from disorder as the poles of a dynamic interchange: "Nature is unnatural, Order is disordering." Amidst the indeterminate and violent fluidity of nature and history, the poem's "truth does not lie outside the art" but, on the contrary, in its own making. Duncan could confess to Levertov: "I *am* apprehensive of my idolatry of the poem ..." Nevertheless, more and more firmly was he convinced that only through "a supreme effort of consciousness" might the poet recover the "gnosis of the ancients" beyond the unremitting "War of Contending Powers" and conjure the hidden truth or "Secret Doctrine" in poems that might constitute "the Gnosis of the modern world." In fact, for him the poem is "an occult document" precisely because language – through the nuances of "syntax, morphology, etymology, psychology" – can strive to apprehend "the exchange of opposites, the indwelling of the one in the other" as "phases of a dynamic unity." "Towards an Open Universe," he told Levertov, proposes "the concept of a poem as a lasting event contributing to the human reality we call language": not the poem as perceived reality but the poem as hermetic reality.[36]

The "wisdom" that Olson dismissed as "pretentious fictions" Duncan saw as *Fictive Certainties*, the title he gave his collection of essays, including "Towards an Open Universe" and "Man's Fulfillment in Order and Strife." For her part, Levertov called her first book of essays, including "Some Notes on Organic Form," *The Poet in the World*.

II

During the late 1960s the seemingly minor dissonances in the loving concord between Duncan and Levertov became an increasingly disruptive discord that finally ended their long friendship. The issue that forced them to face their differences came with their shared opposition to the Vietnam War and turned on the question of how poetry can and should address violence, how the imagination can and should engage politics. After initially trying to minimize their widening differences, they were too true to themselves to dissemble or evade. All the accumulated weight of their long trust in each other makes all the more painful and poignant the barrage of letters in late 1971, when they stood, toe to toe, and battled it out.

The sources of their disagreement were not so much political or even aesthetic as theological: the different religious orientations from family and childhood that informed their adult sensibilities. Born in Oakland in 1919, Duncan was adopted as an infant by theosophical parents, in fact was chosen for adoption astrologically, based on the date and time of his birth. He grew up (first in Oakland and then in Bakersfield) in a household and extended family steeped in a mix of occult traditions: alchemy and astrology, Rosicrucianism and the Kabbala, Mme. Blavatsky and Hermes Trismegistus. Though as an adult he took all symbolic systems not as matters of doctrine but rather as metaphors of the activity of consciousness, his consciousness was thoroughly imbued with the gnosticism at the heart of the various occult symbologies. Jess shared Duncan's hermetic and theosophical interests and painted Duncan's portrait as the "Enamourd Mage," seated at a desk fronted by hefty hermetic volumes with their titles fully legible. Thus Duncan wrote in a continuity and tradition of mages; as we heard him say, "the Secret Doctrine" that offers "the Gnosis of the modern world" makes the activity of imagination a kind of "magic" and the poem "an occult document."[37] The open-ended sequence that was the major labor of the last twenty-five years of his life is called "Passages": verbal passages mapping the maze of his heterodox imagination.

Levertov was born in Ilford, on the eastern periphery of London, in 1923, and she too traced her mystical inclinations, more orthodoxly rooted in the Judeo-Christian tradition, to her parents and her education at home (she and her older sister Olga never went to school). Her father was a Hasidic Jew from Russia who converted to Christianity, married a Welsh woman, and emigrated to England, where he was ordained an Anglican priest and, in addition to ministering to a parish, became a widely published voice in Jewish-Christian dialogue between the two world wars. Levertov's Welsh ancestors numbered a two visionaries well known in their day. She was not a practicing Christian and described herself as a religious agnostic at the time she began her friendship with Duncan. However, the incarnational and sacramental character of the faith in which she was raised made her poems, certainly by the time of *Here and Now*, epiphanies of the everyday sacredness of the perceived world.

From the beginning, then, the poetic explorations of Duncan and Levertov proceeded in directions more divergent than they could for a long time fully recognize: the poem as hermetic gnosis, the poem as natural allegory. Historically, gnosticism is hermetic and platonist; radically dualistic in its conception of physical, moral, and spiritual life, it posits an irreconcilable opposition between spirit and matter, good and evil: "the War of Contending Powers," Duncan called it. In the various formulations of different hermetic cults, gnosis – a spiritual insight open only to a gifted elite of initiated individuals – reveals spirit as fallen into material bodies, trapped in mortal flesh and threatened constantly by physical and moral corruption, so that spirit must strive to hold itself untainted by physical existence until death releases it back into immortality. Duncan adapted the theosophy he learned at home to his own humanist purposes, eliding the agon of spirit into the agon of consciousness: "Consciousness is God, the occult tradition says. 'Consciousness is self,' Olson puts it." For Duncan, God, insofar as we can know him, is consciousness, and consciousness, insofar as we realize it, is godlike. As he put it to Levertov, "ποιειν [*poiein*] the process of Making is Creation itself, our individual awakening to creation we are involved in." The godlike consciousness realizes its own apotheosis by making the contentions of the material, temporal existence into "the poem as a supreme effort of consciousness." Already in 1953 Duncan had cited Plato and St. Augustine (who was himself steeped in Manicheism before his conversion to Christianity) to declare: "Soul is the body's dream of its continuity in eternity – a wraith of mind. Poetry is the very life of the soul: the body's discovery that it can dream. And perish into its own imagination."[38]

In contrast to gnosticism, the Judeo-Christian tradition proclaims not just a personal God but Emmanuel, God-with-us, engaged in material and social existence, immersed in human history, for Christians incarnate in the flesh and bone of Jesus. There has been and is a persistent strain of asceticism and gnosticism in Judaism and Christianity, absorbed from the neoplatonist philosophies and gnostic sects of the centuries just before and after the birth of Christ, but that inclination runs counter to the radical vision of God-with-us. Salvation is not redemption *from* the body but redemption *of* the body. God-with-us reconciled the dualism of matter and spirit, once for all but to be realized, generation by generation and person by person. In the Judeo-Christian tradition, therefore, redemption is not a privilege reserved for the initiated individual or elite but is the personal and public responsibility of the whole people in communion. During the stresses of the 1960s, Levertov did not belong to a religious community, Jewish or Christian. However, in rallying the poetic community to oppose the war and in joining the larger community of resisters, she found herself justifying her ethic of collective action by recourse to theological and moral assumptions rooted in her religious upbringing at home.

The letters and poems of the 1960s record the gradual and then sudden divergence between Duncan and Levertov. A letter of January 12, 1964 reflects how close the symbiosis between anima and animus still was. After chatting about a number of things, including poems they have written, Duncan breaks unexpectedly into a poem that names Levertov muse to the musings of his consciousness:[39]

> I'd
> been in the course of a letter, I am
> in the course of a letter to a friend
> who comes close in to my thought so that
> the day is hers, my hand writing
> in thought shakes in the currents, of air?
> of an inner anticipation of? ghostly
> exhilarations in the thought of her
>
> ....
>
> You stand behind the where-I-am.
> The deep tones and shadows I will call a woman.

> The quick high notes ... you are a girl there too,
> and I would play Orpheus for you again

The letter concludes with "I'm a little shaky with this having happened here" and signs off "with love still shaking a bit." By return mail Levertov recognized how special that moment was: "That's a beautiful poem. Thanks, for it & for the letter"; and in 1968 she wrote a long-ish poem called "A Tree Telling of Orpheus," that can be read on one level as a response to Duncan's playing Orpheus. Duncan's spontaneous poem became the title poem of *Bending the Bow* (1968) and it led, in the weeks immediately after the letter, to the first poems in the long series of "Passages" that would be the central undertaking of his poetry for the rest of his life. *Bending the Bow* contains the first thirty "Passages," written between 1964 and 1968.

"Passages" is a challenging series (rather than sequence) of poems, dense with literary, mythological, historical, and personal allusions, lines spaced out across the page to indicate the pauses and transitions and associative leaps in the poet's consciousness. The text requires and rewards the kind of sleuthing explication that readers have given Pound's *Cantos*, and indeed "Passages" and Olson's *Maximus Poems*, well under way when Duncan began "Passages," follow *The Cantos* in the evolution of the Modernist epic of consciousness from Romantic prototypes like *The Prelude* and *Leaves of Grass*.

The opening "Passages" establish the terms and tones of Duncan's undertaking. The epigraph for the whole series comes from Julian the Apostate's gnostic *Hymn to the Mother of the Gods*, and the first poem, "Tribal Memories," transforms the archetypal woman/muse of "Bending the Bow" into Mnemosyne, mother of the muses, and the "World-Egg" into the matrix of the poet-offspring's consciousness: "enclosed, in a shell of murmurings, // rimed round, / sound-chamberd child." "At the Loom: Passages 2," dated "Feb. 4–11 1964" and citing *The Cantos*, invokes the image of Kirke at the loom, weaving her song into words. In her witch-woman's weaving the warp stands metaphorically for the "set strings of the music": the conventions of syntax and metrics, the historically accumulated denotations and connotations of words. If the "cords [chords] that bind" become too tight, they become "a warp of the will," constricting the free movement of the imagination. However, "my mind" as "shuttle" in Kirke's hands moves through the warp; its "weft of dream" in "the word-flow / the rivering web" gathers "the wool into its full cloth" so that the design in the poem's fabric reveals "[t]he secret! the secret! It's hid / in its showing forth."[40]

By "Where It Appears: Passages 4," Duncan seeks complete release from "the warp of the will," into the boundless freedom of the open universe:

> I'd cut the warp
> to weave that web
>   in the air
>   and here
> let image perish in image,
>   leave writer and reader
>   up in the air
>   to draw
>   momentous
>   inconclusions ...

"Passages" becomes a venture into an undetermined and indeterminate "area of self-creation." The Enamourd Mage, seated in Jess's portrait behind his occult texts, floats his airy inconclusions to counter the "magi of the probable," who think that the art work is a reflecting "mirror" that "I hold in the palm of my hand," a circle that can define and "surround / what is boundless."[41] Duncan wants instead to be a mage of the improbable gnosis, whose inconclusive images, though "up in the air" and of the moment, are nonetheless "momentous" intimations of the numinous secret shadowed forth in the perishing images of material existence.

By July 1964, Levertov had received the first fifteen "Passages," and in a long letter, beginning "Chèr Robèrt," she voiced, amidst the admiring praise, several questions and two revealing criticisms. The last lines of "At the Loom" about the battle she found "tacked on" to "the loom poem," not growing out "of what precedes it but ... irrelevant to it"; and "Where It Appears," she had to admit, is just "obscure to me." What is at issue for her is clarity of focus in the organic integration of the poem. Duncan pushed back on these two objections. Her suggestion that the "tacked on" section be either cut or made into a separate poem would have merit, he tells her, "if the poem is thought of as an organic form ... But what I have in mind ... is to be free of that 'forge, loom, lyre' and work in the air." Indeed, "Where It Appears" is "obscure to you" precisely because it "states as a purpose what you wouldn't accept – that the poem, woven in air, is to be cut loose from its warp ... and that I propose 'momentous inconclusions' ..." His proposed purpose is not, like hers, to connect but, on the contrary, "to *disconnect*."[42]

Levertov's objections, however, had more than a literary basis. During the mid-1960s, while the Mage, inspired by his anima, was seeking in "Passages" the "widest range for the play of the poem,"[43] the Poet in

the World was finding her own poems moving oppositely into political engagement. Through her childhood and girlhood Levertov's parents
had been staunch advocates for social justice and against anti-Semitism,
and her sister Olga had remained a left-wing activist in England. By the
mid-1960s the accelerating violence in Vietnam was drawing Levertov
and her husband into nonviolent protest against the imperialist war
driven by the same capitalist structures that made for racism, classism, and ecological devastation at home. "During the Eichmann Trial,"
Levertov's first political poem, stands out from the poems of celebratory
wonder that surround it in *The Jacob's Ladder*, but *The Sorrow Dance*
(1967), despite celebratory poems like "Psalm Concerning the Castle"
and "A Vision," marks a distinctly darkening tone and deepening political awareness.

"A Lamentation" is an elegy for Olga Levertoff, who died in 1964 after
a stormy life, often estranged from parents and younger sister – "Grief,
have I denied thee? / Grief, I have denied thee" – and the "Olga Poems"
that followed "A Lamentation" mourn her tragic life while acknowledging
her unflagging fight for radical social change. In "A Note to Olga (1966)"
Levertov associates her own turn to political action with her reconnection to Olga, as she imagines Olga behind her in a Stop-the-War march
in Times Square, singing "We Shall Overcome" with her and the other
protesters as they are arrested.[44] Duncan commended the Olga poems, but
the concluding poems of *The Sorrow Dance*, a section titled "Life at War,"
contains the poems that would become an increasingly contested issue
with Duncan through the last years of the decade.

In a letter of January 25, 1966, Levertov submitted the poem "Life at
War" to Duncan with some anxiety as her first "absolutely direct anti-war
poem (finished this very day, though 'brewed' & begun with false starts
back in, oh, October I guess)." Here are the lines from the poem that
would provoke the dispute:[45]

> We have breathed the grits of it in, all our lives,
> our lungs are pocked with it,
> the mucous membrane of our dreams
> coated with it, the imagination
> filmed over with the gray filth of it:
>
> the knowledge that humankind,
>
> delicate Man, whose flesh
> responds to a caress, whose eyes
> are flowers that perceive the stars,

whose music excels the music of birds,
whose laughter matches the laughter of dogs,
whose understanding manifests designs
fairer than the spider's most intricate web,

still turns without surprise, with mere regret
to the scheduled breaking open of breasts whose milk
runs out over the entrails of still-alive babies,
transformation of witnessing eyes to pulp-fragments,
implosion of skinned penises into carcass-gulleys.

We are the humans, men who can make;
whose language imagines *mercy*,
lovingkindness; we have believed one another
mirrored forms of a God we felt as good –

who do these acts, who convince ourselves
it is necessary; these acts are done
to our own flesh; burned humanflesh
is smelling in Vietnam as I write.

Along with "Life at War," Levertov's letter included "A Vision," "a completely *dis*engaged poem about angels," and she nervously voiced uncertainty about the new turn in her poetry, perhaps in anticipation of his response: "I'm very unsure if the 'political' one is a good poem but it is even so a tremendous relief to have at least opened my mouth."

Duncan had recently sent "Earth's Winter Song," a "Xmas poem" that used the Annunciation and Nativity as ironic frame for his own outrage at the Vietnam War. In the next paragraph of her letter Levertov proceeds to state her "considerable reservations" about "Earth's Winter Song" on the very grounds that Duncan will later use to indict "Life At War": the inadequacy of diction and imagery for the emotional weight they are intended to carry, and the judgmental self-righteousness in personal denunciations like the following: "Wearing the unctuous mask of Johnson, / from his ass-hole emerging the hed [sic] of Humphrey, / he bellows and begins over Asia and America / the slaughter of the innocents and the reign of wrath." She could see that "exactly what I am saying about 'Earth's Winter Song' may be true of 'Life at War,'" and her uneasiness in making the critique, she tells him, is intensified by her sense of a widening rift between them.[46]

Her trepidation over challenging "[m]y Master, my Orpheus" only increased when he did not reply for weeks and then months, and in April she anxiously sent a letter that is a poem, acknowledging that their opposition to the war has created a crisis between them. The poem-letter ends:

> I send you therefore
> as if on a seagull's wing
> one word –
>
> what word shall it be? –
> 'Love'? – I love you but
> I love
>   another, as you do.
> Love I send, but I send it
> in another word.
>   Longing?
>   Poetry.

The irony was, as Levertov must have known, that it was precisely poetry that was the pressing issue between them. She was relieved when Duncan at last wrote to thank her for the "lovely" letter-poem and to call "A Vision" "one of your miraculously beautiful and realized poems." However, he made no immediate comment about either "Earth's Winter Song" or "Life at War" and instead discussed "Soldiers," one of a spate of antiwar "Passages," published as *Of the War: Passages 22–27* (1966). Only in 1970, after he had distanced himself from the war in his poetry and was condemning "Life at War" and others of Levertov's war poems, did he admit "how right you were about my 'Earth's Winter Song.' "[47]

Their roles, however, were soon reversed. With her rapidly deepening commitment to the protest movement, Levertov praised the Vietnam "Passages" and published "Up Rising" in the *Nation*, where she was at the time poetry editor. But for his part Duncan recoiled from her Christmas poem "Advent 1966" with "an agonizing sense of how the monstrosity of this nation's War is taking over your life." The Orpheus-master instructed her sternly that despite the war they must both "continue as constantly in our work ... now more than ever" and not betray their vocations as visionary poets. Even as *Of the War* was being published, he attributed the vehemence of his outrage in part to his high blood pressure and warned her against being consumed and transformed by the violence she was protesting. Aware that his war poems are at least as violent and graphic in language and imagery as hers are, he set about sublimating the violence into a "larger context." *Of the War*, he told her, had to be read within the encompassing vision of "Passages," wherein a poem like "Up Rising" underwent a "sea change or alchemical phase towards rendering up its purely poetic identity, where the figures do not *refer* to contemporary history only but are happenings in the poem itself." He distinguished "Up Rising" from Levertov's "kind of witness" because "ultimately it belongs to the reality of that poem ["Passages"] and a vision of Man. And

I do not answer for myself in my work but for Poetry."[48] He would keep the man and the poet in separate activities, faithfully wearing a black armband against the war but striving (not entirely successfully) to keep the war from overtaking the larger poetic vision.

Duncan went on to deconstruct Levertov's witness by questioning the genuineness of her engagement with the war. In August 1966, even before the admonition to Levertov cited above, he quoted to her the lines from "Life at War" about the "breaking open of breasts" and the "implosion of skinned penises" and, apparently without a sense of condescension, expressed concern that the strong emotion here arose not from her compassionate concern for the victims of war but from an unacknowledged neurotic tangle of repressed anger and resentment: 'The words in their lines are the clotted mass of some operation ... having what root in you I wonder?" Her long response by return mail countered, with underlinings, that the poem came from "the extreme *strangeness* of men actually *planning* violence to each other" and argued that "my participation in the Peace Movement" helped her "to grasp with the imagination what does happen in war – so that even if one hasn't been there, in the flesh, one doesn't let the horror of war just be an *empty* word – all our words have to be filled up with, be backed by imaginative experience." She did allow herself to wonder whether "the horror *at* violence" might have some connection with "my own violent temper" or "my anxieties, my 'imagination of disaster,'" but added: "I'm not sure where such questions lead."[49]

Despite their efforts to avoid a showdown, lines of differentiation and opposition were being drawn. Duncan to Levertov: "the question of poetry is *not* whether one feels outrage at the war or feels whatever – other than the imperative of the poem. It's the force of word-work ... that I miss." Levertov to Duncan:

> I stand fast by what has caused me to *feel*. And the range of response in you & me overlaps – & that is a large area – but beyond the area of overlap extends in quite different directions. Years ago that shamed & embarrassed me – but not now. You are more the Master, a Master poet in my world, not less, just because I feel that the only emulation of such a master is to be *more oneself.*

The declension from "the Master" to "a Master" to herself as "master" did not go unnoticed: "It does seem clear, Denny, that you are more an expressive poet than a formalist: the poem so often bears the burden of conveying the feel of something or the emotion aroused by something or a thought – giving rise to the poem instead of the poem giving rise to its own objects."⁵⁰ There was the breaking point, out in the clear: experience giving rise to the poem, the poem giving rise to itself.

Levertov's increasing involvement in speeches, marches, demonstrations, and in her husband's much-publicized trial with five others for conspiring against the military draft law slowed and tempered but did not stop their correspondence, and the dialogue between their differences carried over into the poems themselves. Just as reading "Claritas" with and against his "Answering" encapsulates where Levertov and Duncan stood in 1962, reading Duncan's "Santa Cruz Propositions" and "A Seventeenth Century Suite" with and against Levertov's book length notebook poem "Staying Alive" encapsulates where they stood by the late 1960s. "Staying Alive," written in pieces between 1968 and 1971 out of the same cultural and personal crisis as Lowell's *Notebook* and Rich's *Leaflets*, is unlike any other Levertov poem in its length and diffuseness. A mélange of fragments and short poems interspersed with prose, quotations, headlines, and newspaper excerpts, "Staying Alive," while following her involvement in protest and resistance, also bravely raises the very question that Duncan pressed home: whether her political activism was not sapping her creative energies and visionary wonder.

Duncan derided the refrain "Revolution or death" in Part I of "Staying Alive" as hollow propaganda and pointed out that the word "revolution" meant not change but turning in place ("an endless rolling of the wheel"). Responding in Part II, Levertov admitted the imprecision of the word but clarified her meaning: "A new life / isn't the old life in reverse, negative of the same photo. / But it's the only / word we have …" For her, a line from a Rilke notebook caught the moral and existential imperative behind her anxiety: *"Life that / wants to live. / / (Unlived life / of which one can die.)"*⁵¹ The contention with Duncan impelled Levertov to return to Rilke, her first mentor before "I first came to America and began to read Williams, Pound, and Stevens." From the Modernists she had engaged formal issues of style and technique, but from Rilke she had learned at the outset the essentially moral "concept of the artist's task – a serious, indeed a lofty concept": "my first lesson from Rilke – *experience* what you live: to the artist, whatever is *felt through* is not without value, for it becomes part of the ground from which one grows." Rilke's "passion for 'inseeing'" proposed a "sense of aesthetic ethics" that ran counter to Duncan's hermetic aestheticism. By making "no distinction between meeting art and meeting life," Rilke "shows the poet a way to bridge the gap between the conduct of living and the conduct of art," and in that effort "the underlying necessity was to ask not others but *oneself* for confirmation."⁵²

In October 1968, Duncan saw with dismay a televised film clip of Levertov in a red dress speaking at a protest demonstration with what seemed to him unrestrained fury, and he associated her image with the passage from "Staying Alive" in which Levertov quotes folksinger Judy Collins's plea at an antiwar rally ("We must *not* be angry, we must L-O-O-O-V-E") and then questions it: "Judy understand: / there comes a time when only anger / is love." Duncan responded with Part III of "Santa Cruz Propositions" whose opening line "It is Denise I am thinking of – " unleashes a furious invocation of her as Kali, the Hindu goddess of death and destruction:[53]

> *SHE* appears, Kālī dancing, whirling her necklace of skulls,
> trampling the despoiling armies and the exploiters of natural resources
> under her feet. Revolution or Death!
> Wine! The wine of men's blood in the vat
> of the Woman's anger, whirling,
>
> ⋯⋯
>
> Madame Outrage of the Central Committee
> forms a storm cloud around her where she is brooding.
>
> ⋯⋯
>
> She has put on her dress of murderous red.
> She has put on her mini-skirt and the trampling begins.
> She has put on her make-up of the Mother of Hell,
>
> ⋯⋯
>
>   from the center of terror
>   that is the still eye of the storm in her:
>
> *"There comes a time when only Anger is Love."*

The fury in these lines raises the question of just who was running out of control, but Duncan sent Levertov "Santa Cruz Propositions" in October 1970, merely with the bland notation that she comes into the text as Kali dancing. Her hurt and baffled response comes in Part IV of "Staying Alive": "And meanwhile Robert / sees me as Kali! No, / I am not Kali, I can't sustain for a day / that anger." Later she would explain to him that what he took as rage was really her anxious nervousness when she was told, as she was rushed on stage, that her longer prepared remarks had to be cut to "exactly 3 minutes." Yes, she had blurted out her message, but, she told him, if he had listened to what she actually said, he would have heard a message of nonviolent resistance to the carnage of war.[54]

These later remarks came in the extraordinary exchange of very long letters in October–November 1971, in which the old friends stood their ground and had it out at last. On the psychology of the poems, Duncan to Levertov: "I think the poems like 'Life at War,' 'What They Were Like,' 'Tenebrae,' and 'Enquiry' are not to be read properly in relation to Viet Nam ... but in relation to the deep underlying consciousness of the woman as a victim in war with the Man." Levertov to Duncan: "You say my poems which talk about Viet Nam aren't at bottom about Viet Nam at all but about the sex war. That is unmitigated bullshit, Robert." On the didacticism of the poems as her evasion of their neurotic source in her psyche, Duncan to Levertov: "it is moralizing that sets in"; "it is the *poem* itself that is not listening, that has turned to the vanity that all moralizing is in order to evade the imminent content of the announced theme." Levertov to Duncan: "People in general *have* shared this belief, basically, in many times and places. A faith in man's potential, his capacity for goodness. Certainly in Christian times at least. The concept of the Incarnation is the concept of Man's redeemability, however fallen into corruption, for man was made in God's image. Even sceptics and atheists cannot help being culturally affected by that concept."[55]

The single sentence that epitomizes their differences is Duncan's flat declaration: "The poet's role is not to oppose evil, but to imagine it ..." In the 1968 essay "Man's Fulfillment in Order and Strife" Duncan had made a similar assertion: "Hitler cannot be defeated; he must be acknowledged and understood." Behind these assertions lies the gnostic dualism that sees good and evil as the irreconcilable but constituent poles of temporal existence, so that "the War of Contending Powers" is the inescapable human condition. In Duncan's insistent caps to Levertov, "THERE HAS BEEN NO TIME IN HUMAN HISTORY THAT WAS NOT A TIME OF WAR." Since "the very nature of man" is thus at war with itself, the only transcendence possible is acknowledging the stain of evil, as he had done, in a hermetic poem visionary enough to imagine a cosmic harmony beyond or behind the irreconcilable clash of opposites. "[M]y sense in *Up Rising*," he would insist in the heat of argument, "was not that the war was or was not important to me, but how come it was of import to the poem. Nor was I concerned to attack the war in the poem, but to follow thru the vision of the war ..."[56] Duncan inscribed my copy of *Of the War* with the gnostic injunction: "in the slaughter of men's hopes distil the divine potion that stirs sight of the hidden"; he inscribed my copy of *Bending the Bow* with the neoplatonist line: "In the War now I make a Celestial Cave."

His notion of conscience and moral responsibility was the anarchist injunction "to stand by the individual life." "[T]he righteous

Conscience – what Freudians call The Super Ego" urges opposing evil and doing good, but "I draw back from commanding conscience as I wld avoid whatever tyranny of the will ..." Even Christ's "writing in the place of 'Thou shalt not kill' his 'Thou shalt love'" bound the "free immediate individual experience of choice" into a coercive morality which said that "no man is free until *all* be free; no man has life until *all* have life." For Duncan the only ethics were individualist, and the only politics anarchist: "I would evade the inner command, even as I would evade the social command." Such a position could hardly be more different from Levertov's conviction that "the concept of the Incarnation" means that "'We are members one of another.' I've always believed that even if it was St Paul, whom I dislike on many counts, who said it." Realizing that with these sharp exchanges they were only hurting each other, Levertov declared a "truce, in all courtesy and good faith," in which for a year and a half they would not discuss poetry.[57]

Despite the truce, Duncan could not let go of their wrangle. In March 1972, he sent Levertov "A Seventeenth Century Suite," pointing Levertov to two middle sections of the suite to signal their differences: "Sections 4 and 5 are drawn from your 'Advent 1966' poem – tho not from your poem ... but from your reference points: (a) Southwell's poem and (b) photographs of napalm victims." Levertov's "Advent 1966" recalled Robert Southwell's Christmas poem "The Burning Babe" to contrast Southwell's Christian vision of the birth and death of Jesus as redemptive with the unredeemable and senseless slaughter and incineration of Vietnamese children. Six years after the blow-up, Duncan responded to Levertov's poem by rewriting its message in his own version of "The Burning Babe." Duncan's Christ-child is "no more than an image in Poetry," transformed by "Imagination's alchemy" into "Art's epiphany of Art new born, / a Christ of Poetry, the burning spirit's show ..."[58]

What Levertov called their "love and co-respondence" as visionary poets had reached an unbridgeable "rupture."[59] Where Duncan was metaphysically platonist and gnostic, religiously polytheist, morally manichaean and individualist, politically anarchist, and linguistically self-reflexive, Levertov was metaphysically incarnationalist, religiously monotheist and Christian, morally communitarian, politically socialist, and linguistically referential. Their divergent conceptions of the imagination and of poetry were at base the divergence between a gnostic theology and an incarnational theology. From this point on, as Duncan's conceptual poetry revealed ever more unmistakably its hermetic character, Levertov's perceptual poetry revealed ever more unmistakably its sacramental character.

In "Passages 36," part of "A Seventeenth Century Suite" dated December 16, 1971, Duncan wrote of "the end of an old friendship, / the admission of neglect rancoring, / mine of her, hers of what I am." Their friendship might still have survived on some different basis had Duncan not allowed James Mersmann to publish, in his book on poets and the Vietnam War, Duncan's vicious description of Levertov's war poems as her own sexual fantasies. In 1973, Duncan admitted to Levertov that "my adverse readings" of her war poems arose from "an inner disturbance with what the Jungians call the *Anima*," but that he hoped to "rearrive at what I feel to be a just reading" of her work. However, in the interview quoted in Mersmann's book the year before this conciliatory letter to Levertov, Duncan had said that the depiction of violence in a poem like "Life at War" with its "charged, bloody, sexual" imagery revealed "her own sadism, and masochism" so that the war acts only as "a magnet" for her own violence and "the poem is not a protest though she thinks she's protesting." Levertov told him flatly that she expected him to "apologize and perhaps print a retraction some place," but in the next letter he did not address her demand, merely reporting that "a little suite of poems has begun that are dedicated to you." Only in November 1978 did he send the completed poem "The Torn Cloth," which begins: "We reaving / –'re-weaving' I had meant / to write." The Freudian slip substituting "reaving" for "re-weaving" indicates his ambivalence in the effort to "weave the reaving / into the heart of my / wedding clothes," "into the fabric of intentions." She wrote back sadly that though she felt no "negative emotion," even anger "so long after," he'd "waited too long" to respond, "and so although I would have *liked* to feel ... the relief and joy and deep satisfaction that I might once have felt, the fact is that I *did* not, and do not." She felt only "our friendship twice broken, deeply betrayed."[60]

Levertov would come to feel that "I was too stubborn ... unChristianly stiffnecked" about his failure to apologize or retract, but "at the time I was unable to think that way." At a reading in 1984 Duncan prefaced "The Torn Cloth" with the admission that he was driven by some inner "daemon" to push their friendship to the breaking point.[61] Her response to "The Torn Cloth" would come in "To R. D., March 4, 1988," which records "an extraordinarily vivid dream" that she had the month after his death. Echoing his last poem to her, she tells him that although she had "put you away like a folded cloth," in the dream she is sitting in the Lady Chapel of a church when he takes the seat beside her:

> I put a welcoming hand
> over yours, and your hand was warm.
> I had no need
> for a mentor, nor you to be one;
> but I was once more
> your chosen sister, and you
> my chosen brother.
> We heard strong harmonies rise and begin to fill
> the arching stone,
> sounds that had risen here through centuries.

She immediately sent the poem to Jess, and he "assured me that Robert's affection for me had remained intact."[62]

III

In 1984, the Poetry Society of America recognized the long and fruitful association between Duncan and Levertov by conferring on them jointly the Shelley Memorial Award. In her last letter to Duncan, Levertov wrote solicitously about the kidney failure that would take his life four years later, and added: "felicitations on the 1/2 a Shelley prize – I expect they told you I am getting the other 1/2!"[63] But the fatal break in the fall of 1971 marks the increasingly divergent directions of their later poems.

In Duncan's work, war as the condition of existence runs from the 1950 poem "An Essay at War" through *Of the War* to "Man's Fulfillment in Order and Strife." Language enacts the contention of order in disorder, of disorder toward order, and "God" is the capacity in the human consciousness to imagine order in disorder, to write the poem toward Poetry. "The word 'God' becomes necessary where there is an intense feeling of presence and oneness in opposites, an awe that cannot let go of contradictory elements, of an otherness in which I am more truly 'I.'" Reading Emerson's Transcendentalist "Self-Reliance" in the "Hermetic and Rosicrucian tradition," Duncan marvels at "how Emersonian my spirit is," but at the same time his "Calvinist predisposition" makes him "read my Emerson dark." Duncan rejects the metaphysics of the ancient Gnostics in which the material word is a "grand trap" from which the human spirit must be sublimated into Spirit and instead grounds his gnosticism in the material world with God as "the largest consciousness we have of our 'I' in our belonging to the process of the Cosmos." In effect, God is "the labor of Spirit in every being and thing towards Its Self-realization."[64]

Poems, then, are the "ground work" in the divinization of the visionary consciousness, and the paradoxical culmination of the work is the sublimation of consciousness into the language of the poem: "not myself, or *the* Self, but yet another dimension, the work Itself, the poem Itself, where Poetry Itself appeard." The poet expires into the poem, into Poetry itself: "The poem, not the poet, seeks to be immortal."[65] In 1968, the year not only of "Man's Fulfillment in Order and Strife" but also of the publication of *Bending the Bow*, Duncan declared his intention to free his poetry from the encumbering expectations of readers, critics, and publishers so that it might evolve into its largest consciousness of the process of the Cosmos, and in that pursuit he would publish no collection of poems for at least fifteen years. *Ground Work: Before the War* was published in 1984, fifteen years after *Bending the Bow*, and *Ground Work: In the Dark* in 1988, the year of his death. *Before the War* suggests the poems' aspiration toward a state of consciousness antecedent to and beyond the contentions of mortal existence, and *In the Dark* acknowledges that the progression toward the light is, paradoxically, a progression toward death.

So the enamoured Mage withdrew to his desk and books, and the poems draw on and proceed from favorite sources: neoplatonist philosophers and theosophists, Dante and the seventeenth-century metaphysicals, Baudelaire and Mallarmé, Pound and H.D. and Stevens. There continue to be marvelous short, individual poems like "Achilles' Song" and "Bring It Up from the Dark," "Styx" and "The Sentinels." But Duncan's psychological and imaginative withdrawal in the 1970s and 1980s increasingly made for long sequences ("Dante Etudes" is forty pages long), at the same time that the ongoing series of "Passages" and "The Structure of Rime" continued through *Ground Work*.

Citing Emerson's "Self-Reliance," Duncan described "Passages" as "a work in which I seek to lose myself in the hearing of the voice of the work itself, a work not of personality or oneself but of structures and passages."[66] What Duncan called "structures" were not fixed boundaries but labyrinths of branching and intersecting openings. As a result, the "Passages" become more Poundian as they unfold across the page, with the elusive and allusive openness of the later *Cantos*. Duncan even stopped numbering the "Passages" after 36, in order to avoid any implication of sequentiality and teleological order. He was distressed that Olson, like Pound in *The Cantos*, thought of his *Maximus Poems* as moving to a conclusion that would define its direction and design. Stevens too shared that Modernist aspiration and thought of calling his collected poems "The Whole of Harmonium." But Duncan's notion of a "Grand Collage" was more indeterminate and shifting, less like a collage and (as he told Levertov early on) more like a mobile, the poems circulating in the gyre of "Poetry Itself."

"Passages 31: The Concert" turns on the separateness and connectedness of all things in the cosmos, and the suspended phrases and irregular lines drift and sift down the page, turning on each other. Here is the opening:[67]

> Out of the sun and the dispersing stars
>   go forth the elemental sparks,
>   outpouring vitalities,
> stir in the *Salitter* of the earth
>   a *living* Spirit,
> and the stars, mothers of light, remain,
>   having each
> its own "organic decorum, the complete
> loyalty of a work of art to a shaping
>   principle
>   within itself" –
>
>   that lonely spirit
>
> having in its derivation likewise
> the quality of the stars and yet
> a severd *distinct* thing ...

"Out" and "in," the sun and stars disperse their light; the "*living* Spirit" illuminates the "lonely spirit" of each "severd *distinct* thing." And at the end of "The Concert" the rhythm of expansion completes itself as the "I" of the poem – "the isolated satyr each man is, / severd distinct thing" – explodes into the farthest reaches of the open universe:

>   I saw
>
> willingly the strain of my heart break
>   and pour its blood thundering at the life-locks
>
>   to release   full   my man's share of the stars'
>
>   majesty   thwarted.

In Michael Palmer's introduction to the reissuing of both segments of *Ground Work* in a single volume, he writes of Duncan's quest for "an 'open form' sufficiently responsive to what is, essentially, an ungovernable vision." As a result, Palmer goes on to say, "[p]oetic form is stretched almost to the point of dissolution. The poem-as-object yields to the exigencies of process."[68] But, for Duncan, the dissolution of form into formlessness was indistinguishable from the coalescence of formlessness toward form. That reciprocity is what "The Concert" is celebrating. It is no accident that the poem that first drew Duncan to Levertov was "The Shifting," and, as time went on, he insisted more and more that the gaps between and juxtapositions of words, the orchestrated placement of phrases and images within the rhythmic play of the line, the fine and accurate timing in the length and turning of the lines adumbrate the unique form to which the disparate elements aspire and move, as the poem aspires and moves to "Poetry Itself." As Duncan read poems to audiences, he marked and measured the timing and rhythm with his hand, like the conductor of a private orchestra playing in public, like a mage spelling out his vatic lines.

Here, for example, are lines from one of the final unnumbered Passages called "Et," that begins in French and ends:[69]

> the Cave   the Birds   the Sources   the Trees
> ancestral leavings   seek   first of all
> the Springs   in these passages   back of Pound's cantos
> my keys.
> The Moon is full
> whose sheath of reflections flows out over the shining strand below us
> *ici*   franchissons ces parages
> the silken light   the silver fountain therein
> the dark metal
> *mobiles,   obscurs,   capricieux,   changeants* ...

The French "Et" – "And" – and the French phrases suggest a movement beyond the known and familiar words into a dimension of speech that is other but expressible. Once again, the words cast a spell, spell out the runic invocation. The wide-open lines do not quite vanish; the white spaces suspend the images and phrases in the irregular but steady flow that moves through the sinuous passages of time and measure. Here, from the cave above the shining strand, through the circulations of the obscure, capricious, changing mobile of the poem, let "us" leap over these watery passages to the sources of the flow. Let us pass through the silken light of the silver fountain to the dark metal keys that unlock the gnostic riddle; here – "*ici*" – we are at last: before the war and in the light of the dark.

As Duncan's poems became more gnostic, Levertov's became more incarnational. Her poetic development is often seen as falling into three phases: the earlier lyrics of visionary wonder, the political poems of the 1960s and 1970s, and the religious poems of her last decades, but she saw in these phases no discontinuity but a continuity. She often spoke of her life as a pilgrimage guided by the "acknowledgement, and celebration, of mystery," and the convulsions of postwar politics impelled her to see that the pilgrimage moved through the social world, that pilgrims were "members one of another." "Being the child of a socially conscious family," she said, "conscience and circumstances virtually forced me into the politics of the anti-war movement of the 1960s and on into the broader anti-nuclear, environmental, and social justice concerns which evolved from it …" Moreover, her association in the cause of peace and justice with Catholics like Daniel Berrigan, Thomas Merton, and Dorothy Day served to confirm her realization that her sense of the sacramental mystery of daily experience and her commitment to a community of peace and love were both rooted in Judeo-Christian values, and specifically in the incarnational theology that she had absorbed from her childhood. To her mind, then, the poems traced a pilgrimage at once more expansive yet more centered and grounded: a "mandala or wheel," as Duncan said, in contrast to his "mobile," a "form that maintains a disequilibrium."[70]

"A Poet's View," written in 1984, traces the course of Levertov's religious sensibility. From the beginning she had felt that "[t]he concept of 'inspiration' presupposes a power that enters the individual and is not a personal attribute," but more recently that power "began to be defined for me as God, and further, as God revealed in the Incarnation." Thus "[i]n the matter of religion … I have moved in the last few years from a regretful skepticism which sought relief in some measure of pantheism (while it acknowledged both the ethical and emotional influence of my Jewish-Christian roots and early education) to a position of Christian belief." When she had undertaken to write "Mass for the Day of St. Thomas Didymus," first published as a chapbook in 1981, she thought of the sequence as adopting the traditional parts of the liturgy for "an agnostic Mass" for doubting Thomas. However, "a few months later, when I arrived at the Agnus Dei, I discovered myself to be in a different relation to the material and to the liturgical form from that in which I had begun. The experience of writing the poem – that long swim through waters of unknown depth – had been also a conversion process, if you will."[71]

Levertov's copious notebooks and diaries, in addition to the poems and essays, examine the long pilgrimage that would bring her in the fall of 1990 to becoming a Roman Catholic. The inner journey was matched by a move from the East Coast – with residences in New York, Boston, and Cambridge, summers in Maine, and teaching positions at various colleges and universities – to the West Coast, teaching at Stanford part of the year and living in Seattle, where she died of lymphoma in December 1997. In "A Poet's View," however, she sees herself as never finally settled, always searching out: "[t]hough I own a house and have steady work, I am by nature, heritage, and as an artist, forever a stranger and a pilgrim."[72]

"Agnostic" can cover a range of skeptical positions, but the invocations in the early sections of "Mass for the Day of St. Thomas Didymus" move from "O deep, remote unknown" to "Thou / unknown I know" and "the known / Unknown unknowable." The turning point comes at the end of the "Benedictus": "The word / chose to become / flesh. In the blur of flesh / we bow, baffled." And the concluding "Agnus Dei" completes the "conversion process" by pondering the double paradox of God incarnate in our mortal bodies and our bloody history: omnipotence vulnerable to the fallible human will, yet thereby the fallible human will empowered to choose to incorporate the divine spirit:[73]

> Let's try
> if something human still
> can shield you,
>   spark
> of remote light.

Levertov's later poetry constellates around that paradox. In *A Door in the Hive* (1989), she wrote another poem for Thomas as the patron saint of self-questioning believers who need to verify vision in the physical world, to see and touch the divine mysteries. So there are poem-meditations on the crucial events in Jesus' life – the annunciation, nativity, crucifixion, resurrection, ascension. Levertov would study the *Spiritual Exercises* of St. Ignatius with a Jesuit spiritual director in Seattle in the mid-1990s, but she had already found for herself the Ignatian practice of personalizing and vitalizing the Gospel moments by imagining them in graphic physical and sensory detail. And, since for her the Incarnation is not an isolated historical moment but an indwelling presence, sequences like "Of God and of the Gods" and "Lake Mountain Moon" seek God's continuing immanence in the natural and the human world.

"The Many Mansions," the poem that immediately follows the "Mass for the Day of St. Thomas Didymus" and closes *Candles in Babylon*, is explicit about her vocation:[74]

> What I must not forget
> is the knowledge that vision gave me
> ....
>
> This is what, remembering,
> I must try, telling myself again,

> to tell you. For that the vision
> was given to me: to know and share . . .

The poems of the 1980s and 1990s contain some of the most quietly beautiful and moving religious poems in modern letters. Levertov had described inspiration in "Some Notes on Organic Form" in its root sense of "breathing in," and in "A Poet's View" as "a power that enters in the individual." But what embodies inspiration in moving and effective poems is craftsmanship: the economy of form, clarity of voice, precision of diction and image, rhythmic control of the line that she learned in the 1940s.

Here, for example, is a trio of poems, written separately in different forms but all imaging air or wind as the spirit animating material life. "Passage" is the last poem in the sequence "Of God and of the Gods." There is no reason to suppose that Levertov had Duncan's "Passages" explicitly in mind, but her poem offers a telling contrast to Duncan's. The four sets of tercets quietly develop the multiple sense of the Latin "spiritus" as "spirit" and "wind" and "breath" and project the Hebrew *ruach* – God's breath blowing over the primordial waters in Genesis – into the landscape "here and now."[75]

> The spirit that walked upon the face of the waters
> walks the meadow of long grass;
> green shines to silver where the spirit passes.
>
> Wind from the compass points, sun at meridian,
> these are the forms the spirit enters,
> breath, *ruach*, light that is witness and by which we witness.
>
> The grasses numberless, bowing and rising, silently
> cry hosanna as the spirit
> moves them and moves burnishing
>
> over and over upon mountain pastures
> a day of spring, a needle's eye
> space and time are passing through like a swathe of silk.

The longish (for Levertov) lines follow the sweep of spirit/breath/wind, and the enjambments keep it moving through the verses. At the same time, the repetition of sound and syllable sustains the continuity of movement while also giving it momentary material instantiation. The alliteration of initial "w"s ("walked," "waters," "walks," "wind") thickens in the middle line to give the "breath, *ruach*, light" palpable heft and presence in its reciprocal agency as both its own "witness" and that "by which we witness." The first syllable of the title-word "Passage" blows through the poem – "grass," "passes," "compass," "grasses," "pastures" – to the last line "passing"; and the "s" sounds in every line build to the exquisitely sibilant revelation of "space and time ... passing through [the spring day] like a swathe of silk." The poem itself becomes "the needle's eye" through which we see the vision of that spring day passing.

"The Avowal," written in homage to the seventeenth-century metaphysical poet George Herbert, adopts Herbert's device of centering the text on the page, so that the verses seem to spin (very differently from Duncan's) on a stabilizing pivot:[76]

> As swimmers dare
> to lie face to the sky
> and water bears them,
> as hawks rest upon air
> and air sustains them,
> so would I learn to attain
> freefall, and float
> into Creator Spirit's deep embrace,
> knowing no effort earns
> that all-surrounding grace.

The effortless simplicity of the language in its floating circulations gathers to a concluding consonance in the alliteration of the closing lines ("freefall," "float"; "knowing no") closed by the single rhyme ("embrace," "grace").

In *Sands of the Well*, the last volume that Levertov put together before her death, the poem "In Whom We Live and Move and Have Our Being" takes its title from Paul's sermon on the Acropolis (*The Acts of the Apostles*, chapter 17), in which he tells the Athenians that it is God who has given us life and breath. Levertov's poem insists that "breath of God" is no metaphor or figure of speech but fact: "God / the air enveloping the whole / globe of being" so that "[i]t's we who breathe, in, out, in, the sacred," "we inhale, exhale, inhale, / encompassed, encompassed."[77] In, out, in: here, in contrast to Duncan's isolated and severed individual exploding into the open universe, it's the rhythm of inspiration and incarnation.

"On Belief in the Physical Resurrection of Jesus," near the end of *Sands of the Well*, identifies Levertov with the "literalists of the imagination." The often-cited phrase comes from Marianne Moore's "Poetry," but the poet whom Levertov has more expressly in mind, both technically and thematically, is Williams, who taught her, perhaps more than anyone, how to find her own voice. The poem is written in the variable foot that Williams developed in his own late work: tercets with lines of varying length (the variable feet) spaced by indentation across and down the page. Moreover, her rejection of abstract concepts that are "not / grounded in dust, grit, / heavy / carnal clay" adapts Williams's famous dictum "no ideas but in things" to her Didymus incarnationalism. Resurrection is, for her, no "internal power" of renewal, but "a matter of flesh," a verifiable fact:[78]

<pre>
                        miracles (ultimate need, bread
        of life) are miracles just because
                        people so tuned
                                to the humdrum laws:
        gravity, mortality –
                        can't open
                                to symbol's power
        unless convinced of its ground,
                                its roots
                                        in bone and blood.
        We must feel
                        the pulse in the wound
                                        to believe
        that 'with God
                        all things
                                are possible,'
        taste
                bread at Emmaus
                                that warm hands
        broke and blessed.
</pre>

As in Williams's triadic poems, the openness of the variable feet allow Levertov a prosy discursiveness that suddenly coalesces in the final dramatic image that melds two Resurrection moments: Thomas knowing the risen Christ by touching his wounds, and the two disciples at Emmaus recognizing him in the breaking of the bread.

Levertov wrote an essay on "The Ideas in the Things" (1983) and another "On Williams' Triadic Line" (1984), and this poem brought her full circle back to Williams, as the later "Passages" brought Duncan back to Pound. Their late work marks the end-points of the divergent courses that Duncan and Levertov took through years of "co-respondence."

IV

In 1959, Levertov wrote: "I think of Robert Duncan and Robert Creeley as the chief poets among my contemporaries."[79] Within the Black Mountain poetics of composition by field they represented for her the distinct but intersecting influences of Pound and Williams. Williams thought of Creeley and Levertov as the two poets of the next generation who most successfully carried forward his notions of diction, line, and form, and Creeley was important for Levertov in the late 1940s and early 1950s. But her empathy with Duncan ran deeper because they shared a Romantic conception of the imagination as a visionary faculty; both saw no disjunction between Romanticism and Modernism and sought, in Duncan's words, "a style and temperament in which the Romantic spirit is revived" within a Modernist aesthetic.[80] Nonetheless, as we have seen, their very different theological orientations made finally not only for a different politics but a different poetics – and specifically for different notions of the correlation of language and meaning.

In "A Further Definition" Levertov posited three types of poetry: conventional poems impose "pre-existing, re-usable metric molds" to contain and form experience; free verse accepts and reproduces the "formlessness" of experience; organic poems, with "the utmost *attentiveness*," discover and express the "immanence of form" that is "peculiar to" and "inherent in content." That schema had already been formulated in a lecture that Levertov had given at Wabash College in 1962 with the Emersonian title "Ask the fact for the form." Duncan admired the "clarity" of the lecture but added as a fourth category "'linguistic' poetry," in which language itself constitutes the experience of the poem and its autotelic content: "the linguistic follows emotions and images that appear in the language itself as a third 'world'; true to what is happening in the syntax as another man might be true to what he sees or feels." At first Duncan distinguished his poetry from hers – "'linguistic' poetry – and I think of my own as linguistic – is different from organic" – but almost immediately he corrected himself: "I am organic as well as linguistic." Her response was to accept linguistic poetry as a category that "I'd dimly felt I'd left out of that lecture," and acknowledged that much "in your work" – for example, "puns & multiple meanings" – "didn't really fit in the scheme of things I'd posited there." Consequently, when she revised the lecture into "Some Notes on Organic Form," she added to her schema "the poetry of linguistic impulse," though she preferred to see it as "perhaps a variety of organic poetry": "It seems to me that the absorption in language itself, the awareness of the world of multiple meaning revealed in sound, word, syntax, and the entering into this world in the poem, is as much an experience or constellation of perceptions as the instress of nonverbal sensuous and psychic events."[81]

In fact, however, Levertov was always uneasy about language as primary or originary in the creative process. Painstaking about craft though she was, she saw language as an instrumental means, secondary to inspiration; the poet "is *brought to speech*" by a generating experience. Consequently, in a single sentence paragraph immediately after admitting "the poetry of linguistic impulse," she adds this specification: "Form is never more than a *revelation* of content." The italics on "*revelation*" call attention to the fact that she is revising the fundamental dictum of Black Mountain poetics, blazoned in capital letters in "Projective Verse": "FORM IS NEVER MORE THAN AN EXTENSION OF CONTENT." Levertov said that at the Vancouver Poetry Festival of August 1963 (the single occasion in which all four of the principal Black Mountain poets participated), she proposed her revised dictum to Creeley, "the originator of this now famous formula," and "he agreed." She does not elaborate on the terms of Creeley's understanding of the formula, but hers are clear.[82]

If form as an extension of content meant that content informed form and made it organic to the experience, she would agree, for "thought and feeling remain unexpressed until they become Word, become Flesh (i.e., there is no *prior paraphrase*)."[83] However, if the formula were construed to mean that content was only an extension of form, then language makes meaning and constitutes the "third world" of Duncan's linguistic poetry. Her sense of form as revelation of content stuck by Emerson's principle: "Ask the fact for the form." In their epistolary showdown, Duncan wrote of "form as the direct vehicle and medium of content. Which means and still means for me that we do not say something by means of the poem but the poem is itself the immediacy of saying – it has its own meaning." To which Levertov shot back:

> To me it *does* mean that "one says something by means of the poem" – but not in the sense of "using" (exploiting) the poem: rather that the writer only fully experiences his "content" (that which he is impelled to say by means of the poem) through the process of writing it ... Which is to say that the poem reveals the content, which is apprehended only dimly (in varying degrees) till that revelation takes place. If it (the poem) "has its own meaning," it is only that the revelation is not only the realization, concretization, clarification, affirmation, of what one knows one knows but also of what one didn't know one knew. I do not believe, as you seem to, in the *contradictory* (& autonomous) "meaning" of the poem, and I think your insistence on that leads you wildly astray often ...

Citing again Emerson on the form of the fact as well as his statement that "it is not metres but a metre-making argument that makes a poem," she reiterates, this time with her own caps replacing the italics: "Form is never more than a REVELATION (not extension) of content."[84]

The fundamental issue here is whether language creates meaning or expresses meaning, whether the poem is a confabulated, autotelic construct or a verbal inscape into objective reality. The debate runs through the history of American poetry, formulated in each age in different terms and emphases: for the Puritans, the issue was the distinction between types and tropes; for the Romantics, the distinction between Imagination and fancy; for the Modernist poets, the distinction between Imagism and Symbolism. In an early notebook Duncan saw in Stevens the accommodation of "the Romantic spirit" to a Modernist sensibility and craftsmanship; he was drawn to Stevens's identification of God with the Imagination in its ability to create in the poem a *mundo* or "third world" alternative to the contradictory, conflicted world we live in. Levertov agreed with Stevens and Duncan that "Imagination is the chief of human faculties," but made this distinction: "Where Wallace Stevens says, 'God and the imagination are one,' I would say that the imagination, which synergizes intellect, emotion, and instinct, is the perceptive organ through which it is possible, though not inevitable, to experience God."[85]

Duncan was correct in judging that he could be organic as well as linguistic, but his linguistic impulse led him to speak, even early on, of "the privacy of my craft," "a happening in language" within the hermetic consciousness so that "the truth does not lie outside the art." In the late essay, "The Self in Postmodern Poetry," he seems to associate himself with the emergent Postmodernist deconstruction of self and language: "the multiphasic proposition of voice in my poetry"; "impersonations, personifications, transpersonations, and depersonations"; "the play of 'I,'" the "play of meanings." "Back of the 'Self,' which was but a rime," is the "Elf" lost in "the workings of language." Associating himself with Freud as a "gnostic" in "his profound sense of the nature and operation of language," Duncan notes as one of the "underlying currents" of his work "the weaving of a figure unweaving, an art of unsaying what it says, of saying what it would not say." It is this interest in the fluidity of pronouns, the slippage of signification, the multiplicity of perspectives that in the 1950s drew Duncan to Stein and in the 1970s drew the emerging Language poets, who saw Stein as a forebear of their Postmodernist poetics, to Duncan.[86]

"Most of Gertrude Stein bores me," Levertov told Duncan, and, not surprisingly, her sense of poetic language excluded Language poetry: "the arrogantly self-named 'Language' (or L-A-N-G-U-A-G-E) poets" represent "sterile and elitist manifestations of creative bankruptcy," "rehashed Gertrude Stein veneered with 70's semantics."[87] What's more, in the end, Duncan's own Neoromantic adherences trumped his Postmodernist inclinations. In the first paragraph of "The Self in Postmodern Poetry" he explicitly disavows the label: "'postmodern' is a term used, I understand, to discuss even my work, but it is not a term of my own proposition." Creeley reported that when he asked Duncan what he thought about the Language poets, "he said, 'I can't – I'm moved by this or that person, but I can't finally buy it. I can't accept it, because they have no story.' Well, he didn't actually say all that. He just said, 'They have no story.' And I knew what he meant." Duncan was gnostic but not agnostic: "our belonging to the process of the Cosmos" meant that "[t]his music of man's speech ... has its verity in the music of the inner structure of Nature." In a 1983 sermon published as "Crisis of Spirit in the Word," he reaffirmed the power of the word to tell a story against the very poststructuralist semioticians and semanticists whom Levertov deplored:[88]

> I have none of the trouble that semiotics seem to have of how could a word refer to something. No word refers. Every word is the presence of. Tree is the very presence of the tree, and I have no way of being in the presence of the word alone or in my will that I saw a tree, but in this communion, this communication in which the revelation flows through and through.

These sentences could have been written by Levertov.

In their "co-respondence" and their differences, therefore, Levertov and Duncan stand at the center and turning point of postwar American poetics. The dialogue that runs through their poems, essays, and letters rehearses the interplay between the two aspects of the Romantic imagination, turning its visionary powers out toward the world or in toward its own convolutions. Moreover, their accommodation of the Romantic imagination to the Modernist formalism of Pound and Williams comes just at the point when postwar disillusionment and Cold War anxiety were deconstructing the claims of the Romantic imagination to vision and of Modernist formalism to aesthetic coherence. The poetic poles of the next generation were, on the one hand, the modest, tempered, ecological Neoromanticism of poets like Robert Hass in Marin County and Mary Oliver on Cape Cod and, on the other, the combative, highly theorized Postmodernism of the Language poets on both coasts.

CHAPTER 7

The Language of L=A=N=G=U=A=G=E

Robert Creeley

Michael Palmer

Lyn Hejinian

Robert Grenier

Susan Howe

Fanny Howe

I

Robert Creeley was fond of naming the company of poets to which he felt he belonged, because "in that company one has found a particular life of insistent and sustaining kind."[1] More than any other major poet of his generation, he embraced the whole and varied sweep of twentieth-century poetry from honored forebears in the Modernist period (Williams, Pound, Stein, Stevens, Crane), to the Objectivists of the previous generation (Zukofsky, Oppen), to the various groups of his own poetry scene: the Black Mountain group (and not just the big four but also Edward Dorn, Larry Eigner, and Paul Blackburn), the Beats (Ginsberg, McClure, LeRoi Jones), the San Francisco poets (Philip Whalen, Gary Snyder), New York poets (Kenneth Koch, Ted Berrigan), as well as Language poets of the next generation (Ron Silliman, Charles Bernstein, Michael Palmer, Robert Grenier). Notable absences from Creeley's company of contemporaries were closed-form poets such as Richard Wilbur and James Merrill and poets associated with the East Coast literary/academic establishment and the New Criticism, such as Lowell and Berryman. The only notable absences among Modernist forebears were Frost and Eliot (except to echo Williams's and Olson's deploring of Eliot's retrograde influence on modern poetry). These particular exclusions are not surprising since experimental poets distanced themselves from Frost and the later Eliot as traditionalists. But in a cultural rather than literary context those exclusions are notable, since Creeley, as we shall see, insisted on his New England roots and sensibility. With his chosen and capacious company of poets, however, he was unfailingly generous and enthusiastic, writing essays about them, reviewing and providing forewords for their books, contributing to their magazines and reviews, and maintaining running and often voluminous correspondences.

Creeley's early poems explain his call for and need of company. They voice the tentative, balked efforts of an alienated consciousness to break out of its solipsist anxiety, and their halting, insistently enjambed movement sound like no one else. "I Know a Man" is a much-anthologized poem from the mid-1950s:[2]

> As I sd to my
> friend, because I am
> always talking, – John, I
> sd, which was not his
> name, the darkness sur-
> rounds us, what
>
> can we do against
> it, or else, shall we &
> why not, buy a goddamn big car,
>
> drive, he sd, for
> christ's sake, look
> out where yr going.

Colloquial, almost entirely monosyllabic words, punctuated by profanities and unadorned by poetic diction or metaphor, are stammered out in short lines, all but one enjambed against the flow of grammatical connections; even the word "surrounds" is spliced in two. The clauses of this single, disjointed sentence stop and veer off through a series of twists and turns, and, when reading poems like this aloud, Creeley emphasized the enjambment with a marked pause at each linebreak, interrupting the speaker's compulsive but hesitant need to communicate his dread of the "sur- / rounding" darkness. So pervasive yet undefined is this existential dread that the speaker can find no intellectual or emotional resolution, only the obviously futile physical escape ("& / why not") of a big, speedy car. At this point his anonymous friend (John is "not his / name") breaks in to warn of an imminent crackup, and if the anonymous friend is in fact the speaker's alter ego, then the title "I Know a Man" marks and masks the soliloquy of a divided mind.

"The Riddle" tells us that "[t]he question / is a mute question," too amorphous and all-surrounding for words, but of course the poem is not mute – its words question the question. Consequently in "The Dishonest Mailmen," although the wily speaker blames his isolation and indifference on the anonymous "they" of the conniving and dishonest mailmen, he affirms the supremacy of the isolate poet's language (in a stripped down, bare-bones version of Stevens's "supreme fiction"):[3]

> They are taking all my letters, and they
> put them into a fire.
>
>   I see the flames, etc.
> But do not care, etc.
>
> They burn everything I have, or what little
> I have. I don't care, etc.
>
> The poem supreme, addressed to
> emptiness – this is the courage
>
> necessary. This is something
> quite different.

Different, that is, from a poem addressed to something or someone; all the more different from a poem addressed to wholeness or fullness of being.

On several occasions Creeley mentioned that, as a confused and shy beginner finding his sense of the poem, he was deeply struck by Williams's introduction to *The Wedge* (1944), which defined the poem as a machine made of words. So in 1953 Creeley could say that while "[t]he process of definition is the intent of the poem," its definition is not "any *descriptive* act, I mean any act which leaves the attention outside the poem." What a poet has is words, and the poem is, first and last, a linguistic construction. "A Note" from 1960, citing Williams and Pound, summarizes his stance more fully:

> I believe in a poetry determined by the language of which it is made ... I look to words, and nothing else, for my own redemption either as man or poet ... I mean then *words* – as opposed to content ... I think the poem's morality is contained as a term of its structure, and is there to be determined and nowhere else ... Only craft determines the morality of the poem.

In the opposition of words and content, Creeley meant content as anterior or extrinsic to the poem; content *is* the words of the poem. Hence Creeley's scrupulous and much-touted attention to organizing rhythms, vowel and consonant sounds, internal rhymes, word placement, and line breaks. When Denise Levertov, who shared his sense of craft to different ends, suggested to Creeley that his formula "Form is never more than an extension of content" really meant "Form is never more than a *revelation* of content," she took his silence as agreement, but his own later gloss clarifies his actual intention: "Content is never more than an extension of form."[4]

The title of Creeley's second collection of poems is simply *Words* (1967). When Duncan proposed to Levertov a primarily linguistic impulse in certain kinds of poems, he admitted that he was organic as well as linguistic, but Creeley makes no Romantic claims to organic form. For him, the poem is organic only in its own integral coherence. Obviously, poems arise in response to the stresses and circumstances of the poet's experience, but they change the experience into words: "I care what the poem says, only as a poem – I am no longer interested in the exterior attitude to which the poem may well point, as signboard. That concern I have found it best to settle elsewhere." Since "I have never, to my own recollection, anticipated ... what I was about to say" nor "the necessary conclusions of the activity," in the poem "I write what I don't know." Language becomes the agent of knowing beyond the self-expression of autobiographical or confessional poetry: "[a] poem is a peculiar instance of language's uses" that "goes well beyond the man writing – finally to the anonymity of any song." Consequently, "in this sense it may be that a poet works toward a final obliteration of himself, making that all the song – at last free of his own time and place."[5]

It is easy to see how the Language poets of the 1970s would read Creeley's pronouncements about the obliteration of the lyric speaker and primacy of language in the determination of content as anticipating their own Postmodernist semiotic deconstruction of language. What that reading of Creeley missed, however, was his Modernist sense of not just the constructed but also the constructive character of the poem: "words gave instant reality to this insistent flux, which otherwise blurred, faded, was gone ..." Words may be, as the semioticians claim, "simple markers" that the alienated "mind" uses "in place of" the world it lost. What Creeley claimed as the "redemption" in words is precisely their capacity to tell "what I don't know" and thus open a way back to the world: "Again and again I find myself saved, in words – helped, allowed, returned to possibility and hope." Creeley said that he sought "the anonymity of song" (and many of his poems are called simply "Song"), and, as Duncan pointed out, Creeley's poems place him in the lyric tradition of love song and lament that extends from medieval lyrics to the jazz and blues of the twentieth century. But it is also true that Creeley's talk about the obliteration of "the thought of myself – that specious concept of identity" serves as the self-protective defense of a confessedly introverted person in poems that he well knew were nakedly personal.[6]

Creeley seldom missed a chance to trace his ingrained anxiety to his New England sensibility. New England was the home ground from which he came and to which he always returned in imagination as well as fact: especially to the area of Maine from which his mother came and where he later had a house, and the area around West Acton near Concord, Massachusetts, where he grew up amid the woods and ponds, including Walden Pond, and where he said he felt at times a kind of immanent presence not unlike the presence that Edwards, Emerson, and Thoreau experienced. Creeley came to see himself as an agnostic Puritan in a broken world without the prospect of redemptive grace; his redemption came, as he said, through words. He defined Puritanism not in terms of Calvinist doctrine but in terms of a radical psychological fracture that divided the individual consciousness from the body and the physical world and so from itself. The opening sentences of his "Autobiography" are: "I've spent all my life with a nagging sense I had somehow the responsibility of that curious fact, that is, a substantial *life* . . . This must be what's thought of as Puritanism, a curious split between the physical fact of a person and that thing they otherwise think with, or about, the so-called mind."[7]

The Cartesian split between mind and material world, which Carlyle said was the tragic dilemma of the modern mind, took on additional Calvinist angst in the United States and especially in New England. Emerson defined original sin psychologically rather than theologically as the fall into consciousness, and Dickinson, whose poetry Creeley knew well, described that fall in her own experience:

> A loss of something ever felt I –
> The first that I could recollect
> Bereft I was – of what I knew not
> Too young that any should suspect
>
> A Mourner walked among the children

The fracture of the integrity of self and world, the fall into consciousness and so into self-consciousness, made Dickinson, Emerson, and Thoreau – and Creeley – (in her phrase) "see – New Englandly."[8] That loss generates the individual responsibility ("the one and only one for each of us") to account for a substantial life by testing and negotiating the gap between the mind and the bodily world. And, for Creeley as for the other New Englanders, words are what we have to bridge the gap; seeing New Englandly enjoins writing New Englandly.

The Puritans kept diaries, wrote histories, tracts, and sermons, and set up a printing press soon after their arrival in the American wilderness. The first page of Creeley's *Autobiography* goes on to say: "It is the pleasure and authority of writing that it invents a life to live in the first place."[9] Tom Clark is correct, therefore, in placing Creeley in "that Puritan self-exegetical tradition that goes back ... to the seventeenth century and the first [Puritan] spiritual autobiographer, John Bunyan." Creeley said that as a churchgoing boy his "interest wasn't the Bible" but "certainly the hymnal," and he "really loved" the old hymns because "the language of the hymns brings back for me that still, small voice, that curious immanence."[10]

In Creeley's early poems, however, the Puritan's self-questioning and self-anatomizing, finding no assuagement or resolution in the prospect of a saving grace, turns on itself with the skeptic's ironic wit, at once self-protective and self-wounding. Creeley described himself as "a young man raised in the New England manner, compact of puritanically deprived senses of speech and sensuality," and "the Puritan aura of where I grew up" made him share the Puritan suspicion of tropes and imaginative fictions as decorative lies and blinders: "I distrusted fiction, feeling the term 'something made-up' argued an intentional distortion of the 'truth.' "[11] He could never join Duncan's and Levertov's tracing out of symbol and metaphor, nor indulge in Ashbery's surrealist flights of fantasy and daydream. The minimalism for which the poems have been acclaimed is Creeley's secular, agnostic variation on the Puritan plain style, dubious about the veracity of ornamentation and figuration, and uttering, however stammeringly, the unsparing, self-incriminating truth about one's self. Creeley saw clearly that the Puritan self-involvement could close solipsistically on itself:[12]

> A face that is no face
> but the features, of a face, pasted
>
> on a face until that face
> is faceless, answers by
>
> a being nothing there
> where there was a man.

"The Immoral Proposition" puts solipsism ironically: "If you never do anything for anyone else / you are spared the tragedy of human relation- // ships"; then irony subverts the immoral proposition with the understated conclusion: "The unsure // egotist is not / good for himself." Instead Creeley chooses the moral proposition: "I want, as Charles Olson says, to come into the world." Locality and place become major concerns of Creeley's poetry, and since "[t]he local is not a place but a place in a given man," language can serve "[n]ot merely [as] an escape from the world – the difficulty was how to get *into* it, not away – " but as a place for the local: "a man and his objects must both be presences in this field of force we call a poem." "Measure, then," Creeley says, "is my testament" and "witness" to finding a place in the world.[13]

"Oh No" imagines finally coming to one's own place in a shared and peopled world:[14]

> If you wander far enough
> you will come to it
> and when you get there
> they will give you a place to sit
>
> for yourself only, in a nice chair,
> and all your friends will be there
> with smiles on their faces
> and they will likewise all have places.

The line breaks here work with rather than against the syntax, so that the sentence moves smoothly to its period. But the negative exclamation of the title and the hypothetical "if" from which the poem depends express alarmed uncertainty about reaching such a company of comrades. Creeley's early poems – terse, edgy, elliptical – present a wounded and wounding individual in a wounded and wounding world. They sing the blues of an "unsure // egotist" risking "the tragedy of human relation- // ships," and, most anxiously, the intimate vulnerability between man and spouse.

For Love – Creeley's first substantial collection, compiling the hundred or so published poems of the fifties – returns again and again to this central concern in all its exposed honesty and ambivalence:[15]

> I could not touch you.
> I wanted very much to
> touch you
> but could not.
>
> . . . .
>
> But I love you.
> Do you love me.
> What to say
> when you see me.

Early in the volume there is a "Song" to his first wife, Ann Mackinnon, from whom he was divorced in 1955, and the title (and final) poem of the volume is dedicated to Bobbie Louise Hawkins, an artist with whom Creeley lived from the mid-1950s to the mid-1970s and with whom he collaborated on a number of books during those years. But even the lines of "For Love" twist on their enjambed reversals:[16]

> Love, what do I think
> to say. I cannot say it.
> What have you become to ask,
> what have I made you into ...
>
> . . . .
>
> Nothing says anything
> but that which it wishes
> would come true, fears
> what else might happen ...

The poem needs its unusual length of two pages to work torturously toward "some time beyond place, or / place beyond time" where there is "no / mind left to // say anything at all"; there and then "into the company of love / it all returns." The surrender of self-tormenting "mind" to the consummation of "love" promises to encompass the particular and immediate ("it") in the totality ("all"). The present-tense "returns" suggests that the consummation is reached, but there the poem and the volume end.

What these poems give us, then, are the words working toward "the company of love." For example, "The Language" (in the next volume, *Words*) seeks to realize the mental abstraction of the words "I love you" in physical and realized fact:[17]

> Locate *I*
> *love you* some-
> where in
>
> teeth and
> eyes, bite
> it but
>
> take care not
> to hurt, you
> want so
>
> much so
> little. Words
> say everything.

> *I*
> *love you*
> again,
>
> then what
> is emptiness
> for. To
>
> fill, fill.
> I heard words
> and words full
>
> of holes
> aching. Speech
> is a mouth.

The sentences of simple, monosyllabic words are all declarative, but broken into bits in which subjects are split from verbs and prepositions from objects. Paradoxes pose the conundrum in various ways. Can verbal connection become physical connection? Can mouths kiss without biting? Can "I" touch "you" without hurting you? Can eyes (I's) meet? "*I / love you*" twice isolates "*I*" in its own separate line. Can "words // full of holes" fill holes to make emptiness whole? Can these "so / little" lines do "so / much"?

"Sometime in the mid-sixties," Creeley said, "I grew inexorably bored with the tidy containment of clusters of words on a single piece of paper called 'poems,'"[18] and, abandoning "this single hits theory," he began to let poems, even fragments, collect or accumulate without plan or intentional design to render the randomness of flux. Thus *Words* was followed by the linguistic bricolage of *Pieces* (1969), dedicated to Zukofsky. The psychological and even metaphysical issue behind the experiment in *Pieces* is posited in "A Piece," a gnomic, much-discussed poem toward the end of *Words*. It is the ultimate instance of Creeley's minimalism:[19]

> One and
> one, two,
> three.

One is never alone (all-one); singularity splits and multiplies. "One" immediately leads to the conjunction "and," and, after the line break, to another "one," which makes "two"; and "two" just as immediately leads to "three," the commas separating yet also linking "one, two, / three." In the essay on Plato in *Representative Men* Emerson described the metaphysical dilemma consequent to the Cartesian split as the reckoning of "the one, and the two": the need to reconcile oneness with multiplicity, identity with difference and otherness. But where Emerson sublimated the many into a Transcendental Mind or Spirit, the skeptical Creeley can only count on counting as the abstracting mind's strategy to maintain itself against or within the proliferation of the many. One of the fragments in *Pieces* says: "Want to get the sense of 'I' into Zukofsky's 'eye' – a locus of experience, not a presumption of expected value."[20] The mind/eye can at least play with the sequencing of numbers, so as to conceptualize the many not as a whole but as a collectivity of pieces.

The bricolage of *Pieces* accounts for the pieces by counting. Constellated around Creeley's extraordinary sequence "Numbers" (published first in a limited edition with color prints of the numbers by Robert Indiana), the often fragmentary poems (verses have traditionally been called "numbers") sustain the meditation on numerals as a systematic attempt to apprehend the enigma of reality:[21]

> *What law*
> *or*
> *mystery*
>
> *is involved*
> *protects*
> *itself.*

In the lines, as in "A Piece," the first numeral predicates the profusion and potential confusion of the rest: not a negation but an affirmation (the double "nots" – knots? – untie themselves) of a way for consciousness to enter and engage ("in in") the world of multiple location ("Here here / here. Here."):

> One thing
> done, the
> rest follows.
>
> .
>
> Not from not
> but in in.
>
> .
>
> Here here
> here. Here.

"Gemini" (Creeley's astrological sign) acknowledges the Cartesian split that fractures the world and divides consciousness:

> From one to two,
> is the first rule.
>
> Of two minds the twin
> is to double life given.

However, once again as in "A Piece," the progression from double-
ness to thirdness is a big move: trinity constellates three in one. But now
Creeley's "3 in 1" (one thinks of Stevens's "Thirteen Ways of Looking at a
Blackbird") is open-ended. Its three clusters of verses piece out not three
but four apprehensions of the bird's flight with increasing concentration
and emphasis (five lines to four to three):[22]

> The bird
> flies
> out the
> window. She
> flies.
>
> .
>
> The bird flies
> out the
> window. She
> flies.
>
> .
>
> The bird
> flies. She
> flies.

The number four carries something of its traditional sense of the compact completeness of four-square. Creeley's four "befores" seem to sum up
the whole of mortal life:

> FOUR
> Before I die.
> Before I die.
> Before I die.
> Before I die.

But the stability of four-square proves temporary and illusory; the following lines reverse the closure in the nursery rhyme that says "one, two,
buckle my shoe / three, four, shut the door":

> One, two,
> is the rule –
>
> from there to three
> simple enough.

> Now four
> makes the door
>
> back again
> to one and one.

Thus it is no surprise that when the "Numbers" sequence reaches "Nine," "[t]here is no point / of rest here":[23]

> More. The nine months
> of waiting that discover
> life or death –
>
> *another* life or death –
> not yours, not
> mine, as we watch.

"Zero," the final poem in the "Numbers" sequence, also reaches no finality but at once turns back and opens up. Zero is the source from which one and the subsequent numerals had emerged and the endpoint to which they return, but it is also the point at which nine can begin again as ten, initiating all the numbers that follow to infinity. Earlier in *Pieces* zero is imaged as the uroboros, at once circling and encircled, the snake with its tail in its mouth:

> A circling with
> snake-tail in mouth –
>
> what the head was
> looked *forward*,
>
> what backward is,
> then guess.
>
> Either way,
> it will stay.

In the end, then, counting does not account for the flux; it only enumerates the elements of the flux. The system perpetuates itself without unriddling the psychological and metaphysical problem of the one and the two: forward or backward, "[e]ither way, / it will stay."

Creeley's experiment in bricolage in *Pieces* and, to a lesser extent, in *Hello: A Journal* (about his 1976 residence in Australia and New Zealand, where he met his second wife, Penelope Highton) was important in pushing his poetics of words as far as he could, but the experiment was relatively short-lived. By the mid-1970s, he realized, "I felt neither ease nor possibility in the jumbled or blurred contexts of language," and began assimilating the intensified focus on the word in *Pieces* with his "accumulated habits of order"[24] in poems organized, for the most part, in his customary clusters of two, three, or four lines. Creeley remained prolific to the end, with a new collection appearing every three or four years, but these later poems, gathered in the second volume of his *Collected Poems*, have a different, steadier rhythm, rest in themselves less anxiously. He has answered none of his existential questions, but he is older, mellower, happier in his married and family life. A changing sensibility needed a different measure. These poems tend to be less elliptical and clenched, more discursive, played out with more relaxed rhythms, less angular enjambment, more regular rhymes than the earlier work. The loss in nervous energy and edgy intensity made for a different inflection of Creeley's plain style: a greater steadiness, poise, focus – even at times a kind of stoic serenity in the face of life's uncertainties.

Here, for example, is "As If" from *If I Were Writing This* (2003):[25]

> As if a feeling, come from nought,
> Suspended time in fascinated concentration,
> So that all the world therein became
> Of that necessity its own reward –
>
> I lifted to mind a piece
> Of bright blue air and then another.
> Then clouds in fluffy substance floated by.
> Below I felt a lake of azure waited.
>
> I cried, *Here, here I am – the only place I'll ever be* ...
> Whether it made common sense or found a world,
> Years flood their gate, the company dispersed.
> This person still is me.

The completed sentences of these mostly end-stopped lines (even the few enjambments come at grammatical pauses) confirm the speaker's identity in the momentary equipoise between the mind's abstracted images and the world outside. "As if" suspended in a timeless moment, "I" locate myself. For this instant at least, "[t]he local is not a place but a place in a given man"; "a man and his objects" are both "presences in this field of force we call a poem."

The later poems increasingly find the comforts and solace, rather than the tragedy, of "human relation- // ships." Again and again they return to the company and memory of family, friends, wife and children, as aging takes its toll and mortality approaches its term. There are dedications to family and friends, collaborations with fellow artists, poems for

Penelope and their children. The poems often link into sequences, like "A Calendar" in *Memory Gardens* (1986), "Histoire de Florida" and "The Dogs of Auckland" in *Life & Death* (1998), and "Caves" in the posthumous *On Earth* (2005). With the years the Puritan introvert took as "my dilemma" the challenge of seeking the common language and common ground of human relationships: "The dream of a common language ... in Adrienne Rich's proposal, becomes the hope for, the wish for, the desire for, the working toward, literally ... the place where the company of that dilemma will find a bonding and a way of having a life in common, a common life."[26] Rather than semiotic signs of disconnection, words need to be agents of reconnection in the shared human lot. Creeley understood Duncan's criticism of Language poets because "[t]hey have no story." "It could be," Creeley said, "the hierarchic, mythic story of a tribe's collective experience [as Pound's, Olson's, and Duncan's poetry sought to be], or it could be the imagination of significant values within the social group [as Williams's and Levertov's sought to be]. It could be many things, but it's the common story."[27]

With no large claims or pretensions, with only personal integrity and honesty as touchstones, the agnostic Puritan was feeling his way toward his version of the common story: "I want no sentimentality. I want no more than home." "Credo," from *Life & Death*, reaches an affirmation compounded of negatives:[28]

> I'd as lief
> not leave, not
> go away, not
> not believe.
>
> *I believe in belief* ...
> All said, whatever I can think of
> comes from there,
> goes there.

In the later poems images of echoes and mirrors (also the titles of two collections) register the Gemini's sense of unresolved dualities: "Oneself is instance, an echo / mirrored, doubled. Oneself is twin." Nonetheless, the divided mind, in seeking home, seeks connection:[29]

> Like likes itself, sees similarities
> Everywhere it goes.
> But what that means,
> Nobody knows.

Creeley wrote "Caves" in 2004, the year before his death, after visiting
the French caves with their mysterious prehistoric wall paintings. This
first home seems the final location, and there, in this place of origins and
endings, the aging skeptic finds the riddling enigma of human consciousness and human expression:[30]

> This is where it connects,
> not meaning anything one
> can know. This is where
> one goes in and that's what's to find
> beyond any thought or habit,
> an arched, dark space, the rock,
> and what survives of what's left.

Yet in "As If," quoted above, and in other poems, there are moments
when the echo rings true, when mirrors become windows (the title of
another collection), when mind and world reach reciprocity and inclusion, if not reconciliation:[31]

> Trees stay outside one's thought.
> The water stays stable in its shifting.
> The road from here to there continues.
> One is included.
>
> Here it all is then –
> as if expected,
> waited for and found
> again.

"One is included": the pronoun suggests that Creeley is making something
of a general statement. The only enjambment in these lines serves to give particular force and emphasis to "again," punning perhaps with "a gain."

"To Think ...," one of Creeley's last poems, imagines coming home
as a final return to self, at once completion and emptiness: at peace
with letting words go and letting the world remain where it was, is, and
will be:[32]

> To think oneself again
> into a tiny hole of self
> and pull the covers round
> and close the mouth –
>
> shut down the eyes and hands,
> keep still the feet,
> and think of nothing if one can
> not think of it –

> a space in whose embrace
> such substance is,
> a place of emptiness
> the heart's regret.
>
> World's mind is after all
> an afterthought
> of what was there before
> and is there still.

The lonely Puritan wanted, and found, company and home. He had lived in many places and taught at many universities, and when he died from pulmonary fibrosis in March 2005, he was far from his native New England, in residence at the Lannan Foundation in Texas. But Penelope and their children were at his side in the hospital in Odessa, and when she expressed regret that they were away from home, he told her that he wanted nothing else but what was there in that place. The last sentence of his "Autobiography" says simply: "One had the company."[33]

II

As the chapters in this book have been suggesting, American poetry after Modernism was defined not by Postmodernism but rather by a dialectic between Postmodernism and Neoromanticism that was inherent in the Modernist aesthetic itself. But in that complex configuration how was Postmodernism a response to Modernism?

The Modernist period, bracketed by the two world wars, bore a complicated and ambivalent relation to Romanticism, the dominant aesthetic and cultural ideology of the nineteenth century. And Romanticism, in its turn, evolved out of and against Enlightenment rationalism, which had deepened the skepticism, growing in the West since the Renaissance, about theological or philosophical absolutes capable of sustaining a reliable relation between subject and object, mind and matter, physics and metaphysics. The Romantic's response to this epistemological and religious crisis was to ground certitude not in reason or institutional systems of belief but in the felt experience of the individual. Such moments of intuitive insight constituted acts of genuine signification and proceeded from the highest human faculty of cognition, which philosophers called transcendental Reason and artists called Imagination. Romanticism put such stress on the individual's momentary experience that the Romantic synthesis of subject and object through the agency of the Imagination began to deconstruct almost as soon as it was ventured.

The High Modernism of the early twentieth century advanced a counter-ideology to an exhausted Romanticism, explicitly rejecting its epistemological and metaphysical idealism, its aggrandizement of the individual ego, its organic model for the instantiation of seer and seen, word and meaning. The Modernist work of art proceeded not out of a conviction of organic continuity or even correlation with nature, but instead out of a conviction that the discontinuity between subject and object and the consequent fragmentation of self and experience required the tight construction of the art object from the fragments. The critical discussion of Modernism has often tended to concentrate on the shattering of formal conventions as an expression of the disintegration of traditional values, and this tendency to deconstruct the accepted techniques of the medium itself produced Picasso's Cubism, Kandinsky's abstract designs, Pound's ideogrammic method, Stein's verbal experiments, Schönberg's jarring atonalities, Duchamp's Dada. In Stevens's terms, the Modernist imagination decreated in order to create its own forms. But it is the decreative aspect of Modernism that anticipated and led to Postmodernism.

Much as *Poetry* (Chicago) and *Blast* and *The Dial* had campaigned for Modernists half a century before and *The Kenyon Review* and *The Southern Review* consolidated the New Criticism as the academic institutionalization of certain Modernist values during the 1940s and 1950s, so in the 1970s the Postmodernist poet-critics, based in New York and the San Francisco Bay Area, grouped themselves under the mastheads of such journals as *L=A=N=G=U=A=G=E*, edited by Bruce Andrews and Charles Bernstein, *Poetics Journal*, edited by Barrett Watten and Lyn Hejinian, and *this*, edited by Barrett Watten and Robert Grenier. Anthologies like Ron Silliman's *In the American Tree* (1986) and Douglas Messerli's *"Language" Poetries* (1987) assembled the Language poets, much as Donald Allen's *The New American Poetry* had mapped out the open-form poets of the 1950s and 1960s. Andrews and Bernstein's *The L=A=N=G=U=A=G=E Book* (1984) and Michael Palmer's *Code of Signals: Recent Writings on Poetics* (1983) collected manifestoes and position papers that staked out their claim as the new and combative avant-garde.

In the introductory chapter I suggested the formula: Modernism minus Romanticism = Postmodernism. A more nuanced way of putting it is to say that Postmodernism saw the iconoclastic and deconstructive energies of early Modernism thwarted by its residual Romanticism: the Modernist exaltation of the artist as genius and maker, the emphasis on the integrity of the art-object, the insistence on the medium in the construction of meaning. So Silliman characterizes Modernism as "a lingering hangover" from Romanticism and dismisses it as "but the moment in which the postmodern becomes visible," calling Stein and Duchamp "outright postmodernists, *avant la lettre*."[34] To the Postmodernist the vaunted claims of Modernism were spurious and elitist. Poststructuralist theory, emerging from the disillusionment and anxiety of the Cold War decades, postulated instead the illusoriness of ego, the death of the author, the slipperiness of words, the arbitrary fraudulence of formal construction. Words are signs not of presence but absence, not of connection with and insight into the phenomena of experience, but instead signs of discontinuity and rupture between subject and object. Language is not so much the expression of consciousness as the fabrication of consciousness, and we are trapped in what Frederic Jameson called, in the title of his influential book, the prison house of language. The paradox is that language, indeterminate in its meaning, is at the same time a closed system or code of signals determined in its usage and grammar by the dominant social and economic power structures of an entrenched but decadent capitalism. The responsibility of the poet, then, was to express the indeterminacy of signification by subverting and dismantling the structures and grammar of the linguistic code.

Language poetics is explicitly and vehemently not a poetics of reference and representation but of deconstruction and demystification. For the rigorous theorists of Language poetry, Ashbery, for all his promise, copped out and settled for a soft, accommodating kind of Postmodernism. Ron Silliman openly calls for "a writing that no longer yearns for a unified sign," a non-referential writing that emphasizes the word as signifier rather than as signified. Bruce Andrews writes in "Code Words": "Author dies, writing begins ... Subject is *deconstructed*, lost ... deconstituted as writing ranges over the surface." Steve McCaffery writes in "Sound Poetry" of "the deformation of poetic form at the level of the signifier": "To align, realign and misalign within the anarchy of language ... Cuttings. Fissures. Decompositions (inventions). Not intention so much as intensions. Plasticizations. Non-functionalities. Shattered sphericities. Marginalities."[35] It is easy to see why Levertov, despite her leftist politics, saw Language poetry as a perversion of poetic language, and why Rich, while agreeing that capitalist politics co-opted and corrupted language into a tool of oppression, never flagged in the effort to find a common language powerful enough to stand effective witness against the structures of power.

Barrett Watten's "Introduction" to Silliman's book-length *Tjanting* (1981) sums up in three pages the theory behind Language poetry.

"Writing looks at itself first … makes a reality by taking itself apart …"
Because the extrinsic "materials" of experience "have no motive force,"
the imagination has "no option but … to turn back on itself," even
though it "will generally find itself lacking at that point." The artist is no
Modernist "hero"; that Romantic figure has been "concealed," "broken
down," "replaced by a chain of objectivized situations and surrounding
objects, both animate and inanimate." The "self-consciousness" capable
of fighting back against the paralyzing structures of decadent capitalism
requires "the recognition of non-identity" rather than of identity as "the
first step in the appropriation of one's fate." Because "non-identity is the
term common to all," "the deconstructive activity of the text finds the
destroyed centers of other lives," and "the power of writing to construct"
is a future possibility dependent at the present moment on the "deconstructive activity of the text."[36]

To start dismantling the language, several experiments devise arbitrary
systems so intricate and idiosyncratic that the results look like showy
stunts. Christopher Dewdney's "Fractal Diffusion," for example, mechan-
ically and in stages replaces the vowels in his flat, manual-like prose with
another phoneme: starting with substituting "ave" for "a," "but" for "b,"
"co" for "c," "dio" for "d," "et" for "e," "far" for "f." "Fractal Diffusion"
thus begins: "In this article I am going to reify a progressive syllabic/
letter transposition in units of ten. Starting with the letter A and working through the alphabet I will replavece eavech letter with ave syllave-
ble normavelly starting with the paverticulaver letter in question. The
effects will be cumulavetive, the system is avepplied aves it works its
wavey through the avelphavebutet." In this last word the b's begin to be
replaced, so that by the time the first six transpositions are in play we
reach this point: "Six letttetrs into thet avelphavebutett, mavenifaretstave-
tion petrfaretcotetdio-farlowetr ofar farondiouet – ave faraver/farettcohet-
dio coonconcolusion."[37] It looks less like *Finnegans Wake* than like pig Latin
punched out purposelessly but systematically by a madly logical computer.

Jackson Mac Low's *Words nd Ends from Ez* (1989) is a Postmodernist
deconstruction of a Modernist masterpiece through Mac Low's favorite
device of combining chance and arbitrary rules in the composition of the
text. In an "Afterword" Mac Low describes the "diastic chance selection
method" by which he mined from Pound's *Cantos* for "letter strings" "in
which the letters of Pound's first and last names occupy places correspond-
ing to those they fill in the names."[38] Thus, looking for "E," the first letter
in "Ezra," Mac Low takes up Canto l and runs his finger along the text till
he hits the first "e" and makes the "letter string" that begins with "e" and

continues, as will always be the rule, to the end of the word in Pound's text to constitute the "letter string." Line 1 provides "then" as its second word, and so "En" becomes the first element of Mac Low's text. Running his finger along, he does not find a "z" (the second letter in "Ezra") till line 32 in "bronze," and since "Z" must be in the second place in Mac Low's "letter string," "nZe" becomes the second element. Line 33 almost immediately supplies "R" and "A" in the phrase "beaRing yet dreory Arms," which means that for the "R" to be the third letter and "A" the fourth in his series of "letter strings" Mac Low hacks "eaRing ory Arms" out of Pound's phrase. Moving on to Pound's last name, Mac Low finds "Pallor" in line 35, with "P" in the initial place; hence "Pallor" goes into his crazy acrostic. And so on with "O," "U," "N," "D," and then back to E-Z-R-A – again and again through the letters of the name tirelessly ripping out "letter strings" in a predetermined chance sequence from the texts of all 120 cantos. Line endings are determined by "all punctuation marks that follow the selected letter strings in *The Cantos*, hyphens that are included within those strings, and final letters that end lines in later cantos without punctuation." By the strictly enforced chance of these rules the opening of *Words nd Ends from Ez* (dated January 9, 1981) reads, or rather looks like:[39]

> En nZe eaRing ory Arms,
>
> Pallor pOn laUghtered laiN oureD Ent,
>
> aZure teR,
>
> un-
>
> tAwny Pping cOme d oUt r wiNg-
>
> joints,
>
> preaD Et aZzle.
>
> spRing-
>
> water,
>
> ool A P."

On the back cover Bernstein solemnly puffs Mac Low's book as "an act of homage and a topographical map of features of the work otherwise obscured by its narrative thrusts," which "reveals a purer, inhering paradise within Pound's poem." Pound's actual intention, of course, was that his ideogrammic construction would constellate into a vision so psychologically and politically powerful that the reader would feel: "what // SPLENDOUR // IT ALL COHERES." He would have snorted his contempt both at Mac Low's subversion of his purpose and at Bernstein's pontificating about it.

Ron Silliman's *Tjanting* is another book-length exercise in writing
that "ranges over the surface." *Tjanting* starts with "Not this. / What
then? / I started over and over. Not this."[40] A negation generates a question, which in turn initiates a new start and then a new negation. If not
this, then what? There follows the first in a series of steadily lengthening
paragraphs listing a random, staccato proliferation of words, phrases, and
short sentences. The verbal elements ring changes on one another, and the
paragraphs lengthen as new elements are added to the mix until the last
paragraph swells to 85 of the 200-plus pages. The accumulating welter of
bits and pieces is punctuated by definitive-sounding but mutually incon-
sistent pronouncements: "Each sentence accounts for its place" (p. 15);
"Each sentence accounts for all the rest" (p. 16); "Each word invents
words"(p. 17); "Each mark is a new place" (p. 20); "Each sentence stakes
out" (p. 20); "Each statement is a mask" (p. 21); "Each sentence is itself"
(p. 23); "All words are some language" (p. 25); "Each mask is a statement"
(p. 31); "Sentence itself is each" (p. 34); "This sentence is another" (p. 38);
"The sentence does not occur in nature, save as writing, tho something
very much like it does" (p. 45); "Are all words some language?" (p. 43);
"Sentence each stake out" (p. 55); and on and on.

In between these pronouncements, series of verbal variations begin to
play out from page to page and paragraph to paragraph. For example,
the first-page sentence "Last week I wrote 'the muscles in my palm so
sore from halving the rump roast I cld barely grip the pen'" becomes,
two short paragraphs down the page, "Last week I wrote 'the muscle at
thumb's root so taut from carving that beef I thought it wld cramp,'"
and then, two short paragraphs down the same page, "Last week I can
barely grip this pen" and, a couple of short paragraphs further down,
"Last week I cld barely write 'I grip this pen.'" More variations follow: "I
cld barely write 'last week I gripped this pen'" (p. 18); "Barely I write"
(p. 23), and so on, with the variations spaced out more widely as the new
elements crowd into the lengthening paragraphs. Another element from
the first page, "Hot grease had spilled on the stove top" (p. 15) leads to
"Grease on the stove top sizzled & spat" (p. 15), thence to: "Grease sizzles & spits on the stove top" (p. 16); "On the stove top grease sizzles &
spits" (p. 17); "Grease sizzles, spits on the stove top" (p. 20); "Grease
sizzles, spitting on the stove top" (p. 30), and so on. Another series riff-
ing on prepositions begins its run on the first page: "Of about to within
which" (p. 15); "Of about to within which what without" (p. 16); "Of
about under to within which what without" (p. 17); "Of about under
to within which of what without into by" (p. 19); and so on, and so

forth. Both "Not this" and "Not not this" on the first page (p. 15), followed by "Not not not-this" (p. 16) and "Not not not-not this" (p. 17). "Again and again I began" (p. 15): necessarily so, since *Tjanting* does not seek consequence or development toward a middle or end. Lyn Hejinian remarked on the dust jacket that "the presence (and presentness) of each detail is palpable. The reader recognizes every word." Perhaps, but it is unclear how, as the words and sentences pile up, "the deconstructive activity of the text," in Watten's words, will provide "the power of writing to construct." It is not only, as Duncan observed about the Language poets, that they have no story to tell; sometimes they do not want to tell a story, they want *not* to tell a story.

A footnote to Bernstein's "Dysraphism" teases out etymological connections between this abstruse medical term meaning a kind of birth defect – literally a "mis-seaming" – and the stringing (stitching) of words: "disturbance of stress, pitch, and rhythm of speech." The textual seaming and mis-seaming (seeming and mis-seeming) concludes with these lines:[41]

> Dominion demands distraction – the circus
> ponies of the slaughter home. Braced
> by harmony, bludgeoned by decoration
> the dream surgeon hobbles three steps over, two
> steps beside. "In those days you didn't have to
> shout to come off as expressive." One by one
> the clay feet are sanded, the sorrows remanded.
> *A fleet of ferries, forever merry.*
> Show folks know that what the fighting man wants
> is to win the war and come home.

The short, direct, discrete statements are intelligible individually but not in relation to one another. They are stitched together not by discursive sense but by verbal repetition (seaming) and counterpoint (mis-seaming). Repetitions include such customary devices as alliteration (for example, the d's and b's in the first two sentences), assonance ("Show folks know," "*ferries, forever merry*," "demands"/ "sanded"/ "remanded," "feet"/ "fleet"), verbal associations ("slaughter"/ "fighting"/ "war," "hobbles"/ "clay feet"), and the same word in different senses ("come off as expressive," "come home." Instances of verbal counterpoint (mis-seaming) threading the lines include: "braced"/ "bludgeoned"; "three steps"/ "two steps"/ "One by one"; "slaughter"/ "surgeon"; "hobbles"/ "*fleet*"; "circus ponies"/ "fighting man"; "sorrows"/ "*merry*"; "slaughter home"/ "come home." "Dysraphism" is an extreme demonstration of Duncan's notion of a poem

that unweaves as it weaves, un-seems as it seems. Without the ego of
the Romantic-Modernist centering the text, the deliberately disoriented
reader is adrift in the fun of word play and sound play. The last sentence
of the concluding lines quoted above – "Show folks know that what the
fighting man wants / is to win the war and come home" – is not really
saying anything about the compassionate insight of entertainers or the
attitudes of soldiers toward war, but is phrasing a sentimental platitude so
as to savor the shape and weight of its monosyllables as verbal "facts." The
shapeless poem is six pages long, but it could just as easily have been two,
or twenty, or two hundred.

III

Not all Language poetry is games and gimmicks, but most of its purportedly readerly as opposed to writerly text presents – deliberately and programmatically – challenges to the reader. However, some poets associated
with the movement at the beginning – Michael Palmer, Lyn Hejinian,
Robert Grenier, Susan Howe, and Fanny Howe – developed a Language
poetry that, in their tellingly different and differently difficult ways,
pressed the word games into a serious exploration of how "the deconstruction of the text" can sustain "the power of writing to construct" and sustain the reader's close attention.

Palmer was already resisting the New Critical approach of his Harvard
undergraduate education and the confessional poetry centered on Lowell
before his participation in the Vancouver Poetry Festival of 1963 put him
in touch with Duncan and Creeley. After his move to San Francisco in
1969, he became a voice in the emergence of a West Coast Language
poetry; *Code of Signals*, the 1983 essay collection that he edited and contributed to, is a major consolidation of Language theory. But in a 1995
interview he voiced his growing concern: "There's nothing wrong with all
discourse coming into a framework of doubt, but then you do wonder at
what point – in the face of such massive interrogation, such massive skeptical interrogation – how does one (and I think that's much of the problem now) reassert the force of these words themselves."[42] In an interview
for the first issue of the journal *jubilat* in 2000, Palmer was more explicit
in rejecting the restrictions that Language theory imposed on what the
poet could say and do: "My own hesitancy comes when you try to create,
let's say, a fixed theoretical matrix and begin to work from an ideology of
prohibitions about expressivity and the self – there I depart quite dramat-
ically from a few of the L=A=N=G=U=A=G=E poets."

As for "expressivity," Palmer's poems turn this way and that the permutations of the seeming conjunctions and disjunctions between subject and object, word and fact, the imagined and the seen, and he invests those images and sentences with an intellectual and emotional gravitas and a beauty of phrasing and measure unlike anything in the work of his contemporaries. "The White Notebook" is the first poem in *The Promises of Glass*. Glass, like language, is the medium that interposes between the seer and the seen. But does glass promise to let us see through to the world beyond, or does it merely reflect back the seer's world? Do words image and "name" reality? Or obscure it with "figures-which-are-not"? Here are the opening lines of "The White Notebook":[43]

> But we have painted over the chalky folds,
> the snow- and smoke-folds, so carefully,
> so deftly that many (Did you bet
>
> on the margins, the clouds?) that many
> will have gone, unnoticed,
> under. Water under water,
>
> "earth that moves beneath earth."
> We have added
> silver to the river, dots of silver,
>
> red, figures-which-are-not. Tell
> me what their names might have been,
> what were last and first, what spells
>
> the unfamiliar, awkwardly whispered, syllable?

Who can tell and spell the misplaced syllable?

The fifteen lines of "Study" make the "strange conversation" of these strangers a terse "study" or parable of the Postmodernist dilemma:[44]

> In a darkened room they
> speak as one against the
> religion of the word, against
> the prophetic, the sublime, the
> orphic call. It is a
> strange conversation, coming as it
> does after hours of making
> love, mid-afternoon till now, at
> this their second meeting, shutters
> closed to block the lamplight
> outside. Seated on the bed,
> the curve of her back

toward him, she is smoking.
It is unclear whether they
believe what they are saying.

The poem presents a scene like one of Edward Hopper's images of human alienation in a bleak hotel room. Shuttered in a darkened room against the light outside, the couple, who barely know each other despite their just-completed sexual intercourse, can agree and "speak as one" in denying any metaphysical dimension or visionary insight in language; "the prophetic, the sublime, the / orphic call" would constitute "the / religion of the word." But their shared denial leaves them alone with each other, without a shared language. Back to back, they can't be sure that they even "believe what they are saying."

Palmer inscribed my copy of *First Figure* (1984) with the phrase "scalings of a sentence," from the last line of "The Book of the Yellow Castle": "These are scalings of a sentence."[45] His highlighting that phrase indicates how important a statement this is for him. (He called a sequence that appeared in *Company of Moths* [2005] "Scale.") "Scale" indicates a precisely defined calibration of measurement, as in musical scale or prosodic measurement; hence, "scalings of a sentence." But the line measures the distance between the plural "These" and the singular "sentence," seesawing on the copulative "are." How are the words and sentences of the preceding poem (and, by implication, all of Palmer's poems) scalings of a single sentence? Is that sentence the poem itself, the aggregate of the preceding lines? But "scale" in certain contexts derives from its Middle English root of "shell" or "husk," and can mean "to come off in layers or scales, to flake" or, contrariwise, "to become encrusted with layers or scales." Does "scalings of a sentence," then, mean disintegration or reconstitution? And in other usages "scale" derives from its Latin root as "ladder" or "steps," so that "to scale" means "to ascend by measured steps." Might "these" words measuring the poem, then, be approaches to a meta-sentence that will never be spelled out? Latin "sententia" means "a way of thinking."[46] Is Palmer, without making orphic or prophetic claims, acknowledging the Logos ("the religion of the word") of that lost syllable or sentence? Or do his "scalings" just confirm that loss?

Palmer resists Poststructuralist assertions about the "non-identity" of the author and ideological "prohibitions against expressivity and the self." In an essay titled "Autobiography, Memory and Mechanisms of Concealment" he wrote that "[p]oetry seems often a talking to self as well as other as well as self as other, a simultaneity that recognizes the elusive multiplicity of what is called 'identity.'" "The Promises of Glass" is a sequence of eighteen poems, each titled "Autobiography," but his oblique and elusive approach to autobiography through the mechanisms of concealment could hardly be farther from the self-exposure of the Beats and the confessional poets. The first "Autobiography" consists of seemingly random single-sentence observations of varying length, separated each to a line and six lines to a group. Here are the first two groupings:[47]

> All clocks are clouds.
> Parts are greater than the whole.
> A philosopher is starving in a rooming house, while it rains outside.
> He regards the self as just another sign.
> Winter roses are invisible.
> Late ice sometimes sings.
>
> *A* and *Not-A* are the same.
> My dog does not know me.
> Violins, like dreams, are suspect.
> I come from Kolophon, or perhaps some small island.
> The strait has frozen, and people are walking – a few skating – across it.
> On the crescent beach, a drowned deer.

And the last grouping of six, with perhaps a nod to Duncan's "Passages":

> That all planes are infinite, by extension.
> She asks, Is there a map of these gates?
> She asks, Is this the one called Passages, or is it that one to the west?
> Thus released, the dark angels converse with the angels of light.
> They are not angels.
> Something else.

This approach to autobiography, Palmer acknowledges, is far from the "linear narrative" of, say, "Life Studies" or even *The Dream Songs*. The "I" makes only one appearance, almost lost in the succession of potentially infinite facets and planes: one-line observations, philosophical speculations, questions about origins and directions. Is there a map? It is "She," not "I" who asks, but then "*A* and *Not-A* are the same." Does "I" come from a particular island, or is "I" a linguistic compilation, "colophon" (Greek "kolophon") being the emblem at the beginning or end of a book, indicating its source of publication? But Palmer insists that what seems the indirection of such an exploration of "the inherent complexities and complex possibilities" of self "becomes paradoxically more direct in its presentation than apparently simpler forms of writing."[48] In these passages of concealment the dark angels are released to converse with the angels of light.

Lyn Hejinian's kind of Language writing extends back through the Objectivists – Zukofsky, Oppen, Lorine Niedecker – to, most importantly, Stein. Her ongoing poem *My Life* is another, and very influential, project in "autobiography," very different from Palmer's, and it recalls in particular Stein's prose poetry in *Tender Buttons*, though without Stein's mannerisms of repeating, with variations, words and simple syntactical forms. *My Life* consists of block paragraphs with italicized captions; written in 1978, when Hejinian was thirty-seven, the 1980 edition contains thirty-seven paragraphs of thirty-seven sentences each; the 1987 expansion adds eight sentences to each existing paragraph and adds eight new paragraphs to match her forty-five years. *My Life in the Nineties* was issued separately in 2003, and then with the 1987 *My Life* in 2013; it contains ten paragraphs, for the decade of the 1990s, of sixty sentences each, for Hejinian's age in 2001.

The deliberate structuring of *My Life* thus parallels Hejinian's life, but the sentences in each paragraph just as deliberately subvert chronology, logical sequence, and discursive connection. Each paragraph of *My Life* renders the effort of consciousness to meet and render the blur of time and the jumble of experience in language. The rush of sentences registers the interpenetration of sensation and reflection, moment and memory, literary allusion and political observation, so that *My Life* is not an organized narrative but an ongoing and fluid language event, lived out on the page, paragraph by paragraph, year by year. For Hejinian, an open text like *My Life* denies the reader the relatively passive and secure pleasure of absorbing the text, and instead propels the reader into experiencing the fluidity of self through the rapid succession of discontinuous sentences. Texts like Mac Low's dismantling of Pound's *Cantos* are, almost literally, unreadable, but how might one "read" an open text like *My Life*?

Let's take a representative paragraph.[49] The italicized caption, "*What is the meaning hung from that depend*," takes off from the famous first lines of Williams's poem: "So much depends / upon." But Hejinian turns the momentous implications ("So much") of Williams's declaration into an open-ended question ("What is the meaning"). Both are punning on the Latin derivation of "depend" as "hang from." However, the concise concentration of Williams's Modernist arrangement of words and their objects hanging literally as well as conceptually from that "so much" ("a red wheel / barrow // glazed with rain / water // beside the white / chickens") is replaced by a block paragraph of prose two and a half pages long. Here are the sentences immediately depending from the question "What is the meaning":

A dog bark, the engine of a truck, an airplane hidden by the trees and roof-tops. My mother's childhood seemed a kind of holy melodrama. She ate her pudding in a pattern, carving a rim around the circumference of the pudding, working her way inward toward the center, scooping with the spoon, to see how far she could separate the pudding from the edge of the bowl before the center collapsed, spreading the pudding out again, lower, back to the edge of the bowl. You could tell that it was improvisational because at that point they closed their eyes. A pause, a rose, something on paper. Solitude was the essential companion. The branches of the redwood trees hung in a fog whose moisture they absorbed. Lasting, "what might be," its present a future, like the life of a child. The greatest solitudes are quickly strewn with rubbish. All night the radio covered the fall of a child in the valley down an abandoned well-fitting, a clammy narrow pipe 56 feet deep, in which he was wedged, recorded, and died. Stanza there. The synchronous, which I have characterized as spatial, is accurate to reality but it has been debased.

Most of the sentences and sentence fragments are clear enough in themselves; seeing their interaction is what demands the reader's participation. The last sentence quoted above suggests that there is a kind of synchronicity (etymologically "time with"), a convergence or constellation of the elements disparate in time and relevance, and that the synchronicity spaced out in this paragraph, however seemingly compromised, is in fact more "accurate to reality" than a chronological consistency with its implication of consequentiality. In the middle of the excerpt the tag "A pause, a rose, something on paper" repeats the italicized caption of the first paragraph of the book, and begins to suggest that if one takes the time ("a pause"), one will begin to see a series of exfoliations right there on the page under one's eye.

The opening trio of images of things heard but not seen – "A dog bark, the engine of a truck, an airplane hidden by the trees and rooftops" – intimates the "solitude" of the speaker, although the only first-person pronoun in the paragraph is buried in the phrase "my mother." But solitude is the "essential companion" because it is the inescapable and shared experience of each individual life. The lonesomeness of childhood is rendered not through autobiographical anecdotes from the speaker's own early years, but first through the vignette of her mother as child, and then through the recalled account on the radio of a boy's ghastly death in a well-fitting. The melodrama of her mother's childhood is enacted by her attempt to test and forestall the imminence of collapse while eating her pudding, and what makes that mundane incident "holy" rather than bathetic is that it reveals the "essential" reality as we improvise futilely against the passage from life to death: the past present, the "present a future." "Lasting"? Even the majestic redwoods (known botanically as "sempervirens," always living), which hang on by absorbing and dissipating the fog, in time fall. We live in a world of fall. The Valley boy fell down a narrow well-fitting (not a good fit at all) and died: another closed "[s]tanza there." None of our doomed solitudes is heroic or noble; even the "greatest" are "strewn with rubbish" and "debased" with the litter of a fallen world. The phrase "the center collapsed" echoes Yeats's famous phrase "the center will not hold." As the last quoted sentence says, the exfoliation ("rose") of time away from the center is spatialized here in the paragraph ("on paper"), and its synchronicities, however peripheral and improvisational, are "accurate to reality."

The close reading in the previous paragraph engages only about a fifth of a single paragraph of the forty-five in *My Life*. Yet, for all the demands and challenges that the text presents, *My Life*, in its various iterations, has proved one of the most widely discussed and admired texts in the whole range of Language poetry.

IV

Even before $L=A=N=G=U=A=G=E$ magazine, the journal *this*, edited by Barrett Watten and Robert Grenier in the early 1970s, signaled the formulation of a Postmodern poetics and provided a bridge between post-Olson "composition by field" and the Language poets. Language poetry became the banner movement of a Postmodern poetics when it adopted a post-structural linguistics to extend a dissident strain of Modernist poetics that ran from Stein through Zukofsky to Creeley, and thence to the Language group. That poetic line, from Stein to Bernstein, represents an exploration of the materiality of language, now re-enforced by the post-Saussurean focus on the referential slippage between word and thing, signifier and signified. Grenier's calculatedly provocative exclamation in the first issue of *this*, "I HATE SPEECH," all in caps, rejected the performative, oral inclinations of the Beats for the writerly material on the page. However, as it has turned out, Grenier's own poetic development represents, in many ways, the most radical experiment in Language poetry because it takes the theoretical assumptions of Language poetry and turns them inside out.

Creeley is the key to Grenier's development. As a Harvard undergraduate, Grenier studied with Lowell and found in Lowell not only encouragement for his own writing but the example of a poet totally committed to his craft; from the start, however, Grenier's own inclinations sought another way with language and form than Lowell offered. Reading Creeley's *For Love* in the spring of 1962, during a leave of absence from Harvard, was the defining moment; "the way it sounded, the way the lines were organized, the condensed way that it was" initiated Grenier's "apprenticeship in a craft."[50] Creeley said that in poems he looked "to words, and nothing else," and in Grenier he recognized someone who would push his emphasis on words to the next level. "Bob's 'I hate speech,'" Creeley would say, "means let words talk. Don't just talk for them ... Make words physical, write them as such – they say more than we do. Now and again someone becomes both innovator and paradigm for an art's next necessary step."[51] Creeley showed his high regard for Grenier's poetic sense by asking Grenier to make the editorial choices for his 1976 *Selected Poems*.

Creeley led Grenier back to Williams, Stein, and Pound (none of whom were taught at the time at Harvard), and, as we shall see, forward to Larry Eigner. Returning to Harvard, Grenier wrote his senior honors essay on Williams's prosody, specifically on Williams's use of the line, and he began writing the poems that went into his first book, *Dusk Road Games* (1967). Here is "The Depth Of Fall":[52]

> The silent frenzied fly
> on the window –
> pain is so sheltered –
> peer, pry
>
> hours – and that fly –
> now on the sill
> in the yellow light
> listening to its feet –

Whether or not Grenier had somewhere in mind Dickinson's "I saw a fly buzz when I died," he, like Dickinson, makes every word in the quatrains count, investing an otherwise insignificant occurrence with the energy of observation and empathy. The enjambment he learned from Williams and Creeley catches the trapped fly's zig-sagging frenzy, as does the pun on "pain/pane"; and the erratic rhyme of "fly/pry/fly" links the stanzas as the fly's frenzy subsides in time ("hours," "now") into defeated stillness, suspended in the alliterated "l"s and slant rhyme of "sill / in the yellow light / listening to its feet."

But the effect is too studiedly literary and artificial for Grenier, and his discovery of Eigner's poems around 1963 helped him connect the object of observation with its material word directly in the mechanics of marking down the words. Eigner's short poems, almost telegraphic registrations of

sights and sounds, were typed out on a typewriter with the index finger
of his right hand because Eigner had been severely disabled from birth
by cerebral palsy. Grenier's 1971 visit to Eigner in his family's home in
Swampscott, Massachusetts, began a long association, and when they
both moved to the Bay Area, Grenier, with his partner and his daughter, moved with Eigner into a shared house in Berkeley, where for ten
years Grenier was caretaker and amanuensis: organizing Eigner's scattered
manuscripts, typing out final drafts of poems, editing several collections
of Eigner's poems for publication. And, more than a decade after Eigner's
death, Grenier undertook the monumental task of coediting, with Curtis
Faville, the four-volume *Collected Poems of Larry Eigner*. Eigner used the
spacebar and the keys of the typewriter very deliberately to organize the
precise spacing and placement of letters, words, and lines on the page,
and, because of his disability, as Grenier saw, "he literally had to exert
himself to physically *type*, each letter." Watching Eigner work and then
making final typescripts of the poems, Grenier came to regard "the physical act of typing, having to pay close attention to the position of the
letters and their relation to each other in space, as like a gift to me." As
a result, his own work became "actually a matter of making words out of
letters, as I go along."[53] Eigner's battered Royal portable typewriter still
occupies a special, totemic place on Grenier's worktable.

The typewriter sharpened Grenier's attention to "the combinatorial
possibilities of letters into sounds and words."[54] *Series* (1978), his second
published collection, shows him paring the writing down, sometimes to
single lines and even single words. That clearing of space around words
and phrases also led to *Sentences Toward Birds* (1975), forty typed phrases
and short sentences printed separately, each centered on a 4x6 inch card,
and included unbound, in no given order or sequence, in an envelope.
Here is a random selection:[55]

> birds leave ever trees love birds
> why you say you see later
> if rain it's raining
> repetitive bird and black

Three years later an expanded *Sentences* (1978) was a box of 500 such
phrases, again unbound on 5x8 inch index cards, and these were offset
from Grenier's typewriter images, as were the poems in *A Day at the Beach*
(1985) and *Phantom Anthems* (1986), so that the words appeared on the
card or page as typed. Instead of theorizing about indeterminacy and
slippage between signifier and signified, Grenier went to work, focus-
ing on the words, one by one and in syntactical combinations, starting

at the level of the letter and its sound. The progression in Grenier can be described as moving from a focus on the phrase (Williams, Pound) to the word (Creeley) to the letter (Eigner).

In 1986, Grenier switched from his Selectric typewriter to his old Remington manual for its darker, denser image of the words, and those poems went into the sequences of *What I Believe transpiration/transpiring Minnesota* (1988), a black box containing sheets reproducing pages of 8½ x 11 inch typed text. But the closing pages of *What I Believe* show Grenier moving from typed words to words written by hand with a pen. And then, in 1989, came the final transition to "drawing letters into words" with red, green, blue, and black Uniball pens onto the pages of "blank, bound, 5½ x 8½ inch sketchbooks." Grenier had used colored pens in his job as a legal proofreader in San Francisco, and now these four-color "('calligraphic') *marks in space*" became "the essential act of *naming* that writing (perhaps even more than speaking/sounding words?) for me enacts." These handwritten "drawing poems," as he came to call them, accumulated rapidly; "[s]ince 1989," he could say in 2011, "I have completed about 170, 212-page sketchbooks filled with drawing poems."[56]

Through these years Grenier lived in Bolinas, a small town near the base of the Point Reyes peninsula between Tomales Bay and the Pacific Ocean. The drawing poems inscribe his daily responses – seeing/hearing/thinking – to the California landscape and now, since his move to upstate Vermont in the fall of 2012, to the New England landscape. Characteristically, each poem occupies a page of the sketchbook; most consist of four words (occasionally split or hyphenated), written in the four colors of ballpoint pen with underlining that serves as a rough blocking out of the lines on the page. Here are examples, reduced to conventional typography:

FISH	OWL	AFTER
HAWK	ON	NOON
WITH	BOU	SUN
FISH	GH	SHINE

SIRIUS	DEER
THE	TO
DOG	DO
STAR	OR

The defamiliarization of the words in their odd calligraphy emphasizes the material composition of each word as letters (sometimes even breaking words into clusters of letters) and thereby allows a fresh cognitive

encounter with the word and, through the word, with the material phenomenon. The experience of recognition runs from letters to words to
things.

In the first instance above, which consists of four four-letter words, the
word FISH occurs as the first and last words, but in different parts of
speech (adjective and noun), and the repetition confirms the conjunction
between hawk and fish, designated by the intervening preposition WITH.
In the second instance above, breaking the word BOUGH highlights the
assonance of OWL and BOU, thus connecting the bird and its perch
and perhaps suggesting the owl's repeated call. Occasionally the drawing
poems come in pairs (or even in short series):

RAIN	RAIN
RAIN	ING
ING	RAIN
RAIN	RAIN

Here the repetition of the word renders the persistence of the "RAIN," but
each calligraphic or ideogrammic iteration of the word is different, like
each moment of seeing and hearing and experiencing "RAIN." And the
interplay of noun and present participle links the thing and its activity, as
Pound said the Chinese written character does. Grenier's drawing poems
are an experiment, following Pound's *Cantos*, in finding some equivalent
of Chinese ideograms.

The drawing poems need to be seen and read as written in four colors.
Black-and-white reproductions tend to reduce the image to a scrawl of
lines that are very difficult to read. To give the reader some notion of what
Grenier wrote, I include black-and-white reproductions of FISH / HAWK
/ WITH / FISH, OWL / ON / BOU / GH, and the pair of RAIN poems
(on facing pages of one of Grenier's sketchbooks), but I urge the reader to
go to the following websites to see a number of the drawing poems online
in color: www.bombmagazine.org/article/10022/portfolio; www.writing
.upenn.edu/pennsound/x/On-Natural-Language.php

Conventional print typography cannot render the visual impact and
effect of the four-colour images made on the spot, without revision, and
the spontaneous interplay of lines and curves makes it difficult, at first
glance, to recognize letters and words. A page of the sketchbook confronts
the reader with a stylized version of Grenier's usual distinctive handwriting. The text is written in separate letters rather than cursive script,
and certain letters are rendered in an idiosyncratic but fairly consistent
shape: for example, the lower-case "b" as a curved hook to the right,

FISH
HAWK
WITH
FISH

adapting the curve at the base of the letter; "d" rendered as a curved hook to the left; capital "R" as two verticles connected at the top. In addition to the orthographic quirks, the angularities and overlappings of lines present the words as we have never seen them before; we have to learn to read anew with conscious attention in order to make out the letters that make the words that make the poem. Grenier described "the essential act of *naming*" as "looking/thinking/wording," but by "thinking" he means not abstract cogitation but realization of what one sees, hears, feels: "perception itself involves organized understanding"; "one sees shapes directly as one looks, sees shapes forming as part of the perceptual process, not just sensory data," so that perceptual "thinking," in that sense, shapes the letters into words on the page. The strokes of the pen render the spontaneous gestalt of the verbal moment without the normalizing and mechanical flattening of the typewriter or the letterpress. The poet's hand follows the perceptual process in the calligraphy on the page, and with comparable concentration and focus the reader can enter and follow out the "looking/

OWL
ON
BOU
GH

thinking/wording." Not surprisingly, Grenier has refused to consider typographic publications of the drawing poems as an abnegation of his poetics. But, without an economically feasible means of reproducing the pages in color, only a small sampling of the by-now thousands of drawing

```
RAIN     RAIN
RAIN     ING
ING      RAIN
RAIN     RAIN
```

poems is available, outside of the sketchbooks themselves, in several (but readily accessible) online sites and in three collections of limited-edition color prints: *12 from r h y m m s* (1996); thirty-two drawing poems in *OWL/ON/BOU/GH* (1997); and *16 from r h y m m s* (2014).[57]

Williams maintained in *Spring and All* that "writing deals with words and words only," but he also maintained just as strongly that the words of the poem, while disjunct from nature, were nonetheless in apposition to nature because they "recreated everything afresh in the likeness of that which it was."[58] The progression from Williams to Creeley to Eigner to Grenier traces a clear trajectory in American poetry, and in Grenier, orthography stands in apposition to geography. Writing / reading words is writing / reading the world; we come to know the world as words and words as world. Grenier's drawing poems are a kind of American haiku, and behind them stands Pound's notion of the ideogram as a more accurate analogy. Pound thought the Chinese language superior to English in having words written as pictographs of the things they represent, thus fusing word and thing. The progression from Pound's Imagism to his ideogrammic method in *The Cantos* marks stages in his effort to write an English equivalent of the Chinese ideogram and then to organize a long poem as a compilation and juxtaposition of such ideograms. Grenier has no Poundian ambitions toward epic, but each of the drawing poems is a rough-hewn, handcrafted ideogram. Rough-hewn but not naïve; spare and unpretentious in its tone but sophisticated in its epistemological intentions. What continues to sustain his singular commitment is "a concern for embodiment of words in these constructed spaces / places wherein they can 'live' / do whatever work they do / manifest themselves as verbal objects for a reader's hands / eyes."[59]

Williams's *In the American Grain* has been an important book for Grenier since his Harvard days, and the passionate concern for the truth of words and images has been in the American grain since the Puritans. Grenier was born in Minneapolis, but in spirit he is a New Englander. He taught at Franconia College in northern New Hampshire in the 1970s, and after decades in California, he has moved to a farmhouse in northern Vermont. With Thoreau, Emerson, and Dickinson, with Creeley and, as we shall see, with Susan Howe, he shares a Protestant antinomian sensibility, concentrating the energies of mind and spirit on discerning one's individual experience in and through words. Grenier has acknowledged the "onliness" (punning on "one" and "only" and "lonely") of that pursuit.[60] In some ways Grenier is a kind of latter-day Thoreau, in his Bolinas cabin and now his farmhouse. Like Thoreau he has traveled a great deal in his local place, and the sketchbooks, like Thoreau's many volumes of journals, authenticate, day by day, his explorations of the local by, in Thoreau's phrase, nailing words down to the things they are trying to represent. Each page of the sketchbooks, like the pages of Dickinson's fascicles, inscribes a single, intense moment of experience.

Grenier's resumed engagement with Emerson's essays in the mid-1990s sparked an ongoing dialogue with the Transcendentalists that has clarified his own thinking about words and things, and in turn his response to Emerson indicates how the drawing poems have turned Language poetics inside out. Emerson's Romanticism, his idealistic Platonism and metaphysical claims for the visionary imagination made him seem even more suspect and outmoded to the Postmodernists than to Modernists like Williams and Stein. The three axioms at the beginning of the "Language" chapter of *Nature* (1836) sum up Emerson's poetics: "1. Words are signs of natural facts. 2. Particular natural facts are symbols of particular spiritual facts. 3. Nature is the symbol of spirit." Grenier is no Transcendentalist; the drawing poems insist on their materiality as the condition of their being. Through his reading in Heidegger, Saussure, and Wittgenstein, Grenier sees language as a man-made system of arbitrary signs with all the ensuing gaps that complicate and undermine signification. For Grenier, then, Emerson's notion of the word signing the thing that symbolizes a spiritual truth is "an impossibly grandiose prospect." Yet, despite his Postmodernist doubts, he is drawn to and impelled by the prospect it opens; "it has the virtue of directing my attention toward the thing," so that "the energy that goes into symbolism can, sort of, 'redouble' upon perception of the object" without demanding "that it *be* anything other than itself." Grenier would amend Emerson's dictum "Nature is the symbol of Spirit" to read "Word is a symbol of Nature."[61]

That concentrating energy and focus allow the drawing poems to resist the slippage of signification and instead seek to connect word and things in the immediate moment of experience by the stroke of pen on page, letter by letter, word by word. Each poem negotiates the tension between sensation and semiotics and, in the act of writing, disputes the epistemological skepticism of the deconstructionists. Although Grenier rejects the metaphysics and moralizing of the Romantic doctrine of correspondences, he acknowledges his "very mysterious" sense that, in the act of "looking/thinking/wording," the word exists "in accord with" the thing and "corresponds to" it.[62] Despite the "utter distinction" between word and thing, the appositional correspondence between word and thing makes him "able to go into the metamorphosis, the flow through things that Emerson speaks of," and the consequent act of "creating a new name" is a "joy and affirmation." Reading Emerson's essay on "The Poet," he says, "brought tears to my eyes"; "it was, like, *recognition* … I can acknowledge this to be how I understand what I do, in ways that I experience …"[63] Emerson called the poet the Namer and Language-maker, and at such moments "[p]art of me is utterly convinced that I am this 'Secretary of Nature' that Emerson calls for."[64]

The reader of a drawing poem moves from puzzlement to recognition. However, the textual difficulty is of a radically different sort from the difficulty in reading "Tjanting," "Dysraphism," or even "My Life": less cerebral, more primary. Confronted with what seems a four-colored snarl of jagged lines and sharp bends, the reader wonders: quite literally, what is the text? Can it be read? Grenier would say: engage and enter the image, follow the colored lines. The "looking/thinking" required to discover the "wording" restores the act of naming as pen touched page and letters shaped words. The wide-eyed reader blinks and says, in the sudden wonder and clarity of recognition: "Ah, yes … AFTER / NOON / SUN / SHINE … Of course. Right in front of me, all the time, for me to read and see … OWL / ON / BOU / GH … Yes. Exactly. Right there." The words found, recognized, realized, as if for the first time; and through the agency of the words a moment in time and place seen, felt, encrypted into text.

Eccentric as the ideogrammic drawing poems may initially appear to be, they are in fact in the mainstream of the American poetic tradition. In their revision of Language theory they represent a finally affirming exploration of Emerson's Romantic dictum "Words are signs of natural facts" and of Williams's Modernist dictum that language recreates the world anew in the likeness of that which it was. Grenier's ideograms (literally, writing the idea of the form of a thing) demonstrate, in his words. "the power of the Imagination, grounded in perception and working with the materials of words."

V

The poet as namer and language-maker: Emerson's concept was of vital interest to another poet associated with the Language group. In fact, no poet of her generation is more self-consciously identified with the mind and spirit of New England – its diarists, sermonists, and theologians, its historians, writers, and poets – than Susan Howe. In the sequence "Thorow," punning on "Thoreau" by giving its phonetic New England pronunciation, Howe is specifically concerned with the act of naming. The wobble in the name – Thoreau or Thorow – anticipates both the concern and the direction of the sequence. For where Grenier is bent on reinterpreting Thoreau's injunction to nail words down to things, Howe's historical consciousness is struck by "the ambiguity and instability of names, the multiple layering of names over time that obscures as well as reveals identity and meaning." The foreword quotes the philosophers Gilles DeLeuze and Felix Guattari: "The proper name (*nom propre*) does not designate an individual: it is on the contrary when the individual opens up to the multiplicities pervading him or her, at the outcome of the most severe operation of depersonalization, that he or she acquires his or her true proper name." One epigraph for the sequence cites Thoreau's desire to study "the history of the ponds in order to get the Indian names straightened – which means made more crooked – &c., &c." And another epigraph quotes a farmer-neighbor denying the accuracy of Thoreau's own given name: "His name ain't no Henry D. Thoreau ... His name's Da-a-vid Henry and it ain't been nothing but Da-a-vid Henry. And he knows that!"[65]

A brief "Narrative" before the "Non-Narrative" of the poem establishes Howe's own Thoreauvian situation. As a resident poet at the Lake George Arts Project in upstate New York during the first months of 1987, she was living alone in "a cabin off the road ... at the edge of the lake." Her solitary experience of the lake and surrounding fields and mountains made her feel as though she "stood on the shores of a history of the world," so that her experience of that particular locale encapsulated the universal human drive – including that of her forebears, those "[p]athfinding believers in God and grammar" – to possess and name and desecrate inhuman and word-less nature. In that history "[e]very name driven will be as another rivet in the machine of a universe flux." Instead, her excursions in the Lake George landscape move, in her imagination, against the course of history to reverse the American "errand into the wilderness"; as "Scout," as "surveyor of the Wood," as pioneer in reverse. The pathfinder follows the regressive direction of Thoreau's "Walking" back toward, in Howe's words, "unknown regions of indifferentiation. The Adirondacks occupied me"; possessed by the spirit of place, "my whole being is Vision." In a 1989 interview Howe, thinking about "Thorow," said: "Language is a wild interiority. I am lost in the refuge of its dark life." From the wild interiority of language came an "interior assembling of forces under the earth's eye": "I heard poems inhabited by voices."[66]

The poems in the first two sections of "Thorow" employ clipped phrases, sharp images, and taut lines to hack a regressive path through his-tory to the pathless "primal indeterminacy." The last poem of the second section is poised at the tipping point between elegy and vision:[67]

Elegiac western Imagination

Mysterious confined enigma
a possible field of work

The expanse of unconcealment
so different from all maps

Spiritual typography of elegy

Nature in us as a Nature
the actual one the ideal Self

tent tree sere leaf spectre
Unconscious demarkations range

I pick my compass to pieces

Dark here in the driftings
in the spaces of drifting

Complicity battling redemption

Howe recognizes that her inescapable place in history makes for a complic-ity in the record of violence and corruption that resists "redemption," even as she disassembles her man-made compass in the push to lose herself and perhaps find herself in "driftings" among "[u]nconscious demarkations."

What follows in the third section of "Thorow" is a series of verbal paste-ups or collages intended to image the capitulation of consciousness and coherence to those driftings. Here is the first of those collages, on page 56 of *Singularities*; it is repeated, upside down, on the opposite page of the text:[68]

Cannot be
every
where I   Parted with the Otterware
entreat
snapt   at the three Rivers, & are
Re s o lu t i o n   picked up arrowhead
picked up arrowhead   hieroglyph   Gone to have a Treaty
                                          battered
                          with the French at Oswego
At this end of the carry   islet
                          & singing their war song
                                          neck
sheen   The French Hatchet

Their Plenipo   squall   Messages   dusk

disc   coin   splint   cedar
lily root   chip   grease   cusk
          a very deep Rabbit
swamp   wavelet
          of which will not per[mit] of
          fitted to the paper, the Margins   shrub

Encampt Fires by   Frames should be exactly   mud
canoes wood night   waterbug
          c o v er y
                                          Cove
                          places to walk out to
          Tranquillity of a garrison
                          Escalade
Traverse canon night siege Constant firing
Traverse canon night siege Constant firing

Gabion
Parapet

Is this an image of losing self in primal indeterminacy? Or does losing self then yield the "[u]nconscious demarkations" of an "ideal Self"? The final poem in "Thorow" looks simpler, but it provides no answer. Alphabetical clusters float across the page free of grammatical connection and coherence, and most are not even immediately recognizable words.[69]

anthen	uplispth	enend
adamap	blue wov	thefthe
folled	floted	keen
		Themis
thouscullingme		
Thiefth		

"Themis" and "Thiefth" are singled out by the capitalized opening syllable "The," "Thie," but is the blind goddess of law and order paired with a law-breaker? The adjectives "blue" and "keen" are suspended without noun referents. The other words seem to be in fluid metamorphosis, dissolving and recombining syllables. Are they dissolving into gibberish and the engulfing silence? Or entering new, as yet incomprehensible combinations, as they approach, in Howe's words, the "central mystery" ("God or the Word, a supreme fiction"),[70] wherein "my whole being is Vision"?

These are questions left deliberately open. Bruce Campbell has called Howe a "post-structuralist visionary" because, "while attuned to a transcendental possibility, she is fully aware of how mediated both language and consciousness are."[71] Or, to invert the emphasis of the statement, while fully aware of how mediated language and consciousness are, she remains attuned to a transcendental possibility. In the spring of 1990, when Howe was a fellow at the Stanford Humanities Center and attended a presentation by another fellow on Shelley's "Mont Blanc," a battery of objections from literal-minded members of the audience complained that Shelley's vague words and images had no clear meaning or coherent reference. To the repeated question as to what the poem was about, Howe spontaneously exclaimed: "It's about language! It's about God!"

In "Thorow," she wanted to experience Lake George "pure, enchanted, nameless," but she knew that "[t]here never was such a place," or at least that no human had known it.[72] She had gone as far as she could in the direction of the undifferentiated nameless. Worthy and even necessary as is the effort to look beyond history lest we be trapped by it, Howe's historical imagination knows that there is no human way out of history: we live it out even as we look beyond. And she is clear about the ground of her intellectual, spiritual, and imaginative engagement with history: "I can't get away from New England. It's in my heart and practice." Not the New England of Frost and Lowell and Creeley, but the New England of the Puritans and their nineteenth-century Romantic successors. What holds and impels her, she has said, is their passionate commitment to testing out, in their own experience, the "idea of grace as part of an infinite mystery in us but beyond us."[73] Their writings – in history and autobiography, in fiction and poetry – ponder the paradox that the American wilderness against which they contended brought them into an immediate encounter with the divine. The nameless reality spelled God. Howe's poems, again and again, arise as responses to one or the other of those earlier texts. In *Singularities*, for instance, the "Thorow" sequence is preceded by "Articulation of Sound Forms in Time," which recreates the wanderings of the Rev. Hope Atherton in the Connecticut River Valley woods following a bloody colonial raid on an Indian camp, and it is followed by "Scattering as Behavior toward Risks," which takes off from Melville's *Billy Budd*.

Of course, the New Englander with whom Howe as woman and poet most intimately identified herself is Emily Dickinson. *My Emily Dickinson* (1985), at once a revisionist interpretation of Dickinson and a prose poem by Howe, takes Dickinson's texts as points of departure for Howe's own psychologically acute and historically aware meditations and explications. *The Birth-Mark: Unsettling the Wilderness in American Literary History* (1993) follows with a broader critique of America's historic errand, but Dickinson is the touchstone throughout. In Howe's reading, Dickinson's antinomian independence combined with a clear-eyed feminism to undertake a radical antinomian experiment in poetic form for her singular negotiations with self, society, nature, and God. What were taken as irregularities of grammar and punctuation, of meter and rhyme and stanza, constitute her dissent from the conventions of her culture and designated social role in the unyielding pursuit of personal vision. Dickinson's early decision to withdraw not just from patriarchal culture but from the conformities of publication and print culture freed her to capitalize, punctuate, arrange, and break her lines on the blank space of the page.

Howe had been a painter before she became a poet. For her, each Dickinson poem is a particular and unique visual creation shaping the sound of the words specifically to the sheet of paper on which she was writing. The printed texts that have been "normalized" into type and even at times reworded by male editors distort Dickinson's conception and intention. Aside from the holograph manuscripts at Harvard and Amherst, Howe would say, the most authentic texts are the facsimiles

reproduced in *The Manuscript Books of Emily Dickinson*. In this view of
Dickinson as a crypto-Language poet, the holographs, bound by hand
into fascicles, can be seen to anticipate experiments in Language poetry
like Grenier's drawing poems and Howe's own type collages.

In point of fact, however, Howe's poems, including the type collages,
do not, most of the time, read like Dickinson's, precisely because Howe
has a historical imagination where Dickinson has a lyric imagination. In
contrast to Howe, Dickinson compresses thought and feeling, image and
metaphor into a dense moment of verbal realization, rendered characteristically in a few tight, rhymed quatrains. Howe's poems have such lyrical passages, but her commitment to history needs to follow out ideas,
images, issues through a narrative, however discontinuous and nonlinear,
that extends itself into sequences, often quite long sequences.

The following passage from *My Emily Dickinson* – the opening of a
section called "Architecture of Meaning" – illustrates how Howe recon-
figures Dickinson. After citing lines from Robert Browning's "Childe
Roland to the Dark Tower Came," Howe quotes the opening quatrain
of a Dickinson poem (a poem that recurs in different contexts through
the book). Then, alluding to Dickinson's assertion in another poem that
"I dwell in Possibility – / A fairer House than Prose – ," Howe unwinds
and deciphers the elliptical metaphor in Dickinson's quatrain, spinning
elements from Dickinson's biography and psychology, her literary enthu-
siasms and historical moment into a cadenza that is unmistakably a Howe
prose poem:[74]

> *My Life had stood – a Loaded Gun*
> *In Corners – till a Day*
> *The Owner passed – identified –*
> *And carried Me away –*

My and me. In this unsettling New England lexical landscape nothing is
sure. In a shorter space (woman's quick voice) Dickinson went further than
Browning, coding and erasing – deciphering the idea of herself, dissimula-
tion in revelation. Really alone at a real frontier, dwelling in Possibility was
what she had learned to do.

POSSIBILITIES:

My Life: A Soul finding God.
My Life: A Soul finding herself.
My Life: A poet's admiring heart born into voice by idealizing
a precursor poet's song.
My Life: Dickinson herself, waiting in corners of neglect for
Higginson to recognize her ability and help her to
join the ranks of other published American poets.

My Life: The American continent and its westward moving
frontier. Two centuries of pioneer literature and
myth had insistently compared the land to a virgin
woman (bride and queen). Exploration and
settlement were pictured in terms of masculine
erotic discovery and domination of
alluring/threatening feminine territory.
My Life: The savage source of American myth.
My Life: The United States in the grip of violence that
threatened to break apart its original Union.
My Life: A white woman taken captive by
Indians.
My Life: A slave.
My Life: An unmarried woman (Emily Brontë's Catherine
Earnshaw) wating to be chosen (identified) by her
Lover-husband-Owner (Edgar Linton).
My Life: A frontiersman's gun.

In Howe's delineation, the possibilities in which "My Life" dwells run the
gamut between "[a] soul finding God" and "[a] frontiersman's gun."

Reflecting on "Thorow" shortly after it was published, Howe
observed: "The older I get the more Calvinist I grow … The Puritans or
Calvinists knew that what we see is nothing to the unseen." The word "errand"
denotes both a wandering or straying and a journey with a mission and on a
mission. It was, she felt, the Calvinist sense of sin that impelled the Puritan
errand to look for "America before the fall," and "I think my own poetry
is only a search by an investigator for the point where the crime began …
Will I ever capture it in words?" Or was it only a "dream of Arcadia"?[75]

None of her writings demonstrate her "Puritan" search more personally
and powerfully than *That This* (2010). Its three sequences, in their very
different styles and tones, trace a single sweeping trajectory back through
time and loss toward that perhaps irrecoverable end-point of origin. *That
This*: two demonstrative pronouns without any designated referent: "Will
I ever capture it in words?"

"The Disappearance Approach" immediately states the tragic personal
loss from which the sequences arise: the sudden and unexpected death
of Howe's husband, Peter Hare, from an embolism in January 2008.
He was a philosopher, and their minds and imaginations ran parallel
courses, including a shared interest in the thought and writings of Charles
Sanders Pierce, the central figure in Howe's *Pierce-Arrow* (1999). "The
Disappearance Approach" evolved from a journal that Howe began in the
first shock of her husband's death before she had any notion of shaping
parts of it into a prose poem. The narrative sections recount those dark

days with a spare and muted understatement necessitated by emotions whose depths are deflected and objectified in the interspersed sections that allow Howe to approach her loss through other cherished texts.[76]

At the Metropolitan Museum Howe had been deeply moved by an exhibit of the landscapes of the neoclassical painter Nicholas Poussin, and she was reading T. J. Clark's *The Sight of Death*, a detailed examination (also written in journal form) of two Poussin landscapes. In her own journal Howe sees the inclusion of mythological figures in Poussin's classical landscapes, like those in Ovid's *Metamorphoses*, as recognitions of the entrance of death and suffering into the doomed "dream of Arcadia." For several years before Peter Hare's death, Howe had been working in the vast archive of Jonathan Edwards, the great Puritan theologian, and his family in the Beinecke Library at Yale. "Poussin," Howe said, "lived a hundred years before Edwards and in such a different place! But the world of the imagination has its similarities." So now, along with Poussin, Edwards and his sisters move through Howe's reflections, and she tells of finding in the archive what remains of Edwards's married sister Hannah's diary ("on bits and scraps of paper") as well as a transcription of Hannah's diary ("with commentary") by her daughter Lucy "on folded sheets of paper (rather like a Dickinson fascicle)."[77]

From the first sentence of Hannah's diary – "Oh! that I had the wings of a dove, that I might fly away and be at Rest" – Howe "felt that she was a shadow of me or I was one of her," and that sense of profound identification, losing and finding herself in Hannah, led to "Frolic Architecture," the sequence after "The Disappearance Approach" in the volume, so that "the two sections came together." The opening words of "Frolic Architecture" designate the poem to follow as one attempt to capture "That This" in words:[78]

> That this book is a history of
> a shadow that is a shadow of
>
> me mystically one in another
> Another another to subserve

Me, Hannah, and Another another: the doubling with Hannah moves into a further dimension of realization that the philosopher Pierce called a thirdness. The capital A of "Another" suggests that Howe's "book," through identification with the Puritan Hannah, lies open to the possibility of some shadowy, mystical subservience to the divine.

In her grief, Howe has said, she sought solace in the words of Edwards, especially the "Personal Narrative" and *Images or Shadows of Divine Things*, and of Emerson, especially the essay on "Experience." The title of the sequence comes from the last line of Emerson's poem "The Snow Storm," in which the wind is the irrepressible creative spirit of Nature, even in winter, transforming the world and challenging "astonished Art" to imitate "the frolic architecture of the snow." Emerson's poem "always evokes" for Howe as its polar antithesis Stevens's "The Snow Man" in the death-grip of winter.[79] Between these poles Howe set about making her own "frolic architecture" of text: copying out passages from Hannah's diary on the computer in different fonts, cutting the printed passages up into "bits and scraps" (like the fragments of diary), and pasting them with Scotch tape into collaged texts that create "a landscape out of print traces."[80] At times other snippets mix with the bits of diary: Hawthorne's "The Snow Maiden," references to Poussin, phrases from Ovid (for reasons suggested earlier). That interior landscape visualizes, in a series of images, a consciousness splintered by lonely desolation yet aching for wholeness. "[A]lways in sight of happiness & never get to it," the speaker is "so separate," "weary and heavy laden," "my body slipping down" without "an arm of flesh to lean on," "pursuing shadows and things"; yet she is fleetingly "ravished" by "the light movement," "the flash of lightning," the glitter of cloud – "surprisingly Beautiful" moments that might be intimations or "stepping stones / [pe]rhaps to a complete." The hopeful phrase (even the qualifying "perhaps") is incomplete, and the speaker is left torn between the "bleak account" of her life and the weary injunction to "[l]ook forward Oh my soul."[81]

Such a rearrangement of phrases gives an accurate enough linear summary of what is in the textual collages, but it gives no sense of what engaging them on the page is like. Here is a pair of collages on facing pages (56 and 57) near the end of the sequence:[82]

e set at great distance from this world,

t, it then appeared to me a vain, toilsom·

bitants were strangely wandered, lost, &

comfort to me that I was so separatec

vorldly affairs, by my present affliction&

il tho melancholy was yet in a quiet frame

ngers I was in, it was not without a deep

_ prepared for Death, & I did set myself to

 field, &c, the alterations, which he produces, caus
belonged to no body ... as ...

green hi ng the voices of a vast number of beings in
y mind and soon carried my ideas much into
o be very much ravishd with it & sometimes
nce. had scarce any definite ideas her ty kn
felt like a wave in the air, held there by the
omething delirious & sometimes soft yet I w
gree Rational, and consulted with myself abc
s in my imagination only I thought of speak

But :
it dif
my c
oler
o hi
place
jewil
rom
lang
whe
on
ee

It is important to note that visual constructions like these are meant to be read and heard as rhythms of speech. Howe insists that the language of poems, even of seemingly unreadable collages like these, arises from and resides in sound and rhythm: "sound creates meaning. Sound is the core ... if my ear tells me it's wrong, I have to get rid of it, or change it ..." The first sequence in *Singularities* is "Articulation of Sound Forms in Time." Sound is fundamental because "[s]ound is part of the mystery ... sounds are only echoes of a place of first love," as words resonate from and back into primal soundlessness.[83] Howe recorded a number of her poems, including "Frolic Architecture," and hearing the voice of Howe/Hannah utter these phrases, even to the broken, whispered syllables, is a haunted and haunting, deeply moving experience.

On the last page of "Frolic Architecture" the word "sudden," with the initial "s" and the concluding "n" slightly clipped off, is suspended on the blankness of the page. Does "sudden" portend sudden death or sudden revelation? Although some of the poems of the final and title sequence, "That This," were written before the other sequences, most were written after them, and the sequence came together as a response and even resolution to the questions of life and death that the earlier sequences raise. In the poem "That This," the volume *That This* finds its emotional and spiritual completion. After the puzzling collages of "Frolic Architecture," these poems have a grave clarity and cleanly defined shape; each consists of two couplets centered on the page (except for the penultimate poem with three couplets), and the language has the simplicity and directness of the Puritan plain style. Though Edwards is a Calvinist Puritan and Emerson a Romantic Transcendentalist, what they share is a conviction of the typology of nature, and Howe's sequence tests out the proposition of nature as typological.

The Puritans, like other Christians, read the Bible typologically; that is to say, they read the events of the Old Testament as types – as veiled but prefigured revelations – of the events in the New Testament, which they called, clumsily, the antitypes. Thus the three days of Jonah in the whale's belly was read as a type whose full meaning is revealed in the antitype of Christ's resurrection. The Puritans also extended typology into their daily lives, reading the natural world as another "book" of revelation. Edwards's *Images or Shadows of Divine Things*, one of Howe's treasured texts, is a notebook in which he recorded and meditated on observations from his daily experience and from his walks in the wilderness as types (Emerson would say symbols) of spiritual truths. Here is the first poem of "That This":[84]

> Day is a type when visible
> objects change then put
>
> on form but the antitype
> That thing not shadowed

A type that recurs frequently in Edwards's notebook is the dawning of sunrise (son-rise) as a daily reminder of the resurrection, and Howe echoes Edwards when she takes "Day" as the visible form of the antitype. By this point "That This" has become "That thing not shadowed," Being itself; for, in a line later in the sequence, "non-being cannot be 'this.' "

For all her empathy with Edwards and Emerson, Howe cannot easily feel the comfort of their assurance. The penultimate poem asks the question:[85]

> Is one mind put into another
> in us unknown to ourselves
> by going about among trees
> and fields in moonlight or in
> a garden to ease distance to
> fetch home spiritual things

But the closing poem is another 'That' clause that seems to answer with Edwards and Emerson:

That a solitary person bears
witness to law in the ark to

an altar of snow and every
age or century for a day *is*

"This" is the individual's witness to the testament of the Puritan "law of the ark" and the Transcendentalist "altar of snow": despite the ravages of history and the desolations of individual lives, time and nature unfold and enclose a thirdness. The last italicized word affirms that through "every / age or century" each shadowed dawning "*is*" for that day, a type of the unshadowed "I am." The poet is the namer, and the type is the name for the nameless.

Howe said: "A poet is a foreigner in her own language. I don't want to stay inside." If language is a "wild interiority" in which we can lose the way in blurred indifferentiality, its "dark life" may also be a "refuge" in which we can find the words to open the path, if not to the lost Eden, then to day's clear typological expanse. Knowing full well life's entangling limits, Howe can still say: "I hope my sense of limit is never fixed."[86]

VI

Fanny Howe stands even further on the periphery of the Language group than her slightly older sister Susan Howe. But she was included in Ron Silliman's anthology *In the American Tree*, and her work was praised by Creeley (for whom she wrote an elegy, included in *The Lyrics*), Palmer, Hejinian, and Grenier.

Palmer included her essay "The Contemporary Logos" in *Code of Signals*, and he said about "her lifelong parsing of the exchange between matter and spirit": "Writes Emerson, 'The poet is the sayer, the namer, and represents beauty.' Here is the luminous and incontrovertible proof."[87] In *The Lives of a Spirit/Glasstown: Where Something Got Broken* Fanny Howe includes pages of visual design in her own handwriting that recall Grenier's drawing poems, and a page of print collage that recalls Susan Howe's paste-ups. However, Fanny Howe's poems propose a different conception of the poet as sayer and namer from the versions we encountered earlier in the chapter in Susan Howe and Grenier.

Fanny Howe's wry caricature of herself as "Communist, Catholic and overexcited" indicates what sets her apart from Grenier and from Susan Howe.[88] She was no Party member, but the alliteration of "Communist, Catholic" links her critique of the injustices of capitalist society with her religious vision. Where Susan Howe turned to New England Puritans and Transcendentalists, Fanny Howe turned to Catholic mystics and reformers. Moreover, where her sister's is fundamentally a historical imagination, finding voice intertextually through other voices, hers is a lyric imagination, as the title of her 2007 volume *The Lyrics* underscores. For that reason, despite Susan Howe's identification with Dickinson in mind and spirit, Fanny Howe's poems feel and sound more like Dickinson's in shape and intention, as the speaker encapsulates an intense, even "overexcited" moment of consciousness in lyric form, word by loaded word, image by edged image.

The first poem in Howe's *Introduction to the World* (1986) sounds an unmistakably lyric voice:[89]

> I'd speak if I wasn't afraid of inhaling
> A memory I want to forget
> Like I trusted the world which wasn't mine
> The hollyhock in the tall vase is wide awake
> And feelings are only overcome by fleeing
> To their opposite. Moisture and dirt
> Have entered the space between threshold and floor
> A lot is my estimate when I step on it
> Sorrow can be a home to stand on so
> And see far to: another earth, a place I might know

As with Dickinson, the "I" in this poem, distinctively personal without being descriptively autobiographical, is a creation and creature of the poem; and, in Dickinson's phrase, the speaker tries to "Tell all the Truth but tell it slant –" with surprising sidewise leaps and oblique metaphorical connections to grasp the emotional and spiritual stresses of the immediate moment: "Success in Circuit lies."[90]

Each poem in *Introduction to the World* is ten lines long, and the first nineteen poems are revised and revisioned in the second nineteen. Here is the revisioning of the poem above:[91]

> I wasn't just a memory but a lot
> Like the one you forget
> When you're not afraid. Take the space
> I leave, it's not mine. I am a place for you
> To see far to: a vase, a threshold
> Entering a floor of earth
> Moisture meaning sorrow
> My home was only overcome by an estimate
> And step. No door you could flee for
> Inhaling I'm free

The space in which she speaks in this poem is different from enclosed space of the first poem. She has inhaled and, no longer held by fear, has freed herself to or toward that other, still unspecified, as yet unrealized place she longs to know. Now "you" (the reader or an aspect of the speaker) are where "I" was; "I" am "your" new "threshold," already in a liminal place "for you / To see far to."

A poem like the one below records a moment that suddenly opens out into a "wild" epiphany of cosmic sublimity:[92]

> There is nothing I hear as well as my name
> Called when I'm wild. The grace of God
> Places a person in the truth
> And is always expressed as a taste in the mouth
> Walking with your arms wide open
> And 263 days to follow, four morning stars
> And Yuri Gagarin orbiting Earth
> I know I may never be found or returned
> When Peter, Henri or Mary call me
> Fanny, as if they know who owns me

Here the "I" discovers who she is by responding to the "call" of the "grace of God." Her identity is as individual as her name and as physical as "a taste in the mouth" yet "wide open" to the universe. As in a number of Dickinson's ecstatic poems, she circulates through time and space; she feels like the first astronaut, out so far that she may not be able to return when summoned back by old friends and earthly companions. Now that she knows "who owns me," is she still Fanny? Does she have a new identity?

Commentators all echo Palmer's recognition that Howe's poetry is a metaphysical quest, a spiritual inquiry into material and social life. In the essay "Footsteps Over Ground" she describes her conversion to Catholicism in 1980 as a lifetime marriage commitment:

> In 1961 I dropped out of college and married. In 1963 I left the marriage, and I fell apart. In 1968 I married again and had three children in four years, and that marriage fell apart. In 1980 I married for the third time, with determination to fulfill my vow. You see, I married the Catholic Church this time ...

Her Harvard professor father came from an old and distinguished New England family, but neither he nor her Irish actress mother were believers. She and her sister Susan grew up in a secular and skeptical household, but in response, where Susan's mind and imagination sought out her Puritan forebears, Fanny became a Catholic. She found, however, that "[t]he

Catholic church turns a person into a Protestant mentally ... arguing with texts, testing them, and feeling indignation against dogma, dull vocabulary, hierarchies, moralizing, and patronizing vocabulary." The Protestant in her tested the power and limits of language, the capacity of our "vocabulary" to resolve its ambiguities and distortions and grasp ultimate reality. But, she said, while "all Catholics are Protestants ... not all Protestants are Catholic." The reason that she could not "just *be* a Protestant" and instead became a Catholic was a search for a different kind of language: not the language of theological disquisition but the language of the mystics and of the liturgies celebrating the sacramental mysteries. As a Catholic, she said, you could "argue yourself to the abyss of understanding, slip over the edges, grasp onto the Gospel teachings for dear life, and hear the same words over and over and over – morning, noon, and Sunday – in every city in the world." The epigraph for the essay indicates the efficacy of that language: "*The Mass is an account of the cooperation of transcendence with the ordinary.*"[93]

What she took from the Mass as the basis for her poetry and fiction is the conviction that truth can break through the fissures and obliquities of slant-wise language:[94]

> As it is in the liturgy, so it is in the world: Truth is as fleeting as a sunbeam, and each time you go to Mass, you see truth drop in a place it hadn't before. A word here, a phrase there, and each time a different one is as potent as the little sip of wine at the end. The truth exists, but it surrounds rather than informs people's acts, which are constructed around evasion and resistance.

The Eucharist, while "totally mad in terms of human reason," inscribes "another kind of intelligence ... both earthy and cosmological."

Where William Everson and Denise Levertov came to experience the Incarnation as the central and galvanizing force in nature and human nature and so in language, Howe finds the Incarnation so absent in the public world, finds the world so hostile to the significance of the Word of the Eucharist that our words can only circulate around the missing center. "[T]he incarnational experience of being" consists of the realization "that one is inhabited by the witness who is oneself and by that witness's creator simultaneously." But for the most part our fumbling words have to approach that experience slant-wise through a *via negativa*, through what it is not. Nevertheless, what sustains Howe in the act of language is the conviction she cites from the theologian Martin Buber: "Every name is a step toward the consummate Name, as everything broken points to the unbroken."[95]

But because humans are in fact so broken, so caught in "a double bind established in childhood, or a sudden confrontation with evil in the world – that is, in themselves," the *via negativa* of faith follows what Howe calls an existential state of bewilderment. In the theology of bewilderment God is "present" in time and space "as the embodied names of animals, minerals, and vegetables" and "in the hearts of humans who carry the pulse of the One's own wanting to be known by the ones who want in return to be known by it," but humanity, alienated from the incarnate presence and so from itself, knows only "the longing to be loved" and misses "the very quality that inhabits itself."[96]

In the essay "Immanence" Howe recalls her first memories as the dawning awareness of loss and longing:[97]

> When I was a child I was hyperconscious of the silence surrounding all matter and at first this silence was a dynamic that encouraged me. As time went by, however, the silence became increasingly erratic in the lengths and directions of its waves and not so partial to me.
>
> Being a child of the twentieth century I suppose that the emotional source of this fixation on silence may have come from my father's absence during the Second World War and my yearning for his return. On the other hand, my attention to what was missing may have begun earlier, when this fullness in the air vanished because it vanished the minute I welcomed it consciously.

Her "introduction to the world" was a vanishing, and the vanishing is simultaneous with and caused by the coming to consciousness.

> That body of light and listening around my crib simply moved on as soon as I let it know that I knew it was there. After that it actually seemed to thicken and collaborate with the world in a larger plan for my personal isolation. I began to wonder if the negative emotional responses that emerge in a lifetime aren't generated by that first loss of stability and containment – one that precedes even the loss of security among parents and other people – because it is the loss of a feeling of enfoldment in the whole cosmos, not just in a household.

As we have seen, Emerson psychologized New England theology by contending that the fall into consciousness was the original sin that fractured our perceptions thereafter, and Dickinson's haunted description of that moment, cited earlier in the chapter, gives the fall into consciousness poignant lyric expression: "A loss of something ever felt I – / The first that I could recollect / Bereft I was."[98] Howe has said that we should read her poems like a record or notebook of a life's passage. It is a record of a lifelong mourning,[99] a lost child's search for home in an alien world.

Howe's fixation on that initiating point of primal bereavement is recorded throughout her writings in the many poignant images of children and childhood, of a sheltering mother or grandmother with a child, of a child with or without a mother or father:[100]

> I dreamed I was a closed book
> ending: *Mother, why this me?*
>
> Her face looked like an oncoming car,
> she had no answer, driving by
>
> It was my hand that wrote me:
> *Pull the covers over your story and say*
> *light, light again and again.*
> *Illuminate your pages this way.*

The unmothered speaker pries open again the closed book of herself to answer her existential question (*"why this me?"*) by writing, in the darkness, her own illuminated text. Howe would look back and say: "I was always in a state of shock and awe at existing. It was inevitable that I would end up Catholic ..." Moreover, the religious and political commitments she made in answering her question, *"why this me?,"* only confirmed her unparented isolation:

> Father got worried when I went to the far left
> And called me self-indulgent. Mother laughed
> When I became a Catholic. She didn't believe it. I left the blackened house
> And walked in the dark, throwing ballast overboard
> For the sake of a future of solitariness.

In this suspension of bewildered estrangement, "I preferred animals and strangers to my forefathers."[101]

Howe's theology of bewilderment developed, she said, "from living in the world and also through testing it out in my poems and through the characters in my fiction," and thus it developed as well into "a poetics and a politics." "The politics of bewilderment" is a "grassroots" politics of "the little and weak": "circling the facts, seeing the problem from varying directions, showing the weaknesses from the bottom up, the conspiracies, the lies, the plans, the false rhetoric" of competitive, profit-driven capitalism.[102] But Howe's political poems, unlike those of Adrienne Rich or Denise Levertov, are less bent on advocating action to change the system than on relating its failings to the underlying moral and spiritual dilemma of bewilderment.

In the end, Howe realized, bewilderment is a "language problem." When we fall into consciousness, we fall into language, as impaired and fractured as we are. Since "[l]anguage, as we have it, fails to deal with confusion," bewilderment can either remain passively confounded and paralyzed, or it "begins to form, for me, more than an attitude – but an actual approach, a way – to settle with the unresolvable." This is what she meant by arguing yourself to the abyss of understanding and slipping over the edge so that "a complete collapse of reference and reconcilability ... breaks open the lock of dualism (*it's this or that*) and peers out into space (*not this, not that*)" until absence reveals presence. Bewilderment opens into a further wild place on 'the threshold of love's sanctuary which lies above that of reason.' "[103]

The aesthetic "form" that Howe's bewilderment takes is, characteristically, "the serial poem" because such an open form does not seek finality and closure "around a set of interlocking symbols and metaphors," but instead spins out flawed phrases and images to circle around their absent center in the hope of catching some adumbration of presence. "[T]he spiral poem" is "cyclical, returning, but empty at its axis," and its "circling can take form as sublimations, inversions, echolalia, digressions, glossolalia, and rhymes": human speech insistently seeking the lost Logos. Excerpting individual poems from their serial sequences in a critical argument like this one fails to give the effect of the sequences' spiraling. On the contrary, "[t]he maze and the spiral have aesthetic value" precisely because "Success," if it is to come, "in Circuit lies."[104]

In the essay "The Contemporary Logos" Howe rehearses the argument between the Gnostic Marcion and the Platonist Philo of Alexandria as two interpretations of the devolution from the voice of "Yahweh, the Law, the Logos" into the lacunae and indeterminacy of human language. Philo contended that "the Logos (our source) showed us the way to understand ourselves and our actions. That is, Scripture." On the other hand, Gnostics like Marcion read "the Passion of Jesus" as the failure of the Scriptural Logos demonstrating that "God was distant, alien, indifferent"; "[t]he Gnostics felt it [the Logos] fading into eternity and becoming that eternity." Howe comments that "[m]any recent thinkers share this attitude" and clearly understands their bewilderment, but in the end she resists contemporary gnostic pessimism. It is true that "[p]oets tend to hover over words in this troubled state of mind," but "[w]hat holds them poised in this position is the occasional eruption of happiness ... poets act out the problem with their words."[105]

The prose poem "Doubt" reflects on three women forebears who "sought salvation in a choice of words": Virginia Woolf, Edith Stein, and Simone Weil. For Howe, their words and lives chart three possible responses to the question: "Is it possible to imagine another world ('God'?) or are we condemned to a knowing that is based in our limited perceptions?" Woolf's tragic suicide confirms for Howe that "[a]nyone who tries, as she did, out of a systematic training in secularism, to forge a rhetoric of belief is fighting against the odds." Weil took a different course: despite her "rational prose line," Weil "could be called a poet ... because of the longing for a conversion that words might produce," and "[h]er prose is tense with effort." But the linguistic "sign of conversion" eventuates in "a whole change in discourse." And Howe sees the conversion of Edith Stein, the existential philosopher and disciple of Husserl and Heidegger, inscribed in her ability "to transform an existential vocabulary into a theological one." In other writings as well as "Doubt" Howe reflects on the witness of Weil and Stein. Weil represents to her the state of "active" bewilderment and doubt that "nourishes willpower, and ... is the invisible engine behind every step taken." But Stein represents the further step of a "deliberate choice of one epistemology over another as an act of self-salvation": "a skeptical Jewish philosopher who poured meaning back into the abyss, who 'found God,' who came to believe that Catholicism was the fulfillment of Judaism – its outcome, its offspring – and who changed her way of thinking and living during the ruthless flow of mid-twentieth century history."[106] Stein became a Catholic in 1922 and a Carmelite nun (as Sister Teresa Benedicta of the Cross) in 1934; she was arrested by the Nazis, sent to the gas chamber at Auschwitz in August 1942 and canonized as a saint and martyr in 1998.

Howe empathized with Stein's entering the Carmelite convent: "in Carmel one is wedded to Christ ... The body becomes an easy channel for the invisible." Howe's lifelong mourning, like Dickinson's, is drawn to that mystical marriage, in which the child can become a bride and the bride remain an inviolate child:[107]

> If I'd known all along
> I'd be alone
> I'd have gone
> to Mount Carmel
> as a child-bride calling
>
> *Marry me, God!*

And, although she followed instead the more conflicted way of bewilderment, she called her own embrace of Catholicism an inviolable marriage and titled her "Reflections on Word and Life" *The Wedding Dress.*

Musing in "Doubt" on her three exemplary forebears, Howe poses a crucial question for her life in language: "Is there, perhaps, a quality in each person – hidden like a laugh inside a sob – that loves even more than it loves to live? / If there is, can it be expressed in the form of the lyric line?"[108] "The Passion" occupies half of the volume *Gone*, in which "Doubt" appears. One of Howe's longest serial poems, divided into fourteen clusters of poems, it is a sustained effort to test whether the lyric line can express the human hunger for love greater than life. The word "passion" denotes both erotic love and suffering, and near the center of the sequence a litany of infinitives turns the heart's bewilderment around and around the presence and absence of love:[109]

> To die for love
> to die of love
> to die in love
> to die with love
> to die over love
> to die without love
> to die to love
> to die in the mine
> and be a "mine"
> in the arms of someone's
> chest wound, "Here I will die of the above."

The turns and reversals, the connections and gaps in the individual lyrics of "The Passion" swirl around the longing of the speaker ("I" but sometimes "you" and even "she") for an elusive "he," a beloved who (as in Dickinson's poems) comes and goes and finally disappears. The last lyric is:

> He didn't answer
> The market crashed, rebounded
> and the mourning doves cooed
>
> He couldn't answer
>
> Between my brain and this silence
> time lifted and measured
>
> There was no more reason to die

Without love there is no reason to live or to die. *Gone* is the title of the volume, and the word "gone" occurs more than once in "The Passion." In all the spiraling, the redemptive Passion of Jesus receives only glancing allusion as ironic counterpoint, but the failure of erotic love is intuited long before the end:

> Blood when I dreamed of love
> Love is the dream's blood
> Blood on the way to the past
> Red path red heart white dust

In Howe's poems the unparented child becomes the abandoned lover and, recently, the sheltering mother with child or children. Most recently, the mother in second childhood. The title poem of the 2014 volume *Second Childhood* imagines second childhood not as decline into senility but, on the contrary, as a reversal of adult bewilderment into some recovery of the lost sense of wholeness in an inspirited world. The whimsical playfulness of the speaker in "Second Childhood" makes her sound at first like a child; she is even rebuked by grown-ups for her seeming simplicity: "One cruel female said, 'Don't laugh so much. You're not a child.' / My cheeks burned and my eyes grew hot." The speaker is stung by adult judgment, but in the next poem affirms her choice of a second childhood: "So my commitment to childhood has once again been affirmed. / Read the signs, not the authorities / You might think I am just old but I have finally / decided to make the decision to never grow up." Then she can happily ride the skies in her dreams, sitting "beside my / daughter to watch the wind" and "see the stars and the storm." "If we'd been grown-ups," she says, we "would have perished." In another poem in the sequence ego-consciousness is "spider-dust" from a "web of its own making" that "turns to enamel and hardens on fulfillment"; but second childhood spins "another kind of web of a type that doesn't harden but swings and shimmers" and is "the web-hood of a lost spirit." Through that shimmering web she sees the everyday world transformed into fairytale, with gods and goddesses who are good mothers and fathers and answer "their mortal children's prayers ... sometimes in the form of mist, sometimes as needles of sunlight."[110]

When Jesus' disciples acted too much like bickering, competitive grown-ups, he warned them that unless they became again like little children, they would not enter the Kingdom. But "Second Childhood," with its whimsical return to a child's enchanted world, is an uncharacteristic lark among Howe's poems. Another recent poem catches the lost spirit's longing for another world in a grittier image, as the alliterations push toward the surprise of the last word: we are "[l]ike fish in a secular city / / flipping through sewers for a flash of Christ."[111] For a way out of bewilderment toward what might be called an adult second childhood, Howe's mind and imagination have increasingly turned to the renunciations and reorientations of the monastic life, realized most fully in mystics like John of the Cross, Catherine of Siena, Francis of Assisi, and Teresa of Avila. Another poem in *Second Childhood* is called "A Child in Old Age."[112] As we heard earlier, the mourning child and the bereft lover long to become the child-bride of Mount Carmel, "calling / / *Marry me, God!*": "You may be lonely but you are not empty"; "Unlike the body of a beloved lover whose arms and legs enfold you, give you joy, then part and depart, the air and your own senses of hearing, seeing, feeling become your companions and spiritual oxygen. They stay with you. The visible world is soon emblematic of the intentions of the invisible."[113]

Howe did not enter Mount Carmel, but she has regularly spent periods of retreat in various monasteries and convents in the United States, Ireland, and Italy. "Outremer," an earlier version of "A Vision" in *Second Childhood,* acknowledges the affinity between the monastic life and her life as a poet: "A friend entered my studio and cried out, '*The Diary of a Country Priest!*' / because it was such a monastic space, / and the light in the window solidified for a minute." The next line quotes the priest in the film version of Georges Bernanos's novel: "'What does it matter?' the young priest asks at the end of that film. 'Everything is grace.'"[114] Howe makes no claims to mystical experience, but she describes the inclination and direction of her life and poetry not in terms of literary experimentation but in terms of receptivity to the slanted adumbrations of Logos:[115]

> [F]or some reason, my attention has always been focused on absent presences, invisible forces, the Beyond, and I have found these are located in thought and the body, not in material texts and objects. So I wait for chance interventions to come through me, visions or hints of presences, and go to Mass. My poems are "revelations" rather than experiments. I have steeped myself in Jewish mystical thought, Augustine, Dante, Francis ... more than in poetry.

Poems written from life rather than from other poems; language, poised on the possibility of incarnation, coiling not around other words but around the imminence/immanence of "absent presences, invisible forces."

The first half of "A Vision," which closes *Second Childhood*, describes Howe's residence at a monastery near Assisi. She went because "[s]ome old people want to leave this earth and experience another. / They don't want to commit suicide. They want to wander out of sight / without comrades or luggage." Her lodging in what used to be the granary opens that other world: "From the moment I entered the long strange space, / I foresaw an otherworldly light taking shape." Her long walks through the Umbrian countryside are a pilgrimage in Francis's footsteps, and her meditations lead her to him:[116]

> Some people's lives are more poetic than a poem,
> and Francis is certainly one of these.
>
> I know, because he walked beside me for that short time
> whether you believe it or not. He was thirteen.

Thirteen: precisely the right age for the mystical marriage of the child-bride.

The poetics of revelation she is following could hardly be further from the Postmodernist slippages of $L=A=N=G=U=A=G=E$ writing. She sees language as the flawed medium of human bewilderment, but not as a closed semiotic code. Palmer is correct in seeing her instead as a language-maker and namer. But her naming has less in common with Emerson's Romantic Transcendentalism than with Dickinson's sense that doubt is the janus-face of faith and that bewilderment requires that we tell the Truth (Dickinson uses a capital T) only by telling it slant: the encircling of Logos. She makes no large Romantic claims for the power of words, but she persists in language, both in poetry and fiction, because, with luck and attention, words can catch the revelations of "invisible forces" momentarily "located in thought and the body."

"For the Book" is the dedicatory poem for *Second Childhood*, but it can stand as the preface to and summary of all Howe's slanting and spiraling poems:[117]

> Yellow goblins
> and a god I can swallow.
> Eyes in the evergreens
> under ice.
>
> Interior monologue
> and some voice.

> Weary fears, the
> usual trials and
>
> a place to surmise
> blessedness.

Howe chose as epigraph for *Second Childhood* Blake's line, "*Fear & hope are – Vision*"; the sentence leaps over the dash to follow through the theology of bewilderment. Her own poem "For the Book" marks a similar turn from bewilderment to vision. These ten spare lines compress the circlings of the serial poems, as the swift line-enjambments and the repeated conjunction "and" elide a series of oppositions ("*Fear & hope*") into metamorphic revelations. With a flip of a letter, "b" to "d," "goblins" become "a god I can swallow"; in a play on homonyms, "eyes" see and are seen through "ice"; an "interior monologue" finds "voice"; "fears" and "trials" yield to "blessedness."

The American Poetic Tradition
The Power of the Word

This historical and critical argument about the development of an American poetic tradition has evolved through three volumes written over almost four decades, and after the detailed examination of poets whose work spans several centuries, it is time to look back and retrace the line of argument.

Politicians talk about the "special relation" between the United States and England, and, in arts and letters, Americans have been drawn to and envious of the history, traditions, and literature of the country from which we declared our political independence. In the Massachusetts wilderness, the Puritans Anne Bradstreet and Edward Taylor had only English Renaissance poets as models. In the first generation of professional writers, William Cullen Bryant was praised as "the American Wordsworth," and James Fenimore Cooper as "the American Scott." Nineteenth-century American writers visited and paid homage to the old country: Washington Irving with *Bracewell Hall*, Emerson with *English Traits*, Nathaniel Hawthorne with *Our Old Home*. Hudson River artists knew the English landscapes of Constable, Turner, and Martin and turned to John Ruskin for their aesthetic theory. All-American Whitman treasured Tennyson's acknowledgment and was even willing to expurgate his poems to have a British edition. A number of Americans settled in England: Benjamin West, John Singer Sargent, Henry James, James Whistler; and, in the twentieth century, T. S. Eliot, H.D., and for a while Ezra Pound and Robert Frost, whose first two books of poems about New England were published in Old England. American cultural Anglophilia persisted well into the twentieth century. Moreover, if American writers and artists often felt diminished by the lack of settled traditions and an acknowledged place in the economic hustle of the new democratic society, their insecurity was often confirmed by a British conviction of superiority, expressed most smugly by the critic Sydney Smith in *The Edinburgh Review* in 1820: "In the four quarters of the globe, who reads an American book? Or goes to an American play? Or looks at an American picture or statue?" American writers and artists were soon to refute Smith's taunt, but the import of his questions nevertheless reverberated for a long time in the cultural psyches of both the old and the new countries.

At the same time, the conjunction of envious Anglophilia with British condescension generated, right from the start, the counter, even stronger impulse to match our political independence with a declaration of cultural and artistic independence. The first literary publication from the New World was Anne Bradstreet's book of poems, printed in Britain but ostentatiously called, for all its indebtedness to English antecedents, *The Tenth Muse, lately Sprung up in America*. The very marginalization of writers and artists in the rough-and-tumble, as "Nature's Nation" rapidly transformed itself into a capitalist economy and an industrial power, gave them this paradoxical advantage: they had to determine, for themselves first of all, the means and ends of their art. American individualism informed not just our public and economic life but our psychological and religious – and cultural – life. One by one, generation by generation, each for himself or herself, writers have felt compelled to invent, more or less *ex nihilo*, what to say and how to say it. American art and literature proceed less on convention than discovery: forms and terms of expression distinct not only from English precedents but from other American precedents. Each time we start, or feel that we start, more or less with a clean slate, a blank page, a fresh canvas. What characterizes even those writers concerned with history and tradition – Cooper, Hawthorne, James, Eliot, Pound, Faulkner, Lowell, Susan Howe – is their individuality and difference.

Standing alone and on the outside, the American poet could assume no given role, no accepted function, and so had to draw from within himself or herself the sources, terms, and ends of literary practice. In Britain, the existence of a rich and honored tradition and an acknowledged literary class meant that British poets – Dryden and Pope, Wordsworth and Keats, Tennyson and Arnold, Hardy and Auden and Larkin – did not have the same anxiety and need to justify and prove themselves as American poets did. For Americans, therefore, poetry was inseparable from poetics; poetics had to precede and justify the poetry. Thus the American poetic tradition works itself out through a series of debates about the resources and limits of language. The particular terminology and cultural context change over the years, but the determining issue remains essentially the same: whether language gives form and expression to an objective truth or in its formal expression creates its own meaning. The continuity and discontinuity in American poetics consists in a persistent but shifting dialectic about the truth-telling and fictive capacities of language.

Justification was a major concern of Puritan theology, and the Puritans, prolific though they were in the spoken and printed word, maintained a wary suspicion of literature and art. History and biography, theology and sermons aimed at discerning, recording, and disseminating the truth of experience under the guidance of Providence. But pictures, poems, and novels? Images of saints and of Jesus were forbidden as fabrications and so falsifications. Novels and plays were made-up fictions and so untruths, lies. Music and poetry lulled rational control and inflamed emotions and passions. Puritan commentators made a categorical distinction between two kinds of verbal and visual images: types and tropes. Types were images that revealed meanings ordained by God; thus meaning was not accidental or invented, but embodied in and intrinsic to the objects and people imaged. Typology began as a system of scriptural interpretation, reading people and events and images in the Old Testament as divinely intended prefigurations of people, events, and images in the New Testament. But the Puritans came to extend typology to the reading of natural creation as the other book of revelation. Among Puritan writings Jonathan Edwards's prose journal *Images or Shadows of Divine Things*, recording his excursions into the woods and fields of Massachusetts, is the fullest and richest exploration of the typology of Nature.

In contrast to types, tropes were mere figures of speech, metaphors and similes made up by the fertile human imagination and invested with dubious fictive meaning by the ingenuity of the writer. Besides being a distraction from the pursuit of the eternal truths, the appeal of tropes to the fleshly senses and to the emotions could awaken demonic temptations to sin. Such poetry as might be written – hymns and prayers – was to be composed in the plain style, trimmed of decorative metaphorical artifice, as in the best of Bradstreet's domestic poems. Taylor's elaborately and magnificently tropological poems look like a glaring exception, but in his mind they were written to serve a typological purpose; they were unpublished and private meditations on scriptural passages composed in preparation for writing his sermon for the next Sabbath service.

The typology of Nature provided the continuity from Puritan poetics to the Romantic Transcendentalist poetics of the nineteenth century. Where the Puritans made a distinction between types and tropes, the Romantics distinguished between works of the Imagination (often with a capital letter to indicate its metaphysical source and scope) and works of fancy. Imagination was the supreme human faculty, resolving the dualistic and increasingly skeptical arguments advanced by Enlightenment reason. For the Romantic, sight became insight, intuiting the Creator in Creation; that visionary moment grasped the transcendental reality manifest in the physical phenomena of experience. The metaphorical figurations of fancy might serve to explore and realize the implications of that moment, but its human tropes had to be distinguished from the essential insights of the Imagination. By affirming the truthfulness of imaginative perception and expression, the Romantics personalized and psychologized the notion of types outside the framework of Puritan theology and made the poet in Emerson's words, the namer and language maker.

Emerson regularly used the word "type" to designate those sublime moments when the human seer becomes "a transparent eyeball": "I am nothing; I see all ... I am part or parcel of God." Emerson's *Nature* is his manifesto, and the three axioms in the "Language," cited in the previous chapter, are the most concise American statement of the Romantic aesthetic. Whitman and Dickinson, different as they are from each other, both acknowledged Emerson as inspiration and point of departure in finding their own distinctive language and form: Whitman's expansive free verse catching the rhythms of divine energy animating not just nature but the human body and the comradely life of cities; Dickinson's involuted and divided consciousness, probing in tight quatrains for confirming evidence of cosmic purpose and supernatural meaning in the microcosm of house and garden.

As Dickinson well knew, transcendental moments are not easy to attain, much less to sustain, and then poets were left with the metaphors and tropes of fancy to make their poems. With Emerson enviously in mind, Poe cast himself as the archetypal poet of fancy. In the poem "Israfel" he sets himself against the angelic singer as an earthbound poet, adrift in a dualistic "world of sweets and sours." For Poe, "flowers are merely – flowers"; consequently, his words and images, he feels, can only spin out insubstantial aesthetic fantasies of a dream world: in the title of late poem, "A Dream Within a Dream."

By the end of the nineteenth century, Poe's aestheticism had outlasted Emerson's Transcendentalism, and Modernist manifestos set out to dismiss Romantic metaphysics and idealism in the name of poetry and art expressive of a violent world of broken systems and deracinated individuals. New forms and techniques had, by dint of individual will, to be devised or invented to express and yet contain the psychological, spiritual, and social fragmentation that characterized the modern condition. The poet, Pound declared, had to break the pentameter that had measured English verse for centuries in favor of *vers libre*, collaging images like Cubist canvases. *The Cantos*, *The Waste Land*, Stein's *Tender Buttons*, and Williams's *Spring and All* followed. Whatever meaning the poem attained adhered in the aesthetic construction of fragmented and often seemingly unrelated elements; a poem was its form, however fractured, its own assembled artifice, self-contained and self-sustaining. Archibald MacLeish neatly summed up this aspect of Modernism in the last lines of "Ars Poetica": "A poem should not mean / But be." Imagination, Stevens said, was the only force left to oppose the violence of reality. Even Frost, who still wrote in meter, could only think of the poem as "a momentary stay against confusion."[1]

Yet, despite the anti-Romantic drum-rolling of its manifestos and the rupturing of traditional forms and procedures, Modernism did not, in practice or even in theory, reject Romanticism so much as adapt and reformulate to different cultural circumstances the poetic and linguistic issues central to Romanticism and to the American poetic tradition. Where the Puritans had talked about types and tropes and the nineteenth-century Romantics about Imagination and fancy, Modernist poetics undertook a comparable dialogue about perception and expression in opposing inclinations toward Imagism and Symbolism, exemplified most unmistakably perhaps in Pound and Stevens.

Pound's early iconoclasm rested on the notion of the Image (with a capital I like the Romantic Imagination) as recording the *gestalt* between words and things in an authentic experience of reality. Pound soon came to see in the Chinese ideogram the fusion of word and thing in the linguistic sign, and became determined to devise a comparable technique in the English language. What Pound called the ideogrammic method freed him from a single-image poem like "In a Station of the Metro" into the lifelong venture of *The Cantos*, juxtaposing, without logical or narrative continuity, ideogrammic elements whose emergent interconnections were meant to constitute the inherent form of the poem and thus present a vision of reality that strove to be as comprehensive as Dante's. Pound's linguistics found its source not in Emerson (despite obvious parallels) but in a fusion of Eastern Taoism and Western Neoplatonism. And for Pound, for all his Modernist emphasis on form, the poem, as in Emerson, followed from the vision, so that, even when in his last years he felt that he had failed to achieve the sublime intention in *The Cantos*, he could still say that the failure was his own, not that of his poetics or metaphysics: "it [i.e., the cosmos, the *tao*] coheres all right / even if my notes [i.e., the poem] do not cohere."[2] H.D., whom Pound called the *echt* Imagist, moved in a similar direction from *Sea Garden* to the mystical metaphysics of the later, longer poetic sequences and the autobiographical prose, infusing the Moravian Christianity of her childhood with various gnostic and occult traditions.

Among the Imagists Williams had none of Pound's and H.D.'s religious and metaphysical bent and remained a resolute materialist. In *Spring and All,* which alternated prose enunciating his poetics with poems that exemplified that poetics, he stoutly maintained the disjunction between word and thing. Williams cited Poe for his anti-Transcendentalist insistence on the poem as an artifact, but, far from following Poe into a fanciful dreamland, Williams's Imagism insisted on the inventive power of the imagination to construct a verbal object that was so apposite to nature that it "destroyed and recreated everything afresh in the likeness of that which it was" and thus presented "reality itself."[3]

The French Symbolistes, from Baudelaire and Rimbaud to Valéry, acknowledged Poe as their immediate forebear, and Eliot wrote an essay to trace the line "From Poe to Valéry." And the American Symbolists had a more substantial claim than did Williams to Poe's kind of aestheticism. Where Emerson saw the symbol as type, they, like Poe, internalized the symbol as fancy, evoking elusive states of consciousness through subtle rhythms and metaphorical indirections. Among the American Modernists, both Eliot and Stevens acknowledged their indebtedness to and affinity with the Symbolistes. Eliot said that Laforgue and Baudelaire helped him find a voice for the alienated consciousness and soulless circumstances of urban living. However, by the mid-1920s, Eliot came to see the Symboliste inclination as a symptom of modern sickness, and, after *The Waste Land* and "The Hollow Men," he sought to ground his newfound Christian incarnationalism in a sense of place in the *Quartets* and in the action of verse drama.

Stevens's Symbolistes were Mallarmé and Valéry, and his poems and essays give the fullest statement of an American Symbolist poetics. On one level, Williams could agree with Stevens that, without the Transcendentalist correlation between word and thing, "the difference between philosophic truth and poetic truth appears to become final." However, where Williams the Imagist stresses the poem's recreation of the world as reality itself, Stevens the Symbolist sees the imagination as a force "pressing back against the pressure of reality" by creating its own alternate world, what Stevens calls "the *mundo* of the imagination." Poetic truth is, then, (in the title of Stevens's most famous poem) a "Supreme Fiction." The tropological and metrical artifice of the poetic *mundo* "makes its own constructions" to conjure, in the poet's and reader's minds, the illusory sense of an "agreement with reality" that reasoning can never attain.[4] Stevens's affirmation of the positive, even necessary function of poetic fictions, however, masks a longing for a transcendental connection that would satisfy the alienated mind. For this reason, Stevens says, theorizing about poetry "often seems to become in time a mystical theology or more simply, a mystique." Stevens's famous declaration "We say God and the imagination are one" can mean that God is, as Freud contended, only a projection of human need, but it can also mean that the imagination is the divine power in human consciousness.[5] Stevens's poems "say" both, but the metaphysical diction and sacramental imagery of the later poems increasingly intimate an affinity between word and thing and spirit and foreshadow the account of his deathbed conversion. What we encounter again in Stevens is the fusion of Christian incarnationalism and Romantic idealism deep in the American psyche and spirit that accounts for the metaphysical, often explicitly religious bent of so many of our major poets from the Puritans to the present.

Just as World War I coincides roughly with the advent of the Modernist concentration on art as at least a momentary stay against confusion, so the horrors of World War II precipitated an existential disillusionment that seemed to many to expose Modernist aestheticism as only the residual sham of Romantic claims for the authority of the artist and the integrity of the art work. As an anti-aesthetic, Postmodernism produced more theory than significant poetry: marxist, neo-freudian, sociological, semantic theory that propounded uncertainty and ambiguity with an unambiguous finality. But deconstructing the poetic subject and language as referential signifier left the poet with words that had reference to themselves in a semantic code that, at once predetermined and indeterminate, could only play with its own fluid lacunae and multivalent slippages. Ashbery is the most important Postmodern poet. Some of the more rigorous theoreticians of the Language generation found him disappointingly soft, perhaps because his poems float free of heavy theorizing, lightened by a lingering lyricism, a wacky wit, and a rich engagement with other poets – Stevens and Stein, Auden and Bishop. But Ashbery's work sounds a jazzy, cock-eyed Postmodern riff on Poe's anxiety-ridden Romantic dreamland.

Commentary on American poetry after Modernism has tended to characterize it loosely, for lack of a more substantive term, as Postmodernist. And, as the chapters in this book have indicated, there are Postmodernist aspects and elements in the work of many poets of the postwar period: in Lowell's proliferating and endlessly revised sonnets, in the shifting pronouns and multiple perspectives of Berryman's *Dream Songs*, in the self-reflexiveness of Creeley's *Words* and *Pieces* and Hejinian's *My Life*, in the obliquities of Duncan's "linguistic" poems and Palmer's surrealist poems. But the chapters have also noted a persistent Neoromanticism flexible and varied enough to manifest itself in the work of poets as different as Lowell and Berryman, Ginsberg and Everson, Duncan, Levertov and Rich, as well as (even in the Language group) Grenier and Susan and Fanny Howe.

Some of these poets would resist the label "Romantic" as harking back to a nineteenth-century sensibility that they do not identify themselves with philosophically or formally. However, the essence of Romanticism as a literary and critical term is the affirmation of the poet as seer and sayer. The persistent issue for American poets, in different cultural terms and circumstances, is the capacity of language to locate the inner world of consciousness in the outer world of experience through an understanding or vision of reality – religious or humanist, ethical or political – larger than the sayer and extrinsic to language. The burden of this book has been, therefore, to argue that the postwar period should be seen most accurately in terms of a dialectic between the Postmodernist deconstruction and the Neoromantic affirmation of the poet's role.

No poet of the period was more self-consciously concerned with poetics, traditional and experimental, Romantic and Modernist, than Duncan; his many-sided sensibility put him at the crossroads of the divergent and convergent energies of what has been called the poetry wars that energized the second half of the century. Duncan's early imitations of Stein and his speculations about a purely linguistic poetry made the Language poets claim him as a precursor, and one of his late essays reflects on his own poetic development to illustrate "The Self in Postmodern Poetry." But in fact he was deeply suspicious of Language poetry, because his gnostic imagination convinced him, as we have seen, of "the unbroken continuity" between Romanticism and Modernism. To the assertion by a critic that Modernism precipitated Postmodernism, Duncan offered a contrary genealogy: "I read Modernism as Romanticism."[6]

The long exchange between Duncan and Levertov about how poems mean resumes, more incisively perhaps than anything else in the period, the recurring question that defines the American poetic tradition all the way from the Puritan distinction between types and tropes down to the present day. Does the poem tell the truth or spell out a fiction? Should the poem mean or be? Is what the poem says merely an extension and invention of the form, or does the form function rather to express an insight into experience and reveal a meaning outside the poem? The issues are fundamental, and the various –isms that map literary history record the ways in which those issues have been engaged. But the argument will never be finally settled, will be resumed again and again, because the terms are in fact not dichotomous and exclusive but complementary. They operate not in essential opposition but in dialogic tension with each other. Poems must be to mean, must mean to fulfill their being; they are in various ways the co-instantiation of form and content. What is most interesting and instructive, therefore, are the ways in which the language of each poetic act calibrates the interplay and counterplay of type and trope, imagination and fancy, image and symbol, referential meaning and formal integrity. Puzzling out those subtle and complex negotiations, poet by poet and chapter by chapter, constitutes the historical/critical argument about an American poetic tradition that this book carries forward from the two preceding volumes.

It is too early to make large claims about how poetry will take shape in the twenty-first century. In my very preliminary reading of the present situation, Postmodernism has been deconstructing itself, and aspects of the Neoromantic impulse inform the work of poets like Robert Hass and Mary Oliver, Jorie Graham and Louise Glück. The contemporary poetry scene, however, remains diffuse and diverse, and I await a commanding figure or figures or a catalytic movement to constellate the next phase of the American argument about the power of the word.

Notes

Chapter 1 Twentieth-Century American Poetics: An Overview

1 T. S. Eliot, *Selected Essays* (New York: Harcourt, Brace, 1950), p. 19.
2 Wallace Stevens, *The Necessary Angel: Essays on Reality and the Imagination* (New York: Alfred A. Knopf, 1950), p. 36.
3 T. S. Eliot, *Collected Poems 1909–1962* (New York: Harcourt, Brace, 1963), pp. 208, 184.
4 *The Cantos of Ezra Pound* (New York: New Directions, 1970), pp. 438, 460, 528, 802, 521, 797, 803.
5 *The Collected Poems of Wallace Stevens* (New York: Alfred A. Knopf, 1954), p. 346.
6 *The Cantos of Ezra Pound*, p. 147.
7 *Selected Essays of William Carlos Williams* (New York: Random House, 1954), pp. 283, 287, 337–40.
8 Kathy Acker, "Symposium: Postmodern?," *Poetics Journal Number 7*, ed. Barrett Watten and Lyn Hejinian, p. 117.
9 Ron Silliman, "Postmodernism: Sign for a Struggle, The Struggle for the Sign," *Poetics Journal Number 7*, pp. 38, 24.
10 Nick Piombino, "Writing as Reverie," *The L=A=N=G=U=A=G=E Book*, ed. Bruce Andrews & Charles Bernstein (Carbondale & Edwardsville: Southern Illinois University Press), p. 5.
11 Silliman, p. 39.
12 Wallace Stevens, *The Necessary Angel: Essays on Reality and the Imagination* (New York: Alfred A. Knopf, 1951), p. 36.
13 Charles Bernstein, "Stray Straws and Straw Men" in *The L=A=N=G=U=A=G=E Book*, pp. 42, 39, 42.
14 Silliman, pp. 38, 36, 19.
15 Stevens, *The Necessary Angel*, p. 32.
16 Jonathan Edwards, *Images or Shadows of Divine Things*, ed. Perry Miller (New Haven: Yale University Press, 1948).
17 Ralph Waldo Emerson, *Essays and Lectures*, ed. Joel Porte (New York: The Library of America), p. 20.
18 Edgar Allan Poe, *Poetry and Tales*, ed. Patrick F. Quinn (New York: Library of America, 1984), p. 64.

19 *The Poetry of Robert Frost*, ed. Edward Connery Latham (New York: Holt, Rinehart, & Winston, 1969), pp. 120, 225; *Selected Prose of Robert Frost*, ed. Hyde Cox & Edward *Connery Latham*, (New York: Holt, Rinehart & Winston, 1966), p. 18.

20 Ezra Pound, *Literary Essays*, ed. T. S. Eliot (New York: New Directions, 1954), p. 3.

21 William Carlos Williams, *Imaginations*, ed. Webster Schott (New York: New Directions, 1970), pp. 115, 91, 89, 88, 120, 93, 121.

22 T. S. Eliot, *Selected Essays*, pp. 19, 124, 8.

23 *The Necessary Angel*, pp. 32–33, 57–58, 46.

24 *The Necessary Angel*, pp. 30, 54, 153.

25 *The Cantos of Ezra Pound*, p. 429.

26 Eliot, *Collected Poems*, pp. 184, 199, 92.

27 *The Letters of Hart Crane 1916–1932*, ed. Brom Weber (Berkeley: University of California Press, 1965), p. 237.

28 *The Necessary Angel*, pp. 171, 173–74.

29 *The Collected Poems of Wallace Stevens*, p. 524.

30 *Towards a New American Poetics: Essays & Interviews*, ed. Ekbert Faas (Santa Barbara: Black Sparrow Press, 1978), p. 82.

Chapter 2 The Language of Crisis

1 Herman Melville, "Hawthorne and His Mosses," in *Melville: Pierre, Israel Potter, The Piazza-Tales, The Confidence Man, Uncollected Prose, Billy Budd* ((New York: Library of America, 1985), p. 1159.

2 *The Letters of Robert Lowell*, ed. Saskia Hamilton (New York: Farrar, Straus & Giroux, 2005), p. 3.

3 Ibid., pp. 16, 624.

4 Ibid., pp. 36–7.

5 Philip Hobsbaum, *A Reader's Guide to Robert Lowell* (London: Thames and Hudson, 1988), pp. 15–16.

6 Allen Tate, "Introduction," *The Land of Unlikeness* (Cummington: The Cummington Press, 1944), unnumbered pages.

7 John Berryman, "Robert Lowell and Others," *The Freedom of the Poet* (New York: Farrar, Straus, & Giroux, 1976), p. 286.

8 Irving Eherenpreis, "The Age of Lowell," reprinted in *Robert Lowell: A Portrait of the Artist in His Time*, ed. Michael London and Robert Boyers (New York: David Lewis, 1970), pp. 155–86.

9 Randall Jarrell, "From the Kingdom of Necessity" in *Poetry and the Age* (1953), reprinted in *Robert Lowell: A Portrait of the Artist in His Time*, pp. 19–20.

10 Tate, "Introduction," *The Land of Unlikeness*, unnumbered pages.

11 See "Hopkins' Sanctity" and "*Four Quartets*" in Robert Lowell, *Collected Prose*, ed. Robert Giroux (New York: Farrar, Straus & Giroux, 1987), pp. 167–70 and 45–48. The quotations are on p. 45.

12 *Collected Poems*, ed. Frank Bidart and David Gewanter (New York: Farrar, Straus & Giroux, 2003), p. 230. Subsequent page references from *Collected Poems* are indicated parenthetically in the text of the chapter.

13 Steven Gould Axelrod, *Robert Lowell: Life and Art* (Princeton: Princeton University Press, 1978), p. 54.

14 Early on, as Christianity began to spread, it encountered and absorbed some of the dualism of various Gnostic sects, whose radical metaphysical dualism saw spirit as trapped in a corrupt and sinful body and seeking release. That dualism, antithetical to the holism of the Incarnation, has persisted in the Christian tradition, expressing itself in some forms of asceticism, in Calvinist thinking, and in the Jansenism of the seventeenth century and later.

15 Allen Tate, "Introduction," *The Land of Unlikeness*, unnumbered pages.

16 *The Freedom of the Poet*, p. 290.

17 Axelrod, p. 55.

18 Hobsbaum, p. 42.

19 *The Letters of Robert Lowell*, p. 51.

20 Ibid., p. 248.

21 Ibid., p. 153.

22 Ibid., p. 200.

23 Ibid., p. 632.

24 Ibid., pp. 293–94.

25 *The Contemporary Poet as Artist and Critic: Eight Symposia*, ed. Anthony Ostroff (Boston: Little Brown, 1964), pp. 107–08, 99, 104. See also *The Freedom of the Poet*, p. 316.

26 *The Contemporary Poet as Artist and Critic: Eight Symposia*, pp. 104, 107. See also *The Freedom of the Poet*, p. 320.

27 Axelrod, *Robert Lowell: Life As Art*, pp. 158–159.

28 *The Letters of Robert Lowell*, p. 354.

29 Ian Hamilton, *Robert Lowell: A Biography* (New York: Random House, 1982), pp. 278–79.

30 William Everson, "A Conversation with Brother Antoninus," in *Naked Heart: Talking on Poetry, Mysticism and the Erotic* (Albuquerque: An American Poetry Book, 1992), p. 47.

31 Fredric Jameson, *The Prison-House of Language: A Critical Account of Structuralism and Russian Formalism* (Princeton: Princeton University Press, 1975).

32 *The Letters of Robert Lowell*, p. 154.

33 Ibid., p. 555.

34 Ibid., p. 520.

35 Ibid., p. 450.

36 Ibid., p. 440.

37 Ibid., p. 557.

38 Ibid., p. 577.

39 Elizabeth Bishop, *The Complete Poems 1927–1979* (New York: Farrar, Straus, & Giroux, 1983), pp. 188–89.

40 Helen Vendler, *The Given and the Made: Strategies of Poetic Redefinition* (Cambridge, MA: Harvard University Press, 1995), pp. 1–28.

41 Vereen M. Bell, *Robert Lowell: Nihilist As Hero* (Cambridge, MA: Harvard University Press, 1983).

42 "A Conversation with Ian Hamilton," *Collected Prose*, ed. Robert Giroux (New York: Farrar, Straus & Giroux, 1987), p. 272.

43 "A Conversation with Brother Antoninus," *Naked Heart*, p. 50.

44 *The Letters of Robert Lowell*, pp. 397–98, 423, 401, 449, 548.

45 Ibid., p. 632.

46 "A Conversation with Ian Hamilton," p. 290.

47 Donald Hall, "The State of Poetry – A Symposium," *The Review 2930* (Spring–Summer 1972), p. 40.

48 *The Letters of Robert Lowell*, p. 666.

49 Ibid., p. 671.

50 Robert Lowell, *Collected Poems*, p. 600.

51 John Haffenden, "Introduction" to *Henry's Fate & Other Poems* (New York: Farrar, Straus & Giroux, 1977), p. xviii.

52 Berryman, "The Art of Poetry XVI," *The Paris Review*, XIV, 53 (Winter 1972), pp. 204, 192.

53 Charles Thornbury, "Introduction," to John Berryman *Collected Poems 1937–1971*, ed. Charles Thornbury (New York: Farrar, Straus, & Giroux, 1989), p. xxvii.

54 "From the Middle and Senior Generations," *The Freedom of the Poet* (New York: Farrar, Straus & Giroux, 1976), p. 312.

55 "The Art of Poetry XVI," *The Paris Review*, p. 185.

56 "An Interview with John Berryman," *The Harvard Advocate*, CII 1 (Spring 1966, John Berryman Issue), p. 5.

57 Robert Giroux, "Preface" to *The Freedom of the Poet*, p. viii.

58 "One Answer to a Question: Changes," *The Freedom of the Poet*, p. 324.

59 *Collected Poems 1937–1971*, pp. 4–5, 11, 6, 12.

60 "One Answer to a Question: Changes," *The Freedom of the Poet*, p. 324.

61 *Collected Poems 1937–1971*, p. 11.

62 "One Answer to a Question: Changes," *The Freedom of the Poet*, pp. 326–27.

63 Thornbury, "Introduction" to *The Collected Poems*, p. xix.

64 *The Freedom of the Poet*, pp. 227, 228, 230, 232.

65 "Interview," *The Harvard Advocate*, p. 9.

66 "The Art of Poetry XVI," *The Paris Review*, XIV, 53 (Winter 1972), 185.

67 *The Freedom of the Poet*, p. 327.

68 Ibid., pp. 230, 234.

69 Ibid., p. 328; *The Harvard Advocate*, p. 7.

70 *The Freedom of the Poet*, p. 328.

71 *Collected Poems 1937–1971*, pp. 133, 135.

72 *The Works of Anne Bradstreet*, ed. Jeannine Hensley (Cambridge, MA: Harvard University Press, 1967), p. 241.

73 *Collected Poems 1937–1971*, pp. 143, 133, 139.

74 "The Art of Poetry XVI," *The Paris Review*, p. 195.

75 *Collected Poems 1937–1971*, pp. 140, 142.

76 Ibid., p. 141.

77 Ibid., pp. 146, 147.

78 "The Art of Poetry XVI," *The Paris Review*, p. 198.

79 *The Freedom of the Poet*, p. 330; *The Paris Review*, pp. 199, 190–91.

80 *The Freedom of the Poet*, p. 330; *The Paris Review*, pp. 191, 193, 183; *The Dream Songs* (New York: Farrar, Straus & Giroux, 1969), p. 284.

81 *The Freedom of the Poet*, p. 330. For Berryman there is a fluidity of names as well as pronouns. His baptismal name was John Allyn Smith Jr., but after his father's suicide in 1926 and his mother's marriage to John Angus Berryman the same year, he took the name of the stepfather who adopted him and his younger brother. As for the name Henry, Berryman and his second wife, Ann Levine, called each other by the nicknames Henry and Mabel after they jokingly decided that Henry and Mabel were "the worst names you could think of" for a man and a woman. The first Dream Song Berryman wrote but never published was about Henry and Mabel, and Mabel never appeared again in the texts of the songs. *The Harvard Advocate*, p. 6, and *The Paris Review*, pp. 193–94.

82 *The Paris Review*, p. 191; *The Freedom of the Poet*, p. 330.

83 Adrienne Rich, "Living with Henry," *The Harvard Advocate*, p. 11.

84 *The Dream Songs*, p. 15.

85 Ibid., p. 23.

86 Ibid., pp. 83, 84.

87 Ibid., pp. 191, 367, 381, 278, 194, 178.

88 Ibid., p. 82.

89 "The Art of Poetry XVI," *The Paris Review*, p. 183.

90 *The Dream Songs*, pp. 84, 71, 3, 28, 220; *Henry's Fate and Other Poems*, ed. John Haffenden (New York: Farrar, Straus & Giroux, 1977), p. 14.

91 *The Dream Songs*, pp. 285, 275, 213.

92 Ibid., pp. 33, 51.

93 Ibid., p. 52.

94 Ibid., pp. 253, 187, 219, 22, 65. For the reference to St. Augustine, see *The Paris Review*, p. 183.

95 *The Paris Review*, p. 200.

96 *Collected Poems 1937–1971*, p. 290.

97 *Collected Poems 1937–1971*, p. 256. The text quoted here read in the separate edition of *Delusions, Etc.* "my procedures and ends" and "my insights."

98 *Collected Poems 1937–1971*, p. 221; "The Art of Poetry XVI," *The Paris Review*, p. 180; *The Correspondence of Gerard Manley Hopkins & Richard Watson Dixon*, ed. Claude Colleer Abbott (London: Oxford University Press, 1955), p. 8.

99 William Heyen, "A Memoir and an Interview," *The Ohio Review*, XV, 2 (Winter 1974), 48.
100 Tom Rogers, *God of Rescue: John Berryman and Christianity* (London: Peter Lang, 2011), pp. 279–400.
101 *The Letters of Robert Lowell*, pp. 583, 563.
102 His experiences in alcohol treatment are described, only slightly fictionalized, in the unfinished novel *Recovery*, published posthumously in 1973.
103 "The Art of Poetry XVI," *The Paris Review*, pp. 202, 204.
104 *Collected Poems 1937–1971*, pp. 220, 225–26, 259–60, 251–52, 252–53. For Mary as Queen of Heaven, see Lowell's late poem "Home."
105 Ibid., p. 217. For years Berryman worked on a critical edition of *King Lear*.
106 Ibid., pp. 262, 235. Origen was a third century theologian who inclined to the belief that a good God, through the mediation of Christ, would bring all His creatures into final reconciliation with Himself (apocatastasis) in heaven.
107 *A New Catechism: Catholic Faith for Adults* (New York: Herder & Herder, 1967). See *God of Rescue: John Berryman and Christianity*, p. 27.
108 *Collected Poems 1937–1971*, pp. 262, 263; Paul Mariani, *Dream Song: The Life of John Berryman* (New York: Paragon House, 1989) pp. 482–83.
109 Ibid., p. 264.
110 Ibid., p. 221.

Chapter 3 The Language of Flux

1 *Words in Air: The Complete Correspondence Between Elizabeth Bishop and Robert Lowell*, ed. Thomas Travisano with Saskia Hamilton (New York: Farrar, Straus & Giroux, 2008), p. 407.
2 Robert Lowell, "Elizabeth Bishop's *North & South*," *Collected Prose*, p. 78.
3 *Words in Air*, p. 390.
4 Elizabeth Bishop, *One Art: Selected Letters*, ed. Robert Giroux (New York: Farrar, Straus & Giroux, 1994), p. 477.
5 *Words in Air*, p. 225.
6 Robert Lowell, *Collected Poems*, pp. 321–22.
7 *Words in Air*, pp. 59, 430, 402, 643.
8 Ibid., p. 225.
9 *The Complete Poems 1927–1979* (New York: Farrar, Straus & Giroux, 1983), pp. 3, 89, 157, 131. All quotations from Bishop's poems come from this edition, and the pages are indicated parenthetically in the text.
10 Robert Lowell, "Elizabeth Bishop's *North & South*," *Collected Prose*, pp. 76–77.
11 Robert Lowell, *Collected Prose*, pp. 76–7; Robert Frost, *Selected Prose*, ed. Hyde Cox & Edward Connery Latham (New York: Holt, Rinehart & Winston, 1966), p. 18.
12 Elizabeth Bishop, *The Collected Prose*, ed. Robert Giroux (New York: Farrar, Straus & Giroux, 1984), pp. 121–56.

13 Lynn Keller, *Re-making It New: Contemporary American Poetry and the Modernist Tradition* (Cambridge: Cambridge University Press, 1987), pp. 104–05.

14 *One Art*, pp. 44–45, 67, 48, 596, 89; Brett Millier, *Elizabeth Bishop: Life and the Memory of It* (Berkeley: University of California Press, 1993), p. 424.

15 *One Art*, p. 48.

16 *The Letters of Wallace Stevens*, ed. Holly Stevens (New York: Alfred A Knopf, 1966), p. 544.

17 *The Collected Poems of Wallace Stevens* (New York: Alfred A. Knopf, 1954), pp. 128–30.

18 *Words in Air*, p. 26.

19 Ibid., p. 23.

20 William Aggeler, *The Flowers of Evil* (Fresno: Academy Library Guild, 1954).

21 *One Art*, p. 184.

22 *Words in Air*, p. 784.

23 Ibid., p. 767.

24 Brett C. Millier, p. 492.

25 Ibid. p. 495.

26 *Words in Air*, p. 7.

27 Wallace Stevens, *The Necessary Angel: Essays on Reality and the Imagination* (New York: Alfred A. Knopf, 1951), p. 36.

28 John Ashbery, *Selected Prose*, ed. Eugene Ritchie (Ann Arbor: University of Michigan Press, 2004), pp. 120, 122, 171.

29 *The Collected Poems of Wallace Stevens*, pp. 424–5.

30 John Ashbery, *A Wave* (New York: Viking Press, 1984), p. 89.

31 Interview with John Tranter, first published in *Scripsi (Ormond College, University of Melbourne)*, *IV* 1 (1986), and reprinted in *Jacket 2* (January 1998).

32 *Self-Portrait in a Convex Mirror* (New York: Viking Press, 1975), p. 83. Henceforth page references for quoted passages from this poem will be included in the text at the end of the discussion or of the paragraph in which the quotations appear.

33 *Contemporary Poets of the English Language*, ed. Rosalie Murphy and James Vinson (Chicago and London: St. James Press, 1970), p. 33; *Selected Prose*, p. 217.

34 T.S. Eliot, *Collected Poems 1909–1962*, pp. 184, 180; *Collected Poems of Wallace Stevens*, pp. 76, 130.

35 *Selected Prose*, pp. 15, 12, 242.

36 Ibid., pp. 21, 44, 45, 53.

37 Marjorie Perloff, "Mysteries of Construction: The Dream Songs of John Ashbery" in *The Poetics of Indeterminacy: Rimbaud to Cage* (Princeton: Princeton University Press, 1981), pp. 248–87.

38 *The Contemporary Poets of the English Language*, p. 33; "Interview with John Tranter," *Jacket 2*; *The Paris Review Interviews IV*, *pp.* 186, 187, 198. For a detailed account of the drafts of "A Wave," see John Shoptaw, *On the Outside*

Looking Out: John Ashbery's Poetry (Cambridge, MA: Harvard University press, 1994), pp. 343–51.

39 *The Paris Review Interviews IV*, pp. 197, 190.

40 "The System" in *Three Poems* (New York: Viking Press, 1972), pp. 53, 54, 59. The page references for citations from "The System" will henceforth be cited in the text from this edition.

41 Charles Altieri, *Self and Sensibility in Contemporary American Poetry* (Cambridge: Cambridge University Press, 1984), p. 141.

42 Ibid., p. 139.

43 *Three Poems*, p. 5.

44 Ibid., p. 118.

45 Dennis Brown, "John Ashbery's 'A Wave' (1983): Time and Western Man" in *Poetry and the Sense of Panic: Critical Essays on Elizabeth Bishop and John Ashbery*, ed. Lionel Kelly (Amsterdam and Atlanta: Rodopi, 2000), p. 65; Shoptaw, *On the Outside Looking Out*, p. 313.

46 John Ashbery, *A Wave*, p. 68. Page references of passages quoted from "A Wave" will henceforth be inserted into the text from this edition.

47 John Shoptaw, *On the Outside Looking Out: John Ashbery's Poetry*, p. 277.

48 Ibid., pp. 302–03, 372–73.

49 Ibid., pp. 304, 302.

50 *The Poetics of Indeterminacy*, p. 273.

51 See Shoptaw, p. 306.

52 John Ashbery, *Flow Chart* (New York: Alfred A. Knopf, 1991), p. 216. Further page references will be inserted into the text from this edition.

53 Fred Muratori, review of *Flow Chart* in *Library Journal*, CXVI (8), 79.

54 *Self-Portrait in a Convex Mirror*, p. 75.

Chapter 4 The Language of Incarnation

1 Jack Kerouac, "Beatific: The Origins of the Beat Generation," *The Portable Jack Kerouac*, ed. Ann Charters (New York: Viking Press, 1995), pp. 568, 566.

2 In the late 1940s Corso served three years in prison for robbery. In 1944 Kerouac was held in jail briefly as an accomplice after the fact when Lucien Carr killed a homosexual admirer who attempted to rape him; Carr plead guilty to man-slaughter. Kerouac tells of this incident in *Vanity of Duluoz* (1967). In 1951 Kerouac and Cassady were present at a drunken party when Burroughs shot and killed his wife Joan in Mexico City. In 1958 Cassady served time in San Quentin on narcotics charges.

3 "Introduction by William Carlos Williams," *Howl and Other Poems* (San Francisco: City Lights Books, 1956). Kerouac's novel *Desolation Angels* was begun in 1956, before the publication of *On the Road*, completed in 1961, and published in 1965.

4 Jack Kerouac, "Lamb, No Lion," *The Portable Jack Kerouac*, p. 564.

5 Ibid., pp. 570, 562–63, 543, 571.

6 Letter to Richard Eberhart, May 18, 1956, in *Howl: Original Draft Facsimile, Transcript & Variant Versions*, ed. Barry Miles (New York: HarperCollins, 1995), p. 152.

7 After several rounds of revision, *On the Road* came out in 1957, but *On the Road: The Original Scroll* was published posthumously by Viking Press in 2007.

8 *Howl: Original Draft Facsimile, Transcript & Variant Versions*, p. 156.

9 Jack Kerouac, *Selected Letters 1940–1956*, ed. Ann Charters (New York: Viking Press, 1995), pp. 355, 356, 372–73, 595; *Howl: Original Draft Facsimile, Transcript & Variant Versions*, pp. 149, 153.

10 *Selected Letters 1940–1956*, pp. 515, 516.

11 *The Portable Jack Kerouac*, pp. 483, 484, 485.

12 *Howl: Original Draft Facsimile, Transcript & Variant Versions*, p. 153.

13 *The Portable Jack Kerouac*, pp. 486–87; Ginsberg, "First Thought, Best Thought," *Composed on the Tongue: Literary Conversations 1967–1977*, ed. Donald Allen (San Francisco: Grey Fox Press, 1980), pp. 106, 117.

14 *Composed on the* Tongue, p. 106; *The Portable Jack Kerouac*, p. 485; *Howl: Original Draft Facsimile, Transcript & Variant Versions*, p. 153.

15 Blake's phrase is from the poem "The Divine Image" in *Songs of Innocence and Experience*. The first Whitman citation is from the 1860 poem "To One Shortly to Die," and the second from "Eidólons"; cf. *Leaves of Grass*, Norton Critical Edition, ed. Sculley Bradley & Harold Blodgett (New York: W. W. Norton, 1973), pp. 451, 8.

16 *Composed on the Tongue*, p. 106.

17 *The Portable Jack Kerouac*, pp. 564, 488, 485.

18 Ibid., p. 483.

19 *Howl: Original Draft Facsimile, Transcript & Variant Versions*, p. 156.

20 Allen Ginsberg, "Notes Written on Finally Recording 'Howl,'" *On the Poetry of Allen Ginsberg*, ed. Lewis Hyde (Ann Arbor: University of Michigan Press, 1984), p. 80.

21 *Selected Letters 1940–1956*, p. 508.

22 *On the Poetry of Allen Ginsberg*, pp. 81, 121.

23 Ibid., p. 82; *Howl: Original Draft Facsimile, Transcript& Variant Versions*, pp. 152, 153, 163.

24 *On the Poetry of Allen Ginsberg*, pp. 81, 82.

25 Allen Ginsberg, *Collected Poems 1947–1980* (New York: Harper & Row, 1984), pp. 126, 131, 133.

26 Ibid., p. 134.

27 *Howl: Original Draft Facsimile, Transcript & Variant Versions*, p. 152.

28 Kerouac's recollection of the occasion shows his mixture of vulnerability and bluff when challenged by a Harvard undergraduate: "The little kid in the Lowell House in Harvard, whose professor I was for an hour, looked me right in the eye and asked: 'Why do you have no discipline?' I said, 'Is that the way to talk to your professor? Try it if you can. If you can you'll pull the rug out from everybody." Cf. *The Portable Jack Kerouac*, p. 488.

29 *Selected Letters 1940–1956*, p. 94.

30 *Collected Poems 1947–1980*, pp. 224, 225.

31 *On the Poetry of Allen Ginsberg*, p. 82.

32 *Selected Letters, 1940–1956*, p. 416.

33 *Collected Poems 1947–1980*, pp. 138, 139.

34 See "A Blake Experience," *On the Poetry of Allen Ginsberg*, pp. 120–30.

35 In these early poems Ginsberg sometimes uses wit and verbal play to temper and give an ironic edge to the extremity of his feelings. Other often-quoted instances are the fantasy of Whitman, in "A Supermarket in California," "poking among the meats in the refrigerator and eyeing the grocery boys," and the last line of his invective in "America": "America I'm putting my queer shoulder to the wheel." See *Collected Poems 1947–1980*, pp. 136, 148.

36 *Collected Poems 1947–1980*, p. 139.

37 Ibid., pp. 396, 400, 401.

38 Ibid., pp. 397, 395, 406, 407, 404.

39 Ibid., pp. 406, 407, 408, 409, 411.

40 *On the Poetry of Allen Ginsberg*, p. 319.

41 Michael McClure, *Scratching the Beat Surface* (San Francisco: North Point, 1982), p. 71.

42 *Selected Letters 1940–1956*, p. 507.

43 James T Jones, *A Map of Mexico City Blues: Jack Kerouac as Poet* (Carbondale & Edwardsville: Southern Illinois University Press, 1992), p. 30.; Jack Kerouac *Collected Poems* (Library of America, 2012), p. 1.

44 *Scratching the Beat Surface*, p. 71; *A Map of Mexico City Blues*, pp. 4, 11.

45 Jack Kerouac, *On the Road* (New York: Viking, 1957), pp. 309–10.

46 *Selected Letters 1940–1956*, pp. 447, 448.

47 *Collected Poems*, p. 149. Further quotations from the poetry will be indicated in the text with the number of the chorus and page reference.

48 "The First Word," *The Portable Jack Kerouac*, p. 487.

49 In the fiction Kerouac's engagement with Buddhism is reflected by Gary Snyder's displacing Cassady as the hero of *The Dharma Bums* published the year after *On the Road* in 1958. Nineteenth-century Romantics – Emerson, Thoreau, Whitman – had been drawn to Eastern religious thought, and Buddhism became a potent force in the San Francisco Renaissance for Rexroth, Snyder, and Whalen as well as Ginsberg and Kerouac.

50 *A Map of Mexico City Blues*, p. 114.

51 Ed Adler, *Departed Angels – The Lost Paintings – Jack Kerouac* (New York: Thunder Mouth Press, 2004).

52 *Big Sur* (New York: Farrar, Straus & Cudahy, 1962), pp. 204, 205.

53 Ibid., p. 216.

54 *Lonesome Traveler* (New York: Grove Press, 1960), p. vi.

55 Everson delineated that tradition in a pamphlet published by Black Sparrow Press in 1977 under the title "Dionysus & the Beat," reprinted in *Dark God of Eros: A William Everson Reader*, ed. Albert Gelpi (Berkeley, CA: Heyday Books, 2003), pp. 292–301.

56 Kenneth Rexroth, "San Francisco Letter," *The Evergreen Review*, I, 2, 8–9.

57 *The Residual Years: Poems 1934–1948; The Veritable Years: Poems 1949–1966; The Integral Years: Poems 166–1994.*

58 New York: New Directions, 1988.

59 Everson wrote an introduction to *God and the Unconscious* when it was reissued in 1982.

60 *Dark God of Eros*, pp. 275.

61 William Everson, *The Residual Years: Poems 1934–1948* (Santa Rosa: Black Sparrow Press, 1997), p. 12.

62 Though Jeffers did not want disciples or followers, and though Everson never met his master, he acknowledged him throughout his life. His elegy for Jeffers, *The Poet Is Dead* (1964), is one of the great elegies in the language. He introduced a reissue of several Jeffers volumes: *Medea/Cawdor* (1970), *Californians* (1971), *The Double Axe* (1977). He also edited Jeffers's early, unpublished poems: *The Alpine Christ* (1974) and *Brides of the South Wind* (1974). And he wrote two critical studies: *Robinson Jeffers: Fragments of an Older Fury* (1968) and *The Excesses of God: Robinson Jeffers as a Religious Figure* (1988).

63 *Dark God of Eros*, p. 294.

64 *The Residual Years*, p. 25.

65 T. S. Eliot, *Collected Poems 1909–1962* (New York: Harcourt, Brace & World, 1962), p. 100.

66 *The Veritable Years: Poems 1949–1966* (Santa Rosa: Black Sparrow Press, 1998), p. 14.

67 *Collected Poems 1909–1962*, p. 199.

68 *The Veritable Years*, pp. 131–32.

69 *Dark God of Eros*, pp. 316–17.

70 *The Veritable Years*, p, 189.

71 *Collected Poems 1909–1962*, pp. 29, 30.

72 *The Veritable Years*, pp. 77, 78, 79.

73 William Everson, "The Place of Poetry in the West," *Naked Heart: Talking on Poetry, Mysticism, & the Erotic*, ed. Lee Bartlett (Albuquerque: An American Poetry Book, 1992), p. 191.

74 *The Veritable Years*, pp. 104, 105, 107.

75 *Dark God of Eros*, p. 268.

76 *The Veritable Years*, p. 80.

77 Ibid., p. 113.

78 Ibid., pp. 192–93, 194.

79 *The Hazards of Holiness* (New York: Doubleday, 1962), p. 68.

80 *The Veritable Years*, p. 109.

81 Ibid., pp. 110, 111.

82 Ibid., pp. 169, 171–72.

83 *The Integral Years; Poems 1966–1994* (Santa Rosa: Black Sparrow Press, 2000), pp. 100, 110.

84 *The Veritable Years*, p. 112.

Chapter 5 The Language of Witness

1 Wallace Stevens, *The Necessary Angel* (New York: Alfred A Knopf, 1951), pp. 57–58; *Selected Prose of Robert Frost*, ed. Hyde Cox and Edward Connery Latham (New York: Holt, Rinehart & Winston, 1966), p. 18.

2 Adrienne Rich, *Collected Early Poems 1950–1970* (New York: W. W. Norton, 1993), pp. 39, 3, 30.

3 Ibid., pp. 28, 4, 24.

4 *The Necessary Angel*, p. 52.

5 It is worth noting that the dedication to Frost's friend Morrison comes in Rich's first book, written at Harvard, and the dedication to Matthiessen, who was gay and a socialist, comes later.

6 For a memoir of the Boston-area poets of the time, see Peter Davison, *The Fading Smile: Poets in Boston from Robert Lowell to Sylvia Plath* (New York: Alfred A. Knopf, 1996); Adrienne Rich, *Arts of the Possible: Essays and Conversations* (New York: W. W. Norton, 2001), p. 7.

7 Adrienne Cecile Rich, *A Change of World* (New Haven: Yale University Press, 1951), p. 11; Randall Jarrell, "New Books in Review," *The Yale Review* (September 1956), reprinted in *Adrienne Rich's Poetry*, ed. Barbara Charlesworth Gelpi & Albert Gelpi (New York: W.W. Norton, 1975), p. 127; John Ashbery, "Tradition and Talent," *The New York Herald Tribune Book Week* (September 4, 1966) reprinted in *Adrienne Rich's Poetry and Prose*, ed. Barbara Charlesworth & Albert Gelpi (New York: W. W. Norton, 1993), pp. 278, 280.

8 *What Is Found There: Notebooks on Poetry and Politics* (New York: W. W. Norton, (1993), pp. 191, 199.

9 *Collected Early Poems 1950–1970*, p. 138.

10 Ibid., p. 193.

11 Ibid., p. 38.

12 Ibid., p. 149.

13 "Poetry and Experience: Statement at a Poetry Reading" in *Adrienne Rich's Poetry and Prose*, p. 165.

14 *Collected Early Poems 1950–1970*, pp. 212, 205.

15 Ibid., p. 215; *Adrienne Rich's Poetry and Prose*, p. 24.

16 Ibid., pp. 247, 362; Adrienne Rich, *Later Poems Selected and New 1971–2012* (New York: W. W. Norton, 2012), p. 356.

17 *Collected Early Poems 1950–1970*, p. 283.

18 Ibid., pp. 232, 361–62.

19 Ibid., pp. 362, 376, 399.

20 "Living with Henry," *The Harvard Advocate* (CIII, 1, Spring 1969: The John Berryman Issue), p. 10.

21 *Collected Early Poems 1950–1970*, pp. 248, 323.

22 *Later Poems 1971–2012*, p. 15, *Diving into the Wreck Poems 1971–1972* (New York: W. W. Norton, 1973), p. 9; *Collected Early Poems 1950–1970*, p. 367.

23 *Collected Early Poems 1950–1970*, p. 367.

24 Ibid., p. 385.

25 Ibid., pp. 363–65, 401.

26 W. H. Auden, "In Memory of W. B. Yeats," *Collected Poems*, ed. Edward Mendelson (New York: Random House, 1976), p. 197; *Later Poems 1971–2012*, p. 201.

27 Linda K. Bundtzen, "Adrienne Rich's Identity Politics: A Partly Common Language," *Women's Studies* XXVII, 4 (June, 1998), pp. 331–46; *Collected Early Poems 1950–1970*, p. 400.

28 *Diving into the Wreck*, p. 19.

29 *Later Poems 1971–2012*, pp. 15–17.

30 *Diving into the Wreck*, p. 19.

31 See *On Lies, Secrecies, and Silence: Selected Prose 1966–1978* (New York: W. W. Norton, 1979), pp. 33–50, 199–202, and *Blood, Bread, and Poetry: Selected Prose 1979–1985* (New York: W. W. Norton, 1986), pp. 23–75.

32 From Rich's statement for the dust jacket of *Midnight Salvage: Poems 1995–1998* (New York: W. W. Norton, 1999).

33 *Later Poems 1971–2012*, pp. 19–20.

34 Ibid., p. 34; *Arts of the Possible: Essays and Conversations* (New York: W. W. Norton, 2001), p. 135.

35 *Poems Selected and New 1950–1974* (New York: W. W. Norton, 1975), p. 237. For other poems in which Rich continues to address her husband after his death, see "To the Dead" (1972), "From a Survivor" (1972), "Sources" (1981–82), and "Tattered Kaddish" (1989).

36 See Charles Altieri, "Self-Reflection as Action: The Recent Poetry of Adrienne Rich" in *Sense and Sensibility in Contemporary American Poetry* (Cambridge: Cambridge University Press, 1984).

37 *Arts of the Possible*, p. 8.

38 *A Human Eye: Essays on Art in Society 1997–2008* (New York: W. W. Norton, 2009), p. 144.

39 *Arts of the Possible*, pp. 2, 3, 4, 6, 7; *A Human Eye*, pp. 57–69.

40 *Later Poems 1971–2012*, p. 142.

41 Ibid., pp. 162, 160.

42 Ibid., p. 232; *Arts of the Possible*, p. 141.

43 *Arts of the Possible*, pp. 7, 8.

44 Ibid., p. 116; Rich's statement for the dust jacket of *Midnight Salvage*.

45 *Collected Early Poems 1950–1970*, p. 15.

46 *What Is Found There*, p. 193.

47 *Later Poems 1971–2012*, p. 162, 183–85; *Midnight Salvage*, p. 24; Adrienne Rich, *The Dream of a Common Language: Poems 1974–1977* (New York: W. W. Norton, 1978), pp. 75, 76; *Selected Prose of Robert Frost*, p. 115.

48 *The Dream of a Common Language*, pp. 75, 76, 77; *Arts of the Possible*, pp. 64, 65; *A Human Eye*, p. 141; *Time's Power Poems 1985–1988* (New York: W. W. Norton, 1989), p. 50.

49 *Later Poems 1971–2012*, pp. 135, 136.

50 Ibid., p. 200.

51 Ibid., p. 201.
52 Tom Clark, *Robert Creeley and the Genius of the American Common Place* (New York: New Directions, 1993), p. 98.
53 *Later Poems 1971–2012*, pp. 78–79, 167, 172–73, 255, 256.
54 Ibid., pp. 289, 290, 171, 172.
55 Ibid., pp. 344, 348, 346.
56 Ibid., pp. 349, 350, 351.
57 Ibid., pp. 449.
58 Ibid., pp. 453, 454, 471.
59 Ibid., pp. 458, 456.
60 Ibid., pp. 458, 457, 459, 461, 460, 463.
61 Ibid., pp. 478, 481, 482; *Collected Early Poems 1950–1970*, p. 363.
62 E-mail message to Albert Gelpi, Feb. 28, 2012.
63 *Later Poems 1971–2012*, p. 504.

Chapter 6 The Language of Vision

1 Denise Levertov, *New and Selected Essays* (New York: New Directions, 1992), pp. 205, 237, 240.
2 Charles Olson, "Projective Verse" in *The Poetics of the New American Poetry*, ed. Donald Allen and Warren Tallman (New York: Grove Press, 1973), p. 148.
3 Robert Duncan, *Fictive Certainties* (New York: New Directions, 1985), p. 65.
4 *The Letters of Robert Duncan and Denise Levertov*, ed. Robert Bertholf and Albert Gelpi (Stanford: Stanford University Press, 2004), p. 449.
5 *New and Selected Essays*, pp. 194–98.
6 Robert Duncan, *The Collected Early Poems & Plays*, ed. Peter Quartermain (Berkeley: University of California Press, 2012), p. 5.
7 Ibid, pp. 93, 91.
8 *New and Selected Essays*, p. 196.
9 *The Collected Poems of Denise Levertov*, ed. Paul A. Lacey and Anne Dewey (New York: New Directions, 2013), p. 72.
10 *Collected Poems*, p. 32.
11 *Letters*, p. 510.
12 Ibid., pp. 5–6; *New and Selected Essays*, p. 200–01.
13 For Duncan's Stein imitations, cf. *Letters* (1958), *Writing Writing* (1964), *A Book of Resemblances* (1966), *Names of People* (1968), *Play Time Pseudo Stein* (1969), and *Derivations: Selected Poems 1950–1956* (1968), all included in *The Collected Early Poems & Plays*.
14 *Letters*, pp. 3, 4; *Collected Early Poems & Plays*, pp. 639, 641.
15 *Letters*, pp. 5–6.
16 Ibid., pp. 7, 189.
17 Ibid., pp. 6, 5, 576.
18 *New and Selected Essays*, p. 199; *Letters*, p. 268.
19 *Fictive Certainties*, p. 65; *New and Selected Essays*, pp. 199–200.

20 Ekbert Faas, *Towards A New American Poetics: Essays and Interviews* (Santa Barbara: Black Sparrow Press, 1978), p. 82.

21 Robert Duncan, *The Collected Later Poems & Plays*, ed. Peter Quartermain (Berkeley: University of California Press, 2014), p. 3.

22 *Letters*, p. 134.

23 *Collected Poems*, p. 189.

24 *New and Selected Essays*, pp. 77, 79.

25 Ibid., p. 246.

26 *Collected Poems*, p. 143.

27 Ibid., p. 202.

28 *Collected Later Poems & Plays*, p. 210.

29 Ibid., p. 101.

30 *Collected Poems*, p. 213–14.

31 *New and Selected Essays*, pp. 67, 68.

32 Ibid., pp. 67–69, 73.

33 Ibid., pp. 69, 71, 88–92.

34 *Letters*, p. 510; *New and Selected Essays*, pp. 67–68.

35 *Fictive Certainties*, pp. 79, 88, 81, 83, 113.

36 Ibid., pp. 111–12, 116, 78–79, 81, 82; *Letters*, pp. 440, 439; Robert Duncan, "Pages from a Notebook," *A Selected Prose*, ed. Robert J. Bertholf (New York: New Directions, 1995), p. 13.

37 *A Selected Prose*, pp. 13–14.

38 *A Selected Prose*, pp. 147, 14; *Letters*, p. 468; *Fictive Certainties*, pp. 116, 78.

39 *Letters*, pp. 449–50. With slight revisions, the poem was published as the title poem of *Bending the Bow* 1968); see *Collected Later Poems & Plays*, pp. 304–05.

40 *Collected Later Poems & Plays*, pp. 305–08.

41 Ibid., pp. 310–11.

42 *Letters*, pp. 463–64, 467–68.

43 Ibid., p. 463.

44 *Collected Poems*, p. 256, 339–40.

45 *Letters*, p. 519; *Collected Poems*, pp. 340–41.

46 *Letters*, pp. 519–20; *Collected Later Poems & Plays*, p. 376.

47 *Letters*, pp. 520, 524–25, 531, 650.

48 Ibid., pp. 528, 563.

49 Ibid., pp. 530, 532–33.

50 Ibid., pp. 543, 547, 582.

51 *Collected Poems*, pp. 351, 361, 352.

52 *New and Selected Essays*, pp. 231, 232, 237, 238, 233.

53 *Collected Poems*, p. 375; *Collected Later Poems & Plays*, pp. 480, 481, 482.

54 *Collected Poems*, p. 394; *Letters*, pp. 657, 677.

55 *Letters*, pp. 666–67, 678, 684.

56 Ibid., pp. 669, 661, 666; *Fictive Certainties*, pp. 115, 116.

57 *Letters*, pp. 608, 610, 611, 684, 678–79. 693.

58 Ibid., p. 701; *Collected Later Poems & Plays*, pp. 511, 512.

59 *Letters*, p. 712.

60 *Collected Later Poems & Plays*, pp. 520, 582, 584, 585; James F. Mersmann, *Out of the Vietnam Vortex: A Study of Poets and Poetry against the War* (Lawrence: University of Kansas Press, 1974), p. 94; *Letters*, pp. 711, 712, 715–16.

61 Levertov made her remark in correspondence with me dated September 23, 1996; Duncan's reading took place at the end of a conference on H. D. and Marianne Moore (at Bryn Mawr College in 1985) in which we had both participated.

62 *Collected Poems*, p. 784; *New and Selected Essays*, p. 229.

63 *Letters*, p. 717.

64 *Fictive Certainties*, p.122, 224, 225–26, 123, 140.

65 Ibid., p. 230.

66 Ibid., p. 227.

67 *Collected Later Poems & Plays*, pp. 442, 444.

68 *Ground Work: Before the War. In the Dark*, ed. Robert Bertholf and James Maynard (New York: New Directions, 2006), pp. ix, x.

69 *Collected Later Poems & Plays*, pp. 684–85.

70 *New and Selected Essays*, pp. 246, 4; *Letters*, pp. 679, 510; *Fictive Certainties*, p. 78.

71 *New and Selected Essays*, pp. 241–42, 250.

72 Ibid., p. 245.

73 *Collected Poems*, pp. 673, 674, 675, 676, 678.

74 Ibid., p. 678–79.

75 Ibid., p. 735.

76 Ibid., p. 728. "The Avowal" is dedicated to the poet Carolyn Kizer and her husband John Woodbridge, "Recalling Our Celebration of the 300th Birthday of George Herbert, 1983."

77 Ibid, p. 961.

78 Ibid, pp. 967–68.

79 "Statements on Poetics," *The New American Poetry*, ed. Donald M. Allen (New York: Grove Press, 1960), p. 412.

80 *Fictive Certainties*, p. 65.

81 *The Poet in the World* (New York: New Directions, 1973), pp. 14–15; *Letters*, pp. 407, 408, 413; *New and Selected Essays*, p. 73.

82 *New and Selected Essays*, pp. 68, 73; *The Poet in the World*, p. 60.

83 *The Poet in the World*, p. 17. The passage in which this sentence appears also alludes to Levertov's favorite Romantics: Keats, Wordsworth, and Hopkins.

84 *Letters*, pp. 668, 682, 680.

85 *Fictive Certainties*, p. 65; *New and Selected Essays*, p. 246.

86 *Fictive Certainties*, pp. 66, 78–79, 220, 231–32.

87 *Letters*, p. 679. The remarks about Language poetry come from an unpublished letter that Levertov wrote to her colleagues in the Stanford English Department in March 1984, in connection with a faculty appointment under consideration.

88 *Fictive Certainties*, pp. 219, 123, 83; Tom Clark, *Robert Creeley and the Genius of the American Common Place* (New York: New Directions, 1993), p. 104; "Crisis of Spirit in the Word," *Credences: A Journal of Twentieth Century Poetry and Poetics*, New Series 1 (Summer 1983), p. 65.

Chapter 7 The Language of L=A=N=G=U=A=G=E

1 *The Collected Essays of Robert Creeley* (Berkeley: University of California Press, 1989), p. 572.
2 *The Collected Poems of Robert Creeley 1945–1975* (Berkeley: University of California Press, 1982), p. 132.
3 Ibid., pp. 115, 123.
4 *Collected Essays*, pp. 473, 477; Tom Clark, *Robert Creeley and the Genius of the American Common Place* (New York: New Directions, 1993), p. 142.
5 *Collected Essays*, pp. 477, 493, 496, 483.
6 Ibid., pp. 573, 483, 488.
7 Tom Clark, p. 122.
8 *The Poems of Emily Dickinson*, ed. Thomas H. Johnson (Cambridge, MA: Harvard University Press, 1955), II, 694–95; I, 204.
9 Tom Clark, p. 122.
10 Tom Clark, pp. 1, 40–41.
11 *Collected Essays*, p. 496; Tom Clark, p. 142.
12 *Collected Poems 1945–1975*, p. 227.
13 Ibid., p. 125; *Collected Essays*, pp. 488, 479, 497, 464.
14 *Collected Poems 1945–1975*, p. 158.
15 Ibid., pp. 152–53.
16 Ibid., p. 258.
17 Ibid., p. 283.
18 *Collected Essays*, p. 574.
19 *Collected Poems 1945–1975*, p. 352.
20 Ibid., p. 435.
21 For lines cited in this paragraph, see ibid., pp. 405, 388, 390.
22 For lines cited in this paragraph, see ibid., pp. 416, 437, 440.
23 For lines cited n this paragraph, see ibid., pp. 403, 404, 391.
24 *Collected Essays*, p. 575.
25 *The Collected Poems of Robert Creeley 1975–2005* (Berkeley: University of California Press, 2005), p. 570.
26 Tom Clark, pp. 98, 87.
27 Ibid., p. 104.
28 *Collected Poems 1975–2005*, pp. 495, 486.
29 Ibid., pp. 618, 537.
30 Ibid. p. 625.
31 Ibid. p. 511.
32 Ibid., p. 606.
33 Tom Clark, p. 144.

34 Ron Silliman, "'Postmodernism': Sign for a Struggle, the Struggle for the Sign," *Postmodern? Poetics Journal Number 7* (September 1987), pp. 38, 24. 34.

35 Ibid., pp. 39, 35; *The L=A=N=G=U=A=G=E Book*, ed. Bruce Andrews and Charles Bernstein (Carbondale: Southern Illinois Press, 1984), pp. 54, 78.

36 Barrett Watten, "Introduction" to Ron Silliman, *Tjanting* (Berkeley: The Figures, 1981).

37 *The L=A=N=G=U=A=G=E Book*, p. 109.

38 Jackson Mac Low, *Words nd Ends from Ez* (Bolinas: Avenue B, 1989), p. 89.

39 Ibid. p. 11.

40 Ron Silliman, *Tjanting* (Applecross, Australia: Salt Publications, 2002). p. 15. *Tjanting* was first published by The Figures in 1981.

41 Charles Bernstein, *The Sophist* (Los Angeles: Sun and Moon Press, 1987), p. 50.

42 "Interview with Michael Palmer," *Exact Change Yearbook 1995*, p. 163.

43 Michael Palmer, *The Promises of Glass* (New York: New Directions, 2000), p. 3.

44 Ibid., p. 63.

45 Michael Palmer, *First Figure* (San Francisco: North Point Press, 1984), p. 59.

46 For Palmer's etymological interests, it should be noted that the word that follows "scale" in the dictionary is "scalene," which refers to a triangle with uneven sides, and the phrase "a triangle / of unequal sides" occurs in the first tercet of "The Book of the Yellow Castle."

47 *The Promises of Glass*, pp. 9, 10. Michael Palmer, "Autobiography, Memory and Mechanisms of Concealment," *Writing / Talks*, ed. Bob Perelman (Carbondale: Southern Illinois University Press, 1985), pp. 227–28.

48 *Writing / Talks*, pp. 227–28.

49 Lyn Hejinian, *My Life* (Los Angeles: Sun and Moon Press, 1987), p. 16.

50 Typescript of Robert Grenier, "Interview with Phil Davenport," p. 4.

51 Robert Creeley, "Bob's Blessing," *verdure* 34 (September 2000–February 2001), 84.

52 Robert Grenier, *Dusk Road Games: Poems 1960–1966* (Cambridge: Pym-Randall Press, 1967), p. 13.

53 "Interview with Phil Davenport," p. 5.

54 E-mail to Albert Gelpi, June 27, 2009; typescript of "Realizing Things," a talk given at SUNY, Buffalo, to one of Bernstein's classes, October 22, 1998, p. 39.

55 Robert Grenier, *Sentences Toward Birds* (Kensington: L Publications, 1975).

56 Robert Grenier, "Statement of Plans" for a Guggenheim Fellowship, September 2011.

57 Robert Grenier, "Nature Poetry," *Ecopoetics* 1 (Winter 2001), p. 49; email to Albert Gelpi, July 11, 2013. *12 from r h y m m s* (Scotia: Pavement Saw Press, 1996); *OWL/ON/BOU/GH* (Sausalito: Post-Apollo Press, 1997); *16 from r h y m m s* (Marfa: Marfa Books/Impossible Objects, 2014).

58 William Carlos Williams, *Imaginations*, ed. Webster Schott (New York: New Directions, 1970), pp. 145, 121, 93.

59 Robert Grenier, letter to William McPheron, April 6, 2002.

60 Grenier's marginal note, commenting on the typescript of my essay "The Genealogy of Robert Grenier's Drawing Poems," which appeared in the Stanford Library journal *Imprint* (Fall 2004).

61 Typescript of "Robert Grenier and Stephen Ratcliffe in Conversation," November 17, 2001, p. 43. This conversation is also available online at www .writing.upenn.edu/pennsound/x/On-Natural-Language.php. The final quotation is from an e-mail to Albert Gelpi, July 15, 2013.

62 Recording of Robert Grenier and Stephen Ratcliffe in conversation, January 2, 2011; available online at www.writing.upenn.edu/pennsound/x /On-Natural-Language.php.

63 Typescript of "Realizing Things," a talk given at one of Bernstein's classes at SUNY, Buffalo, October 22, 1998, pp. 32, 34, 36, 43; available online at www .epc.buffalo.edu/authors/grenier/rthings.html.

64 Typescript of "Robert Grenier and Stephen Ratcliffe in Conversation" November 17, 2001, p. 35; available online at www.writing.upenn.edu /pennsound/x/On-Natural-Language.php

65 Susan Howe, *Singularities* (Middletown: Wesleyan University Press, 1990), p. 41, 42.

66 Ibid., pp. 40, 41, 43, 48, 51, 49; Susan Howe, "The Difficulties Interview," *The Difficulties*, vol. 3, no 2 (1989), p. 26.

67 *Singularities*, pp. 40, 55.

68 Ibid, pp. 56, 57.

69 Ibid., p. 59.

70 "The Difficulties Interview," p. 21.

71 Bruce Campbell, " 'Ring of Bodies' / 'Sphere of Sound': An Essay on Susan Howe's *Articulation of Sound Forms in Time*," *The Difficulties*, p. 89.

72 "The Difficulties Interview," p. 21.

73 Ibid.

74 Susan Howe, *My Emily Dickinson* (Berkeley: North Atlantic Books, 1985), pp. 76–77. In *The Poems of Emily Dickinson*, ed. Thomas H. Johnson (Cambridge, MA: Harvard University Press, 1955), "My Life had stood – a Loaded Gun" is Poem 754, and "I dwell in Possibility – " is Poem 657.

75 "The Difficulties Interview," p. 21; e-mail from Susan Howe to Albert Gelpi, August 2, 2013.

76 Some of the factual details surrounding the sequences of *That This* come from e-mails from Susan Howe to Albert Gelpi, dated July 18, July 24, August 2, and August 3, 2013.

77 E-mails from Susan Howe to Albert Gelpi, August 3 and July 30, 2013.

78 Susan Howe, *That This* (New York: New Directions, 2010), p. 39.

79 E-mail from Susan Howe to the author, July 30, 2013.

80 E-mail from Susan Howe to the author, August 2, 2013.

81 See *That This*, pp. 89, 85, 63, 45, 92, 62, 82, 86, 84, 84, 78, 87, 89.

82 *That This*, pp. 84–85.

83 Janet Ruth Falon, "Speaking with Susan Howe," *The Difficulties*, p. 311; "The Difficulties Interview," p. 21.
84 *That This*, pp. 99, 102.
85 Ibid., pp. 104, 105.
86 "The Difficulties Interview," pp. 26, 27.
87 Quoted on the back of Fanny Howe, *The Lyrics* (Saint Paul: Graywolf Press, 2007).
88 *The Lyrics*, p. 54. Henceforth in this chapter Howe designates Fanny Howe, unless otherwise indicated.
89 Fanny Howe, *Introduction to the World* (Great Barrington: The Figures, 1986), p. 11; reprinted in Fanny Howe, *Selected Poems* (Berkeley: University of California Press, 2000), p. 5.
90 *The Poems of Emily Dickinson*, ed. Thomas H. Johnson (Cambridge, MA: Harvard University Press, 1955), II, 792.
91 *Introduction to the World*, p. 30; not reprinted in *Selected Poems*.
92 *Introduction to the World*, p. 27; reprinted in *Selected Poems*, p. 10.
93 Fanny Howe, "Footsteps Over Ground," *A God in the House: Poets Talk About Faith*, ed. Ilya Kaminsky and Katherine Fowler (North Adams: Tupelo Press, 2012), pp. 107, 108.
94 Ibid., pp. 108, 109.
95 Ibid.; Fanny Howe, *The Wedding Dress: Meditations on Word and Life* (Berkeley: University of California Press, 2003), p. 13.
96 Ibid., pp. 5, 12.
97 Ibid., pp. 39–40.
98 *The Poems of Emily Dickinson*, ed. Thomas H. Johnson (Cambridge, MA: Harvard University Press, 1955), II, 694–95.
99 The phrase is Margaret Mahler's in *The Psychological Birth of the Human Infant* (New York: Basic Books, 1975) as she describes the infant's "gradual growing away from the maternal state of symbiosis, of one-ness from the mother," p. 333.
100 Fanny Howe, *O'Clock* (London: Reality Street Editions, 1995), p. 68.
101 *A God in the House*, p. 109; Fanny Howe, *Come and See* (Minneapolis: Graywolf Press, 2011), p. 35.
102 *The Wedding Dress*, pp. 5, 23.
103 Ibid., pp. 14, 15, 16.
104 Ibid., pp. 17, 15.
105 Ibid., pp. 73, 74, 75; Fanny Howe, "Doubt," *Gone: Poems* (Berkeley: University of California Press, 2003), p. 23.
106 *The Wedding Dress*, pp. 48, 40; *Gone*, pp. 23, 26–27, 24, 25.
107 *The Wedding Dress*, p. 53; *O'Clock*, p. 37.
108 *Gone*, p. 24.
109 Ibid., pp. 90, 116, 60.
110 Fanny Howe, *Second Childhood* (Minneapolis: Graywolf Press, 2014), pp. 29, 34.
111 *Come and See*, p. 59.

112 *Second Childhood*, pp. 53–55.

113 *The Wedding Dress*, pp. 53–54.

114 "Outremer" is an earlier, longer version of "A Vision," from a typescript sent to Albert Gelpi by Fanny Howe.

115 E-mail to Albert Gelpi, July 17, 2013.

116 *Second Childhood*, pp. 65, 66, 69.

117 Ibid., p. 3.

Coda

1 Archibald MacLeish, *Collected Poems*, p. 40; Wallace Stevens, *The Necessary Angel: Essays on Reality and the Imagination* (New York: Alfred A. Knopf, 1951), p. 36; *Selected Prose of Robert Frost*, ed. Hyde Cox and Edward Connery Latham (New York: Holt, Rinehart & Winston, 1966), p. 18.

2 *The Cantos of Ezra Pound* (New York: New Directions, 1972), p. 797.

3 William Carlos Williams, *Imaginations*, ed. Webster Schott (New York: New Directions, 1970), pp. 111, 93, 117.

4 Wallace Stevens, *The Necessary Angel: Essays on Reality and the Imagination* (New York: Alfred A. Knopf, 1951), pp. 54, 36, 57–58, 164; *Collected Poems of Wallace Stevens* (New York: Alfred A. Knopf, 1955), p. 380.

5 *The Necessary Angel*, p. 173; *Collected Poems*, p. 524.

6 *Towards A New American Poetry: Essays & Interviews*, ed. Ekbert Fass (Santa Barbara: Black Sparrow Press, 1978), p. 82.

Index